MW01164767

# Professional Social Service Delivery in a Multicultural World

*edited by*
*Gwat-Yong Lie*
*and*
*David Este*

Canadian Scholars' Press          Toronto          1999

**Professional Social Service Delivery in a Multicultural World**
edited by Gwat-Yong Lie and David Este

First published in 1999 by
**Canadian Scholars' Press Inc.**
180 Bloor Street West, Ste. 1202
Toronto, Ontario
M5S 2V6

We acknowledge the financial support of the Government of Canada through the Book Publishing Industry Development Programme for our publishing activities.

**Canadian Cataloguing in Publication Data**

Main entry under title:
  Professional social service delivery in a multicultural world

Includes bibliographical references.
ISBN 1-55130-119-9

1. Social work with minorities—Canada. I. Lie, Gwat Yong. II. Este, David, 1953-  .

HV3176.P763 1999          362.847'00971          C98-930790-5

Page layout and cover design by Brad Horning

# Table of Contents

## B: For Management, Administration and Organizational Change

## C: For Evaluation and Research

## D: For Professional Education, Training, and Continuing Education

# Acknowledgements

We would like to thank the following: the contributing authors for allowing us to share their information and insightful work; to our colleagues, friends, and families for the support you provided provided throughout the work and to Canadian Scholars' Press and, in particular, Jack Wayne and Brad Lambertus for their faith in our ability to complete this volume.

# Preface

The impetus for this book began in fall of 1993, when Professor Lie was on sabbatical leave from Arizona State University and affiliated with the Faculty of Social Work at the University of Calgary. She had been assigned to teach a baccalaureate level course on multiculturalism, and in the process of compiling reading assignments for the course found few articles or books that addressed cultural competence practice in the social services field. She approached Professor Este, and together they planned a book that would represent an attempt to address the gap, and include the perspectives of scholar-researchers, administrators, and educators, as well as career social service professionals. The focus of the book is on: (1) the types of competencies to be acquired; and (2) the processes for acquiring the knowledge, values and skills germane to those competencies. Contributors were encouraged to draw from actual experiences and to incorporate true examples to substantiate points and illustrate abstract ideas.

The book is divided into two major parts. The implications of Canada's multicultural policy for professionals in the social service arena is presented first, as "The Challenge"—how the policy came to be, and the resulting emergent call for culturally competent professionals to deliver culturally appropriate social services. The second part addresses the implications of Canada's multicultural policy for social service practice; for management, administration and organizational change in social service agencies and organizations; for research and practice evaluation; and for professional education and training, and continuing education.

The book begins with a chapter by Este documenting the historical circumstances leading to the promulgation of the multicultural policy in Canada. In addition, he shows how, over the years, changing economic circumstances and socio-political sentiments are reflected in changing immigration policies and, in turn, changing attributes of immigrants. At the end of the chapter, Este offers a summary of the current issues and dilemmas connected with multicultural and immigration policies.

In Chapter 2, Este presents the "Cultural Competence" perspective. He begins with a description of the socio-political circumstances that have led to the call for culturally competent social service professionals. He then addresses the array of competencies—knowledge, values and skills—fundamental to the definition of a culturally competent practitioner. Recognizing that a culturally competent practitioner must be supported and nurtured by a culturally competent organizational environment, Este suggests a process by which such competence can be achieved.

But who are these immigrant and culturally diverse groups of people that social service professionals are likely to encounter? What kinds of issues are they likely to present? Why would culturally appropriate services be especially helpful to these individuals, families, groups and communities? The next five chapters, that is, chapters three through seven, draw attention to the human subjects who are an integral part of the multicultural milieu in Canada today, their predicaments, and how culturally appropriate interventions serve to assuage their circumstances.

The plight of immigrant and refugee children and adolescents in Canada is documented by Aldous in Chapter 3. She describes the biological, psychological and social strengths, and needs of these individuals. In addition, through the use of case vignettes, she effectively drives home the reality of their experiences and its impact on their young lives. She advocates for more primary prevention programs staffed by multidisciplinary and multicultural teams who are knowledgeable about the issues concerning these youth (e.g., trauma associated with flight from the home country and post-trauma adjustment). She presents examples of school-based and community-based programs in the United States and Canada that are aimed at assisting multicultural youth to successfully negotiate the adjustment and transition process that occurs post-migration.

In Chapter 4, O'Neill details the challenges of being a person with same-sex orientation living in a predominantly heterosexual and multicultural environment. Even though protections have been written into human rights codes in all but three provinces, the prevalent attitude among Canadians in general towards gays, lesbians and bisexuals is, at best, one of ambivalence. He also contends that Canada's multicultural policy has mixed implications for people with same-sex orientation. By fostering diversity and countering discrimination, the policy may generate tolerance; on the other hand, in supporting the practice of traditional values, "...multiculturalism may sustain homophobia and heterosexism" (see p. 81). He discusses the ramifications of the intersection between sexual orientation and ethnocultural membership and its accompanying dilemmas. He also addresses the implications of being gay, lesbian or bisexual and an ethnocultural minority for social policy, social service practice, program development, and professional education and training.

The observance of *kuan hsi* (that is, the development of mutually beneficial networks of support) by Chinese elderly and Canadian social service entitlements, in particular to senior public housing facilities, appear to be on a collision course. However, according to Saldov in Chapter 5, such an outcome can be averted, and he offers suggestions based on the results of an exploratory research study he conducted in 1994. The underlying thread of his recommendations is, understand and appreciate what *kuan hsi* means to the elderly and how it shapes their interpretation and response to mainstream social services. With this awareness and the means to overcome language barriers, the social service professional is better equipped to respond in culturally appropriate ways, ways which the elders, in turn, are likely to be more receptive and accepting.

Chapter 6 directs attention to the predicament that many immigrant men encounter. Austin and Este, by giving voice to individuals in the group, are able to document the adverse impact that unemployment and underemployment have had on a group of well-qualified immigrant men. The focus of the chapter is on the mechanics of group work, and on how a support group approach can be helpful in alleviating psychic stress and strain as well as addressing strategies for successful job-hunting.

The final chapter in this section of the book, Chapter 7 by Reinberg, describes strategies that mainstream social service organizations could use to reach out to ethnocultural minority individuals, families, group and communities. These strategies are designed to address and overcome barriers that prevent ethno-cultural minority group members from becoming consumers of social services; and, to recognize salient characteristics of culturally appropriate services, so that these organizations could deliver multiculturally competent social services.

The next four chapters deal with the challenges of leadership and supervision with respect to a multicultural workforce. The issues of organizational change in response to changing composition of clientele, and demands for new ways of marketing and delivering services are also examined. Beginning with Chapter 8, McLeod presents the argument that an increasingly diverse workforce has rendered traditional management practices obsolete. This development demands that a new organizational culture be forged with organizational leaders at the helm, cast in the role of change agents. Ms McLeod closes with suggestions on how to promote organizational change that would result in an organizational climate valuing diversity among its staff, and an organizational leadership that is competent and humane in its dealings with its diverse workforce.

Ing and Gabor examine the dynamics of cross-cultural supervision in Chapter 9. The authors contend that intercultural communication is an integral component of the supervisory process. They explain the mechanics of communication and show how this is heavily influenced by cultural beliefs and values. Invariably, good supervision is contingent on good communication. Thus, good supervision would benefit immensely from a good understanding of the role of culture in influencing, for example, perceptions and verbal and nonverbal behaviors. They provide a case to illustrate their point. They conclude that culturally competent supervision must be supported by a culturally competent organization, and suggest strategies for developing cultural competence within an organization.

Chapters 10 and 11 detail the efforts of social service organizations in Calgary, Alberta, which responded to the challenge of transitioning into culturally competent organizations. Amestica, Houlding, Kiegler and Ksienski in Chapter 10 write about the experiences of the Calgary Immigrant Aid Society and the Calgary Family Service Bureau. Both organizations realized that each could benefit from an expansion in services if both were to enter into a partnership serving ethnocultural minority populations. Amestica et al. describe the goals, the rationale, the structure and the process that the partnership underwent in order to be sufficiently prepared, organizationally and individually, to offer culturally appropriate services.

Babins-Wagner, Hoffart and Hoffart detail the effort and experiences of the former Pastoral Institute in its journey through the multicultural organizational change (MOC) process in Chapter 11. The mandate to the Institute was clear: promote the full participation of ethnocultural groups in United Way funded programs and services by dismantling visible and invisible organizational barriers, and serve as a catalyst for multicultural change among member agencies and nonmember agencies. The authors draw on findings from a program evaluation exercise (which was an integral component of the change process) to show that efforts to meet the mandate were successful.

The next two chapters in the section on evaluation and research grapple with the salience of culture in research and practice evaluation activities. In Chapter 12 for instance, Lie advocates for the selection and approval of a set of competencies that a social service provider working with diverse client populations must have in order to be able to deliver culturally appropriate services. In addition, Lie argues for the setting of standards so that multicultural practice can be evaluated for purposes of accountability, credibility, and knowledge and skills-building.

Writing on the subject of culturally competent research, Krysik, in Chapter 13, contends that the research endeavour must factor in the relevance of culture at all phases of the research process, including how data are interpreted, where the results are presented and published, and how they may be interpreted, used and misused. She offers suggestions as to how one can do this, that is, be alert to issues of cultural bias while attending to the nuances and subtleties of culture that affect people's behaviour.

The final section of the book on professional education, training and continuing education opens with a chapter by Christensen. In Chapter 14, Christensen observes that insufficient attention to the issue of race, culture and ethnicity in the education and training of social service providers has adversely affected their ability to provide sensitive and appropriate services to visible minorities and First Nations people. She examines historical and current developments that have contributed to this critical gap in professional training and education. She also reviews course content with respect to what is presently included in those courses and suggests of what should be included. She concludes that the task of infusing a multicultural and anti-racist perspective is not simply a matter of revising the curriculum to include the necessary content, but that it also entails changing faculty and student enrolment profiles to reflect the diversity of Canadian society today. This responsibility is, necessarily, a collective one, and Christensen names key players who have an instrumental role to play in the changeover.

In a similar vein, Razack, in Chapter 15, argues for the inclusion of anti-oppression content in, especially, social work practica or field training. Field training, as a confluence of vital streams of consciousness in social work education—academia, the professional community and social service agencies as community-based settings for the delivery of services—is thus the ideal location for anti-oppression content. She explains the relevance of such content for work with diverse populations and describes a model that exemplifies the application of anti-oppression principles and content in field training.

The final chapter, co-authored by Rogers and Summers, deftly summarizes the issues salient to a comprehensive and informed discussion of multiculturalism and its place in Canadian social services. The authors review the tenets of the cultural competence perspective and pointedly argue the relevance of this perspective, given the historical legacy and current-day realities of Canada. Becoming culturally competent demands changes in perceptions and beliefs at personal and professional levels. Integral to this process is the issue of "whose truth" should prevail. Contrary to conventional directives to pursue universal truth, Rogers and Summers advocate the recognition of different realities and different ways of interpreting reality. However, to do so is not without its attendant set of dilemmas and challenges. Rogers and Summers discuss these and offer a framework to resolve them. The chapter closes with recommendations on how to facilitate a learning process conducive to the promotion and development of multicultural competence.

In summary, there is consensus among the chapter contributors that social service providers must be competent to render culturally appropriate services. The process of becoming multiculturally competent begins with a set of competencies and standards approved by the profession, and followed by the design and development of educational and training curricula that would creatively deliver the knowledge, values and skills integral to the acquisition of the specified competencies at the standard stipulated by the professional collegia. Because the state of knowledge and the accompanying set of skills are continuously being defined and refined, the process of acquiring competencies is an evolutionary one. The cultural competent practitioner is an inveterate learner, progressing from one level of knowing and doing to the next, and the next...the process never ends. The efficiency of the progression from one level to the next can be facilitated by regular attention to practice research and program evaluation findings. Research and evaluation efforts help keep the trajectory of development in multicultural competence on target and in compliance with established standards and competencies. More importantly, the process of becoming multiculturally competent need not be onerous nor overwhelming. But, it does demand that participants appreciate the value of a multicultural milieu, and are willing to invest in the development and promotion of such an environment.

# About the Authors

**Jane Aldous** R.P.N., M.Ed. (Counselling), C. Psych. works as a private practitioner in the Calgary community and is currently affiliated with National Forensic and Medico-Legal Services, Inc.

**Magdalena Amestica**, M.S.W., is a chartered psychologist, and the Executive Director of Child Focus Services, Calgary, Alberta.

**Christopher Austin**, M.S.W., R.S.W., presently works as a counsellor for a national employee assistance provider, CHC.

**Robbie Babins-Wagner**, M.S.W., R.S.W., is the Executive Director of Calgary Counselling Centre, formerly The Pastoral Institute.

**Carole Pigler Christensen**, M.S.W., D.Ed., is Professor at the School of Social Work, The University of British Columbia.

**David Este**, M.A., M.S.W., D.S.W., is Associate Professor at the Faculty of Social Work, University of Calgary. Alberta.

**Peter Gabor**, M.S.W., Ph.D., is Professor at the Faculty of Social Work, University of Calgary, Lethbridge Division.

**Brian Hoffart**, M.S.W., R.S.W., is a director with Synergy Research Group in Calgary, Alberta.

**Irene Hoffart**, M.S.W., is a director with Synergy Research Group in Calgary, Alberta.

**Hilde Houlding** is Director, Counselling Department, Calgary Family Service Bureau in Calgary, Alberta.

**Carol Ing**, M.Sc., is Chair, Child & Youth Care, Lethbridge Community College, Lethbridge, Alberta.

**Elzbieta Kiegler**, M.A., is an immigration consultant with Van Reekum Veress Immigration Consulting Ltd., Calgary, Alberta.

**Judy Krysik**, M.S.W., Ph.D., was at the Faculty of Social Work, University of Calgary. In 1996, she relocated to Arizona, teaching part-time at the School of Social Work, Arizona State University and working as a research and evaluation consultant with L.A.M. and Associates.

**Hadassah Ksienski**, B.S.W., is Chief Executive Officer of the Calgary Immigrant Aid Society, Calgary, Alberta.

**Gwat-Yong Lie**, M.S.W., Ph.D., is Associate Professor at the School of Social Welfare, University of Wisconsin-Milwaukee.

**Jann M. MacLeod**, B.A., B.S.W., M.S.W., LL.B., is beginning a law practice in Calgary, and is currently a member of Lawyers for Social Responsibility.

**Brian J. O'Neill**, D.S.W., R.S.W., taught at Wilfred Laurier University in Kitchener, Ontario. He is currently Assistant Professor at the School of Social Work, University of British Columbia in Vancouver, British Columbia.

**Narda Razack**, M.S.W., C.S.W., is an Assistant Professor and Field Education Coordinator at the School of Social Work, Atkinson College, York University in Downsview, Ontario.

**Viviana Reinberg**, M.S.W., held joint appointments as Coordinator, Multicultural Counseling Internship Program, Catholic Social Services/Alexandra Community Health Centre and Coordinator, Family Conflict: Cross-Cultural Counseling and Referral Service, Calgary Immigrant Women's Association.

**Gayla Rogers**, M.S.W., Ph.D., is Associate Professor and Acting Dean at the Faculty of Social Work, University of Calgary, Alberta.

**Morris Saldov**, M.S.W., R.S.W., Ph.D., taught at University of Toronto in Toronto, Ontario, Memorial University in St. John's, Newfoundland and Hongkong University. He is currently Associate Professor of Social Work at the University of Hawaii.

**Helena Summers**, M.S.W., was Coordinator of Field Instruction at the School of Social Work, University of British Columbia.

PART **1**

# THE CHALLENGE

# CHAPTER 1

# Immigration, Multiculturalism and Social Welfare in Canada

*David Este*

Immigration and multiculturalism are inextricably linked.
Together they are integral to the identity and evolution
of the Canadian policy. (Tepper, 1994, p. 95)

Any discussion of social services in Canada must take into consideration the multicultural reality of Canadian society, as well as the need for the Canadian social welfare system to become more responsive to the country's changing racial and ethnic diversity. As discussed in several chapters in this book, the imperative for helping professionals to become more competent in dealing with individuals, families and groups from diverse backgrounds is inescapable given the numbers of immigrants and refugees who have entered Canada over the past five years.

The focus of this chapter is on the Canadian social welfare system as it relates to immigrants and minority groups in Canada. The following topics will be discussed:

- The history of immigration in Canada
- Canadian immigration policies and practices
- Multiculturalism in Canada
- The majority versus the minority
- Acculturation in Canada

- The life of an immigrant
- Support services to immigrants
- The problem of jurisdiction for immigration policy
- Recent developments

## THE HISTORY OF IMMIGRATION IN CANADA

Why do some countries welcome immigrants while others do not? A number of reasons emerge, all of which play a part in influencing immigration policies and shaping social welfare policies, programs and services for immigrants (Daenzer, 1989). One reason is that some countries are unable to sustain their population numbers through birth rates. As the population ages and declines, where birth rates are so low that death rates outpace birth rates, a country's economic situation becomes increasingly jeopardized because there are decreasing numbers of workers to draw on. In such instances there is a compelling need for an infusion of people from outside the country, which is often accomplished through the use of relatively liberal immigration policies.

A second reason for differential immigration policies across countries is that even though immigrants may be perceived as necessary for the economic development of a country, certain immigrants may be perceived as more desirable than others. Consequently, immigrants with certain attributes, e.g., from northwestern European countries, are welcomed, whereas those from elsewhere are not. As a result, immigration policies tend to be discriminatory and selective.

A third response to immigration is one that actively discourages the phenomenon. Such a policy tends to be practiced by countries that are economically depressed, and it is adopted because of the fear that more people, particularly unskilled workers, will only exacerbate the already depressed conditions. The perception is that ultimately these immigrants will become a burden on society.

Finally, some countries, such as France, allow immigrants into the country for employment purposes, but restrict them from becoming citizens. Such a policy allows for low-paying jobs to be filled, jobs that citizens of the country are unwilling to take, and it ensures that these workers are in the country on a transient basis. The intent is to encourage these workers to return to their country of origin once their ability to participate in the labour force ceases.

Canada has had a long history of immigration, a history distinguished by a fairly humane approach to immigration given the mutual interests that a rather liberal policy would serve. For instance, many immigrants came for economic reasons, fleeing from impoverished conditions in their homelands. Others fled to Canada to escape political and/or religious persecution. In responding to the needs of these immigrants and refugees, Canada was also meeting its own needs: to have sparsely populated areas settled, and to be able to draw on an inexpensive and available labour pool to promote economic growth. It was offering also, on humanitarian grounds, a safe haven to refugees (Christensen, 1995).

The first wave of immigrants came from France between 1667 and 1763 and settled primarily in what is now known as Quebec (Christensen, 1995). Their reasons for emigrating were primarily economic. Canada was rich in natural resources such as lumber, minerals and furs, which were heavily sought after by Europeans. There was demand for labour to work in the forests and in the timber factories, in the mining sector and the fur trapping and processing industries. Through immigration, job openings in these sectors of the economy were filled, and trade in lumber, minerals and fur continued between Canada and Europe.

The second wave came from Britain, beginning about 1759. These immigrants came for economic reasons as well. They settled mainly in the Maritime provinces and what is now known as Ontario and became farmers, manufacturers and exporters of natural resources. Over time the British and French settlers established their own communities and the accompanying social and political institutions, including governing bodies, churches, schools, roads and postal services.

Another influx of immigrants occurred between 1880 and the beginning of World War I. At that time the Canadian government was attempting to quickly settle the land west of Ontario. Although immigrants were still coming from Britain and France, their numbers were not large enough to fully tap the potential and possibilities of Western Canada. The government therefore had to look beyond those two sources. Canada then began to actively recruit immigrants from other European countries, mainly from northern and eastern Europe. Consequently, the new arrivals were Germans, Dutch, Danes, Swedes, Finns, Ukrainians, Poles and Russians. These immigrants, like their British and French counterparts, were motivated to emigrate for economic reasons. The attraction of owning vast tracts of land at a very low purchase price was the main drawing card. During this period, a few groups of immigrants came because of religious persecutions: the Hutterites (from Austria, Bohemia, Hungary, Slovakia and Moravia); the Mennonites (mainly from South Germany and the Netherlands); and the Doukhobors (from Russia). Since many hailed from rural areas in their home countries they were naturally predisposed to settling in similar locales in Canada. Through hard work and perserverence, these immigrants helped build and develop the agricultural economy of the prairie provinces.

The fourth wave of immigrants came between World War I and World War II. Although many came from the same homelands as those in the previous phases, many also came from southern Europe. These immigrants tended to settle in urban areas, taking employment in industry or establishing their own businesses. Some came highly skilled and worked as masons and carpenters.

The fifth wave came after World War II when Canada was ready to produce consumer goods after the rationing during the war. People were prepared to build and buy. However, the population base was still relatively small given the vast size of the land. At the same time, refugees in war-torn Europe who were housed in camps were looking to emigrate. Many were unwilling and unable to return to their homelands, many of which had been overrun by the Soviet Union. Moreover, those who were involved in resistance movements were facing persecution and certain death if they returned to their homelands. It is likely they would not have emigrated had it not been for the war. Canada was willing to accept these refugees. This group of refugees differed from other immigrants in several ways: 1) they came to Canada for political reasons, 2) they were highly educated professionals and entrepreneurs, and 3) they settled primarily in urban areas.

The sixth wave of immigrants to Canada has taken place between 1970 to the present. In response to pressure and adverse criticism from inside and outside Canada, immigration policy concerning emigrants from Asia, Africa and Latin America was revised. Restrictive criteria for admission had previously severely limited the flow of people to Canada from these regions. As a result of changes in the admission criteria, Canadians began to witness the influx of a group of immigrants quite different from themselves. Chinese from Hong Kong and Taiwan, Koreans, East Indians, Pakistanis, Vietnamese, Peruvians, Guatemalans, Chileans, Somalis and people from the Caribbean Islands were becoming increasingly visible and audible. Some of those who came were well-educated and highly skilled, looking to make an even better living here in Canada. These professionals were able to fill local gaps for suitably qualified personnel. Others were monied and were recruited because of their ability to invest financially in Canadian businesses. Still others came as political refugees. This latter group, generally, tended to have suffered numerous losses either prior to leaving their home country and/or en route to Canada. Many were neither well-educated nor well off financially.

## CANADIAN IMMIGRATION POLICIES AND PRACTICES

The British North America Act of 1867 gave the federal government wide-ranging powers over various domestic issues, including immigration. Except for Quebec, the provincial governments exercised no direct authority over immigration policies. Quebec, because it wished to preserve its French culture and language, demanded and was allowed input into the definition of who would be welcomed in the province. This influence has persisted to the present day. In recent years, Quebec's immigrants have come primarily from French-speaking countries, including Haiti, the Ivory Coast and Algeria.

Despite a long history of immigration, Canada had no coherent immigration policy or legislation until the early 1950s. In 1950 the Department of Citizenship and Immigration was established, and in 1952 the first Immigration Act was passed. A historical scrutiny of immigration policies reveals fairly consistent changes reflective of changing societal values and perceptions about immigrants and their impact on prevailing socio-economic conditions.

One such change was the important amendment to the Immigration Act that was made in 1962. The amendment was enacted in response to criticisms that immigration policies hitherto had discriminated against non-white immigrants. The amended act developed a different set of criteria and created a point system that was designed to be less preferential towards certain nationalities and more inclusive.

The new criteria stressed education and skills, not race and place of origin. However, the criteria effectively prevented those from Africa and parts of Asia from applying because they lacked the necessary education and skills (Ramcharan, 1982). Active recruitment of skilled immigrants was done primarily through announcements placed in English-speaking newspapers in Africa and Asia, which systematically excluded those who could not read or speak English. Canadian immigration officers overseas had wide discretionary powers in interpreting the criteria, and many used their powers to screen out applicants (Anderson and Frideres, 1981; Anderson and Marr, 1987; Ramcharan, 1982). Further, there were few Canadian consulates in Africa and parts of Asia as compared with Europe and Britain. Hence, accessibility to interview sites was a significant obstacle for many applicants. To make matters worse, once the individual submitted his or her application, the waiting period was unusually long due to the complex application procedures and shortage of staff. The result was that, even with the revised provisions, immigrants from Europe were still getting into Canada at a much quicker rate.

In 1966 the federal government published the White Paper on Immigration. This document recommended many changes, some of which were incorporated into the 1977 amended Immigration Act. The point system and scale used to evaluate applicants were changed in response to criticisms that these tools were culturally biased. As a result, more non-white and southern European immigrants arrived in Canada. The rapid increase in the number of "visible minorities" created an increase in racist behaviours. For example, a number of politicians demanded that immigration policies revert to the former criteria (Breton et al., 1990).

In addition to amending the Immigration Act, the federal government declared amnesty to illegal immigrants, most of whom had come to Canada as visitors and had outstayed their official welcome. Fifty thousand came forward in the seven years during which the amnesty was in effect, and most were granted landed immigrant status (Anderson and Frideres, 1981; Anderson and Marr, 1987). Some Canadians believed that the 50,000 represented only a small fraction of those who came illegally.

In times of economic recession and depression, immigrants are most likely to become society's scapegoats. Long-time citizens who are unemployed blame immigrants for the loss of their jobs. In addition, immigrants are accused of draining socio-economic resources such as health, education and social services. During lean times the prevailing stereotypic image of the immigrant tends to be that of an excessive and undeserving user of human services—such was the situation in the recessionary period beginning in 1974. The Canadian government responded by placing curbs on immigration. One such curb was the prerequisite that prospective immigrants had to secure prearranged employment or a financial sponsor before permission to come to Canada would be granted (Anderson and Frideres, 1981; Anderson and Marr, 1987; Ramcharan, 1982).

In 1975 the federal government published the Green Paper as a response to the situation, which resulted in the amended Immigration Act of 1978. The major change was the establishment of another class of immigrants, that of refugee. This allowed those living in fear of their lives or well-being to enter Canada above the usual immigrant quotas. In addition, the criteria, or scale, were changed by increasing the quotas for immigrants from Africa, Asia and South and Central America (Anderson and Marr, 1987; Breton et al., 1990; Ramcharan, 1982).

On the issue of factors that render certain immigrants as "desirable" or "undesirable" in the eyes of the host country, Christensen (1995, p. 181) identified the following as among those that determine which of the two labels an immigrant will be saddled with:

1. National and racial origins of prospective immigrants;
2. The need for labour to fill specific job-market categories;
3. The availability of relatives in Canada to act as official sponsors;
4. Internal economic conditions of growth, recession or depression;
5. International conditions affecting the number of people, worldwide, seeking to escape poverty, natural disaster, war or political unrest, and the number of countries willing to accept them;
6. The anticipated short- and long-term effects of specific immigrant groups on the French and English communities.

Over time, changes in immigration policies and practices were manifest in changes in the immigrant profile, the most notable of which was the nationality of the prospective immigrant. Prior to 1880, 60% of the immigrants were British and 35% were French. The remaining 5% were from non-English- and non-French-speaking countries. Of these, 70% were German and 10% were Dutch (Christensen, 1995). After the third wave of immigration (1880-1914), most were from northern and eastern Europe. About 200,000 came yearly during this period. The following table best illustrates the trends in immigration with respect to countries of origin (Christensen, 1995, p. 183).

## Table 1: National Origins of Immigrants*

| Place of Birth | prior to 1960 % | 1971 - 1975 % | 1981 - 1986 % |
|---|---|---|---|
| USA | 7.3 | 8.2 | 7.0 |
| Italy | 28.1 | 38.3 | 28.8 |
| Germany | 8.4 | 1.4 | 2.2 |
| Other European Countries | 13.2 | 14.2 | 8.7 |
| India | 0.4 | 7.3 | 5.8 |
| Other South Asia | 0.0 | 1.5 | 2.1 |
| Southeast Asia | 0.2 | 7.1 | 16.4 |
| East Asia | 1.8 | 10.0 | 13.3 |
| West Asia | 0.4 | 2.0 | 5.4 |
| Africa | 0.5 | 6.0 | 4.5 |
| Caribbean and Bermuda | 0.7 | 10.8 | 5.8 |
| South and Central America | 0.5 | 7.0 | 9.6 |
| Other | 0.5 | 1.9 | 1.4 |

\* Reproduced from Christensen (1995, p.183)

During the past five years the number of immigrants allowed to enter Canada increased. Fleras and Elliot (1992, p. 44) commented on this trend:

> In recent years, the number of immigrants into Canada has moved up gradually from a low of 84,000 in 1985 to 212,000 who arrived in 1990. Current government estimates indicate a gradual relaxation of quotas to a ceiling of about 250,000 by 1992, to be maintained until 1996. Annual immigration totals of around 1 percent of the population (about 260,000) are required just to sustain current population levels in light of declining birth rates and emigration.

How does a nation manage diverse cultures so that harmony is encouraged and conflict discouraged? The Canadian government has attempted to do this with its multiculturalism policy. This policy has a peculiar origin. During Lester Pearson's tenure as prime minister during the mid-1960s, the government proposed a policy on bilingualism that was designed to appease Quebec's concerns that the needs of its residents and French Canadians outside Quebec to speak and write in French were being ignored. The federal civil service at the time was predominantly English speaking. The policy on bilingualism was intended to ensure that French Canadians would be able to conduct their business with any department of the federal government and their regional offices in the French language. In addition, it gave the French Canadians the right to establish French immersion public schools as a way of preserving the language and culture. In many ways this policy officially recognized the French and the English as the two founding nations of Canada.

The policy seemed to misrepresent Canada as a bifurcated nation—people were either English- or French-speaking. Predictably there was a backlash, as such representation oversimplified and masked the diversity that is Canada today. It did not account for First Nations peoples and the different dialects they spoke, nor the mother tongues of whose ancestry was neither French nor English. These groups felt that because they had also contributed significantly to the development of Canada and wanted to be similarly recognized.

In response the federal government, under the leadership of Prime Minister Trudeau in 1971, decided to implement "an official policy of multiculturalism within a bilingual framework" (Minister of State, 1978, p. 10). In announcing this policy Trudeau stated:

> ...there cannot be one cultural policy for Canadians of British and French origin, another for the original peoples and yet a third for all others. For although there are two official languages, there is no official culture, nor does any ethnic group take precedence over any other. No citizen or group of citizens is other than Canadian, and all should be treated fairly. (Minister of State, 1978, p. 4)

The policy of multiculturalism has two main assumptions: 1) encouraging people to maintain and promote their cultures through art, writing and music enables them to better integrate with mainstream Canada; and 2) the promotion of the various cultures enables all Canadians to become aware of the various peoples in Canada, thereby enhancing respect and understanding among Canadians. It has been noted that Canada has never adopted the "cultural melting pot" model for dealing with immigrants and other diverse groups. When Canada attempted to utilize this approach with First Nations peoples and the early immigrants, it did not work.

Canada's supposed tolerance of multiple ethnic and cultural groups is often cited as a primary reason why Canada has not suffered from the extreme types of racial, religious and ethnic tensions that have marred the histories of countries such as Ireland, South Africa and the United States. However, even with the existence of the multicultural policy, immigrants and their descendants have been discriminated against by the cultural majority (Berry, Kalin and Taylor, 1977; Yelaja and O'Neill, 1990). As Berry et al., point out, the term "multiculturalism" has come to refer to the presence of many distinctive cultural groups, each maintaining its different lifestyle within a larger and dominant host culture.

More recently Elliot and Fleras (1992) defined multiculturalism as a doctrine that provides a political framework for the official promotion of cultural differences and social equality as an integral component of the social order. The use of the term "cultural mosaic" describes the combined impact of these various groups, in conjunction with mainstream culture, upon 1) one's perceptions of oneself, both individually and collectively; 2) the way in which people are viewed by those living outside their borders; and 3) how various groups interact with one another in the context of cultural pluralism and its relationship to the unifying whole.

Despite the noble intentions of Canada's multiculturalism policy, discrimination and oppression are still alive and well, as is discussed in a later section. They continue to make life less than ideal for many, while conferring special privileges upon those who are recognized as belonging to the "majority culture." Many argue that even though Canada has no history of lynch-mob justice, segregated institutions, racial ghettos in cities, riots and other racially based disturbances, this does not mean that Canada does not discriminate; the target of discrimination and oppression typically being recent immigrants and visible minorities (Ramcharan, 1982).

Racial and ethnic discrimination have not always been subtle in form, unofficial, or transient, as many Canadians might wish to believe. Rather, racism and xenophobia (a Greek word meaning "fear of strangers") have been present since the days of the early settlers (Ramcharan, 1982). The following are but a few examples of racist and/or xenophobic acts:

- European settlers exterminated the Boethuk Indians in Newfoundland during the 1700s through mass starvation and murder.
- Racially segregated schools operated legally in Ontario from 1839 to 1965.
- In 1899 Indians and Metis in the Northwest Territories were forced to sign treaties giving up their lands and move to reserves. In 1994 much of this land was returned.
- In 1908 immigration from Asia was curtailed by a government policy that insisted that immigrants coming to Canada do so in one continuous trip. In other words, if the ship stopped at a port or ports, the immigrants were disqualified. When 376 Sikhs managed to meet this demand in 1914, they were forced to remain on board their ship in Vancouver for three months, after which the Canadian Navy ordered the ship back to sea.
- During World War I about 5000 Ukrainian immigrants were interred in concentration camps in Banff. The Ukraine was occupied by Austria at that time, so these immigrants came over as "Austrians." The Canadian government perceived Ukrainians as German sympathizers and hence "the enemy." Banff National Park and the Banff Springs Hotel were built by the incarcerated Ukrainians.
- In 1932 Alberta granted a provincial charter to the Ku Klux Klan.
- In 1939 Canada refused entry to Jews trying to escape Nazi Germany.
- During World War II Canadians of Japanese descent living in British Columbia were interred in concentration camps and had their property confiscated. These Canadians were considered the enemy because their ancestors came from Japan.
- Also during World War II Canadians of Italian descent were put under surveillance and some were interred because of the fascist government in Italy.

- Until the late 1940s Canadians of East Indian, Japanese and Chinese descent were disenfranchised. They were barred from professions such as law and pharmacy, which were open to only those who could vote.
- In 1954 Grantly Adams, Prime Minister of Barbados, was denied accommodation in a Montreal hotel because of his colour. The hotel cited "house regulations" as the reason.
- Until 1960 First Nations peoples could not vote.

## THE MAJORITY VERSUS MINORITY

Comte Alexis de Toqueville, a nineteenth-century French philosopher, traveller to the United States, and student of democracy, had much to say about the "tyranny of the majority." What he cautioned against was the ease with which a group of like-minded individuals with a voting majority could use that power to create laws controlling behaviours normally left to social custom or tradition; or, to take away the civil rights of a dissenting minority in the populace (Anderson and Frideres, 1981). The incarceration of the groups mentioned above is a case in point.

Today Canada faces the problem of majority rule and civil rights with respect to cultural minorities. The problem has to do with the difficult situation where the "majority" culture is not the numerical majority and, hence, over time its social and economic power base is eroding. This dilemma illustrates a very important fact about the term "cultural majority." It is a term associated with elite status and a group that has superior political and economic powers but is actually a numerical minority (Berry, Kalin and Taylor, 1977; Ramcharan, 1982; Yelaja and O'Neill, 1990). Still, it is this group that is vested with political as well as social and economic power that controls prevailing opinions and attitudes, and that has the latitude to translate its prejudices into discriminatory behaviour.

In order for a group to be discriminated against, three factors need to be present. The first is that the target group must have less social, political or economic power than the cultural majority. The second is that other, less powerful groups must align themselves with the cultural majority, thereby discriminating against the target group. What occurs here is that the majority and another minority group (or several minority groups) discriminate against the target group. It helps if the target group feels it deserves the discriminatory treatment. The third factor is that the target groups must pose some threat, real or perceived, to the well-being of the majority (Ramcharan, 1982).

## DISCRIMINATION IS STILL ALIVE AND WELL

Porter (1965) identifies two types of discrimination theories—conflict and scapegoat. Conflict theory states that a growing number of people compete for a finite number of resources, available services and existing jobs. This causes conflict and resentment among individuals and groups competing for these resources and opportunities. Decision-making with regard to the distribution of resources tends to be based on notions of who is "deserving" and who is "undeserving." By comparison, scapegoat theory holds that certain factors render a particular group the target of resentment in society.

Both conflict and scapegoat theories acknowledge that common to racism and discrimination are the dynamics of xenophobia. Such fears are both instinctive and primitive in nature, dating back to prehistoric times when nomadic peoples and tribes had good reason to fear unknown people. This instinct influences people to react with fear and suspicion towards those who seem "alien" in either appearance or behaviour. The fear can also turn into lack of respect for those from other cultures. If the majority feels that its culture is superior to all others, then what necessarily follows is that other cultures are inferior and primitive, and thus not worthy.

While education may be the answer, as some feel, to reducing xenophobia and lack of respect, such behaviour is almost impossible to eradicate (Ramcharan, 1982; Yelaja and O'Neill, 1990). A more difficult problem is institutional xenophobia such as racism and other forms of discrimination—when government policies and practices are clearly and systematically adversely targeting certain groups. The incarceration of various groups during World War I and World War II are examples of institutional xenophobia.

Subtle forms of discrimination continue to exist. Subtle or "polite" ways of showing disrespect to persons viewed as "different" are many. One way is the phenomenon of "looking through" someone—typically someone whose differentness is discomforting to the beholder. Many Canadians complain of being made to feel "invisible." Another "polite" way is the air of condescension with which one conducts oneself when interacting with the "different" individual whose cultural heritage is perceived as being of a "lesser" type. Such behaviour is insulting, as it reduces the status of the "different" person to that of a child or someone with less-than-average intelligence. This puts the other person in the role of a powerful adult and intelligent being. Many Canadians plead ignorance to the fact that they may present themselves in these disaffecting ways, and are appalled to learn that they have used these "polite" forms of discrimination (Berry, Kalin, and Taylor, 1977; Ramcharan, 1982; Yelaja and O'Neill, 1990).

Subtle forms of discrimination are as dangerous as those that are overt. They can easily seep into the policies and practices of institutions such as government, education, health, justice, employment and housing. They are also more difficult to confront. Although there are anti-discriminatory laws, subtle and polite forms tend to provide very little documentable evidence. Legal jurisprudence demands that some provable harm be done that can be measured in a tangible manner. In such cases the injured party may not even report the act of discrimination. However, the results are the same: the individual has been denied a rightful opportunity to fair and respectful treatment.

In addition to acts of discrimination against the individual, there are two other types of prejudice and discrimination: institutional and structural. Institutional discrimination is comprised of laws, programs or policies sanctioned by the state that are designed to exclude certain ethnic or racial groups (Elliot and Fleras, 1992). One example was the apartheid policy in South Africa. By comparison, structural discrimination is that which is shown against members of certain identifiable groups (Elliott and Fleras, 1992). In South Africa, as in most countries, a post-secondary education, namely a college or university education, is the key to full integration into the majority culture. Typically, the criteria used to assign students for inclusion in special college preparatory programs are based on such factors as race, ethnicity, culture, country of origin, gender and class—not on ability and merit. After graduation those who were not selected for college preparatory programs also found that they had been denied admission to college or university. These people will not be able to obtain the types of employment available to university graduates. Because of this limitation they are unable to take advantage of post-secondary educational opportunities, even if these became available to their progeny. In other words, the impact of the selection criteria used in high school is not confined to a particular generation. Instead, the ramifications may reverberate through several generations. Over time, these groups come to be under-represented in those occupations, professions and positions of power where the critical social, political and economic decisions are made. Other groups whose members were selected and did participate in college preparatory programs remain entrenched as the powerful elite of society (Berry, Kalin and Taylor, 1977; Ramcharan, 1982).

Another example of structural prejudice is the accepted definition of what is the cultural majority. In Canada, the accepted majority is white and British (Ramcharan, 1982). This effectively leaves out all others including French-Canadians, even though the latter are officially granted equal status with the English. It is interesting that the British in Canada identify themselves as Canadians while all others, including the French, identify themselves as "hyphenated Canadians," such as Polish-Canadian, East Indian-Canadian and Chinese-Canadian, even after many generations (Berry, Kalin and Taylor, 1977). On the other hand, many members of the cultural majority remain unpersuaded that hyphenated Canadians are "real" Canadians. If that is so, then the hyphenated Canadians may never be perceived as equal to the cultural majority.

## ACCULTURATION IN CANADA

Despite overt and covert discriminatory practices by the Canadian government and public and private institutions, many immigrants have acculturated into mainstream Canadian society. This has been possible for two reasons. One is that immigrants tend to adjust themselves to the host culture, both out of necessity and personal motivation. The second factor is Canada's multicultural policy, which encourages acculturation while at the same time encourages cultural groups to maintain traditions from their country of origin.

The first step towards the adoption of an official multicultural policy was the Canadian Bill of Rights in 1960. Prime Minister John Diefenbaker introduced this bill and fought passionately to have the bill passed in parliament. The bill was followed by the Official Languages Act of 1969, which recognized French as one of two official languages. This act gave French-speaking individuals living primarily outside Quebec the right to be educated in French as well as the right to communicate with governments and the courts in French.

As previously stated, in 1971 the federal government adopted an official policy of multiculturalism, a move precipitated by the enactment of a bilingual Canada. This was followed in 1977 by the Canadian Human Rights Act and the Canadian Charter of Rights and Freedoms in 1982. The Charter made it unlawful to discriminate on the basis of sex, race, age or religious affiliation. Finally, in 1988 the Multicultural Act was passed. According to Berry and Laponce (1994, p. 8):

> [The Act] reaffirmed a policy promoting the freedom of all to 'preserve, enhance and share their cultural heritage,' stated that the promotion of multiculturalism was 'a fundamental characteristic of Canadian heritage and identity,' and encouraged Canadian institutions to be 'both respectful and inclusive of Canada's multicultural character.'

Many immigrants to Canada relied on themselves to learn and adapt to the ways of the majority culture. Others received assistance from earlier immigrants in learning the "Canadian ways." For immigrants whose first language was not English, acculturation was more difficult. These immigrants tended to group together with a church or social centre as the focus of their collective lives. In these situations, learning English was only necessary for those members of the family who had transactions with English-speaking officials or business contacts. For others, their native language was sufficient.

For visible minority immigrants acculturation was also more of a challenge (Christensen, 1995). Many were finding that they were being judged by their visible attributes and the stereotypes associated with these attributes instead of, for example, their character or their deeds. Other groups chose not to acculturate primarily for religious reasons. These include the Old Order and Amish branches of the Mennonites, Hutterites and Doukhobors.

The extent to which immigrant efforts to acculturate are successful is significantly contingent on the receptivity or, conversely, the hostility of the mainstream community. Recent immigrants to Canada are quite different from early immigrants in many respects. The majority settle in urban areas. In addition, an increasing number are visible minorities. Further, the cultural and religious practices of many recent newcomers to Canada are not Judeo-Christian. With the changing diversity in Canadian society, and the increasing visibility of that diversity, there is a growing belief on the part of mainstream Canada that the country is being overrun by unprecedented numbers of strangers (Breton, 1990). Such perceptions are likely to have an adverse impact on the efforts of immigrants to acculturate.

## THE LIFE OF AN IMMIGRANT

Achieving entry into Canada is only the beginning of an odyssey. Many immigrants have little knowledge about Canada, and what they know may be based on myths and misconceptions. Except for English language classes, no level of government provides any orientation program to ease the immigrant's adjustment and orientation to a new society. While voluntary organizations and representative racial and ethnic groups do attempt to assist immigrants, their programs tend to be ad hoc and piecemeal. Although these organizations provide material assistance with housing, employment and advocacy, the resulting effect appears to be a tendency for immigrant groups to band together and to keep to themselves. One explanation for this behaviour is that it serves as a coping strategy to address the fear of losing one's ethnic or racial identity over time. It is not unusual, for example, for ethnic organizations to frown on immigrants' children dating or marrying others outside their ethnic group.

The odyssey is easier if the immigrants can maintain in Canada the social and financial status they had in their homelands. This is more likely with those immigrants who were recruited because of their particular skills or expertise. Artists, professors, scientists and physicians come to mind. But for others, life can be very difficult and there are a number of predictable barriers. One is that of needing to learn a new language, one that may have a different alphabet or lettering. Another barrier is that of moving from a rural environment in one country to a large urban centre in Canada. Many of these immigrants who lived in modest, one-floor dwellings now find themselves living on the twenty-third floor of a high-rise apartment building.

Another difficulty is that of the changing values of their children. Most immigrants value education as they see it as a way for their children to better themselves. However, education is either in English or French and espouses the values of the dominant culture. Further, the children of immigrants interact with other children and swap concerns, feelings, etc. In other words, the children are being influenced by external forces, something their parents fear. As a result, conflicts between children and parents arise. Immigrants who strongly believe in acculturation and integration into mainstream society will encourage their children to learn from outsiders. Such a value springs from having a strong ethnic or racial identity. Such immigrants do not fear the loss of ethnic identity but recognize that all cultures change over time. However, many immigrants think otherwise. The schools and family and youth organizations are replete with parents requesting help with their "badly behaving" teenage child who is rebelling against the family's value system.

Women face additional barriers. In many cultures the man is responsible for earning a living and for controlling the wife's choice of friends, access to outside influences such as learning English, reading local newspapers and watching television. When the wife has to work for financial reasons, the husband will have much to say as to location. If the wife disobeys any of her husband's expectations, physical and verbal abuse may be used. Clearly, a woman who wishes to acculturate herself can find herself in a dangerous situation, as can those assisting women to free themselves.

Another difficulty is that of disappointment from not achieving certain goals. Some highly qualified immigrants may find that their qualifications are irrelevant, inadequate or unrecognized. How immigrants deal with this is important. Some will seek retraining or will change careers; others will keep on attempting to get recognized. If successful, regardless of the route taken, the immigrant will be pleased. If unsuccessful the immigrant may decide to return to the country of origin or take an inferior position in Canada. Such a move must be difficult for anyone (Chapter 6 addresses the plight of immigrant men who are unemployed or underemployed as a consequence of their educational or professional training qualifications not being recognized by Canadian authorities).

Allmen (1990, p. 204-205) describes the three stages of the immigrant's settlement:

Stage 1
• A time of urgency, upheaval and struggle
• Anxiety to get going, extensive demand for information
• A need to meet the basic necessities of life
(Stage 1 lasts about six months unless interrupted by a crisis.)

Stage 2
• Emergencies are resolved, basic needs have been met
• A calmer phase, time for reflection and assessment

- The magnitude of the immigration and resultant losses are realized, depression may occur
- Existing personal problems are allowed to emerge

<u>Stage 3</u>
- Initial settlement adjustment has been accomplished
- On the surface the immigrant appears settled
- This is the stage when a great deal of personal adjustment takes place.

These stages are to be expected even though some can be stressful. The path through the stages can be delayed or interrupted through various crises, such as a death in the family, unemployment, severe illness or disability, marriage breakdown, difficulties with children and problems with relatives back home.

## SUPPORT SERVICES TO IMMIGRANTS

This section examines the issues related to developing social services for and with immigrants. A number of difficulties have been identified. Many immigrants are reluctant to accept services for a variety of reasons. For some, the family is expected to be the primary source of support and assistance. While some of these families seek assistance from mainstream organizations when they have exhausted their own resources, others will not. One overriding fear is the belief that seeking help from mainstream organizations will lead to deportation.

Another reason is that mainstream social and health services may be unaware of the services that immigrant and ethnic groups have developed. Many are staffed by non-professionals who may tend to be discounted by professionals in mainstream organizations. Collaborative efforts between immigrant and ethno-specific agencies may be the mechanism needed to address the concerns of the individual immigrants and specific ethnic communities. For example, some ethnic groups have developed an array of services including financial assistance, senior citizen residences, child-care centres and youth programs. In the city of Toronto, the Caribbean community developed a program to assist their members with establishing small businesses.

The issue of client comfort (or lack of it) with mainstream programs is related to the perceived inappropriateness of services—that services are not culturally responsive and do not adequately or appropriately address the needs of the immigrant client. Because ethnic communities recognize the importance of culturally appropriate services, ethnic agencies have even offered "to help train mainstream agency workers in the principles and intricacies of working with clients from their communities" (Herberg and Herberg, 1995, p. 175). Few mainstream agencies have responded to these offers.

Another reason may be that mainstream organizations are unaware of what immigrants need in order to adjust to life in Canada. As emphasized in a subsequent chapter in this book, there is increasing pressure on, for example, the social work profession, to broaden its curricula to include knowledge about various cultures, how various immigrant groups perceive help and what the best ways are to provide assistance. As part of the educative process there needs to be a focus on individual self-awareness. One of the main types of knowledge required by a social service professional is an awareness of one's own feelings and attitudes towards individuals and groups that are different.

Finally, another difficulty is funding services for immigrants. The provision of federal and provincial funds to assist immigrants in the settlement process is based on four criteria. First, immigrants should be given information for assistance in settling. Second, ethnic communities are capable of providing such services given the necessary funding. Third, such assistance can be provided by untrained and non-professional personnel as long as they can speak the language and understand the culture. Fourth, any other services which immigrants consider as necessary should be provided by mainstream organizations (Allmen, 1990; pp. 207-208). However, as Christensen (1995, p. 206) stresses, the provision of ongoing, long term funding is the major obstacle: "Lack of funding is perhaps the major long-standing problem relating to services for immigrants. For this reason, programs often seem to be temporary or inadequate." As a consequence, social service agencies are now actively engaging in a variety of fund-raising activities in order to sustain existing programs and develop innovative services for immigrants and refugees.

## THE PROBLEM OF JURISDICTION

As previously discussed, the federal government is responsibile for immigration policy and practices and for setting quotas. However, once immigrants arrive in Canada, they also reside in provinces and municipalities. Provincial and municipal governments also spend money on immigrants—health care, education and social services. However, it must be noted that the provinces, as defined in the British North America Act of 1867, have the responsibility to ensure that immigrants have access to necessary social services.

This provision of services to immigrants continues to be a contentious issue with some provinces. Overwhelmingly the majority of immigrants settle in Canada's major urban areas, where there are jobs and people from their homeland. Almost half of the immigrants settle in Ontario, with the majority residing in Toronto. Vancouver and Montreal are also attractive areas of settlement. However, provinces such as Ontario and British Columbia, because of the extent of services they provide to newcomers, contend that they should have a greater role in the nation's immigration policy.

## RECENT DEVELOPMENTS

In recent years Canada's immigration and multicultural policies have been subjected to considerable criticism. According to Fleras and Elliot (1996, p. 298) the major issues raised in relation to the two policies include:

- Concern about the numbers of newcomers entering Canada (255,725 in 1993 and 218,976 in 1994) at a time of double digit unemployment rates;
- Concern about the type of immigrant allowed to reside in Canada. Some of the critics contend that there needs to be an increase in the number of "independent" immigrants, that is, individuals who meet the socio-economic criteria specified in current immigration policies. More specifically, there is a strong belief the more business-class individuals who are deemed investors and entrepreneurs should be the prime targets of the immigration policy;
- Concern over the high proportion of immigrants from Third World countries;
- The impact that the high number of newcomers is having on Canada's social cohesion and cultural identity.

Under the leadership of Sergio Marchi, the minister responsible for immigration under the federal Liberal government, the following changes were announced designed to address some of the concerns discussed above:

- Immigration levels would be reduced from 256,000 in 1993 to 215,000 from 1995 and onwards to the year 2000 without necessarily losing sight of the eventual target of 1 percent of Canada's population (or nearly 280,000);
- Immigration would focus increasingly on independent immigrants rather than family reunification;
- The number of refugees would be increased to approximately 32,000 per year;
- Permanent residents who sponsor relatives may be asked to post a bond or collateral of sorts to ensure continuing support (Fleras and Elliot, 1996, pp. 298-299).

The changes put forth by the Liberal government brought about by the emerging concerns previously presented signifies that immigration and multiculturalism will continue to be very contentious issues.

## REFERENCES

Allmen, E. (1990). Counselling and settlement: The current and futures roles of mainstream and settlement services. In Shankar Yelaja (ed.), *Proceedings of the settlement and integration of new immigrants to Canada.* (Conference February 17-19, 1988). Centre for Social Welfare Studies, Waterloo: Wilfrid Laurier University.

Anderson, A. and Frideres, J. (1981). *Ethnicity in Canada: Theoretical perspectives.* Toronto: Butterworths.

Anderson, G. and Marr, W. (1987). Immigration and social policy. In Shankar Yelaja (ed.), *Canadian social policy* (rev. ed.). Waterloo, Ont: Wilfrid Laurier University Press.

Berry, J. W. , Kalin, R. and Taylor, D. (1976). *Multiculturalism and ethnic attitudes in Canada.* Ottawa: Ministry of Supply and Services Canada.

Berry, J. W. and Laponce, J. A. (1994). Evaluating research on Canada's multiethnic and multicultural society: An introduction. In J. W. Berry and J. A. Laponce (eds.), *Ethnicity and culture in Canada: The research landscape.* Toronto: University of Toronto Press.

Bissondath, N. (1994). *Selling illusions: The cult of multiculturalism in Canada.* Toronto: Penguin Books.

Breton, R., Isajiw, W. W., Kalbach, W. E., and Reitz, G. J. (1990). *Ethnic identity and equality: Varieties of experience in a Canadian city.* Toronto, Ontario: University of Toronto Press.

Cannon, M. (1995). *The invisible empire: Racism in Canada.* Toronto: Random House.

Christensen, C. (1995). Immigrant minorities in Canada. In Joanne Turner and Francis Turner (eds.), *Canadian social welfare* (3rd ed.). Toronto: Allyn and Bacon.

Daenzer, P. (1989). *The post migration labour-force adaptation of racial minorities in Canada.* Toronto: Faculty of Social Work, University of Toronto.

Elliott, J. and Fleras, A. (1992). *Unequal relations: An introduction to race and ethnic dynamics in Canada.* Scarborough: Prentice-Hall.

Fleras, A. and Elliot, J. (1996). *Unequal relations: An introduction to race and ethnic dynamics in Canada* (2nd ed.). Scarborough: Prentice-Hall

Fleras, A. and Elliot, J. (1992). *The challenge of diversity: Multiculturalism in Canada.* Scarborough: Nelson Canada.

Herberg, D. and Herberg, E. (1995). Canada's ethno-racial diversity: Policies and programs for Canadian social welfare. In Joanne Turner and Francis Turner (eds.), *Canadian social welfare* (3rd ed.). Toronto: Allyn and Bacon.

Minister of State, Multiculturalism (1978). *Multiculturalism and the Government of Canada.* Ottawa:Minister of Supply and Services.

Porter, J. (1965). *The vertical mosaic.* Toronto: University of Toronto Press.

Ramcharan, S.(1982). *Racism - Nonwhites in Canada.* Toronto: Butterworths.

Tepper, E. (1994). Immigration policy and multiculturalism. In J. W. Berry and J. A. Laponce (eds.), *Ethnicity and culture in Canada.* Toronto: University of Toronto Press.

Yelaja, S. and O'Neill, B. (1990). Introduction. In Shankar Yelaja (ed.), *Proceedings of the settlement and integration of new immigrants to Canada* (Conference, February 17-19, 1988). Centre for Social Welfare Studies, Waterloo: Wilfrid Laurier University.

# CHAPTER 2

# Social Work and Cultural Competency

*David Este*

Professional social service academic and training programs such as social work are currently being challenged to address the needs of Canada's changing population. Some of this pressure stems from the perception that professions such as social work have not or are too slowly responding to the ethnic and cultural population diversity. Commenting on this situation, Yelaja and O'Neill (1990, p. 1) state:

> Despite social work's professed commitment to equal treatment of all persons, systemic barriers continue to impede racial and ethnic minorities access to mainstream services. Agencies need to form partnerships with ethnic organizations in order to effectively serve minority clients. Concepts regarding ethnicity have not been incorporated into social work theory, and minority differences are ignored in social work training. There is a consensus that social work education is not adequately preparing students to work with all members of the Canadian population.

As a key part of the human service delivery system, social workers are not immune to increasing pressures to become more comfortable, knowledgeable and skilful in their work with diverse populations. Social services, as well as are health care, educational and other organizations, are now being challenged to develop and provide services that reflect the diversity in their communities. For example, in one city, organizations that receive funding from the local United Way are engaged in a process known as multicultural organizational change. The participating agencies are developing action plans designed to enhance the accessibility and utilization of services provided to members of diverse groups. Part of this process centres on the agencies creating organizational environments that accept, promote and value difference.

## FORCES WARRANTING THE NEED FOR CULTURALLY COMPETENT SOCIAL SERVICE PROVIDERS

Changing demographics in Canada make it highly likely that social workers will interact and work with a variety of clients from different cultural backgrounds and experiences. Canada's immigration policy, which during the period 1990 to 1995 will have admitted approximately 1.25 million newcomers (cited in *Managing Immigration: A Framework*, 1990), is a major reason for the increasing diversity in Canadian society. In commenting on this phenomenon, Kelly (1995, p. 3) states:

> In 1991, the 1.9 million adults in a visible minority in Canada represented 9% of the population aged 15 and over, doubling the 1981 proportion. More than three-quarters (78%) were immigrants.... As was the case during the 1980s, Chinese, Blacks, and South Asians accounted for two-thirds of adults in a visible minority in 1991. During the past decade, however, there have been large increases in some of the smaller visible minority groups such as East Asians and Latin Americans.

Therefore, it is imperative that social service professionals practice in a culturally competent manner. They cannot assume that their training provided them with the knowledge and skills required to work in a pluralistic society.

Green (1982) maintains that ethnic and minority groups are entitled to competent professional services. Inherent in this principle is the recognition that social workers must take into consideration the values, beliefs and norms of the client system receiving the services. In stronger language, Casimir and Morrison (1993, p. 58) contend that "anything other than full commitment to cultural competence in the delivery of mental health services must be viewed as a violation of consumers' civil rights."

Another factor driving enhanced attention towards culturally competent practice is the growing recognition that the traditional approaches have not adequately met the needs of individuals from diverse backgrounds. Hence, there is a need to develop effective methods of dealing with the issues and concerns of these clients.

Increasing demands from diverse populations for service providers to be more sensitive and responsive to the issues and needs of different groups is yet another factor. These diverse populations are also demanding enhanced opportunities to become involved in the planning and delivery of services. For example, aboriginal communities in Canada are demanding greater involvement or complete control of the human service infrastructure in their communities.

Pedersen et al. (1989) note that the influence of the multicultural perspective is growing throughout the social sciences, prompting the need for professionals of all types to become culturally competent. Chau (1990, p. 124), in describing the impact of the perspective on social work education, states:

> The rapid growth and increasing visibility of ethnic and racial groups constitutes an important force that revives and reshapes the ever-growing interest in educating for social work practice in cross-cultural contexts.

There is also an urgent need for social workers to recognize how individual and group backgrounds and experiences may impact on the ways services are utilized (Pedersen et al., 1989). It is equally important for social workers to be aware of how their own cultural values, norms and experiences influence their work with clients who possess different cultural backgrounds, values and experiences.

This chapter focuses on the competencies required by social workers in order to work effectively with diverse populations. The chapter presents select concepts that are critical to any discussion of culturally competent practice; this is followed by a description of the types of competencies needed by social work practitioners. Using frameworks similar to those developed by Moore (1994) and Manoleas (1994), these competencies are divided into the areas of knowledge, skills and values. Finally, a brief overview of the organizational variables required to promote and sustain culturally competent practice is provided.

## Major Concepts

In the literature dealing with culturally competent practice in the social service domain, a variety of terms exist to describe cultural competence (for example, cross-cultural practice, ethnic competency, multi cultural practice), but it is beyond the scope of this chapter to define the array of terms. This chapter, therefore, will use the term cultural competence, first defining the concepts of *culture*, *competence*, and finally, *cultural competence*.

Perhaps the most critical term in any discussion dealing with cultural competence is that of *culture*. According to Webster's Dictionary (1979) culture refers to the concepts, habits, skills, art, instruments, institutions, etc., of a given people in a given period (p. 44). Along similar lines, Olandi (1992) defines culture as "the shared values, norms, traditions, customs, arts, history, folklore, and institutions of a given people (p. vi). Culture, according to Kim (1988), is conceptualized as applying to all aggregates or categories of people whose "life patterns discernibly influence individual communication behaviours" (pp. 12-13).

In their classic work Cross et al. (1989) contend that the word *culture* implies the integrated pattern of human behaviour that includes thoughts, communications, actions, customs, beliefs and values, as well as institutions of racial, ethnic, religious or social groups. Edwards (1994, p. 47) remarks that "culture is one's world view: where one came from, why one is here and where one is going." Within the social service field, acknowledging, understanding and respecting different world views is becoming critical for social workers. English draws on Schiele's (1994, p. 22) definition of world views:

> ...the way in which people perceive their relationship to nature, other people, and objects. They determine how people behave, think, and define events. World views also are significantly influenced by culture. Thus, world views are said to vary by racial/ethnic group.

*Competence* represents the second critical concept. According to Webster's, competence is defined as having ability or capacity. Along similar lines, Cross et al. (1989) maintain that this implies having the capacity to function effectively. As discussed throughout this volume, social workers are expected to possess certain competencies such as assessment, planning, linking, monitoring and advocacy skills.

In defining what is meant by *cultural competence*, Cross et al. (1989) state:

> Cultural competence embraces ... the importance of culture, the assessment of cross-cultural relations, vigilance towards the dynamics that result from cultural differences, the expansion of cultural knowledge, and the adaptation of services to meet culturally unique needs. (p. 13)

They also stress that becoming culturally competent is a developmental process.

Olandi (1992, p. vi) defines cultural competence as:

> ...a set of academic and interpersonal skills that allow individuals to increase their understanding and appreciation of cultural differences and similarities within, among, and between groups. This requires a willingness and ability to draw on community-based values, traditions and customs and to work with knowledgeable persons of and from the community in developing focused interventions, communications, and other supports.

Olandi's definition is especially relevant to social work practice. The extent to which social workers become more knowledgeable about different cultural groups, as well as develop an appreciation that cultural differences do exist, are critical milestones in the process of becoming culturally competent. Stressing the importance for social workers to be more cognizant of the values, beliefs and customs of diverse communities represents another key step for social workers in their quest to become more effective in their practice with clients. Finally, Olandi's insistence that social workers connect and work with individuals from different communities represents, in essence, a vital social work process—the linking of clients with individuals and agencies in the community that will provide appropriate services.

According to Olandi (1992), the concept of cultural competence is multidimensional in nature, involving various aspects of knowledge, attitude and skill development. In addition, he contends that these aspects vary along a continuum from high to low. Figure 1, The Cultural Sophistication Framework, illustrates the developmental nature of the process whereby social workers become culturally competent.

| Figure 1: The Cultural Sophistication Framework | | | |
|---|---|---|---|
| | **Culturally Incompetent** | **Culturally Sensitive** | **Culturally Competent** |
| Cognitive dimension | Oblivious | Aware | Knowledgeable |
| Affective dimension | Apathetic | Sympathetic | Committed to change |
| Skills dimension | Unskilled | Lacking some skills | Highly skilled |
| Overall effect | Destructive | Neutral | Constructive |

*Culturally incompetent* represents the initial phase where social workers are unaware of the need and/or may not possess the desire to become culturally competent. In their practice, they may not give consideration to the impact that cultural factors may have on their work with clients. This can be very destructive, as social workers will likely approach all cases with the same mind set and, as a consequence, their practice with clients from diverse communities will not be effective.

In the second phase, *culturally sensitive* social workers are aware of the nuances of their own and others' cultures. They possess some skills in relation to cultural competency and are likely to be receptive to gaining more knowledge about different outcomes.

The final stage of becoming *culturally competent*, occurs when social workers understand the values, norms and customs of diverse communities and possess the skills required to practice in a culturally competent manner. Practicing at this level represents the ideal that social workers should attempt to achieve.

## KNOWLEDGE COMPETENCIES

In the literature dealing with culturally competent practice, there is a fairly strong consensus that social workers need an understanding of different types of knowledge. For example, various writers maintain that social workers need to be knowledgeable about the characteristics of specific cultural groups such as gays and lesbians; have an understanding of phenomena such as racism, sexism, ageing and discrimination; and finally, be familiar with different theoretical perspectives, such as assimilation, melting pot, social class and ethnic conflict (Aponte, 1995). According to Ronnau (1994) "perhaps the first step in the cultural competency journey is the need for professionals to admit to a lack of knowledge about other cultures and to make a commitment to learn about them" (p. 33).

Lum (1986) describes the knowledge base required of professionals working with minority populations:

> ...the range of information, awareness and understanding of the minority situational experience. It involves history, cognitive-affective behavioral characteristics, and of the societal dilemmas of people of color. (Quoted from Manoleas, 1994, p. 47)

The types of knowledge identified by Lum in relation to visible minority clients are also needed by social workers who work with clients from other diverse populations, such as the disabled, gays and lesbians, the mentally ill and persons with AIDS. Each of these communities has distinctive values, beliefs, norms and histories of which social workers must be aware.

### Types of knowledge required by social workers

Unquestionably, the starting point for social workers who aspire to become culturally competent is to become aware of their own cultures. Culturally sensitive individuals must be cognizant of how their own backgrounds may affect interactions with clients from other backgrounds. Ronnau (1994, p. 34) comments:

> To fully appreciate cultural differences workers must recognize the influence of their own culture on how they think and act. It is important that [workers] become aware that cultural competence necessitates some introspection.

Neukrug (1994) makes the same claim as he remarks that "the culturally sensitive individual has an awareness of his or her own cultural background, biases, stereotypes, and values and has the ability to expect differences" (pp. 6-7). Rodwell and Blankebaker (1992, p. 162) comment on the education of social workers:

> Any educational effort should be one of raising "students' consciousness" to their own biases and the dynamics of those biases in social work practice. Education should result in at least a tolerance of, if not acceptance or comfort with, differences.

According to various writers, social workers need to be knowledgeable about different cultures (Moore, 1994; Neukrug, 1994; Ronnau, 1994; Dungee-Anderson and Beckett, 1995). Ronnau (1994) argues that cultural competence requires continuous efforts to gain more knowledge about the client's culture. The quest for this knowledge is an ongoing process, and it is unrealistic to expect workers to have comprehensive knowledge of all cultures. Gaining knowledge to identify what information is needed as well as knowing whom to ask for it is a desirable goal. By interacting with their clients and other practitioners, social workers have the opportunity to learn more about diverse backgrounds.

Jeff (1994) and Moore (1994) contend that it is important for social workers to be knowledgeable of the world views possessed by clients. Again, acquisition of this type of information is an ongoing process. Moore (1994) states that "the culturally skilled [individual] actively attempts to understand the world view of his (her) culturally different client without negative judgements" (p. 34).

Some writers also contend that the culturally sensitive professional needs to understand how behaviours such as racism, sexism, homophobia and ageism impact on individuals. Edwards (1994) contends that:

Racism victimizes the dominant culture by obliterating any distinction or glory to its heritage, in an effort to define difference as negative and undesirable and its own ways as standard. Consequently the pride of identifying with a culture of one's own is lost. (p. 51)

She notes that one of the benefits of being knowledgeable about topics such as racism, sexism and discrimination is that it provides the opportunity for social workers to acknowledge "their own racist attitudes, beliefs, and feelings" (p. 51).

Ronnau (1994, p. 33) strongly contends that if social workers do not engage in the process of becoming culturally competent, their effectiveness will be limited: "The culturally competent professional...must be helped to accept the fact that ignoring or denying that differences do exist is not helpful and may even be harmful." Edwards (1994, p. 49) comments on the same issue:

The denial of or the inability to address cultural differences in a therapeutic relationship has contributed to many counter-transference issues. The racial conflicts existing in society often contribute to clinicians' fear of confrontation. This results in lack of empathy, discomfort, and awkwardness. All this because one is unsure how to communicate, fear of revelation or ignorance or disrespect. This inevitably leads to insecurity and often resentment on the part of the clinician as well as the client.

As part of the knowledge development process, it is imperative that social workers acknowledge that differences exist between and among cultural groups (Edwards, 1994; Moore, 1994). The "ability to appreciate cultural differences is an important step in the journey to become culturally competent" (Ronnau, 1994, p. 33). Edwards (1994) maintains that the willingness to acknowledge and address valid cultural differences between a human service practitioner and client is the most difficult stage of development in the cultural competency process.

Some writers maintain that social workers should possess more specific knowledge. For example, it is important to have knowledge of family structures, hierarchies, sex roles and kinship networks of different cultural groups (Moore, 1994); caregiving roles that prevail in diverse populations (Manoleas, 1994); and community characteristics (basic demographic data, information on employment status and income, housing, educational facilities, transportation systems, prevailing social problems). Being knowledgeable about the available health and social services is essential. Social workers must also identify the barriers that limit both access and utilization of services by diverse populations.

Although advocacy is considered a generic activity, those working with disadvantaged and marginal populations may have to engage in far more advocacy activities to ensure that these clients receive the services they require. The following comment by Moore (1994, p. 38) is appropriate for social workers: "Culturally skilled counselors should attend to as well as work to eliminate biases, prejudices and discriminatory practices."

It is not enough for social workers to possess the different types of knowledge identified in this section; the greater challenge will be to use them in ways that will benefit the clients they serve. Social workers will encounter situations where they will have to be creative not only in their assessments but also in the types of interventions they employ.

## SKILL COMPETENCIES

The skills base for culturally competent practice centres on "developing a helping relationship with an individual, family, group, and/ or community whose distinctive physical/cultural characteristics and discriminatory experiences require approaches that are sensitive to ethnic and cultural environments" (Lum, 1986, p. 3).

Critical for social workers in the development of a trusting relationship is the ability to show empathic understanding. In describing this particular skill, Neukrug (1994, p. 8) comments that "the empathic person is able to have a deep understanding of another person's point of view, can accept people in their differences, and is able to communicate this sense of acceptance."

Proctor and Davis (1994, p. 318) contend that "one of the major concerns experienced by clients in cross-racial helping relationships is whether their social reality is understood by the helper. Empathic social workers accept their clients regardless of different cultural heritage, values or belief systems."

Social workers must conduct thorough assessments and take into consideration how cultural factors may influence the manifestation of their clients' behaviours. As part of the assessment process, social workers should evaluate their clients' world views and their levels of acculturation, especially if the clients are immigrants. In this context acculturation refers to how well individuals adjust to life in Canada.

As part of the assessment process, Edwards (1994, p. 53) maintains that the following questions be posed to clients who are immigrants:

- When and how did the clients or families migrate to their present communities?
- What prompted the move?
- Was it to escape oppression?
- Was their homeland destroyed by war?
- What was needed for them to effect their escape?
- What has been easiest and what has been most difficult for them to adjust to?

Neukrug (1994) and Moore (1994) stress that social workers should utilize a variety of helping styles and approaches in their daily practice. Having such a repertoire, in their opinion, will enhance the likelihood that social workers will be more effective in their work with diverse clients.

Another important skill required of social workers is the ability to speak a second language. For those who are unilingual, access to translation and interpretation services is extremely important. Using such services not only assists in the communication process but also imparts to the clients that the workers are attempting to serve them in an effective manner.

Social workers must possess the ability to utilize culturally appropriate interviewing techniques as well. It is important, for example, for them to be cognizant of the level of their intrusiveness and directness with clients, social distance, formality and ways of addressing clients (Manoleas, 1994, p. 50):

> Effectiveness of direct or indirect practice is closely
> related to the worker's ability to communicate and form
> positive relationships. The communication of respect
> is especially important for clients who have experienced
> oppression at the hands of the system, for immigrants
> not used to the casualness of this country [Canada],

and for others who may be inherently skeptical about social agencies.

In relation to the communication process with clients from diverse backgrounds, social workers must be aware of and sensitive to the verbal and nonverbal communication imparted by their clients. Being knowledgeable about the specific meanings of nonverbal communication in different groups and being observant in practice will enhance social workers' ability to understand their clients.

The ability to recognize and manage defensiveness and resistance in the client is also necessary. In defining defensiveness in the communication process, Kavanagh and Kennedy (1992, p. 52) state:

> At times communication is associated with risk, such as when there is uncertainty about how exposure of reactions will be received, especially if the others have power or are in some way potentially threatening. When involved in a situation that is uneasy, defensiveness, anger, or hurt may occur.... Defensiveness occurs when personal security is perceived to be threatened.

Kavanagh and Kennedy (1992, pp. 56-57) provide the following strategies to decrease client defensiveness:

1. Defensiveness may be revealed and identified through assessment of a client's expressions, manner, or tone of response; to understand, from the client's perspective, what the client's behavior means.
2. Humor, including that which is self-directed, is often valuable in diminishing defensiveness and building rapport.
3. Disclosing selected, culturally appropriate personal information can decrease defensiveness by promoting sharing and a sense of acceptance.
4. Acknowledging and describing your own or the client's beliefs, behavior, or responses in nonjudgmental ways avoids defensiveness.

5. Eliciting information or help from others, including clients, minimizes defensiveness.

A number of writers maintain that recognizing, acknowledging and reducing resistance is important in minimizing barriers in communication between clients and service providers. Kavanagh and Kennedy (1992, p. 58) define resistance as:

> Resistance involves barriers to trust or opposition to the goal of mutual communication. Providers may find themselves resisting the use of a client's perspectives in problem definition and resolution. Clients, on the other hand, may resist professional views of the problem, strategies, or goals.

Having the skills required to deal with resistance is crucial for social workers. Kavanagh and Kennedy (1992, pp. 58-59) also provide strategies designed to deal with resistance.

1. Demonstrate acceptance and understanding by clearly identifying the client's concern or understanding of the problem, whether or not it is addressed the same way by the client.
2. Carefully assess coping response patterns to stressful and other problematic situations. This includes one's own coping patterns. Such assessment promotes identification of patterns of resistance responses.
3. Ask questions, but alter them according to the client's cultural and linguistic expectations. For members of some groups only open questions are socially acceptable (for example, "How do you handle...?"). For others, closed questions are preferred (such as, "Do you...?"). Still others (including many traditional Native American groups) require indirect inquiries. Questions are cast in story-like scenarios to which the client may respond. For instance, "Some people find that when that happens it is best to...."

4. Accurately reflecting, clarifying, interpreting, and perhaps re-labeling the client's behaviors, beliefs, or ideas can communicate both recognition and understanding of the client's perspective.

5. Develop awareness of and knowledge about the client's informal or natural support systems. The client is part of a larger system and seldom acts or makes decisions truly alone.

It must be noted that client resistance may be viewed as a positive development. Such behaviour, for example, may indicate that the client is assertive and capable of making decisions for herself or himself, thus reinforcing a primary value in social work—client self-determination.

Since the ability to form relationships with individuals, communities and organizations across cultures is important, contacts and networks need to be established. Moore (1994, p. 38) states: "Culturally skilled counselors are not averse to seeking consultation with traditional healers and religious and spiritual leaders and practitioners in the treatment of culturally different clients when appropriate."

In conclusion, development by social workers of the knowledge and skills described above represents major components of the process of their becoming culturally competent. It is false to assume that even the most skilful and knowledgeable culturally competent social worker can deal with the array of situations encountered by clients from diverse backgrounds. In those cases where severe language and/or other barriers exist, social workers will need to refer them to individuals or services that will facilitate the helping process. One can argue that social workers who recognize their limitations in relation to cultural competent practice are indeed working in a culturally competent manner.

## VALUE COMPETENCIES

Specific values, beliefs and attitudes are required to assist in the development of culturally competent social workers. Manoleas (1994, p. 52) maintains that the value base is "arguably most important in cultural competence." Social workers must value cultural diversity and respect its worth (Manoleas, 1994; Edwards, 1994; Ronnau, 1994). Ronnau (1994) maintains that being a culturally competent professional is, to a large degree, an attitude.

Manoleas (1994) states that individuals must acknowledge and accept that cultural differences do exist and that they do impact service delivery and utilization. To not do so may limit the effectiveness of social workers with clients from different cultural backgrounds.

In addition in order to avoid stereotyping, social workers must also recognize that heterogeneity within cultures is as important as diversity between cultures. For example, it would be erroneous to assume that all immigrants from the West Indies share the same cultural values, norms and beliefs since the West Indies is comprised of several different nations, each with distinctive cultures. Commenting on this particular value, Waxler-Morrison et al., (1990, p. 246) state:

> ...while there are usually shared beliefs, values, and experiences among people from a given ethnic group, quite often there is widespread intra-ethnic diversity. Factors such as social class, religion, level of education, and area of origin in the home country (rural or urban) make for major differences....

The third value premise, the practice of cultural relativism, which asserts that there are different ways of viewing and interpreting phenomena, is extremely important. Cultural relativism contends that no specific world view is superior, better or more correct than another— the perspective is simply different. By understanding and accepting this concept, social workers will place themselves in a position to learn about other world views and become creative in their work with clients from diverse backgrounds.

It is also important to stress that belief in these values does not ensure that social workers are or will become culturally competent. Possession and utilization of different types of knowledge and skills are essential. As discussed in the following section, administrators of human service agencies must also ensure that their organizations value and support cultural competency in their practitioners.

## ORGANIZATIONAL CONTEXT

Writers such as Mann (1994), Sue (1995) and Rynes and Rosen (1994) contend that it is imperative for social service administrators to ensure that a climate exists in their organizations that values and promotes cultural competency. Mann (1994, p. 21), on child welfare administrators, states: "Some well-meaning executives recognize the need to have a working environment in which all kinds of people can thrive and at the same time effectively provide services to a diverse group of clients." She also comments on the potential implications of those child welfare executives who do not promote diversity:

> Executives in child welfare who fail to value diversity and prepare for multicultural workforces and client populations place themselves and their organizations at risk for internal conflict among staff as well as external pressure from clients and communities who perceive the agency as unresponsive and unconcerned. (p. 21)

There is consensus in the literature that strong leadership is required in order to begin and sustain the process of achieving a culturally competent organization (Mann, 1994; Sue, 1995). More specifically, it is stressed that commitment must come from the top (Sue, 1995, p. 480):

> Commitment must be manifested in action. It is more than a written policy statement of affirmative action or statements that one is an 'equal opportunity employer.' What specific steps have the leadership taken to implement diversity goals?

Mann (1994) and Rynes and Rosen (1994) provide the following guidelines for social service administrators who are committed to creating a culturally competent agency:

- Conduct an introspective examination of cultural values, biases and stereotypes within the agency;
- Identify a personal and professional philosophy that encompasses a respect for cultural differences;
- Clarify the reasons why cultural competence is so important to the organization;
- Develop a vision around the "place" where the organization would be if it functioned as one that strives to be culturally competent;

- Understand and think through the personal and organizational risks that must be taken in launching cultural competence initiatives;
- Assume responsibility for creating and maintaining a culturally supportive environment for staff and clients;
- Provide training and staff development that encourage non-threatening opportunities for open discussion of problems and issues;
- Assume a leadership role in encouraging boards and other advisory bodies to reflect in their membership the cultural mix of the client population served by the agency;
- Assume a leadership role in communicating the significance of cultural competence to the governance of the organization;
- Recruit and retain staff who are culturally diverse;
- Include all staff in plans for creating a culturally supportive environment;
- Commit to achieving a personal and an organizational lifetime goal of cultural competence.

Collectively the implementation of these initiatives represents tangible evidence that the leadership in human service organizations values and is highly committed to cultural competence. In essence, activities designed to enhance the cultural competence of social workers represent the profession's attempt to fulfil one of the basic social work values— the inherent respect for and dignity of the individual.

## REFERENCES

Aponte, C. (1995). Cultural diversity course model: Cultural competence for content and process. *Arete*, 20, 1, 46-55.

Casimir, G. and Morrison, B. (1993). Rethinking work with multicultural populations. *Community Mental Health Journal*, 29, 6, 547-559.

Chau, K. (1990). A model for teaching cross-cultural practice in social work. *Journal of Social Work Education*, 124-133.

Cross, T., Bazron, B., Dennis, K. and Isaacs, M. (1989). *Towards a culturally competent system of care*. Washington, D.C.: CASSP Technical Assistance Center.

Dungee-Anderson, D. and Beckett, J. (1995). A process model for multicultural social work practice. *Families in Society*, 76, 8, 459-468.

Edwards, V. (1994). Understanding culture as a process. In R. Surber (ed.), (1994), *Clinical case management: A guide to comprehensive treatment of serious mental illness.* Thousand Oaks, CA: Sage.

Employment and Immigration Canada. (1992). *Managing immigration: A framework for the 1990's.* Hull: Government of Canada.

Green, J. (1982). *Cultural awareness in the human services.* Englewood Cliffs, NJ: Prentice-Hall.

Jeff, M. (1994). Afrocentrism and afro-american male youths. In R. Mincy (ed.), *Nurturing young black males.* Washington, D.C.: The Urban Institute Press.

Kavanagh, K. and Kennedy, P. (1992). *Promoting cultural diversity: Strategies for health care professionals.* Newbury Park, CA: Sage.

Kelly, K. (1995). *Visible minorities: A diverse group.* Canadian Social Trends, 3, 1, 3-8.

Kim, Y. Y. (1988). On theorizing intercultural communication. In Y. Y. Kim and W. B. Gudykunst (eds.), *Theories in intercultural communication.* Newbury Park, CA: Sage.

Lum, D. (1986). *Social work practice and people of color.* Pacific Grove, CA: Brooks/Cole.

Mann, J. (1994). Diversity: Professional and personal challenges for executive leadership. *The Child and Youth Care Administrator*, 6, 1, 20-22.

Manoleas, P. (1994). An outcome approach to assessing the cultural competence of MSW students. *Journal of Multicultural Social Work*, 3, 1, 43-57.

Moore, Q. (1994). A whole new world of diversity. *The Journal of Intergroup Relations*, 20, 4, 28-40.

Neukrug, E. (1994). Understanding diversity in a pluralistic world. *The Journal of Intergroup Relations*, 22, 2, 3-12.

Olandi, M. (1992). Defining cultural competence: An organizing framework. In M. Olandi (ed.), *Cultural competence for evaluators: A guide for alcohol and other drug abuse prevention practitioners working with ethnic/racial communities.* Rockville, Maryland: Department of Health and Human Services.

Pedersen, P. , Fukiyama, M. and Health, A. (1989). Client, counselor, and contextual variables in multicultural counseling. In P. Pedersen (ed.), *Counseling across cultures.* Honolulu, Hawaii: University of Hawaii Press.

Ponterotto, J., Casas, J., Suzuki, L. and Alexander, C. (1995) (eds.), *The handbook of multicultural counseling.* Thousand Oaks, CA: Sage.

Proctor, E. and Davis, L. (1994). The challenge of racial difference: Skills for clinical practice. *Social Work*, 39, 3, 314-323.

Rodwell, M. K. and Blankebaker, A. (1992). Strategies for developing cross-cultural sensitivity: Wounding as metaphor. *Journal of Social Education*, 28, 2, 153-165.

Ronnau, J. (1994). Teaching cultural competence: Practical ideas for social work educators. *Journal of Multicultural Social Work*, 5, 1, 29-42.

Rynes, S. and Rosen, B. (1994). What makes diversity programs work? *HR Magazine*, 39, 10, 67-73.

Schiele, J. (1994). Afrocentricity as an alternative world view for equality. *Journal of Progressive Human Services*, 5(1), 5-25.

Sue, D. W. (1995). Multicultural organizational development. In J. Ponterotto, J. Casas, L. Suzuki and C. Alexander (eds.), *The handbook of multicultural counseling*. Thousand Oaks, CA: Sage.

Waxler-Morrison, N., Anderson, J. and Richardson, E. (1990). *Cross-cultural caring: A handbook for health professionals*. Vancouver, BC: University of British Columbia Press.

*Webster's new world dictionary* (1982). New York, NY: New World Dictionaries.

Yelaja, S. and O'Neill, B. (1990). *Multiculturalism and social work education: Resources for change*. Waterloo, ON: Wilfrid Laurier University Press.

# PART 2

# IMPLICATIONS OF MULTICULTURAL POLICY
## a) for practice

# CHAPTER 3

# Immigration and Refugee Children and Adolescents: Expanding the Vision of Possibilities

## Jane Aldous

The way in which we conceptualize the needs of clients affects our operational definitions and therefore our practice. If each discipline views immigrant and refugee (IR) children and adolescents from the perspective of their own practice, using varying languages, conceptual frames and modalities of intervention, the result may be a fragmented patchwork of interventions with gaps or overlaps in certain areas, and a lack of continuity and meaning for the client. Although a great deal of research remains to be done, our current knowledge about effective intervention with IR children and adolescents points to an approach that puts the child's meaning and experience at the centre, in relation to his or her bio-psycho-social needs and strengths as they develop over time and within the context of family and community systems. Such an approach involves the weaving together of intervention modalities by a multicultural, multidisciplinary, professional and paraprofessional team, preferably working at the primary prevention level.

Although various members of a team of human service professionals working with IR children and adolescents will provide expertise in one aspect of intervention, each must have a multidimensional view in order to work in context. The first four sections below are demographics and definitions, followed by descriptions of the biological, psychological and social needs and strengths of IR children and adolescents. In order to create a full picture from which a sense of practice in context can begin to develop, the fifth section brings the reader's multidimensional view alive by including examples of experiences of IR children and adolescents and the effects of these experiences on their continuity of meaning and spirituality. In the subsequent section, a summary of some current and developing programs are provided, including a look at two evolving Canadian programs. This is followed by a discussion of research needs and the effect of Canadian social policy on the implementation of such programs in Canada.

## CREATING A FULL PICTURE OF IR CHILDREN AND ADOLESCENTS

### Demographics and definitions

During the five year period of 1986 to 1991, approximately 157,000 immigrant and refugee children under the age of twelve landed in Canada (Beiser, Dion, Gotowiec, Hyman and Vu, 1995). About one-quarter of all migrant children under age twelve who entered Canada in 1995 were refugees. When we include adolescents in these numbers it is estimated that up to a total of 35,000 children and teenagers under age nineteen were entering Canada each year by 1993 (Beiser et al., 1988).

More than 75% of immigrants now come from Asia, Africa, the Middle East and Latin America. In light of this change, Hicks, Lalonde and Pepler (1993) challenge the very definitions of immigrant and refugee. They suggest that for research and intervention purposes with immigrant children it is essential to make distinctions based on "the extent to which the receiving country differs from their country of birth, their age at migration, and length of residence in receiving country" (p. 73). For example, a young child from the United States who has been in Canada the same length of time as an adolescent from Africa or Asia would have vastly different needs from his or her fellow immigrant.

It is also crucial to be aware of the distinction between immigrant and refugee children. Violence, trauma, persecution and/or severe deprivation, combined with the fact that migration was not chosen, make the needs of refugee children unique. Post-migration these children live with their parents' uncertainty about the outcome of their refugee claims, and families are often forced into poverty during the wait because working is illegal (Beiser et al, 1995).

The terms immigrant and refugee are also the first in a string of labels such as "displaced person" and "illegal alien" that not only hide the complex variables involved in defining their experience, but also serve to erase the image of "the human face" of the immigrant and refugee story from our awareness (Kuoch, Wali and Scully, 1992).

## The biological view

Poor physical health in children has a significant effect on physical, cognitive and related psychological and social development and therefore must be assessed as part of any intervention. Health may be affected prior to or during migration as well as post migration. Although immigrant children may have a variety of health problems, in comparison, refugee children are more likely to have poor physical health related to pre-migration malnutrition, physical injury or abuse, sexual abuse or disease. Following migration, both immigrant and refugee children may continue to suffer nutritional disorders (physical and mental) due to unfamiliar foods and preparation methods, the greater expense of some foods such as fruit, lower resistance to local diseases, as well as possible improper use of medications (Westermeyer, 1991; Hicks, Lalonde and Pepler, 1993; Beiser et al, 1995). In addition, health professionals who work only in Canada may not be aware of some of the diseases present in immigrants and refugees from countries lacking adequate nutrition, healthy environments and health care (Williams, 1991).

## The psychological view

Although there is little known about specific mental disorders in IR children and adolescents, Williams (1991) cites numerous case studies that suggest there is higher prevalence among refugee children and adolescents than in the general population. Westermeyer (1991) extrapolates from the little available research to summarize various diagnoses that could be expected to occur, many of which may have been present pre-migration, but some of which may be a result of the migration experience or acculturation: eating disorders, major depression, paranoid psychosis, conduct disorders, post-traumatic stress disorder or substance use disorders. In general he concludes, however, that these disorders are difficult to assess accurately in children. Even the most prevalent disorder in adult refugees, major depression, is rarely diagnosed in children under sixteen years, perhaps because it does not occur or because it manifests differently or is accompanied by other problems that mask it (Westermeyer, 1991).

Hicks et al. (1993) cite research that suggests psychiatric disturbances in refugee children can be related to mental health problems in other family members and, as would be expected, symptoms can be exacerbated by the separation from or loss of parents. Athey and Ahearn (1991) review the literature on bereavement in children and conclude that because of their refugee experience, when these children lose a parent they are often automatically at higher risk of emotional problems for five of the eleven risk factors: 1) the death is often unanticipated; 2) the death is often violent; 3) there is lack of adequate family or community supports; 4) the child's environment is unstable and inconsistent; and 5) the surviving parent is probably psychologically vulnerable and may have excessive dependence on the child.

Surviving parents who are suffering the trauma of war, torture and the anxiety and stress of flight and resettlement are often unable to care for children adequately and communication may be poor. Also, children may make up their own explanations and take on responsibility and guilt for what has happened (Hicks et al., 1993). Williams (1991, p. 207) provides a quote from one little Pakistani girl that illustrates this acute sense of responsibility for such events: "Oh what have we done now that they need to bomb us again?"

Even though some studies do indicate a higher prevalence of psychological disturbance among IR children, other studies summarized by Hicks et al. (1993) provide evidence of positive adaptation such as success in school and adequate self-esteem. Beiser et al. (1995) point out that the stress of migration itself is not necessarily related to psychological disorder but rather the "context" in which it occurs. For example, Hicks et al. (1993) lists five research studies that support the hypothesis that refugee children experiencing war violence, trauma and extended deprivation are at increased risk of prolonged psychological disturbance. On the other hand, Garmezy (1983) summarizes five studies on the surprising resilience of children to such stress and identifies a triad of resiliency producing factors: 1) positive personality dispositions (active, autonomous, social); 2) supportive family milieu (closeness, rule-setting); and 3) external support system (peers, teachers etc. who strengthen and support coping efforts).

Carlin (1986) emphasizes the importance of the age of the child at various critical points in the flight and resettlement because of the developmental task that may be interrupted. For example, older but still pre-verbal infants will have memories of traumatic events, which will not be represented in language and may present as nightmares. Children who experience trauma at age two to three years when language development is rapid may experience various disruptions in speech. Matsuoka (1990) notes that for adolescents the lack of continuity and meaning due to cultural and family losses is of particular significance when they are establishing an adult identity and looking for a place to belong. Although some attention has been given to ethnic identity development in general in the literature (see Ponterotto, Casas, Suzuki and Alexander, 1995) the interface of adolescence identity development tasks with ethnic identity development has been virtually ignored.

In practice it may be more useful to be aware of the various possible symptoms of distress that may occur in children, rather than to focus on specific diagnoses. Ressler, Boothby and Steinbock (1988) describes the difference of general symptoms of distress in children of various ages; for example, infants in distress may refuse food, have sleep disturbances and cry intensely. Young children may have somatic complaints along with sleep disturbances. Young adolescents may withdraw or be aggressive and exhibit somatic symptoms such as headaches or stomach pains. Hicks et al. (1993, p. 76) summarize studies on children exposed specifically to war violence and trauma and indicates that in general they may have: "confused and disordered memories of events, repetitive unsatisfying play on themes related to trauma, substantial personality change, imitation of violent behaviour, and pessimistic expectations regarding survival." Very young children exposed to war violence may demonstrate regressive behaviour, withdrawal and fearfulness, while school-age children may demonstrate poor concentration, startle responses, flashbacks and somatic and sleep complaints. Adolescents, by comparison, tend to exhibit aggressive behaviours and delinquency, along with nightmares, flashbacks and guilt at their own survival.

Beiser et al. (1988, p. 65) conclude that research regarding the extent of mental health needs and the conditions that create risk for these youth is very much needed: "Patterns of adaptation laid down in childhood and adolescence are important precursors for mental health in later life."

## The social view

Compared to the average Canadian child, 12% more IR children may live in poverty and in unstable or even dangerous environments post-migration. They may also experience interracial conflict, youth unemployment and family instability through death, separation, illness or stress-related conflict. (Beiser et al., 1988). Despite a widespread belief that children are free from racist attitudes, many young children suffer discrimination in the classroom from both peers and teachers. The desire to belong to the Canadian peer group is so strong that many children dream of changing their physical appearance. Youths have reported that they have done such things as play with white towels on their heads to pretend they were blond and have created fantasies in which they married someone white and had blond, blue-eyed children (Mattu, Pruegger, and Grant, 1995). Teachers may fail to actively intervene to stop racist classroom behaviour and further fail to support the self-esteem of an offended child when racist attitudes are expressed (Beiser, et al., 1988).

Youth unemployment is also a neglected problem. Many refugee youth, for example, have experienced disruption in their education but are now too old for the Canadian school system, yet they lack the necessary skills to enter the workforce. The "double alienation" or marginalization that occurs as these youth attempt to relinquish their own culture while not yet accepted in the host culture leaves them wide open for such things as recruitment, often by the adult criminal element, into gangs (Beiser et al., 1998).

Some IR children may find themselves isolated from both the mainstream community by virtue of language, culture and racism, and at the same time isolated from their own ethnic community due to lack of proximity or differences in sub-cultures. Children of refugee families may find their parents wary of involvement in the new culture, while others may be wary of cultural groups from their country of origin because of lack of trust and suspiciousness originating from their pre-migration experiences. Sometimes spies are suspected of reporting information to the homeland that could have severe repercussions for family members who remain there (Athey and Ahearn, 1991). Rosenthal (1984) has found that the adolescents who are the most assimilated to the host culture are the ones associated with higher levels of family conflict. As Anderson, Waxler-Morrison, Richardson, Herbert and Murphy (1990) point out, some immigrant parents may seem to Canadians to be overly indulgent with young children while overly strict with teens. Their hopes for the future may be put into the youth's education so much so that the teen is expected to stay at home and study instead of socializing. The acculturating youth, however, may object to their parents' discipline and demands as they develop language and attitudes outside the home that their parents cannot understand. Rosenthal (1984) suggests that defining these problems broadly as "culture conflict" is too simple. The balance between the two cultures is key. Adolescents need to maintain a positive sense of their culture of origin identity; their parents need to be able to openly value positive aspects of the new culture. Too great an emphasis on rapid assimilation may lead to greater feelings of conflict for adolescents.

It must also be noted that socio-economic and sociological change have been linked to an increase in child maltreatment. Korbin (1991) cites three sources to support this statement, but is quick to point out that this is a complex issue. Korbin (1991) lists a number of possible reasons for this shift: 1) a change to an urban economy makes children "consumers" rather than "producers"; 2) children acculturate faster causing a power shift in the family relationships; 3) parents are less confident in their parenting given different norms and behaviours; and 4) parents and children are separated from extended family members. To add to the complexity is the need for culturally informed definitions of child maltreatment that include an understanding of the intent of certain cultural practices, i.e., the definition of abuse must be considered with regard to intent to harm, for example, use of certain traditional medicines. Some child-rearing practices may be acceptable in one culture but not in another (e.g., corporal punishment) or practices may be altered and misused when transplanted into a new setting (Korbin, 1991).

As mentioned previously, some research shows that despite all of these stressors most families display resiliency. Rosenthal (1984, p. 74):

> ...this study adds further support to previous research in which it has been argued that the prevalence of such conflict [issues related to personal freedom, occupational goals and social behaviour] has been exaggerated. It seems that parents and their adolescents can and do live together in relative harmony although external factors, such as minority group status, may create some degree of familial conflict.

The above diversity of research and conjecture offers complex and often contradictory outcomes regarding IR children and adolescents' problems and their successes in the process of adaptation. Hicks et al. (1993) suggest that, correspondingly, for purposes of intervention we take a more complex and dynamic view that balances the interplay of risk and protective factors that operate in the context of family, school and community. Hicks et al. (1993) use Bronfenbrenner's (1979, p. 72, 74) ecological framework for conceptualizing adaptation as a "multidimensional ... interactive process unfolding over time," in which "children cannot be understood without considering the complex environments they inhabit." Williams (1991a) emphasizes three points regarding the understanding of acculturation in general. First, the culture of the acculturating group must be understood on its own terms and not as a "minority." Second, many acculturation "phenomena" are a result of the interaction of the two cultural groups, not simply that of the newcomers. Third, there are wide individual differences in mental health outcomes that depend on a variety of group and individual variables in the acculturation process.

From the perspective of promoting health development, Hicks et al. (1993) summarize from the available literature the following risk factors for the IR child as he or she functions within the family and community: degree of trauma, loss or deprivation during pre-migratory experience; poor language acquisition; low literacy and education of parents in language of receiving culture; inability of parents to support the child in his or her education due to language and cultural barriers; family disruption in the form of separation or physical and mental health problems; poverty, underemployment and unemployment of parents; isolation from the mainstream community due to discrimination or language and cultural barriers; and finally, isolation from the ethnic community due to marginalization or lack of community development.

The risk factors described above presuppose the protective factors for healthy development: family stability; involvement with the ethnic community to support integration and to validate cultural traditions and values; and school characteristics including, a balance of heritage language and host culture language, training of teachers and students regarding racism and multiculturalism, and creative solutions to problems of communication between parents and school based on the realization that these problems are reciprocal (Hicks et al., 1993). The importance of viewing these protective factors as dynamically interrelated is stressed.

For example, as suggested by Rosenthal (1984), the combination of parents maintaining ties to their ethnic community while demonstrating positive attitudes towards acculturation may be a protective factor.

## A look at experience, meaning and spirituality

The picture created so far of the IR child has consisted of numbers, labels, concepts and frameworks, but as yet a human face has hardly appeared. The stories of these children and youths need to be heard and felt in order to bring these words and numbers to life.

Roberson, (1992, p. 38), tells the story of ten-year-old Muna, a Palestinian refugee forced from her home at gunpoint, who struggled with shame as well as loss and trauma:

> Almost dying of thirst during their walk ... Muna nursed from her mother who had given birth to her brother days earlier. A desperate search for water occurred after mother's collapse. Although they found some, they had no container. Muna's cousin dipped his shirt into the water and returned to her mother to squeeze the moisture into her mouth. Thankfully, Muna's mother survived. Many didn't .... 'We were upset. Being a refugee, you're stigmatized; you're poor; you're nothing. Even though these [refugees] had come from very good homes. Nobody would trust you; nobody would lend you money.' ... Muna recalled with humiliation the time she went to the Red Cross worker and said: 'We need some help. We need clothing.' It was cold, my feet were swollen from chilblains. I had frostbite in one finger ... the Red Cross worker looked at me and said, 'We don't have any; you go home.'... And I went home and never went back again. That was, very, very humiliating. To go and beg for these things and to be told no.

Roberson (1992) traced the process of transformation of Muna's refugee identity and discovered four distinct transformations. Muna's awareness of her refugee identity consisted of becoming "this label." However, she gradually came to think: "'the fact that we are refugees and we are poor, that does not mean that we are poor in mind, that we cannot make things, that we cannot do things'" (p. 38-39). And as transformation to self-acceptance occurred, she "refused to be ashamed." Further transformations included the emergence of refugee pride that claimed the refugee identity card as a "passport" that connected her roots with her future. Finally the death of the refugee identity transformed her from victim to survivor, forever influenced by the refugee experience.

Those caring for refugee children, whether family or health professionals, are often unaware of difficulties and tend to "underidentify problems," and families may be reluctant to seek help (Hicks et al., 1993), perhaps due to a lack of understanding or fear of the host country's health system or the inability to use traditional language and cultural structures such as rituals to make sense of and transform experience. For young people this disturbance of cultural norms and structure occurs before they have had time to internalize them (Matsuoka, 1990). At the same time there may be no structures in place in the host country for them to make meaning of their experiences. The story of an eleven-year-old boy from El Salvador told by Espino (1991, pp. 106-107) illustrates this:

> After a long pause he said that 'when they would come out of hiding there were only dead people.' He proceeded to say, 'One day there were three men by the house, one dead, one alive and one begging for water with all his insides hanging out. There were many asking for water. This would happen when there was fighting or when someone was killed by an enemy. They would come and dump them on the street and there they stayed until they died or their mothers came to get them.' ... Douglas admitted to remembering traumatic events when he did not want to, for example, the sound of a motorcycle brought back a vivid memory of a man who had been shot and whom he had seen crash to the ground. When he did his school work, 'some of the things came out right and others come out wrong' because of thoughts he had about his grandmother being left back home. Douglas had not been referred for treatment nor was he identified by teachers or parents as needing any sort of

intervention. His poor school performance was attributed to his lack of knowledge of English and lack of formal education.

For refugees and immigrants the experience of migration means a disruption of a coherent sense of self, in relation to others and as part of a group. Jeter refers to the work of sociologist Emile Durkheim to emphasize the original function of spiritual beliefs and rituals for aboriginal peoples before religion was "bureaucratized, formalized, and professionalized." He states:

> ...beliefs and rituals foster relationships between people .... Frightening periods of time, such as bereavement, are not faced alone.... The rites remind individuals that they have kin and friends to lessen burdens, to fill voids, to respond through active presence, compassion, empathy, listening, love and physical comforting. (Jeter, 1988, p. 387)

The story of a seventeen-year-old unaccompanied refugee from Cambodia illustrates the power that meaning in the form of ritual has in maintaining the human spirit through loss and trauma:

> He was diagnosed as having severe sclerosis of the liver as a result of untreated hepatitis B and immediately placed in isolation with the requirement that all staff and visitors must wear gowns, gloves, and masks when entering his room. There were no bilingual, bicultural staff available at the hospital and communication was only possible during visits from a social worker and a Cambodian paraprofessional. On the third day following admission, the patient suddenly became unmanageable. He was found cowering under his bed, pulling his intravenous line out of his arm and wrapping the tubing around his neck as if to strangle himself. Following extensive psychological testing, which further agitated the young man and produced no indication of the cause of his behaviour, the social worker was permitted to talk with him. She discovered

that he was 'seeing' his mother, grandmother and four friends, all of whom had died during the Pol Pot regime, surround his bed and call him to join them. He also saw many white ghosts in the room. This was terrifying to him and an indication that he would die soon. With the help of the Cambodian paraprofessional, it was determined that he believed strongly in the power of ancestors and in the protection offered by blessings from the monks. Arrangements were made for a Cambodian monk to come to the hospital room and perform a ceremony of protection around the patient. A knotted string, blessed by holy water, was tied around his waist and an altar was set up next to his bed. Following this ritual, the young man was compliant with treatment and responsive to medication. (Leiper de Monchy, 1991, p. 173)

The importance of maintaining a sense of social identity and connectedness in both cultures, especially during the critical adolescent phase of identity formation, is illustrated in the story of Phuc, a fifteen-year-old from Vietnam:

As a student in Vietnam, this young man excelled in mathematics and was encouraged by his parents to pursue a career in engineering. Although an only child, Phuc was part of a close-knit extended family and was often called upon care for his grandparents and younger cousins. Upon the death of his father, and seeing little future for themselves in Vietnam, Phuc and his mother set out as 'boat people' to seek a better life elsewhere. They eventually resettled in America. After a year, Phuc's mother met and married another Vietnamese refugee and they moved to a home in a middle-class community without a concentrated population of Vietnamese. Because of the lack of a Vietnamese community, reinforcement for appropriate Vietnamese behaviour was unavailable beyond Phuc's family. The loss of reinforcement and role patterns that would ordinarily have given him a strong identity left him confused and depressed. In school, Phuc was having great difficulty understanding the lessons because he could not speak fluent English. Phuc felt inferior because he was doing poorly, and soon he began skipping classes and spending time in the city with other Vietnamese youth who were involved in gang activity.... When his stepfather and mother discovered that their son had not been attending school, they became very angry because back home he was an outstanding scholar. The stepfather felt that Phuc was lazy and disrespectful, so he physically punished him for his truancy. As a result, Phuc ran away from home. The police eventually picked him up, and because he refused to return home he was placed in foster care. (Matsuoka, 1990, p. 344-345)

Jeter (1988, p. 381), in his examination of Georg Simmel's "Socialization of the Spirit" theory, quotes Simmel: "The feeling of isolation is rarely as decisive and intense when one actually finds oneself physically alone, as when one is a stranger without relations." Spirituality and the reenactment of rituals connect kin to each other not only in the present but also across time. In the next section on intervention programs, other personal IR experiences will further illustrate that the ability to relate to others and make meaning of experiences along with opportunities to learn and practice skills fuels growth and health.

## INTERVENTION

### Primary prevention at the community level

Based on a review of the literature and on public hearings across Canada, Beiser et al. made twenty-seven recommendations on prevention and remedial intervention for immigrants and refugees including specific recommendations for children and youth. Overall, the task force concluded that:

while moving from one country and culture to another inevitably entails stress, it does not necessarily threaten mental health. The mental health of immigrants and refugees becomes a concern primarily when additional risk factors combine with the stress of migration (Beiser et al., 1988, p. i).

Such a conclusion points to the need for programs at the primary prevention level. Beiser's abovementioned report for the Canadian government is an example of national primary prevention. International primary prevention intervention may include political action and direct action, such as health promotion in refugee camps. The programs described below are at the community primary prevention level of intervention.

Williams (1991) uses Cowen's (1982) model when she defines primary prevention as intervention that targets a specific group (rather than individuals) within the population who are known to be at risk but have not already encountered difficulties. The goal of such a primary prevention intervention would be to promote health or prevent maladaptation. Since the child does not go through the acculturation process in isolation, but does so in the context of the family and the community, then preventative intervention must take place within this context. There are two public organizations in the community that already bring the child, the family and the community together and have a focus on healthy development: public health programs and schools. A number of programs have already been developed in the United States, and some are developing in Canada, that use public health or the school, as well as ethnic community organizations, as the doors of access to development of networks of community relationships that promote the healthy development of IR children over time.

## Fundamental principles for intervention

Leiper de Monchy (1991, p. 169) proposes four fundamental principles essential to effective practice with IR children and adolescents:

1. Trauma experiences need to be acknowledged as they have impacted the child's development, perception of the world and vision of the future.
2. Recognizing the success of refugees as survivors, and affirming their wisdom and strengths, are essential to helping them improve their self-esteem.
3. Cross-cultural living skills need to be taught in order for refugees to develop positive bicultural identities.

4.  Empowerment and the recovery of control over one's life need to be encouraged, especially for refugees who are re-establishing parental roles with their children.

In order to implement these principles effectively and to reduce risk of further trauma or "second injury" (Symonds, 1980), the program must be run by staff who have knowledge of trauma experiences and post-trauma syndromes. The team must also include bilingual and bicultural staff, there should be linkage with refugee/immigrant communities and there needs to be integration of traditional healing methods.

Knowledge of trauma and post-trauma experience includes training in recognition and understanding of the effects of extreme trauma and violence on children's bio-psycho-social and spiritual development at various ages and on their natural support systems. Understanding one's own reactions to the experiences of these children is also essential. Western professionals may cope by either denying the child's experience or conversely, becoming overprotective. Many interpreters and paraprofessionals may themselves have their own post-trauma needs, which can put additional demands on other team members (Leiper de Monchy, 1991).

The abilities of bilingual, bicultural staff are required not simply to translate but to understand the culture-bound, nonverbal messages of children, especially those who come from cultures where expression of emotion is not expected. Even children and adolescents who are "fluent" in the new language are still learning its meanings and metaphors (Dunnigan, McNall and Mortimer, 1993). Team members also facilitate communication with the children's families and ethnic communities who are part of the needs assessment and intervention process. Working through interpreters and across cultures takes a great deal of patience and skill; initially, Western professionals often have to cope with feelings of powerlessness and loss of control. The bilingual, bicultural team members are the essential link for cross-cultural understanding in terms of communication of culture and values in both directions. Some refugees find the Western health-care system extremely fragmented, impersonal and confusing compared to the family elders and spiritual healers. It is for this reason that it is more helpful for teams to be multidisciplinary and multipurpose in service delivery so that the child's experience has more continuity and trust can develop.

Linkage to immigrant and refugee communities shows respect for the child's cultural identity and encourages enhancement of natural support systems. The community in return can provide credibility to the service provider who sometimes may be viewed with mistrust and apprehension. In addition, the majority of current refugees come from countries where healing methods incorporate spiritual rituals that address beliefs about spiritual wrongdoings and involve the power of ancestors and other higher spirits. IR children and adolescents may have various combinations of beliefs that reflect both Western and ethnic world views depending on their degree of acculturation. As illustrated in some of the examples previously cited, refugee children particularly will need service providers who are willing to be creative and flexible across language, culture and professional disciplines to address their needs (Leiper de Monchy, 1991).

The following section describes programs which are group or mass-oriented, as William's (1991) definition of primary prevention intervention specifies. However, some of the modes of intervention within the programs include family therapy and individual contact. For a more in-depth look at working across and within cultures in family therapy, the reader is referred to other chapters in this volume and to such sources as Gushue and Sciarra (1995) who propose a multidimensional approach that incorporates within-group as well as between-group differences. Differences in language ability, acculturation and racial/cultural identity within the family itself and in relation to the therapist are considered as essential to planning effective intervention.

## Programs

Ready (1991) describes a school-based primary prevention program in Washington, D.C. that incorporates some of the above factors. The Bell Multicultural High School (formerly known as the Multicultural Career Intern Program) was established to meet the acculturation needs of IR youths, largely originating from Central America, especially El Salvador, and many from Vietnam, Cambodia, Afganistan and Ethiopia. The primary objective was to prevent dropping out through "career-oriented curricula, intensive counseling, and internships" (p. 182). Some of the problems these youths faced were: exploitation in the labour market due to undocumented refugee status, poverty and the need to work at a very young age; no close family support in the US; domestic discord in "re-constructed" families; fear for safety of friends and family back home; and adjustment to a foreign language and culture.

The school was open year-round and provided gradually increasing exposure to the new language and culture while also providing credit courses in their heritage culture and language. Most teachers were bilingual and offered courses in either language, but as proficiency in English increased so did the English language course load. Pride in their cultural heritage and in development of cultural participation in the new country were both valued.

Career development was facilitated through career counselling seminars, individual counselling, hands-on experiences, "shadowing" workers in their field of interest and paid internships. Various federal programs were coordinated through the school, such as a summer youth employment program, work experience programs and out of school programs. Kiselica, Changizi, Cureton and Gridley (1995) also recommend hands-on experience to develop skills and provide positive role models for students. They too work with groups of IR youth to develop cohesiveness and ethnic pride and promote a life-planning approach to academic/career counselling

The school employed five mostly bilingual counsellors so that each student could receive in-school academic, career and personal counselling, as well as practical out-of-school assistance and agency liaison with the same counsellor. The counselling room became the informal hub of the school. The needs of these youths were such that their counsellors often performed the role of surrogate parent, and the school was their stable and accepting community. They could receive "a wide variety of services in one location from people whom they knew and trusted" (Kiselica, Changizi, Cureton and Gridley, 1995, p. 185).

Ready's (1991) study registered 80% of the 106 students interviewed as happy with the program. The supportive environment and the career development program was cited as most beneficial, while some saw the school as a bit too Spanish-dominated for learning English. Between five and six years after completion of the study, two-thirds of the graduates, and one-half of all informants, had received some type of post-secondary education and "virtually" all were employed. However, Felipe who later earned an associate degree in medical technology and became employed in a hospital while continuing studies towards pre-law, says there was more to it than just finding a job:

> ... it is not just the [career development], or academics, but what I learned as a human being—as a person. In

that aspect I think that MCIP has helped me to better relate to everything here. Even though I didn't have anyone like family to advise me, I had MCIP counselors who were great, who I will never forget. They were the only source that I had then—to come over and talk. I didn't have parents. They were the only ears that I had to listen to me. They were the only ones who could try to understand me, about the things that I did and I didn't like about this society. At the same time, I learned to relate not only to Hispanics, but to Vietnamese, Chinese, Africans, [and] people from the Middle East. I think that the multicultural way has been really helpful to me because now I can see good in everyone." (Ready, 1991, p. 198)

Leiper de Monchy (1991) also describes a program that exemplifies the "cross-cultural team" approach. The Metropolitan Indochinese Children and Adolescent Services Program (MICAS) provides child welfare/mental health services for Cambodian, Laotian and Vietnamese children and adolescents in Massachusetts. This program includes both primary and secondary prevention (early detection, reduction of prevalence, halt of progression and further occurrence of disorders). The base is an established ethnic community agency with a broad range of comprehensive services in satellite sites such as various schools that provide in-school and home-based adjustment counselling and out-patient and in-patient mental health facilities. Staff follow their clients and the clients' families throughout the system of services to maintain an ongoing therapeutic relationship. Leiper de Monchy (1991, p. 176) concludes: "This continuity in provision of services allows refugee children to develop trust in their helpers. The cross agency funding model provides a cost-effective method for state agencies to address the specialized service needs of a relatively small client population."

Each client is assigned both a Western therapist and a bilingual and bicultural paraprofessional who consult with each other frequently but work together or independently with the client based on the type of intervention required. Paraprofessionals advance through standardized levels of skill development and all staff participate in case consultation with a variety of consultants including a clinical psychologist and social workers with expertise in child welfare, refugee settlement and ESL with a clinical focus. Cross-cultural training is maintained and advocated for by linkages with refugee community leaders and other refugee service providers. Leiper de Monchy (1991, p. 177) notes that participation in ethnic community events and celebrations is critical because these activities help " ... build trust, mutual understanding, and cooperation between Western program staff and the communities of new Americans they serve."

The programs described above incorporate the fundamental principals and specific components identified as necessary by Leiper de Monchy (1991). The MCIP school program in particular is a good example of primary prevention at the community level. In addition to this, these programs also highlight the value the participants place on the continuity of intervention over time in a way that allows relationships and trust to develop. Ready (1991, p. 197) concludes that MCIP provided a "viable social and cultural framework within which most of these young people could reconstruct a coherent image of themselves in their new society."

In Canada not much literature is available regarding specific interventions currently underway with IR children and adolescents. Three programs will be described: the Global Youth Support Program at the Rainbow Youth Centre in Regina and the two associated with the Mosaic Centre in Calgary.

The Global Youth Support Program is comprised of two age groups of new Canadian youth, eleven to fourteen and fifteen to twenty-one years. For three years the program has been part of the Rainbow Youth Centre, which was founded to meet the specific needs of inner-city youth in Regina. Since Rainbow already provided a community-based, multiservice centre where youth of any ancestry, including First Nations youth, could find respect and diversity, development of programming to meet the needs of IR youth was a natural extension.

The youth are provided with transportation to and from school or home. Both groups meet for three hours weekly for fourteen to twenty weeks and enjoy a mixture of sports, activities, outings, tours of local facilities and discussion, with periodic family and community events. The program emphasizes getting out into the community and keeping active since the youth tend to get impatient when there is too much discussion. Getting out into the community also provides other agency staff with information about the needs of these youth.

The group activities are structured so as to take the groups through three phases: 1) developing trust, acceptance and belonging in the group;

2) taking risks in the use of new communication and recreation skills, exploring the cultures of group members, accessing resources; and 3) making choices, identifying accomplishments, moving on, separation and closure. Throughout the group, via involvement in sports, activities, outings and discussions, a number of issues are addressed, such as racism, developing self-esteem and identity, dealing with differences, conflict and learning social skills. The older group also addresses issues around dating and sex roles, as well as having the opportunity to do career planning and learn job search skills.

In Calgary a primary prevention pilot project for immigrant and refugee youth that incorporates a concurrent parenting group is underway (D. Este, personal communication, February 1, 1996). The Mosaic Centre is a project of the Calgary Immigrant Aid Society in cooperation with various other community agencies. The goal of the youth program is to prevent family conflict and reduce the potential for violence in the home and community by increasing open communication within the family and support and coping skills. Polish, Spanish, Serbo-Croation and Chinese teens participate in weekly ethno-specific groups in which they learn communication skills, share problems and solutions, learn about community resources and have fun getting to know each other while playing sports and listening to music. Concurrently their parents learn communication and parenting skills while sharing and supporting each other in their fist language. Combined parent-teen and multicultural activities are built into the program.

The Mosaic Centre also provides a primary prevention program called Brighter Futures for families from the former Yugoslavia with children up to six years of age. In cooperation with public health nurses and a psychologist from the former Yugoslavia, the staff provide a variety of educational and supportive activities to promote the children's health.

## Interdisciplinary intervention

Each discipline is dedicated to promoting the healthy development of IR children and adolescents within their own domain and mode of expertise; however, most disciplines are now venturing beyond traditional views that fragment the child's experience of acculturation.

In education, for example, Auerbach (1989) proposes a "social-contextual" approach to family literacy that works with IR children's and parent's strengths using "real life" content and action such as: children writing down stories from the parents oral tradition, and parents learning to write by constructing letters to the editor about community problems. Kiselica et al. (1995, p. 523) calls for school counsellors to liaise between the families and the school and advocate for "broadening the mission of schools" to make them more relevant:

> Schools can no longer be viewed merely as places where children are educated ... schools should develop partnerships with social and health agencies, remain open 7 days a week, 12 months a year, and provide parents and children struggling to overcome the untold hardships of poverty a safe haven for health care, socializing and recreation.

In nursing, Kemp (1993) also invites practitioners to step outside the traditional role to act as advocates for individuals and communities; and Carrington and Procter (1995) puts the enabling of extensive networking and relationship-building for refugees at the centre of the nurse's role.

Perhaps it is the IR child's process of meaning-making or ongoing reconstruction of a coherent image of self, in relation to both traditional and new cultures and in context of family and community relationships, that is the centre point through which the disciplines can weave their various bio-psycho-social interventions. Team interventions undertaken in this spirit reduce the risk of further fragmenting the experience of the IR child and might give them the chance, as Beiser et al. (1995, p. 71) put it, to "make themselves according to the best vision of their possibilities."

## Research and policy

Beiser et al. (1995) call for more research in a number of areas of IR child and adolescent acculturation, for example: developmental and health patterns; research into the distinctions between immigrant and refugee experience; longitudinal investigations of adaptation; and intensive case studies of identity formation to understand the sources of success as well as difficulty for IR youth. Both Beiser above and Hicks et al. (1993) call for models that reflect the complexity of the adaptation process for the IR child. Three other points are also stressed: 1) researchers must recognize that acculturation is a process of adaptation for both the IR child and members of the host country as well; 2) researchers must be sensitive to the heterogeneity of their subjects in terms of ethnocultural background and migration experiences; and 3) researchers must recognize that the concept of family may differ for children cross-culturally.

Beiser et al. (1988) concludes that despite the fact that there is little definitive research, interventions that change attitudes, change school curricula and provide youth programs must proceed nevertheless. The youths (Mattu et al., 1995) tell us to listen to IR children and teens "as people" and respect what we hear. Listening should also include research that captures the essence of the solutions that evolve from within ethnic communities. For example, one group of refugee families created a huge permanent mural at their community centre to tell their story of loss, pain and re-growth. Another group of women and children put on a musical that traces the story of their grief:

> In one scene I played my brother who was shot and that gave me a feeling of being with him in his hard times, in his death. You know, that's the important thing: to be able to be together with those you love when it's tough. And I didn't feel so guilty anymore that I survived and he didn't. And Miranda played the grief singer, and we did it as we do in my country, you know, where the grief singer comes and sings the story of the whole life of the dead person and we all sit and cry and fill in our own memories. Everybody cried for someone. Your folks cried too. And I've seen it at performances we had later that you people understand how we feel ... that you share our struggle and that we've something really important for which we can struggle together and achieve a result. We still organize a festival for human rights every year, and the work goes on. (Byland, 1992, p. 62)

We no doubt have much to learn from new Canadians.

Hicks et al. (1993) call for Canadian policies that strengthen multicultural knowledge and attitudes and promote acquisition of information about the receiving culture pre-migration for IR children. Policy that more actively supports primary prevention interventions is required to eliminate the discrepancy between Canada's welcoming attitude and the reality that the acculturation process currently has more risk factors than protective factors.

## SUMMARY

In order to experience healthy development, IR children and adolescents need a number of things. They need family stability and involvement with their ethnic community in ways that validate their cultural traditions and values while supporting integration with the host culture. They need school environments that balance heritage and host culture language and have teachers and students who are educated regarding racism and multiculturalism. School environments should promote creative bridging of communication gaps between parent and school based on the belief that communication problems are reciprocal. Although much more research is needed, it is safe to say that we must make interventions that provide an experience of stability, consistency and validation in ways that have meaning for the child and socialize the spirit as well as the body and mind. We can only do this if we challenge ourselves to step outside our own frames of reference and expand our vision of possibilities beyond the stereotypes not only of our clients but also of our own institutions, ourselves and each other as human services workers.

## REFERENCES

Anderson, J. M., Waxler-Morrison, N., Richardson, E., Herbert, C. and Murphy, M. (1990). Conclusion: Delivering culturally sensitive health care. In N. Waxler-Morrison, J. M. Anderson, E. Richardson (eds.), (1990). *Cross-cultural caring: A handbook for health professionals*. Vancouver, B.C.: UBC Press.

Athey, J. L. and Ahearn, F. L. Jr. (1991). The mental health of refugee children: An overview. In F. L. Ahearn and J. L. Athey (eds.), *Refugee children: Theory, research and services*. Baltimore, MD: The John Hopkins University Press.

Auerbach, E. R. (1989). Toward a social-contextual approach to family literacy. *Harvard Education Review*, 59(2), 165-181.

Beiser, M., Dion, R., Gotowiec, A., Hyman, I. and Vu, N. (1995). Immigrant and refugee children in Canada. *Canadian Journal of Psychiatry*, 40(2), 67-72.

Beiser, M., Barwick, C., Berry, J., daCosta, G., Fantino, A. M., Ganesan, S., Lee, C., Milne, W., Naidoo, J., Prince, R., Tousignant, M. and Vela, E. (1988). *After the door has been opened: Mental health issues affecting immigrants and refugees in Canada.* Ottawa, Ont.: Ministry of Multiculturalism and Citizenship, and Health and Welfare Canada.

Berry, J. W. (1991). Refugee adaptation in settlement countries: An overview with an emphasis on primary prevention. In F. L. Ahearn and J. L. Athey (eds.), *Refugee children: Theory, research and services.* Baltimore, MD: The John Hopkins University Press.

Bronfenbrenner, U. (1979). *The ecology of human development: Experiments by nature and design.* Cambridge, MA: Harvard University Press.

Byland, Maria. (1992). Women in exile and their children. Special edition, *Women and Therapy,* 13(1-2), 53-63.

Carlin, J. E. (1979). The catastrophically uprooted child: Southeast Asian refugee children. In J. D. Noshpitz (ed.), *Basic handbook of child psychiatry.* New York, NY: Basic Books.

Carlin, J. E. (1986). Child and adolescent refugees: Psychiatric assessment and treatment. In C. L. Williams and J. Westermeyer (eds.), *Refugee mental health in resettlement countries.* New York, NY: Hemisphere.

Carrington, G. and Procter, N. (1995). Identifying and responding to the needs of refugees: A global nursing concern. *Holistic Nursing Practice,* 9(2), 9-17.

Cowen, E. L. (1982). Primary prevention research: Barriers, needs, and opportunities. *Journal of Primary Prevention,* 2, 131-137.

Dunnigan, T., McNall, M. and Mortimer, J. T. (1993). The problem of metaphorical nonequivalence in cross cultural survey research: Comparing the mental health statuses of Hmong refugee and general population adolescents. *Journal of Cross-Cultural Psychology,* 24(3), 344-365.

Espin, O. M. (1992). Roots uprooted: The psychological impactor historical/ political dislocation. Special edition, *Women and Therapy,* 13(1-2), 9-19.

Espino, C. M. (1991). Trauma and adaptation: The case of central American Children. In F. L. Ahearn and J. L. Athey (eds.), *Refugee children: Theory, research and services.* Baltimore, MD: The John Hopkins University Press.

Garmezy, N. (1983). Stressors of childhood. In N. Garmezy and M. Rutter (eds.), *Stress, coping and development in children.* New York: McGraw Hill.

Gushue, G. V. and Sciarra, D. R. (1995). Culture and families: A multi-dimensional approach. In J. G. Ponterotto, J. M. Casas, L. A. Suzuki and C. M. Alexander (eds.), *Handbook of multicultural counseling.* Thousand Oaks, CA: Sage Publications.

Hicks, R., Lalonde, R. N. and Peplar, D. J. (1993). Psychological considerations in the mental health of immigrant and refugee children. *Canadian Journal of Community Mental Health*, 12(2), 71-87).

Ima, K. and Hohm, C. F. (1991). Child maltreatment among Asian and Pacific Islander refugees and immigrants: The San Diego case. *Journal of Interpersonal Violence*, 6(3), 267-285.

Jeter, K. (1988). "And baby makes three": An examination and application of Georg Simmel's "Socialization of the Spirit" theory. *Marriage and Family Review*, 12(3-4), 377-396.

Kemp, C. (1993). Health services for refugees in countries of second asylum. *International Nursing Review*, 40(1), 21-24.

Kiselica, M. S., Changizi, J. C., Cureton, V. L. and Gridley, B.E. (1995). Counseling children and adolescents in schools. In J. G. Ponterotto, J. M. Casas, L. A. Suzuki and C. M. Alexander (eds.), *Handbook of multicultural counseling*. Thousand Oaks, CA: Sage Publications.

Korbin, J. E. (1991). Child maltreatment and the study of child refugees. In F. L. Ahearn and J. L. Athey (eds.), *Refugee children: Theory, research and services*. Baltimore, MD: The John Hopkins University Press.

Kuoch, T., Wali, S. and Scully, M. F. (1992). Foreword to: Refugee women and their mental health. Special Edition, *Women and Therapy*, 13(1-2), xv-xvi.

Leiper de Monchy, M. (1991). Recovery and rebuilding: The challenge for refugee children and service providers. In F. L. Ahearn and J. L. Athey (eds.), *Refugee children: Theory, research and services*. Baltimore, MD: The John Hopkins University Press.

Lese, K. P. and Robbins, S. B. (1994). Relationship between goal attributes and the academic achievement of Southeast Asian adolescent refugees. *Journal of Counseling Psychology*, 41(1), 45-52.

Liskowich, C. (1995). *Global youth support program: A program manual and curriculum guide for groups*. Regina, Saskatchewan: Paw Prints Publishing.

Matsuoka, J. K. (1990). Differential acculturation among Vietnamese refugees. *Social Work*, 35(4), 341-345.

Mattu, L., Pruegger, V. and Grant, E. (eds.). (1995). Youth symposium '95: Building tomorrow for today, Conference report. Calgary, Alberta: Youth Symposium '95.

Peeks, B. (1989). Strategies for solving children's problems understood as behavioural metaphors. *Journal of Strategic and Systemic Therapies*, 8(1), 22-25.

Ponterotto, J. G., Casas, J. M., Suzuki, Lisa A. and Alexander, C. M. (eds.). (1995). *Handbook of multicultural counseling*. Thousand Oaks, CA: Sage.

Ready, T. (1991). School and the passage of refugee youth from adolescence to adulthood. In F. L. Ahearn and J. L. Athey (eds.), *Refugee children: Theory, research and services*. Baltimore, MD: The John Hopkins University Press.

Ressler, E. M., Boothby, N. and Steinbock, D. J (1988).*Unaccompanied children: Care and protection in wars, natural disasters, and refugee movements*. New York, NY: Oxford University Press.

Roberson, M. K. (1992). Birth, transformation, and death of refugee identity: Women and girls of the Intifada. Special Edition, *Women and Therapy*, 13(1-2), 35-52.

Rosenthal, D. A. (1984). Intergenerational conflict and culture: A study of immigrant and nonimmigrant adolescents and their parents. *Genetic Psychology Monographs*, 109, 53-75.

Rosenthal, D. A., Moore, S. M. and Taylor, M. J. (1983). Ethnicity and adjustment: A study of the self-image of Anglo-, Greek-, and Italian-Australian working class adolescents. *Journal of Youth and Adolescence*, 12(2), 117-135.

Sapir, D. G.(1993). Natural and man-made disasters: The vulnerability of women-headed households and children without families. *World Health Statistics*, 46, 227-233.

Symonds, M. (1980). The "second injury" to victims. *Evaluation and Change*, 1 (Special Issue), 36-38.

Westermeyer, J. (1991). Psychiatric services for refugee children. In F. L. Ahearn and J. L. Athey (eds.), *Refugee children: Theory, research and services*. Baltimore, MD: The John Hopkins University Press.

Williams, C. L. (1991). Toward the development of preventive interventions for youth traumatized by war and refugee flight. In F. L. Ahearn and J. L. Athey (eds.), *Refugee children: Theory, research and services*. Baltimore, MD: The John Hopkins University Press.

Williams, C. L. and Berry, J. W. (1991). Primary prevention of acculturative stress among refugees. *American Psychologist*, 46(6), 632-641.

# CHAPTER 4

# Social Work with Gay, Lesbian and Bisexual Members of Racial and Ethnic Minority Groups

*Brian O'Neill*

Canada has always been a culturally and racially diverse country. In addition to the First Nations peoples who were living in North America when French and British colonists arrived, Canada's population has developed through a continuous process of immigration from countries with various languages, cultures and racial make-ups (Naidoo and Edwards, 1991). As well as ethnocultural heterogeneity, the population is characterized by differences related to gender, age, class, religion and physical and mental ability. This chapter focuses on social work practice at the intersection of two aspects of diversity—ethnicity and sexual orientation.

Although for the most part hidden until recently, there is evidence of same-sex sexual behaviour throughout the history of Canada (Kinsman, 1987). While ethnocultural minority groups face racial and ethnic prejudice, and sexual minority groups encounter discrimination related to sexual orientation, gay, lesbian and bisexual members of racial and cultural minority groups confront multiple oppressions. They may be marginalized in Canadian society at large, as well as in gay and lesbian associations, because of racial and ethnic differences. Conversely, they may be stigmatized in both the dominant and minority ethnic communities because of their sexual orientation. Women and individuals who are poor, handicapped or elderly are subjected to additional prejudice. Thus people who are attracted to members of their own sex and who are also members of aboriginal, racial or ethnic minority groups encounter a complex set of barriers to their full participation in Canadian society.

The *Social Work Code of Ethics* (CASW, 1994) identifies respect for human diversity and opposition to discrimination as central values of Canadian social work. However, responding to ethnocultural differences is a complex task given the ongoing national debate about the multicultural and multiracial nature of Canadian society. Similarly, dealing with issues of same-sex sexual orientation is a difficult undertaking in the light of Canadians' conflicting values and strongly held beliefs regarding human sexuality. Therefore, addressing the concerns of members of First Nations and ethnic minority groups who are gay, lesbian or bisexual is a formidable challenge in that it entails simultaneously confronting issues of both ethnicity and sexuality.

This chapter presents a theoretical framework for considering issues of same-sex sexual orientation in a cross-cultural context. It provides an overview of same-sex sexual behaviour and attitudes towards it in various cultures. The chapter then identifies issues faced by gay, lesbian and bisexual members of ethnocultural minority groups in Canada, which fall within the mandate of social work. Finally, the chapter offers recommendations for social work practice and professional education with respect to these issues.

There is little Canadian literature on gay and lesbian issues in relation to ethnocultural minorities in general and First Nations peoples in particular, a limitation which is reflected in this chapter. In addition, issues related to Francophones are not addressed since they are one of the two dominant cultures in Canada. However, it is assumed that some of the issues discussed here may have application to gays, lesbians and bisexuals from these groups.

## CROSS-CULTURAL PERSPECTIVES ON HUMAN SEXUALITY

Prior to discussing issues specific to cross-cultural social work in relation to same-sex sexual orientation, it is important to consider alternative conceptions of sexuality. In her book on cultural differences and sexuality, Irvine (1995) describes the essentialist perspective, which is that sexuality is primarily a biological drive expressed in the same way irrespective of historical period, locale or culture. In contrast to this view, the social constructionist position is that sexuality is for the most part shaped by culture, and that the meanings attached to sexual attraction and behaviour vary depending on the historical and social context.

De Cecco and Elia (1993) doubt that either essentialist or constructionist theories fully explain the diversity of human sexuality. They argue that biological, social and personal differences are involved in determining sexual behaviour. Whatever the relative balance of these factors, it is clear that cultural norms transmitted and implemented through social institutions such as the family, education, religion, the legal system, as well as health and social services, exert a profound influence on the expression of sexuality.

Given the multitude of factors which influence human sexuality, it is important that Canadian social workers become knowledgeable about how people from various backgrounds define, interpret and value behaviours that may or may not be considered sexual in the Canadian context (Lavee, 1991). The difficulty of this task is compounded by issues related to class, race and gender that interact with cultural values in shaping the social construction of sexuality. For instance, ethnic groups which have highly differentiated gender roles may stigmatize same-sex behaviour more severely than those with more flexible boundaries. To further complicate matters, values and behaviours regarding sexuality are impacted by contact among cultures. This dynamic is particularly important to keep in mind in Canada with its constantly changing ethnic mix.

## DEFINITIONS

Three terms related to sexual identity are often used interchangeably although they have distinct meanings (Berger and Kelly, 1995). "Gender identity" is the sex which a person considers himself or herself to be, while "gender role" refers to the behaviour expected in various cultures of males and females. In the dominant culture of Canada, "sexual orientation" is defined by the gender of people to whom one is sexually and emotionally attracted.

The terms "gay" and "lesbian" are used to refer to people who have accepted their sexual orientation as a positive aspect of their identities and to some extent have acknowledged this with others. "Gay male sexual orientation" is the primary but not necessarily exclusive attraction of men to men and usually includes a sexual component. The term "lesbian sexual orientation" refers to the attraction of women to women and may or may not include a sexual dimension (Tully, 1995). "Bisexual sexual orientation" is some degree of attraction to people of both genders (Gochros, 1995).

There may be apparent inconsistencies in a person's gender identity, gender role and sexual orientation. For instance, typically men who identify as gay think of themselves as male, exhibit most of the behaviour expected of men in our culture and yet are sexually attracted to males. However, it is less widely acknowledged that many men who consider themselves to be heterosexual, participate in sex with other males (McKirnan, Stokes, Doll and Burzette, 1995).

In some cultures, sexual orientation is defined by criteria other than gender. For example, in certain ethnic groups it is the nature of sexual behaviour, rather than the gender of those involved, which determines how participants in sexual encounters are labelled (Irvine, 1995). Thus, in Latin cultures a man who is the inserter in anal intercourse with another man may be seen as heterosexual, while his partner is identified as gay.

## PREVALENCE

In the past it was thought that gay, lesbian and bisexual sexual orientations were rare because same-sex behaviour was largely hidden due to its stigmatization in the Western world. This myth was shattered by Kinsey's classic investigations of human sexuality in the United States (Kinsey, Pomeroy, and Martin, 1948; Kinsey, Pomeroy, Martin, and Gebhard, 1955). These studies revealed that between 5% to 10% of men and 3% to 5% of women had participated exclusively in same-sex sexual behaviour for a significant period of their adult lives (Marmor, 1980). Including data from those who participated sporadically in sex with members of their own gender and those who did not act on their same-sex attraction caused the estimates to double. While Kinsey's methods have been criticized, and more recent surveys have produced lower estimates of same-sex sexual behaviour in the US, the data continue to support the conclusion that a significant proportion of the population is gay, lesbian or bisexual (Binson et al., 1995; Harry, 1990).

Cross-cultural research has found evidence of same-sex sexuality in the majority of cultures, past and present (Churchill, 1967). For instance, same-sex behaviour was accepted among aboriginal peoples in North America and Java (Williams, 1993) and in China (Hinsch, 1990) prior to contact with Europeans. Recent studies have produced similar estimates of the prevalence of same-sex attraction and erotic behaviour in contemporary Europe and Asia as in the United States (Diamond, 1993; Sell, Wells and Wypij, 1995; Whitham and Mathy, 1986). Although data are not available, it is reasonable to assume the incidence of same-sex sexual orientation in Canada to be similar to that in other Western nations.

## ATTITUDES AND DISCRIMINATION TOWARDS SAME-SEX SEXUALITY

Homophobia is individual prejudice related to same-sex sexual orientation (Gramick, 1983; Herek, 1984). It may take the form of negative stereotypes, irrational fears and active discrimination against gay, lesbian and bisexual people. Homophobia is higher among persons with less education and those who hold fundamentalist religious values, make sharp distinctions in the roles of men and women, and live in rural areas. In contrast to homophobia, heterosexism refers to "the continued promotion by the major institutions of society of a heterosexual lifestyle while simultaneously subordinating any other lifestyles (i.e., gay/lesbian/bisexual)" (Neisen, 1990, p. 25). The underlying assumption is that all people are heterosexual (Neiberding, 1989).

Over the past twenty years in Canada, attitudes regarding same-sex sexual orientation have become significantly more positive. While in 1975 only 28% of Canadians were accepting of same-sex sexuality, current data suggest that 48% of the population feels that same-sex sexuality is not wrong (Bibby, 1995). The intensity of the homophobia that endures is suggested by police statistics which indicate that during 1993/94, gay men and lesbians were the victims of 11% of violent hate crimes committed in major Canadian cities (Bronskill, 1996).

Based on his analysis of the history of sexuality in Canada, Kinsman (1987) argues that heterosexism has shaped the functioning of systems of social control such as the law, education and social welfare, with the result that same-sex sexuality has been suppressed. However, significant changes in major institutions have been made over the past thirty years. The *Criminal Code of Canada* was revised in 1969 and 1988 removing provisions that were used primarily against gay men, so that sexual acts between persons of the same-sex are legal in Canada (Adam, 1993; MacDonald, 1994). Seven of the ten Canadian provinces and one territory have included sexual orientation in their human rights codes. However, the continuing ambivalence of Canadians with respect to same-sex sexual orientation is revealed by a decline in support for recognition of equal rights for gay men, lesbians and bisexuals from 80% in 1990 to 67% in 1995 (Bibby, 1995). These attitudes support the heterosexism which is evidenced in the denial, under a variety of federal and provincial laws, of access to financial benefits and legal protection to same-sex couples on the same basis as to heterosexual couples (Schneider and O'Neill, 1993).

In other parts of the world, attitudes towards same-sex sexuality are both more positive and more negative than those in Canada. An international survey reveals that in eleven countries a majority of the population supports equal rights for gay and lesbian people, while in another forty-seven, there is minority support (Tielman and Hammelburg, 1993, p. 250). However, in 144 states there is virtually no support for gays and lesbians; in seventy-four jurisdictions same-sex sexual behaviour is a criminal offence. Former British colonies, satellites of the Soviet Union and predominantly Islamic areas are the most repressive.

## CANADIAN MULTICULTURAL CONTEXT

There is a long history of prejudice and discrimination in Canada against First Nations peoples and members of racial and ethnic minority groups (Naidoo and Edwards, 1991). However, following World War II, Canadian governments enacted laws prohibiting discrimination on the basis of race and ethnicity and certain other criteria (excluding sexual orientation until recently) and promoted equitable access to employment and services. One of these pieces of legislation, the *Canadian Multiculturalism Act* (1988), has goals of countering racism and helping cultural minority groups to maintain their traditions. Despite these initiatives, negative attitudes towards First Nations peoples and racial minorities persist (Bibby, 1995). For example, Bronskill (1996) reported that racial minorities were the targets of 61% of hate crimes while other ethnic minorities were the victims of 5% of attacks.

Canada's multicultural ideology has mixed implications for gay, lesbian and bisexual people. By encouraging acceptance of cultural diversity and countering discrimination, the policy may foster tolerance of same-sex sexual orientation. However, attitudes in many of the countries of Asia, the Caribbean and South America, which are primary sources of immigration to Canada, are hostile towards gay men and lesbians (Tielman and Hammelburg, 1993). For instance, Ho (1995) provides a vivid picture of the lives of gay men in contemporary Hong Kong, a major source of immigration to Canada. Political and social conditions in combination with Chinese values regarding sexuality, the family and gender present almost insurmountable barriers to the recognition and expression of same-sex sexual orientation. These influences may persist among many Chinese immigrants in Canada. Unfortunately, in supporting the traditional values of newcomers from cultures which oppress gays and lesbians, multiculturalism may sustain homophobia and heterosexism within both the dominant and ethnic minority communities.

## RATIONALE FOR SOCIAL WORK INVOLVEMENT

Given the evidence of same-sex attraction among people from all over the world, it is likely that most social workers serve gay, lesbian or bisexual clients or their families and friends. These clients have the same array of social service needs as do heterosexuals. However, due to heterosexism and homophobia, gays and lesbians of all ages may have additional needs related to developing a positive identity, establishing and maintaining supportive relationships and coping with the stress of discrimination and harassment (Shernoff, 1995; Woodman, 1995). For members of racial and ethnic minority groups, these difficulties are exacerbated by racism and ethnocentrism. Even though they may be unaware of the sexual orientation of their clients, social workers in all areas of service may encounter people who are confronting this complex set of issues.

## IDENTITY DEVELOPMENT: COMING OUT

The most fundamental issue which gay, lesbian and bisexual clients may need help with is that of integrating same-sex sexual orientation into their identity, often referred to as "coming out." Coming out entails recognizing attraction to members of one's own sex, participating in same-sex behaviour and emotional relationships, revealing gay or lesbian sexual orientation to others and attaining a feeling of comfort with this identity (Lee, 1992). Barriers presented by heterosexism must be overcome in order to achieve a positive gay or lesbian identity. For instance, many people have some degree of attraction to members of their own sex, but due to internalized homophobia remain unaware of it or do not act on it. Differences related to gender, age, race and culture may cause the coming out process to unfold in various patterns (Schneider, 1991).

Coming out is complicated for racial and ethnic minority gays and lesbians by the need to integrate two kinds of marginalized differences into their identities. Reynolds and Pope (1991) comment that most developmental models which address diversity focus on a single category of difference, such as ethnicity or sexual orientation. However, this approach provides an oversimplified and fragmented view of the lives of ethnic minority gays and lesbians. For instance, a person must deal with being both Asian and gay at the same time.

The "Multidimensional Identity Model" developed by Reynolds and Pope (1991, p. 179) distinguishes several responses to having more than one type of difference. According to this scheme, a person may "... identify with one aspect of self ... with multiple aspects of self in a segmented fashion ... [or] ... with combined aspects of self..." (Reynolds and Pope, 1991, p. 179). Furthermore, an individual may change his or her approach to dealing with minority differences depending on circumstances throughout life.

Each of the various responses to diversity has implications for self-esteem. For instance, the first option would entail identifying with either an ethnic group or the gay and lesbian community and denying membership in the other group. Because this approach results in rejection of a significant part of one's identity, it can impair self-esteem and limit relationships. The second alternative would involve participating in both the ethnocultural group and the gay and lesbian community, but keeping these lives separate. However, this adaptation can increase awareness of conflicts between ethnic identity and sexual orientation and may weaken identification with either community. The third choice would imply embracing both same-sex sexual orientation and ethnic identity simultaneously. Similar to those who identify as bisexual or biracial, this approach would consist of relating to gay, lesbian and bisexual members of one's racial or ethnic group. Although this strategy may limit one to socializing among a relatively small group of people, it offers the possibility of integrating various aspects of diversity into the identity in a positive way. The Multidimensional Identity Model suggests two areas on which social worker intervention should focus: homophobia and heterosexism within ethnic minority families and communities, and racism and ethnocentrism within gay and lesbian communities.

Anti-gay discrimination within ethnocultural minority groups may be associated with racism and ethnocentrism within the dominant culture, and with traditional values within immigrant communities. Homophobia within racial and cultural minority groups may in part be a reaction to racism and ethnocentrism. Groups which face oppression based on race or ethnicity may attempt to avoid additional marginalization related to same-sex sexual orientation. This need may result in particularly strong expressions of homophobia within minority communities (Irvine, 1995). For instance, although data suggest that African American heterosexuals are no more prejudiced than whites (Herek and Capitanio, 1995), the belief that same-sex sexual orientation is "... a white man's disease" is often voiced within black communities (Critchlow, 1995, p. 28). Thus gays and lesbians who encounter racial and ethnic discrimination in the dominant culture may be unwilling to take on a second devalued status related to their same-sex sexual orientation that will marginalize them within their ethnocultural minority communities.

In order to avoid stigmatization, members of racial and cultural minorities may deny being gay or lesbian or identify as bisexual despite the predominance of their same-sex attraction and behaviour. For instance, McKirnan et al. (1995) found black men more likely than white men to identify as bisexual, a phenomenon which they related to homophobia within the black community. The combination of racism, ethnocentrism and heterosexism can cause ethnic minority gays and lesbians to internalize oppression, develop negative self-images and acquire poor life skills (Icard, 1986).

In addition to the influence of the dominant culture, traditional values can also shape the reaction to same-sex sexual orientation within ethnocultural minority communities in Canada. A study of Canadian gay and lesbian youth by Tremble, Schneider and Appathurai (1989) reveals how minority ethnocultural values can be both oppressive and supportive of same-sex sexual orientation. Traditional conceptions of highly differentiated gender roles and conservative religious values can force gay, lesbian and bisexual members of minority groups to conceal their sexual orientation. Individuals who are unwilling to remain in the closet may be excluded from their families and communities. Alternatively, the strong family ties found within many cultures can prevail over community disapproval, so that young people are accepted within their families despite their same-sex sexual orientation. The result can be that gay, lesbian and bisexual members of racial and ethnic minority groups are tolerated, if not completely accepted, and thus may not have to not give up their identification with their cultures completely.

## DISCRIMINATION WITHIN GAY AND LESBIAN COMMUNITIES

Members of ethnocultural minority groups may also encounter racism and ethnocentrism when they participate in gay and lesbian communities (Hidalgo, 1985; Tremble et al., 1989). For example, a black gay man described the racial stereotypes he has encountered within the Canadian gay community (Plowden, 1992). He perceived that some white gay men were attracted to him because they assumed that all black men have large penises, are sexually skilled and are invariably willing to have intercourse. Conversely, other white gay men avoided him because of his race.

An illustration of the complex effects of the interaction of racism and ethnocentrism is provided by a Canadian born gay man of Chinese heritage who described the barriers he encountered within the gay community (Lee, 1995). He was not accepted by either Asian-born gay men or by members of the dominant, white gay community. While socializing within gay and lesbian communities increases cultural assimilation, discrimination prevents racial and ethnic minority gays and lesbians from fully integrating within these groups, which are comprised primarily of members of the dominant culture. Thus, minority gays and lesbians may be left feeling like outsiders in both their ethnic communities and the gay and lesbian communities.

## IMPLICATIONS FOR SOCIAL WORK INTERVENTION

Cross-cultural social work practice with respect to same-sex sexual orientation involves untangling a web of issues at the individual, family, community and institutional levels. Racial and ethnic minorities in Canada may have social service needs related to discrimination as well as to cultural adaptation (Yelaja and O'Neill, 1990). Similarly, gays, lesbians and bisexuals may also have special needs related to oppression as well as differences in same-sex relationships (O'Neill and Naidoo, 1990). In addition to these difficulties, gay, lesbian and bisexual members of racial and ethnic minorities may have unique needs arising from their membership in more than one marginalized group. Special problems may occur in relation to developing an integrated identity, maintaining family and community relationships and coping with discrimination within the gay and lesbian community. However, there is evidence that social services are insensitive to clients who are members of both ethnocultural and sexual minority groups (O'Brien, 1994; Travers, 1994). Effective responses to these concerns necessitate changes in policies, programs, practice and professional education.

## RECOMMENDATIONS FOR POLICY

A prerequisite to the development of effective social services is the creation of an organizational climate which is safe for open discussion of differences of race, culture and sexual orientation. In order to achieve this goal, agencies should officially recognize that same-sex sexual orientation is a legitimate aspect of human diversity and that heterosexism is as unacceptable as racism, ethnocentrism and other forms of oppression. They should provide leadership in community programs to counter all forms of discrimination. Initially, services should advocate for inclusion of sexual orientation in human rights codes and the provision of spousal benefits to those involved in same-sex relationships.

Social services should also review their policies, procedures, forms and public relations materials to ensure that all aspects of their programs recognize and accommodate gays, lesbians and bisexuals. It is particularly important that agencies add sexual orientation to their policies against discrimination based on race, culture and other differences. Brochures geared to various ethnic communities should reflect the organization's position with resect to same-sex sexual orientation and make it clear that the agency serves gay, lesbian and bisexual persons. In addition, where potentially relevant, intake procedures and forms should provide an opportunity for clients to indicate their sexual orientation so that agencies will have data regarding the number of gay, lesbian and bisexual clients and their needs.

The provision of services by social workers who are open about being gay or lesbian makes it easier for clients to discuss their sexual orientation. With agency policies which affirm respect for gays and lesbians, staff members may feel safe enough to be open about their same-sex sexual orientation. In addition, agencies should recruit new staff members from sexual as well as racial and ethnic minority groups.

## Recommendations for Programs

As noted earlier, gay, lesbian and bisexual people have the same range of social service needs as do heterosexuals. Thus, in general, it is not necessary to provide separate programs for them. However, when the focus is on issues in which sexual orientation and ethnicity are particularly relevant, specialized programs may be more effective. For example, in order to facilitate the development of an integrated identity, agencies that provide counselling to both adults and youths should provide "coming out" groups specifically for members of ethnocultural minorities. Other areas in which separate group services may be beneficial are programs for victims of anti-gay and lesbian violence, couple counselling and addiction problems. At the level of community intervention, agencies should support the formation of ethno-specific groups within gay and lesbian communities.

Of particular importance is the need for AIDS prevention programs that focus on racial and ethnic minority gay and bisexual men. Members of racial and ethnic minority groups may deal with conflicts between their cultural values and their same-sex sexual orientation by identifying as bisexual rather than as gay (McKirnan et al., 1995). However, this approach may increase their risk of contracting acquired immunodeficiency syndrome (AIDS). Because many AIDS prevention programs are geared towards dominant culture gay men, ethnic minority bisexuals who do not participate in the gay community may not receive accurate information regarding the transmission of the human immunodeficiency virus (HIV) or may not realize that it is relevant to them. AIDS prevention programs are also an opportunity to provide accurate information regarding same-sex sexual orientation to ethnic groups that proscribe discussion of sexual issues, and thus counter homophobia (Leong, 1995).

## ISSUES IN PRACTICE

There are a number of issues to be considered when working with members of ethnic and sexual minorities, whether individually or in groups. One issue is how clients integrate their sexual orientation and ethnicity into their lives. Individuals may change their approach to dealing with their ethnic and sexual identities throughout their lives. An implication of the "Multidimensional Identity Model" (Reynolds and Pope, 1991) is that social workers need to assist clients in examining all aspects of their identities and assess the benefits and risks of the various approaches to dealing with their sexual orientation in relation to their families and ethnic communities. Social workers should be aware of resources within gay and lesbian communities such as ethno-specific groups which provide individuals with opportunities for relating to gays and lesbians from their own culture, thus avoiding the fragmentation which may result from living separate lives in ethnic communities and gay and lesbian communities.

Another issue social workers may need to address in a variety of services is the relationship between gay or lesbian clients and their families. Social workers may help ethnic minority families to accept a gay or lesbian member by emphasizing the importance of maintaining the bonds among family members rather than conforming to conventional mores regarding gender and sexuality. Knowledge of traditional religious beliefs is essential in working towards this goal (Shernoff, 1995). Enhancing awareness of gay and lesbian members of extended families and the ethnic community, and the provision of information which counters stereotypes and reduces families' feelings that they are responsible for the same-sex sexual orientation of their children, can also contribute to acceptance (Tremble et al., 1989). Presentations to community groups by gay and lesbian speaker panels which include members of the ethnic group can contribute to reaching this objective (Croteau and Kusek, 1992).

## PROFESSIONAL TRAINING

In order to provide ethical and effective services to gay, lesbian and bisexual members of racial and ethnic minority groups, social workers need to be competent to work with clients who are different than they are with respect to culture as well as sexual orientation (Irvine, 1995). In order to achieve this goal, all social workers need to be knowledgeable regarding both same-sex sexual orientation and ethnic minority cultures. In addition, social workers should be helped to become aware of their feelings regarding differences of sexual orientation, race and culture. Social work training should facilitate comparison of workers' personal values regarding sexuality with those in other cultures. Differences with respect to sexuality should be considered in the context of discrimination faced by various disadvantaged groups. Social workers should be helped to develop cross-cultural communication skills regarding sexuality and advocacy skills to counter all forms of systemic discrimination. They should also develop the ability to collaborate with agencies within the ethnic minority and gay and lesbian communities in serving clients.

Social work education with respect to sexuality and cultural differences should be provided by schools of social work as well as by social services. Members of gay and lesbian community organizations may be able to assist in such training. However, it should not be assumed that gay and lesbian staff members from ethnic minorities are responsible for or necessarily competent enough to provide this training.

## CONCLUSION

Heterosexism presents significant barriers to the full participation in society of gay, lesbian and bisexual Canadians. This disadvantage is compounded by the racism, ethnocentrism and sexism encountered by members of the ethnocultural minority groups which comprise the population. However, Canada's multicultural ideals hold out the promise of a society in which differences of all kinds will be recognized, accepted and valued. Social workers can contribute to the realization of this dream by transforming social services to make them responsive to the needs of oppressed groups and by supporting gay, lesbian and bisexual members of all racial and ethnic groups in realizing their full potential.

## REFERENCES

Adam, B. D. (1993). Winning rights and freedoms in Canada. In A. Hendriks, R. Tielman. and E. van der Veen (eds.), *The third pink book: A global view of lesbian and gay liberation and oppression.* Buffalo: Prometheus.

Berger, R. M. and Kelly, J. J. (1995). Gay men overview. In R. L. Edwards (ed.), *Encyclopedia of social work* (19th ed.) (Vol. 1, pp. 1064-1075). Washington, D.C.: National Association of Social Workers.

Bibby, R. (1995). *The Bibby report: Social trends Canadian style.* Toronto: Stoddart.

Binson, D., Michaels, S., Stall, R., Coates, T. J., Gagnon, J. H. and Catania, J. A. (1995). Prevalence and social distribution of men who have sex with men: United States and its urban centers. *Journal of Sex Research*, 32(3), 245-254.

Bronskill, J. (1996, Feb. 12). Most hate crime 'goes unreported.' *Vancouver Sun*, p. B3.

Canadian Association of Social Workers. (1994). *Social work code of ethics.* Ottawa: Author.

Churchill, W. (1967). *Homosexual behavior among males: A cross-cultural and cross-species investigation.* New York: Hawthorn Books.

Critchlow, W. (1995, April 28). Untying the tongue: Black revolutionaries confront the policing of homoerotic desire. *XTRA,* p. 23.

Croteau, J. M., and Kusek, M. T. (1992). Gay and lesbian speaker panels. *Journal of Counseling and Development,* 70, 396-401.

De Cecco, J. P. and Elia, J. P. (1993). A critique and synthesis of biological essentialism and social constructionist views of sexuality and gender. In J. P. De Cecco and J. P. Elia (eds.), *If you seduce a straight person, can you make them gay?* Binghampton, NY: Harrington Park.

Diamond, M. (1993). Homosexuality and bisexuality in different populations. *Archives of Sexual Behavior,* 22(4), 291-310.

Gochros, J. S. (1995). Bisexuality. In R. L. Edwards (ed.), *Encyclopedia of social work* (19th ed.) (Vol. 1, pp. 299-304). Washington, D.C.: National Association of Social Workers.

Gramick, J. (1983). Homophobia: A new challenge. *Social Work,* 28(1), 137-141.

Harry, J. (1990). A probability sample of gay males. *Journal of Homosexuality,* 19(1), 89-104.

Herek, G. M. (1984). Beyond "homophobia": A social psychological perspective on attitudes toward lesbians and gay men. *Journal of Homosexuality,* 10(2), 1-21.

Herek, G. M. and Capitanio, J. P. (1995). Black heterosexuals' attitudes toward lesbians and gay men in the United States. *Journal of Sex Research,* 32(2), 95-105.

Hidalgo, H. (1985). Third world. In H. Hidalgo, T. L. Peterson and N. J. Woodman, (eds.), *Lesbian and gay issues: A resource manual for social workers.* Silver Spring, MA: National Association of Social Workers.

Hinsch, B. (1990). *Passions of the cut sleeve: The male homosexual tradition in China.* Berkeley: University of California.

Ho, P. S. (1995). Male homosexual identity in Hong Kong: A social construction. *Journal of Homosexuality,* 29(1), 71-85.

Icard, L. (1986). Black gay men and conflicting social identities: Sexual orientation versus racial identity. *Journal of social Work and Human Sexuality,* 4, 83-93.

Irvine, J. M. (1995). *Sexuality education across cultures: Working with differences.* San Francisco: Jossey-Bass.

Kinsey, A. C., Pomeroy, W. B. and Martin, C. E. (1948). *Sexual behaviour in the human male.* Philadelphia: W. B. Sanders.

Kinsey, A. C., Pomeroy, W. B., Martin, C. E. and Gebhard, P. (1955). *Sexual behaviour in the human female*. Philadelphia: W. B. Sanders.

Kinsman, G. (1987). *The regulation of desire: Sexuality in Canada*. Montreal: Black Rose Books.

Lavee, Y. (1991). Western and non-western human sexuality: Implications for clinical practice. *Journal of Sex and Marital Therapy*, 17(3), 203-213.

Lee, E. (1995, Dec. 1). Achieving acceptance in Vancouver, on World AIDS Day: Golden mountain gay. *Vancouver Sun*, p. A23.

Lee, J. A. B. (1992). Teaching content related to lesbian and gay identity formation. In N. J. Woodman (ed.), *Lesbian and gay lifestyles: A guide for counseling and education*. New York: Irvington.

Leong, L. W. (1995). Walking the tightrope: The role of Action for AIDS in the provision of social services in Singapore. In G. Sullivan and L. W. Leong (eds.), *Gays and lesbians in Asia and the Pacific: Social and human services* (pp. 11-30). New York: Harrington Park.

MacDonald, M. J. (1994). Sexuality and the criminal law in Canada. *Canadian Journal of Human Sexuality*, 3(1), 15-23.

Marmor, J. (1980). Overview: The multiple roots of homosexual behavior. In J. Marmor (ed.), *Homosexual behavior: A modern reappraisal*. New York: Basic.

McKirnan, D. J., Stokes, J. P., Doll, L. and Burzette, R. G. (1995). Bisexually active men: Social characteristics and sexual behavior. *Journal of Sex Research*, 32(1), 65-76.

Naidoo, J. C. and Edwards, R. G. (1991). Combating racism involving visible minorities. *Canadian Social Work Review*, 8(2), 211-236.

Neisen, J. H. (1990). Heterosexism: Redefining homophobia for the 1990s. *Journal of Gay and Lesbian Psychotherapy*, 1(3), 21-35.

Nieberding, R. A. (ed.). (1989). *In every classroom: The report of the president's select committee for lesbian and gay concerns*. New Brunswick, NJ: The State University of New Jersey, Rutgers.

O'Brien, C. A. (1994). The social organization of the treatment of lesbian, gay and bisexual youth in group homes and youth shelters. *Canadian Review of Social Policy*, 34, 37-57.

O'Neill, B. J. and Naidoo, J. C. (1990). Social services to lesbians and gay men in Ontario. *The Social Worker*, 58, 101-104.

Plowden, N. (1992, Feb.). A gay black man's perspective. *GO INFO*, p. 15. [Newspaper of Gays of Ottawa]

Reynolds, A. L. and Pope, R. L. (1991). The complexities of diversity: Exploring multiple oppressions. *Journal of Counseling and Development*, 70, 174-180.

Schneider, M. (1991). Developing services for lesbian and gay adolescents. *Canadian Journal of Community Mental Health*, 10(1), 133-151.

Schneider, M. and O'Neill, B. (1993). Eligibility of lesbians and gay men for spousal benefits. *Canadian Journal of Human Sexuality,* 2(1), 23-31.

Sell, R. L., Wells, J. A. and Wypij, D. (1995). The prevalence of homosexual behavior and attraction in the United States, the United Kingdom and France: Results of national population-based samples. *Archives of Sexual Behavior,* 24(3), 235-248.

Shernoff, M. (1995). Gay men: Direct practice. In R. L. Edwards (ed.), *Encyclopedia of social work* (19th ed.) (Vol. 1, pp. 1075-1085). Washington, D.C.: National Association of Social Workers.

Tielman, R. and Hammelburg, H. (1993). World survey on the social and legal position of gays and lesbians. In A. Hendriks, R. Tielman. and E. van der Veen (eds.), *The third pink book: A global view of lesbian and gay liberation and oppression.* Buffalo, NY: Prometheus.

Travers, R. N. (1994). *You can feel the wall: Barriers to addictions services for lesbian, gay and bisexual youth.* MA thesis, Graduate Department of Education, University of Toronto, Ontario.

Tremble, B., Schneider, M. and Appathurai, C. (1989). Growing up gay or lesbian in a multicultural context. *Journal of Homosexuality,* 17(3/4), 253-267.

Tully, C. T. (1995). Lesbians overview. In R. L. Edwards (ed.), *Encyclopedia of social work* (19th ed.) (Vol. 1, pp. 1591-1596). Washington, D.C.: National Association of Social Workers.

Williams, W. L. (1993). Being gay and doing research on homosexuality in non-western cultures. *Journal of Sex Research,* 30(2), 115-120.

Whitam, F. L. and Mathy, R. M. (1986). *Male homosexuality in four societies.* New York: Praeger Special Studies.

Woodman, N. J. (1995). Lesbians: Direct practice. In R. L. Edwards (ed.), *Encyclopedia of social work* (19th ed.) (Vol. 1, pp. 1597-1604). Washington, D.C.: National Association of Social Workers.

Yelaja, S. A. and O'Neill, B. J. (1990). Chapter 1: Introduction. In S. A. Yelaja (ed.), *Proceedings of the Settlement and Integration of New Immigrants to Canada Conference.* Waterloo, Ontario: Wilfrid Laurier University, Faculty of Social Work and Centre for Social Welfare Studies.

# CHAPTER 5

# Chinese Elderly in Public Housing: A Challenge for Mainstream Housing and Community Service Providers

*Morris Saldov*

## INTRODUCTION

By the year 2021, the Canadian population of elderly is expected to exceed five million if present immigration levels and mortality rates are maintained, (Secretary of State, 1988).[1] The largest group of people in Canada who are unable to speak either of Canada's two official languages is the Chinese (population: 100,185). Chinese seniors are expected to lead the growth rate among ethnic elders between 1991 and 2006, particularly in Toronto and Vancouver where they are projected to have the highest growth rates in the country (Multiculturalism and Citizenship Canada (MCC), 1993:3).

Since the fastest growth rate in persons age sixty-five and over is occurring in non-white populations, particularly Asians,[2] gerontology research in the field of housing and community services needs to shift its focus from comparative studies to describing and analyzing individual seniors groups' requirements. The service needs of ethnocultural racial minorities, such as those of Chinese seniors, require definition in their own right and not necessarily by comparison with majority groups.

Housing and community services utilized by Asian elderly have largely been ignored by Canadian and US researchers. The ethnic elderly have been under-represented in the aging literature, (Kramer, Barker and Damron-Rodriguez, 1991), (Saldov and Chow, 1994). The paucity of such research has been a persistent problem for service providers. If services to the ethnic elderly in Canada are to be adapted to be more congruent with their needs, policy initiatives will need to be adopted, aided by more ethnographic research.

## The Canadian context for multicultural services

When the official policy of multiculturalism was introduced in 1971, it was the Canadian government's intention to promote institutional changes whereby all cultural groups could gain equal access to public services in Canada. The Multiculturalism Act of 1988, which set out the means by which this was to be accomplished, defined the concept of multiculturalism as *integration* (i.e., equal membership by ethnocultural groups in a communalistic society). This meant that ethnic minorities could expect to access public services which were sensitive to their linguistic and cultural needs (MCC, 1991:9). The government's aim was to: "promote the full and *equitable* [emphasis added] participation of individuals and communities of all origins..." (MCC, 1990:13).

The concept of equity, key to the understanding and implementation of the federal government's policy on multiculturalism, represents a higher standard than equality in promoting the elimination of linguistic and cultural barriers to accessing services. The equity principle demands that those who have the least access should gain the greatest advantages in overcoming barriers. Within the housing field, equal access for ethnic elders to housing and community services has been the goal of various human service organizations. However, this ideal has been difficult to achieve (MacLean and Bonar, 1987).

The ethnic elderly may be faced with additional barriers to accessing services owing to generic problems of ageism and disability (Saldov, 1991). Therefore equity considerations may take on greater significance in designing social programs serving ethnic seniors who experience the multiple jeopardies of ethnoracial discrimination, ageism and disability.

The present study attempts to expand the database on Chinese seniors living in the Canadian institution of public housing by examining the linguistic and cultural problems they face in accessing both the services of the Metro Toronto Housing Company Ltd., (MTHCL) and those of community agencies.

A major defining characteristic of chinese culture is the practice of building social networks of support (*kuan-hsi*) to ensure the availability of help when needed. *Kuan-hsi* has been described as the development of mutually beneficial networks of support between Chinese people. In a relationship where *kuan-hsi* is established, each person can ask a favour of the other with the expectation of future reciprocity (Yang, 1994:1-2). Yang (1994:6) defines *kuan-hsi* as:

> ...the cultivation of personal relationships and networks of mutual dependence; and the manufacturing of obligation and indebtedness. What informs these practices and their native descriptions is the conception of the primacy and binding power of personal relationships and their importance in meeting the needs and desires of everyday life.

According to King (1994), certain *kuan-hsi* relations are preordained and others are voluntarily constructed. Relations between father and son as well as brother and brother are preordained, lifelong and obligatory while husband-wife and friend-friend *kuan-hsi* are a matter of choice and can be ended (King, 1994:112). In cities, non-kin relations can be even more important than kinship, as demonstrated by the popular Chinese saying, "Distant relatives are not as dear as close neighbours." Distance can weaken the kinship bond of "familiarity" and obligation. In the absence of family support, where *kuan-hsi* is operating between neighbours, mutual aid and obligation can develop.

In addition to positive neighbouring relations, *kuan-hsi* may derive from native-place connections. People who originate from the same village, town, country or province or speak the same dialect have an additional basis for *kuan-hsi* relations (Yang, 1994:115). There may also be gender differences in personal relations. According to traditional Chinese culture, many women are expected to follow their husbands when they are young and follow their children, especially sons, when they are old. Chinese elders in public housing may therefore experience a loss of face when not living with family members.

Because many Chinese immigrants to Canada had limited exposure to formal social services in China and Hong Kong when help was needed, they relied on *kuan-hsi* to obtain and exchange favours. Chu and Ju

(1990) studied the importance of *kuan-hsi* to socio-economic well-being in contemporary China. Over two-thirds of those studied (71.7%) stated that they would try connections rather than using "normal channels" to resolve a problem, while only 19.6% said they would go through normal channels (Chu and Ju, 1990:66). In China, housing officials often used their public position as a private possession for the purpose of *kuan-hsi* exchange (Yang, 1994:87). Residents were careful not to offend housing officials and develop *kuan-hsi* to enhance their security of tenure and to promote good service when needed. *Kuan-hsi* may also have been used to protect oneself from fellow tenants who may curry favour with officials by acting as "informers" (Yang, 1994:97).

The Western practice of providing human services "as a right" obviates the necessity of exchanging favours customary in *kuan-hsi* relations. In Canadian public housing, job-related services are viewed as entitlements rather than favours. The practice of *kuan-hsi* by Chinese seniors and the entitlement to services while in Canadian public housing may create cultural conflicts which result in service incongruencies. This study was an attempt to describe and explore the congruence of Chinese seniors' cultural and language needs with the structure of housing and community services available to them in MTHCL.

## PERSON-ENVIRONMENT CONGRUENCE

Person-environment congruence theory provides a common sense model for policy-makers, managers and professionals in the human services field to achieve a better fit between the housing environments they create and the people they purport to serve. A congruence approach may supply a set of culturally sensitive guidelines to assist housing suppliers and managers to accomplish the desired match of housing and community services to the characteristics of the ethnic elderly. According to Kahana:

> ...in the present congruence model goodness of fit is seen as antecedent to well being rather than synonymous with it. Whenever there is a lack of congruence between the individual's needs and life situation—due to either change in environment (especially new housing or institutionalization) or a change in needs or capacities—various adaptive

strategies are called upon to increase the fit between person and environment. Adaptive strategies may serve to reduce mismatch either by changing needs or by changing the environment. Depending on the success of these adaptive strategies, well being or lack of well being may result.... An important role of the environment then is to accommodate as much as possible to the changing needs of the aging individual. (Kahana, 1982:99-103)

Studies of health and community services in Toronto have revealed that serious incongruencies exist between the needs of ethnic seniors and the services they are offered (Doyle and Visano, 1987) and (Saldov and Chow, 1994). Results of health-care research by the Chinese Community Nursing Home (CCNH) for Greater Toronto revealed that, "...the cultural needs of the Chinese senior population, particularly as these needs are reflected in the delivery of health care services, are not being met" (CCNH, 1989:11).

This study has attempted to discover barriers that prevent the matching of housing and community services to the needs of Chinese seniors in Toronto's public housing environment. It represents an effort to assist mainstream agencies like MTHCL to develop strategies that achieve a better fit of services to the needs of ethnic seniors, in particular the Chinese elderly.

## "AGING IN PLACE" AND THE ETHNIC ELDERLY

At the time of the study, MTHCL was engaged with the province of Ontario and the federal government in a process of creating a new vision for housing the elderly within the long-term care concept of "aging in place." As part of this process, MTHCL was committed through a task force on multicultural/anti-racism "to examine issues arising out of the increasingly multi-cultural nature of both the tenants and staff and to develop recommendations which will address those issues." (MTHCL, 1993b:8). In its "Race Relations and Multicultural Policy," regarding race, culture and language, MTHCL committed itself to "identify and eliminate all barriers that may exist in obtaining or accessing services, programs and/or employment" (MTHCL, 1993a:1). In developing its aim of forging new partnerships with tenants, the housing company went on to suggest a strategic direction which "recognizes and responds to the needs of an increasingly diverse ethno-racial and cultural tenant population" (MTHCL, 1994:3).

In some MTHCL housing, the ethnoracial composition of the elderly has become quite homogeneous. With the increasing concentration of ethnic elderly in some developments, housing agencies like MTHCL are being challenged to effectively and equitably adapt their services to meet the needs of shifting balances of residents in their buildings. In 1991, MTHCL found that tenants of foreign origin experienced lower levels of satisfaction owing to greater difficulty in forming social networks due to the language and culture differences from majority groups in their buildings (MTHCL, 1991a:22-3). Within a racially and ethnically diverse population of elders in a mainstream housing agency like MTHCL, when one group becomes the majority, how should services be organized? This study enables Chinese seniors, where they represent the majority of residents, to expound on their experiences when seeking housing and community services.

## METHODOLOGY

### The sample

Interviews were conducted during the summer of 1994 with a random sample of 306 Chinese seniors drawn from nine MTHCL buildings. All buildings contained 50% or more Chinese seniors. The concentration of Chinese seniors ranged from 52% to 84%. The Chinese population of elders in the nine buildings ranged in size from 13 to 237 residents. To control for the effects of the size of populations in buildings with larger numbers of Chinese seniors (i.e., 116-237 Chinese seniors), approximately 30% of potential respondents were selected while about 50% of potential subjects were chosen in buildings with smaller Chinese populations (i.e., 13-63 Chinese seniors).

### Study design

This is an exploratory-descriptive study using an interview approach focused on the relationship of language and culture to accessing housing and community services. Demographic and contextual factors are also described in relation to the social environment of MTHCL housing.

The set of questions contained in the interview guide was developed, translated into Chinese and checked for content validity by asking key informants for appropriate cultural content. These key informants were either currently working with Chinese seniors in metro housing or had previously been accustomed to working with low-income Chinese elderly. To further refine content validity for the interview questions, a focus group was conducted with Chinese seniors from a non-sample MTHCL building of 37% Chinese. The interview guide was pretested in a building where the percentage of Chinese (49%) most closely approximated the minimum requirement for inclusion in the sample.

Other research experiences with Toronto and Vancouver Chinese seniors' communities showed that many elders were minimally literate or semi-literate. Consequently, mail-out questionnaires would likely have yielded a lower response rate than interviews (Chinese Interpreter and Information Services, 1987; Chinese Community Nursing Home, 1989; MTHCL, 1991b; and Lau, 1993).[3] Since many Chinese seniors in Canada lack literacy skills, it was decided to conduct interviews.

## Data collection

A core group of seven Chinese-speaking volunteer interviewers recruited from English as a second language classes, volunteer services and the Asian Studies Department of the University of Toronto assisted the project coordinator (PC) with the interviewing.[4] All of the interviewers spoke Cantonese. Some could also speak Mandarin, Toi San and Shanghainese dialects. The dialect used for the interviews was primarily Cantonese (73%), although a substantial number (20%) were conducted in the Toi San dialect. Additional dialects used were Mandarin and Shanghainese (6%). Training for interviewing was provided to enhance consistency in applying the interview guide. Care was taken to train the interviewers not to apply any pressure to participate that would suggest coercion. Rather, benevolent persuasion to encourage participation was the approach taken through explaining the purpose of the study.

The PC and principal investigator (PI) had spent several years providing voluntary services to Chinese seniors in one of the buildings studied and were therefore known to many of that building's residents. This relationship may have contributed to *kuan-hsi* with the residents and in turn promoted their participation in the study. It was observed that in many of the buildings "natural helpers" (i.e., tenants who had the trust of the Chinese residents) acted as intermediaries in facilitating seniors' access to a variety of housing and community services. By accompanying the research team, the natural helper from the building where the PC and PI were known to the residents was able to help develop relationships with other natural helpers in the remaining eight buildings. Often the introduction to the research team was given by the natural helpers. Some even organized meetings of residents where the interviewers and the study objectives could be introduced to potential participants. The considerable trust which had developed through *kuan-hsi* relations between tenants and natural helpers could have played a major role in "opening doors" to the research team. In addition to the critical role of the natural helpers in promoting the study, the MTHCL manager and her housing staff added their support. The general manager provided a letter, translated into Chinese, which gave an introduction to the study. This letter also made clear to the seniors that the study was being carried out with the co-operation and support of MTHCL and that their participation would not jeopardize their tenancy.[5]

## Data analysis

The data have been analyzed using descriptive statistics to summarize characteristics of the sample and report on the responses of the seniors. Frequencies are given on the knowledge and use of housing and community services and the extent of the seniors' social interaction and participation in meetings within their buildings. To enrich the analysis of the quantitative data, additional notes were taken concerning qualitative statements made by respondents. The interviewers' observations were also recorded during the debriefing sessions following interviewing.

## FINDINGS

## Characteristics of the sample

The Chinese seniors in our sample were mainly female (76%), a larger representation than that found in the MTHCL population (62%) (MTHCL, 1993b:9). Seventy percent of the elders had lived with family members prior to entering MTHCL, 83% were born in China and 79% had lived in Hong Kong or China prior to their arrival in Canada. Their average length of time in Canada was fourteen years. Although not all buildings were in Chinatown areas, there was easy access via public transportation for those seniors living further away.

About 60% of the elders spoke only Chinese while nearly 40% stated that they also spoke some English. Fifty-two percent said they were able to read and 44% stated they could write Chinese. Twenty-three percent stated they could read English. Their level of English understanding was not assessed.

Sixty percent of the sample was between the ages of seventy and eighty-four. There was considerable age variation by housing project with three buildings having mostly younger populations of the elderly (fifty-five to seventy-four), while the remaining buildings had predominantly older populations (seventy-five to ninety-four). Chinese seniors reported that they had good vision (77%), hearing (86%) and mobility (77%). These figures suggest that the Chinese seniors sampled saw themselves as mainly healthy. It is important to note however that seniors generally report high levels of self-assessed health even though they may have significant disabilities that can affect daily activities (Zimmer and Chappell, 1996:73).

## Social environment

To gauge the social atmosphere in their buildings, seniors were asked about the extent of friendliness and racism they had observed. Ninety-four percent of the residents perceived the Chinese seniors in their buildings to be "very friendly" (e.g., helpful, co-operative, confidante, socializing considerably [going out together]) or "friendly" (e.g., greet and chat, seldom go out together) towards them. Since 93% of the interviews were conducted in either Cantonese or Toi San dialects, it may be reasonable to suggest that social relationships are formed because of regionalism, with elders coming from similar areas of China speaking the same dialect of Chinese developing strong social bonds. This may reflect native-place ties (*tongxiang*) described by Yang (1994). People coming from the same village, town, country or province, or speaking the same dialect wherein shared values are likely to occur, may have a special inclination to enter into "friendly" perhaps *kuan-hsi* exchange relations. Fifty-two percent of the non-Chinese were perceived to be "friendly" and 47% "neutral" (e.g., merely greet each other, neither avoiding nor seeking contact). Without special efforts to overcome language and culture differences, it would have been surprising to find the same high levels of "friendly" relations between Chinese and non-Chinese residents.

When asked about their observations of racism in MTHCL housing, 10% reported what they believed to be racist incidents. The Chinese tendency to seek harmony and not "make waves" may have contributed to reduced rates of reporting racism. There was also a degree of uncertainty about the occurrence of a racist incident due to language barriers and cultural differences in interpreting non-verbal actions. Higher rates of reported racism were reported (14% and 20%) in two buildings where the Chinese seniors had better English understanding. In these buildings, the social club executives had also experienced a transition from Anglo to Chinese majority representation, which appeared to generate considerable resentment and alienation among some non-Chinese residents.

To further gauge the seniors' social interaction in their buildings, they were asked about their participation in social activities like birthday parties or festival events. Thirty-eight percent of elders reported participation in such social activities every two weeks while 28% said they never participated. When seniors held parties they always gave foodstuffs to staff as part of the group's efforts to maintain good relations (*kuan-hsi*). Half of the residents stated that they had attended meetings with MTHCL staff. This was sometimes confused with meetings at the buildings arranged by politicians who often turned such occasions into social events where food was served and an interpreter made available.

Sixty-six percent of elders reported that they preferred to live in a building with a majority of Chinese while almost 30% stated that this did not matter to them. The main reason given for wanting to live in a building where a majority of tenants were Chinese was ease of communication. Common language made it possible for the elders to engage in neighbouring behaviour so they could feel more secure in their building. Shared language and native place (*tongxiang*) would likely enhance the possibilities for the development of supportive social networks among Chinese-speaking neighbours in MTHCL housing.

## Housing services

When asked about the duties of different MTHCL staff in their buildings, over 90% of residents (with prompting) stated that they knew the superintendent and custodian were responsible for the maintenance of the buildings. Sixty-eight percent of elders knew about the services provided by the nighttime (key) person while 70% knew about the services of the housing case worker (social worker). Forty-four percent knew about the services of the recreation/community development worker. Most of the elders (97%) knew how to reach the superintendent or custodian either at the general office or by phone. Since the offices were usually located near the entrances of the buildings, superintendents and custodians were readily visible to residents. There was no attempt however to validate the seniors' knowledge by asking for phone numbers or location of the office. About 75% of seniors said they knew how to reach the key person in case of an emergency after hours. Approximately 70% knew how to reach the housing case worker while less than 30% of residents were aware of how to contact their recreation/community development worker.

The study explored the means by which Chinese seniors sought help if they did not or were unable to communicate their service needs directly to staff. In these circumstances about 32% of elders said they sought assistance from other tenants. While a little more than 50% sought help from family members. Elders rarely (less than 12%) contacted a friend from outside their building to assist them. Even fewer residents (8%) contacted a volunteer for help. These figures suggest that Chinese seniors often use other means than direct communication with staff in order to obtain MTHCL services.

In a number of situations elders reported giving gifts (tips) and foodstuff to staff to help develop *kuan-hsi* so that services would be provided when needed. In China, obtaining accommodations and maintaining good relations with housing officials is often achieved through the use of *kuan-hsi* (Yang, 1994:96). Chinese seniors may be expected to base their expectations of staff on these types of past experiences with housing officials in China. The practice of gift giving in exchange for services had become a means of assuring seniors that services would be available when needed, but it presented MTHCL management with a serious dilemma. Staff were not to accept tips for providing job-related services. How MTHCL was to assure residents of the availability of services while remaining sensitive to the seniors' cultural practice of *kuan-hsi* development through gift-giving remained a challenge for policy and program innovation at the conclusion of this study.

## Communication barriers

For 72% of elders, language was the principal barrier in communicating with the superintendents or custodians. Communication problems would also appear to exist in trying to reach key persons (60%). Language barriers were less of a problem for Chinese seniors when contacting the housing caseworker (22%) who could communicate using Cantonese and Toi San dialects. Twenty-one percent had difficulty in communicating with the recreation worker who spoke only Mandarin.

Almost 70% of elders used body language and 40% used broken English to communicate their needs to staff. Despite the language barrier and the problems in trying to reach MTHCL staff, more than 85% of respondents said that they neither gave up trying to reach them nor did they seek alternative services.

The elders gave a clear indication that Chinese is the preferred language for communicating with staff (80%). If the staff cannot speak the seniors' language, they will be severely handicapped in developing a service relationship with them. Ninety percent of seniors felt it was important that the superintendent and custodians be able to speak Chinese. Very few elders (7%) thought that this was unimportant. Almost as many seniors felt it was important for the key person (88%) as for the housing caseworker (87%) to be able to speak Chinese. About 73% felt it was important for the recreation/community development worker to speak Chinese. The importance seniors assigned to speaking Chinese suggests that they would like to feel more comfortable and secure in their communication with housing staff.

## Community services

Community services available to the Chinese seniors in their buildings and the methods they used to learn about them are summarized in Table 1. Most seniors found out about community services through "word of mouth" or by their "own observation." A lesser number used the bulletin boards to get information while few used radio, TV or newspapers. A substantial group of elders did not know about many of the services.

When asked how they would obtain community services if they needed help, 61% said they knew how to contact volunteers, 29% knew how to reach homemakers, 19% and 28% respectively knew how to contact public transport and meals on wheels. Volunteers were mainly

| | Do Not Know | Un- clear | Know | | | | | |
|---|---|---|---|---|---|---|---|---|
| | | | 1 | 2 | 3 | 4 | 5 | 6 |
| Doctor | 17 | 2 | 35 | 0 | 1 | 14 | 20 | 0 |
| Chiropractor | 46 | 4 | 15 | 0 | 0 | 10 | 11 | 0 |
| Public Health Nurse | 31 | 1 | 26 | 0 | 0 | 14 | 17 | 0 |
| Homemaker | 32 | 3 | 37 | 1 | 0 | 5 | 16 | 1 |
| TTC Wheel Trans | 39 | 2 | 16 | 0 | 3 | 4 | 35 | 0 |
| Meals on Wheels | 19 | 2 | 28 | 0 | 1 | 7 | 43 | 0 |
| Police | 20 | 3 · | 28 | 1 | 6 | 6 | 28 | 2 |
| Ambulance | 18 | 2 | 29 | 1 | 6 | 6 | 31 | 2 |
| Fire Protection | 16 | 2 | 28 | 1 | 6 | 6 | 33 | 2 |
| Volunteer Services | | | | | | | | |
| Income tax | 16 | 3 | 41 | 2 | 2 | 8 | 23 | 1 |
| Social | 24 | 3 | 37 | 0 | 2 | 6 | 21 | 0 |
| Contact | | | | | | | | |
| Translation | 23 | 2 | 38 | 1 | 2 | 6 | 22 | 1 |
| Filling Forms | 21 | 2 | 39 | 0 | 2 | 6 | 22 | 1 |
| Others | 0 | 0 | 0 | 0 | 0 | 0 | 0 | 0 |

**Table 1: Knowledge Summary of Community Services and Methods of Finding Out about Them Expressed in Percentages of Respondents**

| | | | | |
|---|---|---|---|---|
| Word of Mouth | = 1 | | Bulletin Board | = 4 |
| Correspondence | = 2 | | Own Observation | = 5 |
| Public Media | = 3 | | In Meetings | = 6 |
| (Radio, TV, Newspapers) | | | | |

supplied by the Chinese Home Support Services of Greater Toronto and represented a point of entry for many Chinese seniors into other community services. It appears that few seniors knew how to reach many of the community services available to them. Unless Chinese seniors or those people in their support networks become oriented to the community services environment in MTHCL, they will be unlikely to get help when needed.

Approximately 75% of the elders said that they knew to call 911 in an emergency. The number of elders who stated that they knew to phone 911 is compromised by their confusion about how their calls would be handled. The seniors were unaware that the 911 operator could locate their address from their telephone number when calling; neither were they familiar with the Language Line Service of AT&T in San Francisco, which Metro Toronto Emergency Services (MTES) uses for interpreter services. Unaware of these services, Chinese seniors may be reluctant to telephone 911 if they believe that their call will be disconnected when the language barrier emerges. Moreover, delays in reaching an interpreter may also be a source of confusion. The 25% of elders who did not even know to call 911, therefore, likely under-represented the extent of the barriers to accessing services of police, fire and ambulance. Chinese seniors were at risk in an emergency situation owing to communication problems and a lack of orientation to MTES's system of providing interpreter services.

## LIMITATIONS OF THE STUDY

One of the major challenges in conducting research with Asian cultures is overcoming Western bias. Several efforts were made here to help overcome this bias. The study was carried out by Chinese interviewers and assisted by natural helpers.[6] The interview guide questions were refined in a focus group and pretested with Chinese seniors. The questions were examined for content validity by key informants from the Chinese community. Despite these efforts, inconsistencies occurred in communication between colloquial expressions and the literal Chinese regarding the questions in the interview guide. This required some flexibility on the part of the interviewers in adapting the language of the questions to the respondents, a process the PI and PC were not always able to monitor for consistency.

Given the cultural tendency of Chinese seniors to seek harmony and maintain face, many of the elders' responses to questions about racism, communication barriers and difficulties with obtaining housing and community services likely under-represent the extent of the problems they experience when seeking help.

The study did not set out to establish the role of *kuan-hsi* in accessing housing and community services. Rather the *post hoc* analysis using this cultural concept is at best suggestive of the need for further research to explore its importance to Chinese seniors seeking housing and community services.

MTHCL staff were not interviewed concerning the communication barriers they faced. However, the researchers were able to make several observations of the services they provided and received numerous comments from them regarding the elders. The social workers and the recreation worker were particularly informative. Their observations and comments helped with the design of the study and the interpretation of the results.

It may not be valid to extrapolate findings on Chinese seniors in MTHCL to other ethnic elders in public housing. Although Chinese seniors' experiences of barriers in accessing services could be similar to those of other ethnic elders, the cultural pattern of responding to these barriers may differ by ethnic group. Research is needed to elucidate the experiences of other ethnic elderly accessing housing and community services.

## SUMMARY

Results of this exploratory descriptive study would appear to support the need to adapt services provided by MTHCL and community agencies to better meet language and cultural requirements of Chinese seniors. Chinese seniors had difficulties in obtaining services from staff who did not speak their language (particularly superintendents/custodians and key persons). Communication barriers were less apparent when trying to reach the social worker and the recreation/community development worker who both spoke Chinese.

Emergency services are critical to well-being and require rationalization if they are to be accessible to Chinese seniors. Most Chinese seniors knew about 911 services but were reluctant to call owing to perceived language barriers. Better information about the MTES response protocol to a non-English-speaking caller could help prevent delays and confusion in an emergency. The help of MTHCL staff becomes even more crucial in creating a socially secure environment during an emergency. The night-time (key) person expected to deal with emergencies, however, is unable to speak Chinese. This presents immediate communication problems and barriers when handling crises. MTES could also improve access to their assistance through finding a less confusing and faster method of obtaining an interpreter. Were emergency services to negotiate with the telephone company to solicit language, age and disability status from their ethnic elderly customers, computer technology now makes it possible for a 911 operator to quickly access this information. To further enhance communication in an emergency, a recorded message in the senior's language could urge the caller to stay on the line until she or he is connected with an interpreter. Cooperation between MTES, MTHCL and the telephone company in seeking these improvements would speed up access to an appropriate emergency service and thereby overcome a significant barrier and source of anxiety for Chinese seniors when seeking assistance in times of an emergency.

Other services provided to MTHCL buildings including homemaking, meals on wheels, public transportation, etc., were largely unfamiliar to Chinese seniors. For most seniors, community services were neither available to them in their native China nor in Hong Kong. Consequently, community agencies need to explore effective ways to acquaint Chinese seniors with their services. Word of mouth communication seems to be a typical method of finding out about services among Chinese seniors. Notices posted in English or in Chinese may be of limited utility in communicating information about services. Effective approaches need to take into account the language of communication and networks of social support used by Chinese seniors to access services.

It appears that roughly half of the Chinese seniors go through their families and one-third seek help from other tenants in their buildings to obtain MTHCL housing services. Whether this indirect approach was due to the language barrier with some staff or related to Chinese seniors' preferences for seeking the assistance of a neighbour, relative or friend using *kuan-hsi* was not determined. The extent of using third parties to obtain services, however, raised speculation as to whether language was the only factor influencing the Chinese seniors' pattern of help-seeking behaviour. Further research aimed at exploring the seniors' networks of support and the effects of the language barrier may help to clarify why so many of them do not seek help directly from staff. Social network analysis is needed to answer Bond and Hwang's (1986) question of who are the supportive people in the lives of Chinese seniors in order to better predict their help-seeking behaviour and, therefore, suggest how congruent housing and community services might be designed and developed.

# NOTES

[1] These estimates will need to be revised in light of changes to immigration rules limiting the sponsorship of parents of Canadian citizens and landed immigrants, which took place in 1995.

[2] Most elderly immigrants in 1991 came from the People's Republic of China (35,025), which may include Hong Kong since it was not listed separately, followed by Vietnam (4195), Malaysia (730) and Taiwan (475) with Chinese seniors from other Southeast Asian countries (2325) (Statscan. 93-316:70).

[3] It was considered culturally and contextually relevant to recruit as interviewers Chinese seniors from the same cohort as the participants in our study. However Dr. Peter Lomas, anthropologist with the gerontology diploma program at Simon Fraser University, who was concurrently conducting a study with Chinese seniors in the Vancouver area, advised against this owing to literacy problems with interviewers when reading and completing interview guides.

[4] Interviewers were paid $4.00 for each completed interview. This was intended to cover their transportation and related expenses. Additional benefits included refreshments on the job and a group meal at the end of the day to debrief interviewers and to build a sense of community and cooperation.

[5] Respondents were screened for cognitive functioning by their ability to answer questions about background characteristics—age, birthplace and length of time in Canada.

[6] Natural helpers, in the context of our study, consisted of Chinese residents who assisted the interviewers by encouraging and organizing residents in their buildings to participate in the study. These elders had the respect of most of the tenants because they had informally helped and supported the residents to obtain services within and outside the buildings (they had perhaps built up considerable *kuan-hsi* with the other residents). Gaining the cooperation of natural helpers was key to increasing participation in our study.

# REFERENCES

Bond, M. H. and Hwang, K. K. (1986). The social psychology of the Chinese people. In M.H. Bond (ed.), *The Psychology of the Chinese People*. Hong Kong: Oxford University Press.

Chinese Community Nursing Home (CCNH) for Greater Toronto. (1989). Health care needs of the Chinese elderly population. A needs assessment. February, p.26.

Chinese Interpretation and Information Service. (1987). A report on the aged Chinese in the City of North York and the City of Scarborough. p.58.

Chu, G. and Ju, J. (1990). The Great Wall in ruins: Cultural change in China. East-West Center, Honolulu.

Doyle, R. and Visano, L. (1987). Social Planning Council of Metropolitan Toronto, a time for action Part I,(1987), Part II, A program for action : Access to health and social services for members of diverse cultural and racial groups in Metropolitan Toronto.

Kahana, E. (1982). A congruence model of person-environment interaction. In M.P. Lawton, P. G. Windley and T.O. Byerts (eds.), *Aging and the environment. Theoretical approaches*. New York: Springer.

King, A. Y. (1994). *Kuan-hsi* and network building: A sociological interpretation. In W. Tu (ed.), *The living tree: The changing meaning of being Chinese today*. Palo Alto, CA: Stanford University Press.

Kramer, B. J., Barker, J. C. and Damron-Rodriguez, J. (1991). Ethnic diversity in aging and aging services in the U.S.: Introduction. *Journal of Cross Cultural Gerontology*, 6 (2), pp.127-133.

Lau, K. K. (1993). An exploratory study on the nature of elder abuse in the Chinese community and the attitude of Chinese seniors towards elder abuse in the City of Toronto. Faculty of Social Work, University of Toronto, pp.49.

Maclean, M. and Bonar, L. (1987). Cooperative practice to overcome socially constructed hardship for ethnic elderly people. In D.E. Gelfand and C.M. Barresi, (eds.), *Ethnic dimensions of aging*. New York: Springer.

Metro Toronto Housing Company Ltd. (1991a). A lifestyle analysis for the Metro Toronto Housing Company Limited. Final report. Volume I: Synthesis report. Hickling Corporation.

Metro Toronto Housing Company Ltd. (1991b). A lifestyle analysis for the Metro Toronto Housing Company Limited. Final report. Volume II: Activity needs and preference analysis. Hickling Corporation.

Metro Toronto Housing Company Ltd. (1994). Building on change. A pamphlet, pp.4.

Metro Toronto Housing Company Limited. (1993a). Race relations and multicultural policy, pp.7.

Metro Toronto Housing Company Limited. (1993b). Anticipating change.

Multiculturalism and Citizenship Canada. (1990). The Canadian Multiculturalism Act. A guide for Canadians. Ministry of Supply and Services Canada.

Multiculturalism and Citizenship Canada. (1991). Multiculturalism. What is it really about? Ministry of Supply and Services Canada.

Multiculturalism and Citizenship Canada. (1993). Projection of Canada's 1991 people in 2006, Ottawa.

Saldov, M. (1991). The ethnic elderly: Communication barriers to health care. *Canadian Social Work Review*, Theme Issue on Multiculturalism and Social Work. 8 (2), 269-277.

Saldov, M., and Chow, P.C. (1994). The ethnic elderly in Metro Toronto hospitals, nursing homes and homes for the aged: Communication and health care. *International Journal on Aging and Human Development*, 38 (2), 117-135.

Secretary of State. (1988). *Aging in a multicultural Canada: A graphic overview. Policy, analysis and research.* Directorate, Ottawa.

Statscanada 93-316. (1991). *People unable to speak English or French.*

Yang, M. (1994). *Gifts, favors and banquets. The art of social relationships in China.* Ithaca, NY: Cornell University Press.

Zimmer, Z. and Chappell, N.L. (1996). Distinguishing the spending preferences of seniors. *Canadian Journal on Aging*, 15 (1), 65-83.

## ACKNOWLEDGMENTS

This study was conducted with the assistance of a grant from the External Research Program of Canada Mortgage and Housing Corporation.

# CHAPTER 6

# Group Work with Immigrant Men

*Christopher Austin and David Este*

## Introduction

Immigrants often journey to other countries in search of greater economic opportunities in the hope of improving their standard of living (Christensen, 1986). For first generation immigrants, this hope is often met with the harsh reality of, for example, job rejection and an interminable series of job search disappointments. Briar (1988, p. 8) notes that, although immigration policy favours well-educated and skilled immigrants, the job market seems to insist that immigrants "start at the bottom of the ladder." Data from the 1986 Census of Canada indicates that descent into the lower end of the labour market is a reality of occupational adaptation upon relocation. Comparisons between "intended" (13% to 14% for 1985-86) participation and "actual" (23% for 1984-85) participation in service occupations reveal that approximately 30% to 40% of immigrants who do not intend to work in menial service jobs eventually find themselves in this lower end of the workforce.

Among those professionals who work with newcomers to Canada, it is common knowledge that the early settlement years and beyond are often characterized by dissatisfaction with unfulfilling low-end job situations. Clearly, immigrants in their eagerness to become employed are vulnerable to exploitation by employers, particularly those in the nonunionized service and industrial sectors. The longer it takes to find a job that is satisfying (at minimum, in terms of renumeration; at maximum, in terms of work responsibilities), the greater the risk of unemployment and occupationally related mental health problems.

In Canada, refugees and immigrants are "[t]ypically the last to be hired and first to be fired ... (and) suffer higher rates of unemployment than the general population" (Report of the Canadian Task Force on Mental Health Issues Affecting Immigrants and Refugees [CTFMH], 1988, p.29). Despite the claim that immigrants are entitled to "full participation... in all aspects of Canadian life" (Employment and Immigration Canada, 1992, p.25), many highly educated and skilled immigrants are forced into dead-end jobs and may repeatedly experience underemployment and unemployment for a number of years. Refugees who are even less prepared for their adjustment in Canada than self-sponsored immigrants commonly find themselves in menial jobs (or situations). The pervasiveness of this unhappy and prolonged tenure among the immigrant and refugee community deserves the attention of the social work profession. As Daenzer (1989, p. 62) notes: "There is evidence that many minority immigrants are failing to achieve congruence between pre-migration aspirations and post-migration status. This social, and presumably cognitive dissonance cannot be achieved without human consequences."

The focus of this chapter is a group work program offered by a community-based agency that was specially designed for immigrant and refugee men who work or have worked in jobs they considered below their educational and work qualifications. The program targets male members of the immigrant and refugee community because in their countries of origin these men were very likely to have been primary breadwinners. Thus, these men have to deal with not only the disruptive effects of relocation and resettlement but also with the ramifications of dashed expectations of working at a level commensurate with their training, education and experience. Since the well-being of immigrant families is related to the well-being of the head of household, a goal of the group work program was to provide a supportive and therapeutic context for men to discuss and address, among other topics, their frustrations with the job search process.

There are numerous barriers preventing immigrants from getting satisfying jobs. Westwood and Ishiyama (1991) single out several factors including language; lack of specific career knowledge and employment skills; culturally biased vocational counselling; racial/ethnic discrimination and intolerance; and psychological problems related to overall cultural adjustment (pp.130-138). One of the major barriers preventing immigrant men from working in fields related to their previous occupations is the failure of institutions and private employers to recognize and help upgrade academic and trade credentials earned outside of Canada (CTFMH, 1988, p.32). Boyd (1985) notes that foreign-obtained credentials are undervalued in relation to their potential Canadian labour market worth. The consequence of this under-recognition of human endeavour and value is that foreign-born males who migrated at age seventeen or older and acquired basic first-level credentials for employment in their home country end up in lower occupational status jobs than same-age Canadian-born males.

The early entry and subsequent entrenchment in menial jobs over a prolonged period of time is, psychosocially, a very taxing period for immigrant males. As Li (1988) observes, dead end jobs further stigmatize minorities, which results in fewer opportunities to obtain higher paying and higher status employment. Ironically, for some immigrant men their educational and vocational qualifications actually handicap them in their competitive struggle to find skilled, decently paid work. These job seekers may be perceived as overqualified for certain well-paying entry level positions. These immigrant men, who see themselves as skilled and well qualified, experience difficulties in obtaining desired employment situations and are particularly vulnerable to mental health problems.

In Canada there appear to be few published studies directly exploring the way immigrant men adapt to assigned work circumstances. What few are available address, for example, first-hand accounts of unemployment and job loss (Borgen and Amundson, 1984) and anecdotal reports of the adverse impact of unemployment and underemployment on the mental health of the men and their families (Thurston, McGrath and Sehgal, 1993). The dearth of empirically based information was evident in the CTFMH (1988) study with an absence of an explicit discussion of the disadvantages immigrant men face finding employment commensurate with their qualifications in Canada. Beyond the comment that immigrant men are "destined to marginal employment" (CTFMH, 1988, p.30), this document gives scant attention to the plight of the un/underemployed immigrant man.

The lack of research may be partly due to the unwillingness of society-at-large to accept that able-bodied immigrant men who are willing to work and who are not "picky" about their first jobs are unable to get jobs commensurate with their qualifications. Further, many Canadians seem to think that those who do obtain employment have workmates to help ease the transition into Canadian society. Thus, Canadians appear to be more attentive to the plight of immigrant wives, generally seen as alone at home and isolated from mainstream Canada. Men tend to be perceived as better able to cope with emotional stress than women, a false pancultural stereotype that has connotations of "man as warrior" (Keen, 1991).

## STARTING THE GROUP

On the evening of the first group session, seven men were present. The group facilitator (the first author, Chris) explained that these meetings were part of his social work research project expressedly designed to examine the occupational experiences of immigrant men. The purpose of group meetings was to provide psychosocial support to unemployed/ underemployed members who were job-hunting. One type of support that members could expect was assistance in planning how each could realize their career goals. Members would be encouraged to verbalize concerns and problems related to their resettlement in Canada. Support and other types of help would be offered through problem-solving and action planning of concerns raised.

After all the participants had signed the "consent to participate" form, the group's co-facilitator (Esau) handed out a list delineating goals for each of the six meetings and provided a short overview of each session. The foci of the six sessions were described as follows:

Session 1.   Types of Employment Experience and Coping with Loss of Occupational Status

Session 2.   Knowledge of Personal Skills and Strengths

Session 3/4.   Job Finding Skills and Interviewing

Session 5.   Building Support for Career Plans

Session 6.   Celebration of Group's Ending

An outline specifying goals for each group session was thought to be helpful to members. It was intended as one more device to reduce the many "unknowns" associated with the group process. As Sue and Sue (1990) note, the culturally different person may not be familiar with Western counselling structure and process. Group members were then asked to clarify their expectations, which were noted and recorded. Group facilitators hoped that by having members speak about how each hoped to benefit from group work, members would develop a sense of commitment and investment in group sessions.

A short round of introductions followed. In an unplanned fashion, the pronunciation of the members' names functioned as an initiation to ethnocultural issues. Esau, for example, emphasized that he felt it was important that people pronounce his name correctly, and he helped members to pronounce his name correctly. Some of the members took Esau's lead and stressed the correct pronunciation of their names as they introduced themselves.

Three of the men were from Central America, one from Eastern Europe, one from South Asia and two from Africa. Five of the men had lived in Canada for more than three years, one for less than a year and one for more than ten years. Variation in length of residence can be helpful in group work because those immigrants in post-settlement have had more experience adapting to the host culture and can share their knowledge with those who are less acculturated. For two of the members—a refugee claimant from Russia, Michael,[1] and a man from Northeast Africa, Mengani—their comments during the introductions indicated they would benefit from the experiences of "older" immigrants. Mengani said that he did not know how to find a "good" job and that he did not know the kind of work he wanted because during the two years that he had been in Canada he had worked in cleaning and parking attendant jobs only. Michael wanted to know what electrical engineering jobs were available to him. Given that half the members of the group had lived in Canada for more than three years, several had helpful information to offer. Some had knowledge of how to access the "hidden" job market, that is, job openings advertised by word of mouth.

To begin a process of sharing job-seeking experiences in greater detail, members were asked if their present work was satisfying. Facilitators were careful to speak slowly and enunciate clearly. It was not at all uncommon to be asked to repeat or simplify questions or statements to accommodate the wide range of English proficiencies. Sometimes the use of gestures was necessary to communicate ideas. This practice was normalized at the group's outset and members were encouraged to seek clarification from each other and the facilitators whenever needed.

Federico, from Guatemala, responded in broken English that the last two and one-half years in Canada were terrible. He was trying to learn English, but no one would hire him because he lacked fluency in English. Federico also added that he felt that not one moment of his time in Canada had been happy. He was not presently employed and all that was available to him was volunteer work—in a library and in his children's school. Another member, Francisco, empathized with Federico. He said that he understood the predicament of having professional qualifications and not being able to land a suitable job.

Throughout the group, members were asked how they had coped, how each had adapted to the loss of their occupational status. This was considered an important part of group process because a loss of self-efficacy may result from underemployment (Chau,1992), and the lack of self-confidence and increase in self-doubt resulting from underemployment affects immigrants in unique ways. Austin (1994), for instance, found that immigrant men resorted to a range of adaptations. Early immobilization resulting from being overwhelmed by barriers to career reconstruction may prevent men from searching for a job for an extended period of time. Early success in overcoming barriers to finding employment often leads to quick acceptance of an underemployed situation or to intensified efforts to redefine one's occupational image. As in Federico's and a few other group members' cases, they had given up on their job search early (within the first three years after arriving in Canada) and accepted their underemployment as a matter of fate.

Francisco had been a philosophy teacher and social researcher in Guatemala for twenty years. His first job in Canada was as a cleaner at a university. After four years at this job, Francisco found a job as a gardener. At the time of the group meetings, he was still working as a gardener in various commercial buildings. With a sad tone he said, "People must think, 'Poor man, he can't do anything else.'" Esau asked Francisco if he enjoyed his work more than his last cleaning job, and Francisco replied that working with "living things" was more enjoyable than cleaning toilets and hallways. To the query, "Didn't you also work with people when you were a janitor?" Francisco replied, "No, No! Canadians don't talk to you when you are cleaning." Most of the members laughed and concurred.

The facilitators addressed the issue of shame that seemed to underlie Francisco's comment by asking if any one else wondered what others thought of them or if they felt ashamed when they worked at jobs for which they were overqualified. The intent in "uncovering" the issue of shame was to normalize this painful emotion as a natural reaction. Adel, who had arrived in Canada sixteen years ago from Egypt, turned to Francisco and said, "Don't give a damn what Canadians think of you. You have to survive; do what you have to!"

Feeling validated by Adel's comment, Francisco volunteered more information: "You know, cleaning, gardening is not my life. I'm sure my life will change in the future. I have to enjoy it.... Now I have been working in this job for three years."

Esau: "You are getting concerned because time, a short time, is getting too long. It's time to look for other alternatives."

Francisco: "Two weeks ago I put an application to work as a teacher's aid because I know my limitations. English is a big problem. I know that in Canada I never can be a teacher in philosophy. I have to speak English as well as a Canadian.... First thing, I am fifty years old. Second thing, I am hard of hearing. Another thing, I haven't ability to learn a language ... but I study English by myself."

Chris (to the group): "Can everyone here understand Francisco?" This checking back with the group is essential. Although Francisco's English pronunciation was difficult to understand at times, with some careful attending, he was very understandable. But one should never presume that this is the case for all members of the group.

As Esau had also struggled to rebuild his career in Canada, he often empathized with the group members' situations and offered strategies to cope with disappointments based on his own experience. Addressing the group Esau said, "At first I thought somehow my English was very, very poor. Then as I studied English, I realized that I used some words better than native speakers." This comment brought some laughter from the group. "After some time, I thought more and more when I had to repeat myself that I spoke two languages and that made me feel strong."

Julio, a doctor from Guatemala, added that he often feels "bad" that he cannot make others understand him easily. His strategy, though, was to just keep on trying to communicate.

Francisco's self-disclosure set the stage for an important area of discussion in career planning. Actualization of occupational goals depends in large part on our perceptions of our ability to overcome the barriers to these goals. Julio had not allowed the language barrier to limit his desire to connect with English speakers. In his own way, Julio had demonstrated the resilience that is so essential to immigrant survival and, ultimately, well-being. Group facilitators took advantage of the opportunity to emphasize the merits of persistence.

The topic of barriers to gainful employment was addressed by asking the group what they believed to be the single most important barrier preventing them from finding satisfying work. All the men agreed that their difficulty with English and nonrecognition by Canadian authorities of foreign-obtained credentials were powerful barriers to satisfying employment.

Jose, the third member from Central America, spoke up in anger against the unwillingness of employers to give immigrant men credit for their skills. Jose had worked with his father crafting various pieces of furniture in his father's shop since he was eight years old. What Jose found difficult to understand was that his employers required him to go back to school to study English and math when he was already skilled as a fine-finish carpenter. His frustration with demands that he retrain as a carpenter was also based on his observation that, "I have friends who take a student loan; they study math, English, science, but they get no work. Why should I waste my money?"

Esau: "I can understand that you see studying English as a waste of time, but do you have the same skills as Canadian carpenters?"

Jose: "I am a carpenter. I don't use power tools. I use handsaws, chisels. I make furniture by hand better than you buy in the shops."

Adel: "My friend, can you learn anything more, or do you know everything about carpentry?"

Chris: "How good are you at reading blueprints?"

Jose: "We didn't use blueprints."

Adel: "You will have to use blueprints in Canada."

Just as it was important to have the men confront the fact that some barriers to their career goals are self-erected, it was also important to acknowledge the unfairness and absurd foundations of systemic barriers. Such recognition was critical to helping the men feel validated. It was also intended to empower them to search for other ways to overcome these barriers.

To prepare for the second session, the facilitators asked members to think of a job they would like to apply for. Their homework assignment was to formulate a response to the question, "What makes you think you are right for this job?" In addition, they were to list their strengths and skills on a sheet of paper, which group facilitators distributed at the end of the session.

## Second Session

Five additional men all new to the group showed up for the second session. After a short round of introductions in which Francisco said to the group that he hoped others would benefit as much he did at the last session, the last two of the new members to introduce themselves felt that the group was not for them. They had just begun looking for work and had not encountered any problems; they then left the group. The suddenness of their departure prompted group facilitators to take the time to process the impact their departure and decision not to join the group had on the others. This began with asking those who were at the last session what they had found personally helpful about the previous session. This question was also intended to provide the three newcomers with a sense of what had been discussed previously.

Julio thought that this kind of group was good because in the first few years of their arrival "immigrants get depressed, and this helps them know they are not alone." Julio's comment was telling in that he spoke in the third person. He was encouraged to reframe his response, "For you, Julio, how did *you* see the group last week being useful or helpful?" "Oh, well," Julio half-laughed, "I think I know really, really *here* I am not alone."

Chris continued, "Last week we talked about some of the jobs men in the group have taken in Canada and aspects of the work they enjoyed and disliked. There were a few members we did not have time to hear from. What about you Rajinder? Have you found any satisfying work over the last year?"

Rajinder began, "For the last five years I have been doing odd jobs only. As an engineering draftsman there are no more jobs. Actually, I am desperate; at times I could end my life, but for my religious beliefs I can not."

One of the new members, Moses, asked Rajinder, "Are you working now?"

"Actually," Rajinder responded, "I am unemployed, except I do some translations, but that too is drying up." Rajinder spoke with great intensity and feeling, and he was clearly feeling helpless as a result of his unemployment. He mentioned entertaining suicidal thoughts. At this juncture, it was important that the group acknowledge his despair and provide him with some encouragement.

However, members found Rajinder difficult to understand. Adel sought further clarification, "Rajinder, what kind of drafting have you done?" Eventually, it became clear to Adel and others that Rajinder had worked as a checker before he was laid off. Adel responded spontaneously, "To be a checker, that is a *real* skill. Lots of people can be draftsman, but *very few* can be checkers." Rajinder smiled.

Esau was among those who had not understood why a checker was more prestigious than a draftsman so he asked, "What is a checker?" Adel explained that a checker is a senior draftsman who reviews the drafting plans of less experienced and skilled technicians. Still further clarification was sought. Chris asked Rajinder what he believed was holding him back from working as a draftsman at this time and whether he wanted to work again as a draftsman. Lack of training opportunities in computer drafting was the major barrier. Chris enquired further as to whether Rajinder had any computer training. He replied that he had; however, he was concerned that in not having had access to a computer over the years he may have forgotten how to work one. Rajinder had given up hope of working as a draftsman again, though it was not completely clear why this was so. He had recently received some upgrade training, had past experience and seemed to identify with his profession. Had Rajinder given up prematurely on a career he may be able to still practice?

In order to ensure that Rajinder would not feel on the "hot seat," he was asked if he minded that the group deliberated further on his situation. Rajinder gave his permission but stressed again that it was his belief that the job market and his lack of experience with computer-guided drafting were the main culprits preventing him from getting a job as a draftsman. Taking the time to check with a group member on their level of comfort with the process is an important way of expressing respect and sensitivity to personal dispositions. The request is also effective in promoting an attitude of receptivity to ideas because the individual member is more likely to see him/herself as asking for the other members' input rather than experiencing it as being inflicted on him/herself.

Chris began to focus the group's attention on Rajinder: "I don't know if Esau and I understand enough why Rajinder is not working in his field as a draftsman. Could you help us out with your ideas?"

Andreas, one of the new members, suggested that when immigrant men believe it is impossible for them to work again in their field they start to lose confidence in their abilities. Esau asked Andreas if this was true for himself.

"Yes," Andreas said, "I was an artist, also an art teacher, now I don't draw any more."

Adel agreed, mentioning that he had tried to find an apprenticeship as a machinist for the last ten years, but added that sometimes he still looks for a way of doing this work again and has not lost all hope.

Francisco said philosophically, "We talk about our past, but we should live in the present."

Chris asked Francisco, "Do you think Rajinder should give up on his drafting skills?" Francisco smiled and said that if it is his dream, he should try to make it a reality.

Esau then reflected on his goal of recapturing the love of his work as a teacher on a part-time basis by giving Spanish lessons. Esau said that he still thought of himself as a teacher and no one would ever stop him from doing so.

To relate the above group comments directly to Rajinder's situation, Chris asked Rajinder if he still wanted to work as a draftsman, and Rajinder said that if it was possible he did.

Without an interest or passion for a particular type of work, one's commitment to an active job search or entrepreneurial effort in that field will be tentative at best. Helping members to recognize and support their passion provides them with more of a focus and reason to continue the job search, but using different strategies can be energizing.

One of the challenges facing group members was to identify in their menial jobs skills and strengths that could be applied to other employment possibilities. Understandably, some members were ashamed of their low-skilled and low-paying jobs and were hard pressed to find anything useful. Another problem that members encountered was their lack of fluency in English. Nonetheless, they were encouraged to persevere, and in the process they acquired new vocabulary.

Turning to the homework assignment that members were given at the end of the last session, Mengani offered that he wanted to try working as a waiter as he saw this as a more interesting and a higher skilled job than his current job as a car park attendant. Asked about the skills a waiter would need to be good at his job, Mengani said "friendly." This was a good start, but it needed expanding. Asked how his last job prepared him to work with customers in a restaurant, Mengani said that he was good at dealing with angry people. When other members volunteered further skills and strengths, "problem solver" and "quick learner" were repeatedly mentioned. The facilitators also contributed to generating words and phrases that helped reframe the work of a janitor or parking attendant. The group was quick to recognize the strength and courage involved in sticking with these jobs: "patience, an optimistic attitude, determination, good at planning and managing time, able to see challenges in even the most mindless of tasks, good at working under pressure and time constraints...."

The facilitators encouraged members to "honour" the qualities they possessed in performing boring, repetitive and physically demanding jobs. Facilitators and group members emphasized the virtues of perseverance in the face of hardship. Levity in group discussions came by way of some members explaining the lengths they had to go to so as not upstage their supervisors. Esau pointed to this use of humour in the group and patience on the job as a coping strategy when belittled by workmates and superiors.

Julio told a story of being asked by a nurse if he knew how to draw blood. He said he may have forgotten, but if she was willing to show him again, he would appreciate her help. Unfortunately for the nurse, she tried to demonstrate on a patient with difficult-to-find veins. Julio, who had trained and practiced as an anaesthetist, took over "very gently" and commented to the nurse that "problem veins in Central America are the same as they are in Canada." Another coping strategy that this anecdote conveys is the importance of not trying to prove to others one's credentials but simply demonstrating these in a nonthreatening way.

Members' limited occupational experience in the Canadian job market rendered them unable to consider other types of work that they may enjoy. In addition, certain occupational designations in Canada carried different meanings in other economic and socio-cultural settings. For example, some Canadians would look upon the job of a salesman as a medium- to high-status job, whereas in certain Central American countries, sales jobs, as Esau noted, are looked upon as "a pick-up job" and the people who fill them are those that "can't or don't want to go to university." Given that there is such a wide range in renumeration between the professions and other jobs in many third world countries, nonprofessional work may also be seen by professionally trained immigrants as menial, and thus may not be sought by them. So, ironically and irrationally, newcomers may never consider taking up jobs with a higher earning potential simply because of the perception that it is nonprofessional, and instead would rather settle, albeit unhappily, for menial, low-paid work

The third new member who joined the group in its second meeting, Ignatio, explained that he had been unemployed for the last few months and that he was preparing to apply for a job cleaning buses in the evenings. He was asked if he had ever considered sales work: he spoke English well, dressed well, was a personable young man and had experience marketing his part-time business as an income tax consultant. He said that he had not.

Chris (to the group): "Ignatio has been thinking about the possibilities of getting into some sales work. What steps do you think you will have to take Ignatio?"

Ignatio: "I don't know exactly what I'll have to do."

Esau: "You feel uncertain because you're not exactly sure if this (sales) is the field you want to go?"

Ignatio: "I feel this, yes, but I certainly want to try it!"

Chris (to the group): "Would anyone here buy furniture from Ignatio? Does Ignatio seem like a salesman to you?"

Adel: "I can imagine Ignatio wearing a suit! He has the face of a salesman" (followed by laughter from the members).

Chris: "What do you think, Andreas?"

Andreas: "Yes, I think he is a salesman."

Chris: "What are this man's characteristics as a salesman?"

Andreas: "Personality."

Chris: "He has personality. What type of personality?

Andreas: "Good speaker."

Julio: "Good listener."

Adel: "Friendly."

Chris: "Also, I see him as open, so that people will trust him."

Francisco: "How do you say in English, extroverted."

Esau: "Yes, extroverted."

Julio: "He's a salesman!" (the group laughs).

By the end of the third meeting, Ignatio indicated that he would like to consider some sales positions. The next task was to locate sales opportunities and apply.

## Third/Fourth Sessions

By the third group meeting, there was evidence that various members had begun to believe in themselves and their ability to improve on their current job situations. Francisco said that he was looking forward to a discussion of job-search strategies because he wanted to be prepared. Adel announced that he had landed an apprenticeship in a machine shop. Mengani felt optimistic about a job interview that one of the facilitators had set up for him for a job waiting on tables. Michael had telephoned a number of engineering companies and made enquiries regarding the Canadian equivalency of his credentials.

To maintain the enthusiasm and support evidenced at group sessions, Esau and Chris kept in telephone contact with the men between group meetings. In particular, members who were unemployed seemed to really appreciate contacts outside of group sessions, e.g., a phone call, help in locating job leads, work on writing cover letters and resumes.

The most difficult aspect of the job-search process appeared to be initiating new contacts through telephone calls and networking. The facilitators framed this difficulty as a loss of self-confidence and normalized it by mentioning that most job seekers have difficulty enquiring about job openings and interviewing for the job. Group members appeared to benefit more from discussions about the effects of losing one's self-confidence and how to restore it than from informational activities such as job finding techniques or how to interview well. Most members appeared to already possess such information.

The facilitators asked members to list the factors that contributed to their loss of self-confidence in presenting themselves at networking sessions and job interviews. The most frequently mentioned issue was the lack of fluency in the English language. Throughout the duration of the group processes, the members related stories of feeling humiliated when asked by employers and workmates the "What's that?" question. Repeatedly asked to clarify themselves, some of the members reacted by withdrawing socially and psychologically. Consequently, the most common means of finding work among the group members was to approach persons in their own ethnic communities rather than reaching out to the community-at-large.

The problem of self-confidence became evident when three of the group members avoided following through on making phone contacts to set interview times. Other members expressed discomfort with having to enquire about job opportunities when these were not being advertised. Julio explained his reaction to the practice of networking: "You feel sometime that you are not really yourself. Somebody has to put you before someone else. He says, 'Okay, let's look at this guy; let's examine him.' It's disgusting." Given that Julio and other men were often applying for work far beneath their skill levels, networking understandably felt like begging for a job.

A distaste for the entire job-search process including the job interview is evident in Andreas' description of a job opportunity referred by a friend: "I remember when I take my first job. My friend called for me, but the owner say: 'Come into my office; I need to see you.' I remember when I was in the office, the man say, 'What is your profession?' I told him, 'I was an art teacher in my country.' Then he makes a face. Then he said, 'What can you do?' 'Everything,' I said. 'What everything!?,' he said. 'I am a carpenter. I can fix some furniture, but I need a job. I don't care what job.' And he say, 'Can you do a mould for a ceramic?' I say 'Yes, I can. If I can't, I go home.'"

The facilitators highlighted Andreas' and other members' descriptions of networking and interviewing experiences. They emphasized that while a lack of self-confidence makes the task more difficult, it should not stop them from job searching. Andreas' case draws attention to the often harsh and insensitive questioning common among unskilled interviewers in blue-collar industries where so many immigrant men with professional training look for work. But, as the facilitators point out, his perserverence paid off.

Moses: "Did you get the job?"

Andreas: "Yes."

Chris: "What is your work there?"

Andreas: "I paint; I clean the floors; I make the moulds."

Esau: "You described your skills clearly and directly; this maybe a part of the reason you got the job."

Chris (to the group): "How did Andreas get the job?"

Julio: "Probably I am dreaming. But if you go to a place as you did yourself, that's what I think is the real thing; they are trusting you, even though they don't know you."

Chris: "But why did they really give Andreas the position? After all he's only an art teacher" (laughter from the men follows).

Adel: "Because people in Canada, they need someone who is positive. If you are sure of yourself, you are the right guy."

Adel's comment was perfect because it stressed the connection between finding a job and self-confidence.

Esau: "That's somehow challenging the employer."

Jose: "The owner discovered that you are going to learn quickly."

From the above and other descriptions of successful job finding experiences, the facilitators prepared the group for job interview situations. Esau conducted interviews with a few of the members in front of the group. The exercise involved members pointing out the weaknesses and strengths of the interview. An interesting insight emerged among the Hispanic members while participating in this exercise: there was a tendency among Spanish-speaking members to explain themselves in what some Anglo employers would consider excessive detail. The group discussed this difference as a culturally based one and developed an interviewee stance that stressed being direct, specific and concise.

## ENDING THE GROUP

By the fifth and sixth sessions, enough trust had been established that the men were prepared for a more intense level of self-disclosure. Adel, who had functioned throughout the group as a guide to other members, approached the group in the fifth session for support when the apprenticeship he had found earlier did not work out to his expectations. Adel's re-experience of unemployment triggered another round of discussions on how to cope with being un/underemployed:

Chris: "What about you Adel? Are you scared now that you are not working?"

Adel: "Well, I would say I was really pissed off about Canada, all Canada. It is a stupid system. Especially if something is wrong with your health; they want to kick you out."

Chris: "Employers don't really care about us—just what they can get out of us."

Adel: "They like to eat your meat and they throw what's left in the garbage. For six years, I worked for one company. I was one of the best workers and I think and work for that company. But when I hurt my back they kicked me out. And that's it. They didn't want to know me anymore. They wouldn't take me back, even for a light job!"

Until this second last group, Adel presented his life in Canada as one marked by successful adaptation. He had studied English, found employment through networking and was a storehouse of information and experience, yet he did not feel ready to share his deepest frustrations. Chris acknowledged Adel's observations and directed the discussion at the frustration of having to start the job search over after a recent termination. "Adel has shared with us his struggles and it is the first time he has done this so directly. Are there times when anyone here really wants to share their worries and difficulties but they feel ashamed or that they have to hide their problems?"

Adel: "I think when a man is not working he is too scared to go out the door. Somebody will ask, 'Are you working?'"

Chris: "Are you afraid of being asked 'Are you working?' Adel?"

Adel: "Not anymore."

Esau: "What about others? I know I am afraid to not work."

Chris: "What about our wives? What do they think about us when we are not working?"

The members debated the role of their wives in providing support for themselves and their families, resulting in further self-disclosure at this late stage of the group. In considering his own situation, Jose commented: "There are times when we cannot handle, and we don't want to believe that our wives can handle that."

Esau: "Women are stronger sometimes. What do you do Jose when you don't think you are not getting enough support from your wife?"

Jose: "I have problems because she is busy, too busy, especially here [in Canada] *everybody is busy*. We have to talk."

Chris: "Who has more problems talking, you or your wife?"

Jose: "The problem is mine because I am not going to her. First, I want to handle the problem by myself, and what happens is that I add more trouble."

Chris: "What is the biggest problem?"

Jose: "The first problem is I don't have a job and she is working."

Julio: "I know what you mean. I say to my wife, 'I need you here at home because I need somebody to talk to me, you were not there.' When we lived in our country with our culture we have the support, in my case the support of the rest of my relatives."

Common among the men was the experience of not feeling supported by their spouses because both were working full time or because the man was employed part time and felt ashamed that his wife was contributing more to their families' financial purse than he was. When asked how they coped with feelings of shame and loneliness, members suggested various solutions: sharing with friends, actively job searching, being honest about one's thoughts and feelings to one's spouse and setting and trying to meet goals.

The facilitators completed the fifth group by discussing the importance of social and family supports. Chris drew Esau's eco-map on a flip chart, illustrating types and quality of interactions within the family and between the family and outside supports. Rajinder made the comment that he could not rely on his own East Asian ethnic community because people there had judged him as a failure for not holding down full-time professional employment. Julio concurred with Rajinder that he had noted in his own Hispanic community a tension between persons holding professional and non-professional jobs. It became clear to the members that a change in status as a result of underemployment emerged as a potential barrier to establishing supportive contacts within one's ethnic group. The rest of the time was spent discussing how to overcome this barrier.

The last meeting celebrated the sharing and support of the past five weeks. The facilitators initiated a common exercise in group work at the beginning of the session. Group members wrote down qualities they appreciated about each other. These were done anonymously and sealed in envelopes to be read at home. The facilitators also asked members what they would have liked to have focused on but did not. Most members said they wanted more practice with interviewing, which reflected their need to develop confidence with their English-language skills. During the remainder of the session, Hispanic members led the group in songs from Guatemala and El Salvador with Francisco strumming his guitar.

Members filled out a questionnaire designed to evaluate their experience in group. In answer to the question, "In what ways do you think you have benefited from the group?" one member wrote: "First I recognized that my struggle was causing some pain in my inner side, but not as hard as others. Second, my value as a person improved. . .I understand that I have the complete right for working and not to feel as a beggar." In answer to the question, "What were the highlights or special times for you in the group?" another member commented: "When the group got confidence and everybody started to share experience, gave opinions, and everybody encouraged each other. Second, when I discovered that my opinions were taken into account."

In summary, the group did meet its goals of providing support to immigrant men in search of gainful employment. Its members were multicultural, and group work was a novel experience for them. Members did eventually develop trust, a sense of safety and self-confidence that enabled them to open up and use the group as a forum for venting frustrations about the system and the unjust and irrational reasons for which they have been denied employment commensurate with their qualifications. At the end of the sessions, members reported feeling an improved sense of self-efficacy about who they were and what they had to offer in spite of a persistent lack of fluency in the English language, which many had identified as a major obstacle to obtaining the employment they desired. Hopefully, each would channel renewed energies into the search for improved opportunities and relationships, both in the job market and on the home front.

## NOTE

[1]  Pseudonyms were used to protect the identity of all group members.

## REFERENCES

Canadian Task Force on Mental Health (CTFMH) (1988). *After the door has been open: Mental health issues affecting immigrants and refugees in Canada.* Report of the Canadian Task Force on Mental Health issues affecting immigrants and refugees (1988). Ottawa: Health and Welfare Canada and Multiculturalism and Citizenship Canada.

Austin, C.G. (1994). *An exploratory study of the occupational adaptations of status inconsistent immigrant men with their needs and problems addressed in a social work group intervention.* Unpublished Master's Project. University of Calgary Faculty of Social Work, Calgary, Alberta.

Borgen, W. and Amundson, N. (1984). *The experience of unemployment: Implications for counselling the unemployed.* Toronto, Ontario: Nelson.

Boyd, M. (1985). Immigration and occupational attainment in Canada. In M. Boyd, J. Goyder, F.E. Jones, H.A. McRoberts, P.C. Pineo and J. Porter (eds.), *Ascription and achievement: Studies in mobility and status attainment in Canada.* Ottawa, Ontario: Carleton University.

Briar, K.H. (1988). *Social work and the unemployed.* Silver Springs, MD: National Association of Social Work.

Chau, K.L. (1992). Needs assessment group work with people of color: A conceptual formulation. *Social Work with Groups*, 53-65.

Christensen, C.P. (1986). Immigrant minorities in Canada. In J.C. Turner and F.J. Turner (eds.), *Canadian social welfare*. Toronto, Ontario: Collier-Macmillian.

Daenzer, P. (1989). *The post-immigration labour force adaptation of racial minorities in Canada*. Toronto: The University of Toronto.

Employment and Immigration Canada. (1992). *Managing immigration: A framework for the 1990's*. Ottawa.

Keen, S. (1991). *Fire in the belly: On being a man*. Toronto, Ontario: Bantam Books.

Li, P. S. (1988). *Ethnic inequality in a class society*. Toronto: Wall & Thompson.

Sue, W. S. and Sue, D. (1990). *Counseling the culturally different* (2nd edition). New York: John Wiley & Sons.

Thurston, WE, McGrath, A. and Sehgal, K. (1993). *With two pennies in my pocket, I just feel not so helpless*. A report on the mental and occupational health promotion needs of immigrants in Calgary, Alberta.

Westwood, M.J. and Ishiyama, F.I. (1991). Challenges in counseling immigrant clients: Understanding intercultural barriers to career adjustment. *Journal of Employment Counseling, 28*, 130-143.

# CHAPTER 7

# Techniques for Engaging Immigrant Clients

*Vivianna Reinberg*

The recent emphasis on multicultural awareness within the Canadian social service delivery system is not only necessary but also overdue. Social workers now more than ever are coming face to face with immigrant populations who not only hold different views but have become more vocal in demanding culturally responsive services. This reflects the diversity of the rapidly changing Canadian population in the 1990s: a diversity that on the one hand poses similar client needs and on the other hand demands the use of culturally appropriate means with which to meet those needs. Existing techniques and tools are no longer "good enough," and social service providers are faced with the challenge of special needs groups whose different world view and ways of being need to be honoured if we are to achieve a truly multiculturally competent social service system.

In order to place this chapter within the larger multicultural perspective, it is necessary to explain some of the beliefs and principles underlying my perspective on working with immigrants. First, the word *immigrant* is used here to describe a group of people who were raised outside Canada in a substantially different culture and who, because of these unique experiences, have significantly different world views and ways of being from the mainstream Canadian population. Second, it is my belief that the immigrant experience plays an important role in determining a client's ethnic and cultural identity and, in turn, in shaping the texture and tone of any helping relationship. Acknowledgment of these differences through the provision of multiculturally appropriate services is not an endorsement of separatism, nor is it a way of granting permission for the promotion of cultural encapsulation. On the contrary, it serves as a gesture of unconditional respect and acceptance and, tacitly, a commitment to the establishment of an honest and egalitarian relationship between providers and immigrant consumers of social services. The client's desire to retain ethnic identities and ethnic ways of being should not be construed as a lack of willingness to acculturate or to assume a Canadian identity. Instead, for many immigrants one's ethnic identity serves as a known and sure reference point in otherwise unchartered and unknown circumstances.

Another belief underlying my approach to successfully engaging immigrant clients is the importance of recognizing the power differential that exists between immigrant groups and mainstream Canadian society, in particular its social service delivery system. Power differences can translate into differential access and, in some cases, non-access to needed services and resources. To be effective providers of services, practitioners must also discern the barriers that deny access. It is our responsibility to bridge the imbalance and to establish a collaborative relationship by actively seeking ways to reach out to a population that may not be aware of the assistance available in Canadian society.

There are numerous reasons why immigrant people do not use services offered by the social service delivery system. Until recently, poor utilization of mainstream health and mental health facilities and services by immigrants was attributed primarily to characteristics thought to be inherent in the immigrant population itself. The literature implicated, for example, norms and values that precluded seeking help from beyond the family or clan group, variant definitions of normality and ill health, and differences in styles of communicating. However, these factors only partly explain immigrants' reluctance to use services. Understanding how services to culturally diverse groups can be truly culturally responsive also involves an understanding of how organizational characteristics deny or hinder clients' access to services and resources (Padilla and DeSnyder, 1985).

This chapter discusses the need for more effective access to social service programs and offers a perspective on techniques and methods for reaching out to and engaging the immigrant population. The perspective presented here is based on my years of experience working with immigrant groups as well as my own personal experience as an immigrant from Latin America. The ideas presented here are meant to be illustrative rather than prescriptive. Also I wish to clarify that the generalizations presented in this chapter were not conceived in denial or ignorance of the existence of the immense variation within cultures. Rather, these generalizations were born of my desire to offer pragmatic suggestions to life situations encountered by the many immigrant clients I have worked with.

## ENGAGEMENT AT THE MACRO LEVEL

### Engaging larger client systems

The ecological systems model, a natural extension of the person-in-environment perspective, is a relevant framework for understanding the immigrant situation. First, the immigrant person works to fit within an immigrant/ethnic community as well as Canadian society. In doing so, the immigrant person or family attempts to negotiate two realities, each having a different, perhaps even conflicting, impact. Second, the larger Canadian societal context is not necessarily an environment that is supportive or nurturing. It is not uncommon, for example, for immigrants to encounter acts of discrimination and oppression, including political, economic and social discrimination, and they may also face psychological oppression, which develops through internalized attitudes that designate the immigrant person as inferior to mainstream North Americans (Espin, 1985).

When attempting to engage immigrant individuals and/or families, the practitioner must take into account the larger socio-cultural-economic context of the immigrant group. Engagement, therefore, needs to take place within the socio-cultural, political and religious context of the ethnic community. For many immigrants the ethnic community is a natural support system, social network and source of identity, particularly for first generation immigrants. I would argue that even for people who choose to isolate themselves from their ethnic community, the psychological ties and invisible loyalty towards that community still have some bearing on their help-seeking behaviours.

As an initial method of outreach, group activities serve multiple purposes. They are often the immigrant person's initial encounter with community-based agencies, and thus can serve as an outreach and engagement point from which to recruit persons needing, for example, counselling services, into the system. Group activities can also serve as support groups for persons undergoing counselling as well as those who have completed their counselling program. For example, my experience in providing counselling services to the Latin American and Farsi communities showed that participants in group activities (e.g., workshops on improving English-language skills) found their involvement in the groups extremely helpful in meeting psychosocial as well as educational needs.

The groups were, in essence, community gatherings, and eventually these became a culturally appropriate network of support for clients undergoing psychotherapy. The groups also offered opportunities for clients to try out new skills learned in counselling and the new roles they found themselves cast in by virtue of their status as immigrants. Group participants identified with the overall goal of group activities, which was the betterment of the community. In becoming active participants in community-building and in seeing their participation as being integral to the well-being of the community, many group members developed a sense of belonging and purpose in the ethnic community. This development contributed to the formation of a positive ethnic identity, an important developmental milestone in the cultural transition process. In short, community outreach reaps important community benefits. It serves the dual purpose of helping to integrate the immigrant individual and family into the fabric of the local ethnic community while serving as an integral part of the therapeutic aftercare process.

## THE IMPORTANCE OF COMMUNITY INVOLVEMENT

As discussed in the previous section, successful integration of immigrants into the local community is predicated on active outreach activities. Effective outreach, on the other hand, is contingent on the immigrant population being accorded genuine acceptance and respect. Thus, when programs and services for immigrants are being designed, consideration should be given to the needs and reality of each specific group. Members of the immigrant population should be actively recruited to help identify those needs and to describe members' realities. For example, these immigrants should be consulted for perspectives on the importance of religion, politics, gender and socio-economic status on critical life situations. Their participation must be fully integrated into the program planning and implementation process, and this prerequisite for successful program development and appropriate service delivery must be recognized at different levels within the structural hierarchy of the sponsoring agency. If no provisions have been made to include members of the immigrant/ethnic community as active participants in the initiation, planning, implementation and evaluation aspects of the program and service, then the relevance and potential success of the program become questionable.

Thus, the first tenet in genuinely engaging an ethnic community is the acknowledgment that their reality may be different from that of mainstream society. This acknowledgment should not be used against the immigrant group, however. Just because their reality is different, that reality should not construed as inferior or even deviant, thus allowing for it to be dismissed as invalid and illegitimate. The second tenet is the acceptance of that reality and the incorporation of immigrant experiences into the program planning and implementation process. The third tenet is the integration of ethnocultural and "mainstream" Canadian perspectives into a coherent master plan that would then guide implementation efforts.

Unfortunately, it is easy to overlook these fundamental principles when planning and implementing programs and services for immigrant populations. Involving the immigrant community in the planning and implementation process may be perceived as too time-consuming and tedious. In the name of expediency, agency representatives may decide that they know better what the immigrant group needs and choose to develop funding proposals independent of feedback from those for whom the programs are being developed. Alternatively, the sponsoring agency may consult with one immigrant person or a segment of a population supposedly representative of the immigrant perspective. Such accommodations are unacceptable and may be perceived as yet another form of oppression.

Further, care must be taken to develop the proper mechanisms for introducing a new service into an immigrant community. For example, prior to publicizing the availability of a new service for battered women in ethnic/immigrant communities, a review should be undertaken to assess whether, for example, there are sufficient numbers of culturally competent providers to work with immigrant women should they present for services. Without culturally competent staff, the potential to do more harm than good unfolds. A word of caution also needs to be sounded with respect to short-term programs. Independent short-term programs with no provisions for follow-up services should not be encouraged. But if such programs do exist, then a community network of agencies offering culturally competent follow-up services to either complement or supplement the direct intervention services already received from independent programs needs to be part of the community infrastructure.

The Coalition on Family Violence in Calgary, Alberta is a good example of how to involve immigrant communities in intervention and prevention efforts. Front-line workers in the coalition identified the need for support groups for immigrant women experiencing family violence. The coalition organized a workshop for all service providers on the topic of family violence and the immigrant community. At the workshop front-line workers began a process of needs identification and brainstorming. The next logical step in this process may be the identification of strategies to deal with family violence and the involvement of all stakeholders at different levels such as executive directors, funders, front-line workers and ethno-specific associations.

## THE ETHNIC COMMUNITY

Cohesiveness in an ethnic community is another important factor to consider in developing programs for the immigrant population. The ethnic community plays a crucial role in the provision of indigenous counselling and/or mental health services. For many immigrants this is their first source of identity as well as a natural support system. Engaging immigrants with a highly cohesive and well-developed sense of community is quite different from engaging those experiencing a fragmented, limited sense of community. The former requires enough understanding of the interests of that community and the methods of mobilizing both its formal and informal social networks.

For example, the experience of Chilean refugees who immigrated in the early 1970s after the military coup in Chile was that of a cohesive community with a highly developed sense of identity and socio-political awareness. Outreach to this group at that time would have required strategies that appealed to their values and belief system. If the purpose was to engage them in a counselling program, strategies geared to their individual well-being, self-growth and future development would not have been effective, as the focus of attention at that time was the collective rather than the individual good, mutual help rather than independence and solidarity with those left behind in their homeland. A more effective way to engage this community would have been through cultural-educational exchange activities where people had the opportunity to present their culture to the mainstream.

On the other hand, community engagement with a noncohesive immigrant group whose members question the merit of a having a close-knit ethnic community, as in the case of the Farsi/Iranian group in the early 1990s, would require very different strategies. Here the appeal would be on building something and generating a sense of pride. Lack of cohesiveness necessarily requires a more neutral stance on the part of the social service provider. His or her role would be primarily to try and bring the different socio-cultural, religious and political factions together to iron out their differences and eventually coalesce into a unified front.

## THE IMPORTANCE OF ENGAGEMENT AND ACCESS

It is well known that there is a pattern of underutilization of mental health/counselling services among immigrant populations. Traditionally the reasons for the lack of access to services was attributed to the particular characteristics of the various immigrant groups. The explanation given for low self-referral from people of Hispanic ancestry to mental health services in the United States was the characteristics of the Hispanic culture—the extended family, religious beliefs and the use of *curanderos* or folk healers. Ruiz and Padilla (1977), however, believe that this ethnic group has resisted traditional counselling services because of institutional characteristics of the service delivery system, linguistic difficulties and cultural/racial characteristics that obstruct communication between service providers and their Hispanic clients.

Similarly, Draguns (1981) believes that failures in the therapeutic process have been too quickly dismissed as client resistance or lack of motivation. More recently research studies offer at least two perspectives to explain this phenomenon:

1.  the alternative-resource theory, which points to the ethno-social organizations serving as therapeutic agents
2.  The barrier theory which explains low use of services as a result of "institutional and structural impediments inherent in the mental-health delivery system" (Padilla and DeSnyder, 1985, p. 158).

The Canadian Task Force on Mental Health (CTFMH) in its 1988 report on issues affecting the well-being of immigrants and refugees expands on the barrier explanation:

> Part of the difficulty in getting appropriate care stem from the extreme specialization which characterizes Canadian society, where mental health services are separate from other aspects of life, including general medical care. (CTFMH, 1988, p. 39)

CTFMH reports two reasons for the inappropriateness or ineffectiveness of present services. First, there are cultural and language barriers leading to inaccurate assessment and treatment. This results in the inability of the provider to collect all relevant information to make an accurate diagnosis, which leaves immigrants feeling negatively towards the counsellor/therapist. This situation indicates a lack of information or awareness of cultural values and background on the part of the health provider. The other reason mainstream services are generally culturally inappropriate for the immigrant population is the fact that most therapeutic modalities used in mainstream agencies have a Eurocentric orientation. The value and belief system undergirding these modalities may conflict with those to which immigrant clients subscribe. Clashes in values, differences in expressive and problem solving styles, and incongruence of expectations are likely to result (Pedersen, 1987).

Engaging with an immigrant ethnic community, therefore, has a dual purpose. First, it paves the way for building trust and building bridges with the ethnic community, bridges that will eventually facilitate the socio-cultural integration of individuals, families and the whole community. Second, engagement at the community level promotes accessibility to community services. Through this process of engagement and outreach, those individual and organizational barriers preventing full participation of the immigrant population are identified, thus giving rise to the beginning of a genuine, culturally responsive social work practice.

## OUTREACH TO THE IMMIGRANT POPULATION

In this chapter "outreach" is defined as efforts to engage people into the social service delivery system by breaking down individual and organizational barriers that prevent immigrant people from accessing and utilizing services. It is my experience that engaging individuals necessarily requires outreach at the community level. The following ideas for outreach have been developed through trial and error in the process of providing counselling services to the immigrant population. In these cases outreach was focused on promoting the concept of seeking help, building trust in a new program, developing credibility of the counsellors, creating a sense of security and confidentiality, and mobilizing the immigrant community to access programs and services.

## 1. Reframing concepts in ways that are culturally appropriate and acceptable

The concept of counselling is virtually non-existent in most immigrant groups. In other countries there are natural support networks built into the fabric of society that are unlike institutionalized forms of helping in Canadian society. These natural support networks include the extended family (and its variation, such as the *compasdrazgo* system or adopting people into the family unit), the church, neighbours, relatives, elders, traditional folk healers, doctors and fortune tellers. There is a stigma attached to going outside the family for help, so it is not within the parameters of immigrant thinking to turn to strangers for help in a transactional relationship such as the one between service provider and client.

For engagement purposes, this relationship can be modified. For example, if professionalism is a deterrent to people seeking help, then help can be offered in a relationship that is friendly rather than formal and professional. For example, a Chinese woman enrolled in a skills training course was referred to me by her program coordinator for difficulties in relating within her work placement. We spent more than an hour talking about her life, her worries, her difficulties learning English and her problems at work. In professional terminology I formed a therapeutic relationship, established a contractual agreement for a single session, did an assessment, did a number of in-session interventions and gave her a homework assignment. This woman, however, insisted that she did not believe in counsellors and that she would never seek help from anybody because there was nothing practical anybody could do to change her situation. At the end of the session, when I asked her how she viewed our conversation, she responded by saying that she thought it was helpful because it had been different with me, as we had talked like friends.*

The formality of intake, signing consent for therapy, establishing parameters of the client-worker relationship and negotiating fees alienates rather than engages people. Most of these activities are important for organizational purposes and need to be done in some way at some point; however, outreach strategies require that at the point of first contact these aspects of professionalism and institutionalism need to be either modified or left out.

Services, therefore, need to be established at a level that fits the immigrants' frame of reference. Making services accessible not only means flexibility of time, place and location but, most importantly, it means offering help within a culture's ground rules. If people are not familiar with the concept of counselling or mental health, then the provision of assistance needs to change to one that best suits that culture and still imparts help. It does not matter how help is provided as long as it helps people. Assistance provided in traditional counselling can be modified into a medium that is culturally acceptable and appropriate.

An example of a modified program is the Family Conflict Program at the Calgary Immigrant Women's Association, which assists women and their families experiencing family violence. As the word "violence" is defined differently acrosss cultures and is usually imbedded with negative connotations, it was decided to use the word conflict, which is more neutral and encompassing. Another example is that of suicide prevention workshops for the Polish community in Calgary. The Polish community has a relatively low sense of identity and cohesion as a community compared to the Spanish community. With the Spanish community, there was no difficulty engaging people in piloting the program, but it became difficult to gather people for the Polish workshops. As the word "suicide" had negative connotations as well as religious implications, it was felt that the workshops would be more acceptable if they also appealed to the unity of the community. The slogan "building a community" was used along with the suicide prevention title, thus attendance at the workshops helped to build a healthy community.

The Multicultural Counselling Internship Program is another example. This program offered a counselling service to the Farsi community in Calgary, an ethnic group which had no previous experience with a counselling service. Engagement with this population took the form of

---

\* This reflects the importance of people's perception of what constitutes help.

outreaching through the provision of English-language workshops, which is a relatively safe and understood concept compared to the concept of "counselling." Farsi-speaking people were more receptive to workshops that addressed their practical everyday needs.

## 2. Capitalize on people's holistic concept of health

Most immigrant groups do not make a distinction between physical and mental pain and suffering. The two aspects of illness are so intertwined that their home countries support the practice of providing help for mental complaints in medical forms. Thus, it is common for immigrant people to express emotional pain through somatic complaints and seek help from doctors rather than a mental health professional. This offers an excellent opportunity a comprehensive service delivery system that addresses the different needs of the immigrant reality. A natural way to engage immigrant people, then, is through the provision of medical and social service assistance as one package. A perfect example of this is the Alexandra Community Health Centre in Calgary where physicians, social workers and counsellors work in a team approach engaging people through health promotion activities. Alternatively, if a physician decides that the patient would be better served by mental health provider, the same patient is more apt to follow through on the doctor's referral than if the referral was made independent of a visit to a physician.

In addition, addressing the physical and psychological/emotional aspects of well-being demonstrates understanding and respect for people's world view. Promoting well-being through medically related themes such as stress management (rather than, e.g., self-esteem) is more appealing to the concrete, practical side of immigrant people's notions about what to seek help for. Thus prenatal care, postnatal care and child-care courses offer perfect opportunities to address couple relationship issues.

Capitalizing on the physical aspects of people's complaints during the first clinical contact can help clients feel understood. In counselling I ask questions related to people's home remedies and nontraditional ways of healing. For example, in the case of child bedwetting, a parallel intervention may involve the use of herbs or steam baths. In cases of stress, my regular parallel interventions include drinking herb tea, taking hot baths and exploring any other ways in which the person takes care of his or her body.

## 3. Addressing loyalty issues

In most immigrant groups there seems to be a particularly strong cultural norm against the disclosure of personal problems. In some cultures, such as the Japanese, the disloyalty implicated in disclosing family secrets is strongly entrenched. Disclosing a family secret brings shame on the family and the ethnic community, and is thus regarded as a personal failure. Outreach requires that the service provider explain the different ways in which agencies and individual practitioners protect the confidences of clients.

## 4. Building trust

Any understanding of the reality of the immigrant population would not be complete without acknowledging the impact of past and current socio-political situations in their home countries. Many refugee survivors still struggle with the horrors of persecution and torture, and they may develop coping mechanisms of distrust and antagonism towards people in a position of power or authority, including those in the helping professions. Even the process of migration and cultural adaptation results in normal imbalances in the trust-mistrust issues of psychological functioning. Outreach efforts need to be carefully balanced between sufficient efforts to engage people and sensitivity to the intrusiveness of such efforts, and enough caring and empathy to build trust in a climate of honesty and congruency.

The Farsi community seemed to be extremely distrustful of strangers in general as a result of the socio-political experiences in Iran. Having Canadians interested in their well-being raised suspicions and had the Farsi immigrants questioning the motivation behind such endeavours. In this case extensive time was devoted to meetings with settlement counsellors and staff to design appropriate ways to introduce topics a nonthreatening manner. Trust can only be developed gradually through individual and face-to-face contacts with people in order to establish agency and staff credibility.

## 5. Personalize the referral/initial contact

It is my experience that most immigrant people need to establish a personal relationship with service providers before being able to trust them. In the Hispanic population this trait is referred to as *personalismo* and is defined in the following manner:

> Personal contact and individualized attention in dealing with power structures, such as social institutions. Anglos, in contrast, seem to favor an organizational approach that follows impersonal regulations (the "chain of command"). ( Ruiz and Padilla, 1977, p. 173)

It has been widely suggested that traditional counselling approaches be modifed to include the concept of *personalismo* in the therapeutic relationship as a form of engagement. (Atkinson, Morten and Sue, 1989). This approach advocates for a more flexible, warm, personable style, which may include home visits and some information-sharing about self on the part of the service provider.

In addition, many immigrants will not access a counselling program unless a personal contact is made by a middle person (intermidiary). Most referrals come through the encouragement of a friend or trusted paraprofessional who channels the person through a direct contact with the helping professional. A perfect example of this was made by counselling agencies with the Family Conflict Program at the Calgary Immigrant Women's Association to have counsellors work in the immigrant community itself, rather than have the immigrant client present at the agency for services. This not only allowed for personalized contact with the immigrant person in his or her natural environment but also offered the opportunity for a team approach working with immigrant staff indigenous to the community.

Most referrals to this program were made through word of mouth as counsellors became known and trusted within the immigrant community. As a staff person in this program I wanted to refer an ambivalent battered woman to a counsellor. As I had already established a relationship of trust with her, my reasurring her that the counsellor was a good, trusted professional whom I personally knew and would vouch for, and who had an interest and understanding of people from other cultures, was sufficient for her to give the referral a try. I subsequently carried out a joint first session with the other counsellor as a means of building trust and personalizing the contact.

## 6. Importance of the relationship

The client-professional relationship takes on a new dimension with the immigrant population. Trust, credibility and a personalized approach are perhaps the most important determinants in building a relationship that is congruent with the immigrant's concept of receiving help. Credibility on the part of the worker/counsellor is a somewhat more difficult thing to pinpoint. I have encountered situations where credibility came from having an inside knowledge of people's culture, other situations required having a dissimilar but neutral background.

For example, one case involved a Latin American woman who had seen a social worker from a hospital regarding conflict with her teenage daughter. She was told that her daugther needed more independence than the mother was allowing her. This woman came to me complaining about the social worker's lack of understanding about her culture, a culture where parental overprotection is more common than in the Canadian culture. In one session I gave the mother the same message as did the social worker and she seemed to accept it. I concluded that she was more receptive to the views of somebody from her own culture. It seemed that she placed more credibilty on my analysis of the situation than that of someone whom she still did not trust. It is not uncommon for immigrant clients to "shop" for and compare opinions as they mull over ways to resolve their problems. Immigrant people often express an exclusive preference for an immigrant counsellor because they perceive that someone with a similar background would be better able to understand their problems and all the cultural nuances associated with them.

Service providers can also build credibility by virtue of their educational background. Many immigrants were raised in social environments where social status, prestige and credibility stem from formal education. Knowing that the service provider has a university degree and work experience is very important, particularly for immigrant clients who see themselves as being of medium or high social class.

For a non-immigrant professional to develop credibility, it is important to share information about herself or himself, including information about the institution where he or she received training; educational qualifications; length and types of experience in working with immigrant people; and the amount and type of personal exposure to another culture.

On the other hand, there are immigrant people who specifically prefer not to see a professional from their own culture or an immigrant professional. Fear of having their problems exposed in the ethnic community is a major concern; thus the importance of reassuring the client about the agency's policy and practice with regard to protecting confidences. Factors that appear to influence the immigrant client's decision to work with an immigrant or a non-immigrant professional include the client's level of acculturation, his or her fluency in the English language and the type of experiences he or she has had in the ethnic community.

## 7. Mobilizing the ethnic community

A crucial factor in outreach is the relationship established with the immigrant settlement agencies, which provide a valuable service in the community and have already established a relationship of trust and credibility within their own ethnic communities. Immigrant-serving agencies provide practical assistance and supportive counselling to a good segment of the immigrant population. As explained earlier, they are important elements in the delivery of social and mental health services. Similarly, ethnocultural associations are also an important stakeholder in the process of engagement, as they have the grassroots connections with the community. Another aspect in mobilizing the community is working in conjunction with para-professional healers who are already providing services in the community. This approach, of course, requires genuine acceptance of and respect for the perspective and work performed by these people.

## 8. Using ideas appealing to family values

Pedersen (1987) noted that the concepts of individualism and independence are Western cultural assumptions upon which traditional theories of mental health and social service practice are based. Individualism, which is the most widely embedded value in the traditional models of practice, emphasizes the growth and development of the individual rather than collectives. Thus, most interventions focus almost exclusively on the benefit of the individual at the cost of the values of obligation and duty to the family, yet these values are highly regarded by all immigrant groups. For this reason it has been suggested that for interventions to be appropriate they need to incorporate values such as familism (Green, 1995). Similarly, it has been suggested numerous times in the literature (LeVine and Padilla, 1980; Sue and Sue, 1990) that family therapy is a natural mode of intervention, as the conceptualization of problems coincides with the importance immigrants place on family. Translating this concept into engagement, it is obvious that outreach strategies need to become inclusive of the whole family and appeal to the sense of family unity.

For example, a family violence program located in an immigrant women's organization emphasized its family perspective. Advertisements about services targeted immigrant women *and their families*; it did not exclude men from receiving services. Programs for immigrant women need to include services with a holistic focus for the whole family. In more practical terms, outreach methods need to include activities for the entire family. For example, outreach to the Latin American community in Calgary included workshops on improving interpersonal communication skills, along with activities for children such as a pinata, games and face painting.

A delicate balance needs to be struck between advocating for a family-based perspective in intervention and attending to women's individual needs. Women do require special consideration because of the unequal power distribution along gender, class and race lines. For immigrant women, their plight is exacerbated by being doubly (gender and immigrant status) or triply (gender, race, immigrant status) disadvantaged. These women might benefit from women's assertiveness workshops. Programs for women are no doubt needed and safety issues must be considered in all programs for women or families. The difference in working with immigrant families is that women's awareness about rights and civil liberties needs to be developed slowly, while still honouring deeply embedded family values.

## 9. Developing practical rather than conceptual modes of helping

Most ethnocultural groups have a different perspective on providing and receiving help. Similarly, there are cultural differences in how help is conceived. Counselling in the North American culture has been described as being highly linear, analytic and verbal (Sue and Sue, 1990). Western society emphasizes the scientific method, which involves objective, rational, linear thinking in conceptualizing problems and looking for solutions. Other cultures tend to emphasize the "harmonious aspects of the world, intuitive functioning, and a holistic approach...[and] ... value different ways of asking and answering questions about the human condition" (Sue and Sue, 1990, p. 41). Pedersen (1987) describes that traditional counselling theories have a tendency towards a high level of abstraction and assumes that concepts such as self-esteem, unconditional positive regard, empathic understanding and empowerment are universally understood. These concepts are difficult to understand for many immigrants who do not value subjective experience. The term "empowerment," for instance, does not have an equivalent in some languages; in Spanish there is no conception of an individual sense of power. Instead, there is a parallel term, *poder popular*, meaning power of the people, along with an extensive vocabulary on community work and social action, exemplifying the value conflict between individualism and collectivism and familism.

In order to be more congruent with the value orientation of diverse cultures, social service interventions need to become more practical and tangible, at least at the engagement level. Sue and Zane (1987) refer to the concept of "giving," providing a tangible, practical thing such as an exercise, piece of advice or written assignment to clients to take home with them. My practice of giving tips on herbal and home-made remedies for the alleviation of stress and physical pain, along with the more abstract interventions, is congruent with this idea of "giving." Many immigrant clients strongly question the value of talking about their problems and getting only "talk" back. When reaching out for help, the expectation is to receive advice, mediation, financial help. Thus, program goals should aim at, for example, strengthening family ties and assisting in improving communication between parents and adolescents instead of promoting the well-being of the individual. These goals are not only more concrete but they are also congruent with the "familism." Once people are engaged in addressing their immediate needs, they usually are able to focus on more abstract problems.

Immigrant people are often engrossed in a multitude of concrete problems that affect their emotional and psychological functioning. People expect that the service provider will be able to address all of their needs at the same time. For example, a couple came to me complaining of their marital problems as well as depression on the part of the wife, for which she was receiving medical treatment. They saw the reason for the stress and depression as coming from an employment situation where they were abused by their employer and unable to leave their jobs or exert their rights. The pressure from work was rending this woman physically ill and unable to work. In order to assist this couple with either marital difficulties or personal stress, I first needed to address the tremendous pressure this woman experienced at work. I assisted her by contacting her employer and filing a complaint at the Employment Standards office. Only after she had resolved her employment issues was she able to address the emotional aspects of her situation. My assistance with the practical aspects of her employment situation gave us the foundation of a relationship where she implicitly trusted me in my helping role.

In addition to receiving help with practical needs, immigrant people usually expect more guidance than the nonstructured, nondirective approach specified by the principles of client self-determination normally endorsed by mainstream Canadian culture. It is quite common for immigrant people to ask for an opinion and seek advice. Providing a balanced opinion is seen as one of the highest forms of respect paid towards such clients. It is also a way of conveying the message that they are seen as competent enough to make an independent decision.

Another difference in working with the immigrant population is accepting their definition of what constitutes the problem. Again, this follows the principle of respecting their reality and beginning at their level of awareness. I have been more effective accepting that an abused woman needs advice on how to change her husband rather than giving in to the impulse of challenging—confronting the fact that she can not change another person and needs to focus on herself.

Accepting the client's definition of the problem can be difficult because it is a matter of professional approach and personal perspective. I have often heard from immigrant people about the evils of the Canadian society; they blame the government, culture and discrimination for their problems. In this case I usually join the person in his or her definition and begin a discussion on the merits and demerits of Canadian culture. I gradually shift to how the individual needs to learn the rules of the game to survive in this society. From there, it is easier to focus on individual change that is still compatible with the socio-cultural value base that he or she subscribes to.

Another helpful consideration is knowing the cultural biases that influence where people place responsibility for change. Draguns (1981) states that cultures differ in how change is perveived and pursued. He calls this the autoplastic/aloplastic dimension, where the autoplastic view "modifies behavior to accommodate external circumstances...[and the alloplastic view]... by imposing changes upon the world at large" (Draguns, 1981, p. 14). This leads to differences in placing of responsibility for behaviours on the self or external sources. North American culture is highly autoplastic, placing responsibility for change on the individual, while other cultures are geared more towards the alloplastic dimension, placing responsibility on external sources.

In the final analysis, appropriate intervention always begins with the individual or family. For interventions to be culturally appropriate and effective, the service provider needs to understand the context in which immigrant clients live—norms, values and beliefs—and how this is handled on a day-to-day basis vis-à-vis the norms, values and beliefs of the larger Canadian society. In addition, all individuals and families are a sum total of their past experiences and current realities. These too need to be factored into the equation for intervention. Finally, let the immigrant client be the "teacher," teaching you the provider what it means to be an immigrant person in Canada today, with all its attendant complications and benefits. In turn, see yourself as a partner, collaborating on meaningful solutions for a healthier person, family and community.

## REFERENCES

Atkinson, D.R., Morten, G. and Sue, D.W. (1989) (eds.), *Counseling American minorities*. Dubuque, IA: W.C. Brown.

Canadian Task Force on Mental Health. (1988). *After the door has been opened: Mental health issues affecting immigrants and refugees in Canada*. Report of the Canadian Task Force on Mental Health Issues Affecting Immigrants and Refugees. Ottawa: Health and Welfare Canada and Multiculturalism and Citizenship Canada.

Draguns, J. G. (1981). Counseling across cultuires: Common themes and distinct approaches. In P.B. Pedersen, J.G Draguns, W.J. Lonner, and J. E. Trimble (eds.), *Counseling across cultures*. Honolulu, HI: University of Hawaii Press.

Espin, O. M. (1985). Psychotherapy with Hispanic women: Some considerations. In P. Pedersen (ed.), *Handbook of cross-cultural counseling and therapy*. Westport, CT: Greenwood Press.

Green, J. (1995). *Cultural awareness in the human services: A multi-ethnic approach*. Needham Heights, MA: Allyn & Bacon.

LeVine, E.S. and Padilla, A.M. (1980). *Crossing cultures in therapy: Pluralistic counseling for the Hispanic*. Monterrey, CA: Brooks/Cole.

Padilla, A.M. and DeSnyder, N.S. (1985). Counseling Hispanics: Strategies for effective intervention. In P.B. Pedersen (ed.), *Handbook of cross-cultural counseling and therapy.* Westport, CT: Greenwood Press.

Pedersen, P.B. (1987). Ten frequent assumptions of cultural bias in counseling. *Journal of Multicultural Counseling and Development*, 15, 16-24.

Ruiz, R.A. and Padilla, A.M. (1977). Counseling latinos. *Personnel Journal*, 55, 401-408.

Sue, D.W. and Sue, D. (1990). *Counseling the culturally different: Theory and practice.* New York, NY: John Wiley.

Sue, S. and Zane, N. (1987). The role of culture and cultural techniques in psychotherapy: A reformation. *American Psychologist*, 42, 37-45.

# IMPLICATIONS OF
# MULTICULTURAL POLICY
## b) for management,
### adminstrations and
### organizational change

# CHAPTER 8

# Valuing Diversity in
# Human Service Organizations

*Jann M. MacLeod*

## INTRODUCTION

Every year about 250,000 people from every part of the world immigrate to Canada. Immigration flow and changes in the pattern of immmigration over the years have had a marked effect on the ethnocultural profile of the Canadian population—a population that is becoming increasingly diverse in culture, colour, religion, ethnic origin, place of origin, education and language (Fallick, 1991). As Canadian communities become increasingly diverse, human service organizations will have to continuously reassess the needs and interests of the community to ensure that appropriate services are delivered.

People who have recently immigrated to Canada often benefit from having access to the following types of programs and services, according to Minna (1986):

- language training
- resettlement assistance
- ongoing integration assistance
- accessible health services
- family counselling
- job search assistance
- assistance in locating housing

However, the continuing immigration of people to Canada and the increasing ethnocultural diversity of Canadian communities have implications for the leader of a human service organization beyond ensuring that programs efficiently and effectively meet the needs of changing client populations. The changing patterns of immigration in combination with demographic changes in the composition of the total population are producing a workforce dramatically different from the workforce of the past. The leader of human service organizations will need to acquire the knowledge and skills necessary to attract, retain, motivate and develop high-potential employees from a variety of ethnocultural backgrounds (Taylor, 1995). The objective of this chapter is to provide background information and a basic framework for understanding how to successfully lead an increasingly diverse workforce.

## UNDERSTANDING DIVERSITY IN THE CANADIAN LABOUR MARKET

### Demographic changes in the Canadian labour supply

The rate of growth of the Canadian population is slowing (Health and Welfare Canada, 1990). The slow population growth increases the likelihood that there will continue to be a significant flow of people into Canada as the government balances a low birth rate with increased immigration. Even with continued immigration, the growth in the Canadian population and labour force is expected to continue to be slow into the beginning of the 21st century (Health and Welfare Canada, 1990).

As growth in the population slows and its composition changes, traditional sources of labour decline. According to Alberta Career and Development (1989), less than 50% of those now entering the workforce are physically able, white and male—the traditional workforce. All employers, including human service organizations, in their search for skilled workers will come to rely more and more on the non-traditional workforce. The non-traditional workforce includes people from many different groups—visible minorities, women, disabled persons and Aboriginal people. The non-traditional workforce also includes people who are different from each other in attributes such as lifestyle, education, religion, personality, political beliefs, sexual orientation, language and income. Sometimes employees drawn from the non-traditional labour pool will require help in overcoming barriers to full workforce participation. A report by Alberta Career Development and Employment (1989) identified the most significant employment barriers as:

- lack of experience
- lack of appropriate education and training
- lack of information
- lack of support services
- stereotypes concerning skills and abilities.

Leaders can acquire the skills needed to assist employees overcome these workforce barriers. More importantly, leaders in organizations can acquire the knowledge, skills and abilities necessary to identify such barriers within the organization and can work towards their elimination.

Today's leaders must begin to appreciate the impact which changing demographics have on recruiting, training and leading the employees within their organizations. As individuals differing in culture, colour, religion, ethnic origin, place of origin, sexual orientation, education and language come together in the workplace, conflicts and tensions arise. Today's leaders must develop the skills to manage the diverse workforce of today and tomorrow. The challenge facing today's leaders is to foster an organizational culture that values differences and maximizes the potential of all employees.

## Employment equity in Canada

As the traditional labour pool began to shrink, there was increasing pressure upon employers to hire from non-traditional sources. As more employees were hired from non-traditional sources, there was accompanying pressure upon organizations to improve the opportunities of those from non-traditional labour sources to obtain work and achieve success in the workplace. The Royal Commission on Equality in Employment was established by the federal government in June 1983 to address some of those concerns. The commission operated under the following terms of reference:

> to explore the most efficient, effective,and equitable means of promoting the equality in employment for four groups: women, native people, disabled people and visible minorities. (Abella, 1984, p. v)

People from these four designated groups were generally found to be underemployed, underpaid and often the victims of forms of hidden or systemic discrimination. The commission concluded that government intervention was necessary to ensure freedom from discrimination and equitable participation in the workforce (Abella, 1984).

The legislation, the Employment Equity Act, received royal assent in 1986. This legislation includes a requirement that federally regulated employers take steps to eliminate discriminatory employment practices. The purpose of the Employment Equity Act is to ensure that unnecessary barriers that restrict employment and promotional opportunities for women, people with disabilities, Aboriginal people and people of colour are identified and eliminated.

While the Employment Equity Act only applies to federally regulated undertakings, the legislation reflects the desire of many Canadians for fairness in the workplace. Many Canadian employers and most employees are increasingly concerned with fairness in the workplace, which encompasses such issues as equal access to training, to employment and to advancement opportunities. Fairness in the workplace also includes fairness in compensation and benefits.

Many private sector employers followed the example set by the federal government through the Employment Equity Act and implemented their own employment equity program (City Of Calgary, 1992). The goal of such programs is to ensure that equal employment opportunities are extended to all employees, including members of the designated groups.

## Traditional management practice

Assimilation of non-traditional employees has been the management norm within most organizations (Cleghorn, 1992). The process of assimilation requires that individuals relinquish their own identity and adopt that of the larger or dominant group (Herberg, 1989). Managers often managed people who were different from members of the traditional labour pool as if there were no differences between people. The burden of changing and adjusting fell on those differing from the members of the traditional labour force. Homogeneity, assimilation and the assumption that equality meant treating all people the same were recurring themes of the traditional organization (Loden and Rosener, 1991). In traditionally managed organizations there is typically one set of policies, practices or systems universally applied. There is no consideration, accounting or accommodating for individual differences, interests or needs (Jamieson and O'Mara, 1991; Loden and Rosener, 1991). In fact, it is not uncommon for managers in traditionally managed organizations to deny that differences exist among their employees (Malmquist, 1993).

Such traditional management behaviour tends to reinforce the behaviours, experiences and values of the dominant group. Loden and Rosener (1991) suggest that the limitations of workplace assimilation must be acknowledged and addressed in any organizational change effort. The basic goal of a valuing diversity management philosophy should be to move the organization from one in which workers are expected to assimilate to one in which all workers are integrated into the workforce. Valuing diversity goes beyond employment equity's focus on the four designated groups; it addresses the need to create a fair work environment for all employees (Taylor, 1995)

## Changing employee values

Today's workforce is changing. The changes are the result of two main factors. One is the increasing diversity in the workforce, and the other is changing employee values. Today's employees want interesting, challenging jobs that they can control. Today's employees want to be treated fairly and equally. They want to have a say in the evaluation of their performance. Employees in today's workplace want to play an active role in training and development needs. They want to be recognized for their individuality and their uniqueness. Today's employees want to have a balanced work and personal life (Fernandez, 1991).

Today's employees hold values relating to work and family which differ significantly from the values held by employees in the past. As a result of changing values, employees are less willing to become assimilated into the organizational culture. Prospective employees are saying,

> I'm different and proud of what makes me so. I can
> help your team, and I would like to join you, but only
> if I can do so without compromising my uniqueness.
> (Cleghorn, 1992, p. 5)

### Costs of continuing with traditional management practices

There are monetary costs to the organization that fails to effectively manage diversity within the workplace. As employees identify the organization as a negative one which provides a poor quality of work life, they will seek employment elsewhere. High turnover rates lead to increased costs as the organization must expend resources in recruiting and training replacement employees. There are also costs to the organization as employees take time off in an attempt to deal with the stress of working in a non-inclusive environment. Other costs may be attributed to such things as:

- reduced efficiency as a result of low morale among employees excluded from work groups;
- work disruptions due to conflicts and tensions among people who differ from one another;
- limited innovation due to the underutilization of skills of the organization's employees;
- problems caused by poor or lack of communication;
- discrimination complaints filed with human rights commissions
- legal actions brought against the employer for harassment injuries suffered during employment (Loden and Rosener, 1991).

## MANAGING DIVERSITY

### The case for managing diversity

Changes in the composition of the workforce, as well as changes in values held by individuals in the workforce, present the opportunity for the human service leaders to re-examine the ways in which the workforce has traditionally been managed. Meeting the needs of the new diverse workforce and maximizing the potential of all employees requires vastly different knowledge, skills and abilities from those required to manage the traditional workforce (Francis, 1992). With regards to managing the new workforce, Francis (1992, p. 2) stated:

> Employees are human resources that must be developed, nurtured and encouraged to mature to their full individual potential. It's this kind of nurturing, this

kind of focusing on the individual talents of all employees regardless of sex, racial background or cultural background or physical ability—that managing workplace diversity is all about.

Leadership itself is the most critical variable in an organization's ability to incorporate the value of diversity into its culture (Taylor, 1995).

Valuing diversity is both morally and economically essential to the future management of all organizations. Studies have shown that fairness, equity and a high quality of work life within the workplace result in performance improvement and increased productivity. Put simply, organizations that have a philosophy of valuing diversity do better (Hayles, 1994). As a result of implementing a valuing diversity management philosophy, the organization will almost certainly benefit from increased service improvement brought about by increased employee motivation and loyalty. In addition diverse work groups can help the human service organization better understand and meet the needs and interests of their increasingly diverse client base. Other advantages of valuing diversity within the organization include:

- increased retention of employees,
- reduction in employer liability,
- decreased sick days,
- decreased costs to assistance and benefits plans,
- full utilization of the organization's human resources,
- reduced interpersonal conflict,
- enhanced work relationships,
- greater innovation and
- greater flexibility and creativity in problem solving (Loden and Rosener, 1991).

It does not take a leap of faith to appreciate that people who feel important, who feel that their employer values their unique perspective enough to manage them as individuals, will feel satisfied as employees. Satisfied employees benefit their employers.

In studies examining task performance, diverse groups have been shown to outperform homogeneous groups on complex tasks both in terms of quality and quantity of solutions (Hayles, 1994). More and better solutions are the result of increased opportunities for expression of different points of view and increased acceptance of different and creative ways of solving problems. People who have all had the same experiences tend to think the same way, to see the world the same way and to come up with similar solutions to problems. Unfortunately, similar people also tend to make the same mistakes. Although it may feel good when everybody agrees with us, it does not create good decisions (Philip, 1989).

## The human service manager as change agent

Leaders who are working towards creating a philosophy of valuing diversity in their organizations are engaged in changing the culture of their organization. It is imperative that leaders at all levels of the organization are committed to achieving the change goal and to engaging in the work necessary if the change in culture is to be achieved (Fernadez, 1991). Wherever organizational culture includes valuing diversity, senior levels of management have endorsed the change in culture and communicated their support throughout the organization (Loden and Rosener, 1991). Organizations which have been successful in achieving a valuing diversity culture frequently linked improvement in a manager's diversity work with their evaluations, bonus or incentive plans. Promotional opportunities were often tied to a manager's commitment and ability to succeed with a diverse work group.

In order to foster a culture of valuing diversity within an organization, a leader requires skills in decision-making, in exercising judgment, in being open to new ideas. The leader should have excellent communication skills. Leaders of diversity need to have an understanding of the values, beliefs and assumptions which they hold about those who differ from themselves. Diversity leaders need to be able to accurately assess employees' character and skill when allocating job assignments and promotions. They must be willing to share information with others, to share the informal rules of the organization and to provide access to mentors to help individuals break through invisible barriers. Diversity leaders must work at removing barriers to opportunities and rewards within the workplace. Diversity leaders will exhibit a willingness to change old rules and to be flexible. Such leaders will also encourage each individual to participate in the success of the organization and achieve their highest level.

## Organizational change

*Measuring diversity within the organization.* Valuing diversity culture within the organization ensures that every employee experiences a high quality of work life. The climate or quality of work life should be the same for all employees regardless of how employees may differ from one another. In order to bring about organizational change, the leader needs to understand existing demographics within the workplace.

The first activity which should be undertaken is the development and implementation of a needs assessment survey of the organization. The needs assessment should measure the diversity within the organization including such characteristics as gender, race, age, sexual orientation, physical ability, education and employment functions.

One of the main purposes of the needs assessment is to provide a snapshot of the organization. Is it diverse at all levels or only at certain levels? The needs assessment should provide information about what the employees believe to be the main issues in the workplace and which employees possess those issues. Are some issues being expressed and seen as issues only by employees from certain groups? Does the needs assessment survey identify some groups of employees as having religious, cultural or language issues and not others?

The needs assessment should also provide a comparison of the quality of work life within the organization for members of different groups. Are members of certain groups experiencing a better quality of work life than members of other groups? If an assessment indicates that there is a difference between groups, then there is a diversity issue to tackle.

Frequently, organizations collect data through their management information systems that can be useful in providing a snapshot of the organization. For example, many organizations collect data on complaint and grievance rates and issues, turnover rates and attrition, voluntary or involuntary terminations, promotions and training. This data can be analyzed by the diversity leader in order to gain an understanding of what is happening within the organization (Hayles, 1994).

The issues may vary, but their foundation will be the same. They all will have to do with the ways in which people differ. The following issues are typical of those frequently identified in a needs assessment survey:

- formation of cliques of workers at breaks and lunch,
- different languages spoken at the workplace,

- name calling and teasing,
- perceived favouritism in promotional processes,
- language barriers making communication difficult,
- gender and cultural tensions in the workplace,
- cultural value differences left unrecognized and
- confusion between discrimination and interpersonal conflict.

Once the needs assessment survey has been completed and the diversity issues identified, it becomes possible for the diversity leader to select areas that need immediate attention. The initial needs assessment should be followed up by ongoing measurement. Ideally the diversity leader should begin by surveying every three months for the first year and then surveying every six months thereafter.

*Diversity education.*The second level of activities that the diversity leader should implement are those directed towards increasing employee awareness about diversity issues. Many leaders are ill prepared to deal with the differences now found in a diverse workforce. Surveys of leaders in corporations and government departments revealed that the vast majority had no contact with other cultures or races until adulthood (Philip, 1990).

Educational programs designed to increase employee awareness about diversity should be implemented. The goal should be to train those at all levels of the organization, beginning with the people in the senior management levels. One of the goals of the education program should be to establish a universal definition of diversity within the organization. The best definition will be one which emphasizes that diversity is about the experience of being alike or different from others. Diversity is "all the ways in which we differ" (Hayles, 1994). Using such a broad definition will ensure that all people who differ from one another in dimensions such as gender, age, ethnic origin, culture, education, colour, physical ability, sexual orientation and function in the organization are included.

Robert Hayles (1994) suggests including the following simple activity in the diversity training program in order to help people understand the concept of diversity. The following experiential exercise can be used to establish a shared universal definition and understanding of diversity within the organization. It consists of providing an opportunity early in the diversity training for employees to reflect on the following question: "Imagine that you are with a group of people similar to yourself. How do you feel?" Most people respond to this question by reporting that they feel connected, good, warm, safe and comfortable. Then people are asked to: "Imagine that you are with a group of people where you are different from everyone around you. How do you feel?" In response to this question, most people report that they felt left out, stressed, resentful, had negative feelings, were uncomfortable or felt intimidated (Hayles, 1994).

Valuing diversity then becomes as simple as checking to see if a person is feeling left out of their workgroup. Is the employee included when others go for coffee, for lunch or during informal conversations? If the employee is feeling left out, then it is up to the manager or supervisor to find ways that the person can be included and become connected to others in the workplace. It is also the responsibility of members of the workgroup and the individual to work on this task. The primary goal of the diversity leader is to help employees find creative ways to ensure that all individuals feel included. In checking up on the progress, the diversity leader need only ask the individual how they are feeling. If the person is not feeling included, then the manager, supervisor and work group have not been successful and the task continues.

The goal of the valuing diversity program is to create an environment within the human service organization in which all employees have the feelings that are associated with sameness, while recognizing that all people are different. The diversity training is around unity, not uniformity; its about understanding the similarities and differences in people (Hayles, 1994).

*Developmental stages of accepting diversity.* Robert Hayles suggests that people typically progress through three stages with respect to accepting diversity. The first stage is one of minimizing difference. In this stage a person typically goes through a process of:

- meeting someone different from them,
- noticing that the other is different from them,
- either acknowledging the difference or trying to deny the difference and, lastly,
- minimizing the difference.

There are many employees, including many managers, in the workplace who maintain that they do not notice when someone working with them differs from them in some way. Hayles suggests that the reason some people minimize differences is that they do not believe that those who differ from themselves can be as good as themselves. In order to get past this mindset, people minimize or deny the differences between themselves and others. The second stage is one in which a person goes beyond minimizing differences and recognizes that people can be different from and as good as themselves. The minimum goal of a valuing diversity program should be to move the majority of employees to this second stage.

The final and third stage is one in which people are able to adopt and borrow from those who differ from themselves in some way. People who have reached the third stage adopt and borrow other styles, approaches and languages in order to enhance their own abilities. People in this third stage recognize that they can learn the most from people who differ from themselves. The ideal valuing diversity training program is one designed to move people developmentally forward through these stages.

*Diversity training.* Loden and Rosener (1991) characterize the education and training phase of implementing valuing diversity in the workplace as one which includes elements such as:

- providing awareness education to minimize culture clash and improve work relationships among all employees;
- enlisting support for change from employees at all organizational levels and creating structures to support organizational change;
- diversifying work groups and decision-making groups;
- tying individual and group rewards to consistent behaviour that values diversity; and
- creating benefit plans that reflect diverse employees priorities.

The individuals responsible for implementing the valuing diversity training program should enlist the support of a group of employees to help move the diversity effort forward. These people, often called process champions, should be volunteers, have the support of their managers, possess good communication skills and, most importantly, should have a personal commitment to achieving a culture of valuing diversity within the workplace. Process champions would be the first to receive the diversity training. Diversity training of process champions typically includes:

- participating in the diversity education training session as a regular participant,
- participating in a train the trainer program,
- participating in a mock training session,
- assisting a senior trainer in an actual training sessions, and
- delivering their own educational session.

The process champions become educators, role models and advocates of the culture of valuing diversity. It will be through support of these individuals that the culture within the organization can be achieved.

*Supporting valuing diversity within the organization.* Upon completion of a diversity training program, leaders must ensure that other organizational activities which support the valuing diversity culture are implemented. The following ongoing maintenance activities are suggested by Loden and Rosener (1991):

- periodic audits which examine organizational practices and their impact on diverse employees;
- periodic employee opinion surveys to identify emerging diversity issues and measure the effectiveness of the current practices; and
- annual surveys and feedback to individual managers to identify specific leadership strengths and areas needing improvement.

As part of the strategic planning process for achieving the culture of diversity the organization could establish diversity advisory groups. The task of such advisory groups is to help the organization move forward in valuing its diverse workforce. It is also beneficial to allow the formation of informal networks of people who will also have the opportunity to discuss diversity issues. These informal networks could be given the responsibility of advising the organization of the things which need to change (Fernandez, 1991; Hayles, 1994).

As the culture of the organization begins to change, the organization will likely go through certain predictable stages. For instance, as the organization begins its diversity work, there are likely to be more complaints and issues than usual. This occurs because the process provides a forum for discussion and resolution. In addition, as the first people of different races and cultures are promoted into leadership positions, and as the organization begins to hire more people who look different from the mainstream, the organization will need to continue to address issues of inclusion and diversity.

## CONCLUSION

As the workplace becomes increasingly diverse, leaders will be unable to defer implementation of valuing diversity programs. Valuing diversity makes sense not only from a social justice perspective but also from a labour market perspective. The costs to the organization of failing to effectively value the diversity within the workplace include, among other things, lost productivity, high turnover rates, limited innovation and underutilization of the skills of all employees. The costs to the individual working in an environment which fails to recognize and support their differences include such things as failure to develop to their full potential, increased stress from working in a negative environment, and low morale caused by conflicts and tensions among people from different groups. Studies have shown that fairness and equity, and a high quality of work life within the workplace, result in performance improvement. Organizations which support a culture of valuing diversity will do better.

The notion of change agent is not an unfamiliar one. Those who work towards achieving valuing diversity in their organizations are engaged in changing the culture of their organization. Organizations, like people, rarely change quickly. The leaders in the organization must be committed to the change process, willing to engage in the work necessary for success, and patient, recognizing that cultural change occurs slowly. After gathering information about the existing diversity within the organization, leaders should implement diversity education training programs. The goal of these programs is to educate all employees about diversity issues and to help people move through the developmental stages of valuing diversity. The goal of the valuing diversity program is to create an environment within the organization in which all employees have the good feelings associated with belonging, while recognizing that all people are different.

Wherever valuing diversity has been a success, the very top levels of managers and the senior managers have endorsed the philosophy and communicated their support throughout the organization. Such transformational leaders have a commitment to encourage each employee to participate in the success of the organization and to achieve at their highest level. Valuing diversity is a legitimate leadership philosophy that is taking its place among other transformational leadership philosophies.

## REFERENCES

Abella, R. (1984). *Equality in employment: A royal commission report.* Ottawa, Ontario: Canadian Government Publishing.

Alberta Career and Development. (1989). *The Alberta Workforce in the Year 2000.* Edmonton.

City of Calgary. (1992). *Employment equity data for the city of Calgary.* Equal Employment Opportunity Division. The City of Calgary, Alberta.

Cleghorn, John E. (1992). Diversity: The key to quality. In Alberta Citizenship and Heritage Secretariat, *Managing diversity: The quality imperative.* Calgary, Alberta.

Clifton, R and Roberts, L. (1982). Exploring the ideology of Canadian multiculturalism. *Canadian Public Policy*, 8, 1, winter, 88-94.

Fallick, A. (1991). People, jobs and immigration: A study of Canada's future workforce. (Unpublished Technical Report prepared for the Laurier Institute, Ottawa, Ontario.)

Fernandez, J. (1991). *Managing a diverse workforce: Regaining the competitive edge.* Toronto, Ontario: Lexington Books. D.C. Heath Company.

Francis, A. K. (1992). Employment equity and workplace diversity at Xerox Canada. In Alberta Citizenship and Heritage Secretariat, *Managing diversity: The quality imperative.* Calgary, Alberta.

Hayles, R. (1994). Keynote address in "Symposium 94: Managing Diversity," Alberta Multi-Cultural Commission.

Health and Welfare Canada. (1990). *Charting Canada's future: A report of the demographic review.* Ottawa, Ontario: Minister of Supply and Services.

Herberg, D.C. (1985). Social work with new immigrants. In S.A.Yelaja. (ed.), *Social work practice in Canada.* Scarborough, Ontario: Prentice-Hall.

Jamieson, D. and O'Mara, J. (1991). *Managing workforce 2000.* San Francisco, CA: Jossey-Bass.

Loden, M. and Rosener, J. (1991). *Workforce America: Managing employee diversity as a vital resource.* Homewood, Illinois: Business One Irwin.

Malmquist, Lynne. (1993). *Managing diversity within the City of Calgary.* Equal Employment Opportunity Division, The City of Calgary, Alberta.

Minna, M. (1986). Focus on gaps in services for immigrant and visible minority communities. Toronto, Ontario. (Unpublished Paper prepared for Multiculturalism Directorate and Secretary of State Department)

Philip, Zac. (1989). Interaction management of a multicultural workforce: A preliminary study with particular reference to people of South Asian origin. In *Management 2000*, Calgary, Alberta.

Taylor, C. (1995). *Dimensions of diversity in Canadian business: Building a case for valuing ethnocultural diversity.* The Conference Board of Canada, Canada.

Workplace Innovations Inc., Calgary. (1993). Diversity initiatives. In The Alberta Citizenship and Heritage Secretariat, *Managing diversity: The quality imperative.* Calgary, Alberta.

# CHAPTER 9

# Cross-Cultural Supervision: From Differences that Divide to Strength in Diversity

*Carol Ing and Peter Gabor*

Canada is a racially and ethnoculturally diverse society made up of a variety of Aboriginal groups, English- and French-speaking populations, and a wide spectrum of visible and non-visible minority groups. Many of these groups immigrated to Canada during the past 150 years. At the time of Confederation, excluding the Aboriginal population, Canada's population consisted of 60% British and 40% French. By 1986, Canadian census indicated that the population had changed to 24.4% French, 33.6% British and 37.5% a variety of ethnic backgrounds such as German, Italian, Ukrainian, Caribbean, Hungarian, Chinese, Japanese and so on. First Nations groups constitute about 4% of Canada's population, totalling close to 1.2 million people. These statistics include status Indians living on and off reserves, non-status Indians, Metis and Inuit.

Statistics Canada's census figures indicate that in 1991 two-thirds of immigrants to Canada were Chinese, blacks or South Asians. The largest concentration of visible minority groups live in Toronto (40%), Vancouver (15%) and Montreal (14%) (Kelly, 1995). As these figures suggest, the fastest increase in population today comes from visible minority groups. Statistics Canada expects the number of visible minorities to triple by 2016, representing 20% of the adult population. Such diversity will, of course, be reflected in the workplace and hence in the supervisory process.

Traditional views of supervision have focused on concrete supervisory functions such as program implementation, monitoring and evaluation. However, these functions are only one part of the supervisory process. Supervision also entails interpersonal processes, the dynamic and complex process of interactions which involves giving and receiving feedback, communicating role and job expectations, support, leadership and personal influence (Evera and Lazar, 1994; Ing, 1990; Kadushin, 1992). Supervision is central for professional development in social work and is a major contributor to quality of work, job satisfaction, staff morale and the reduction of burnout (Munson, 1983, 1989). By paying attention to the relationship-oriented aspects of their work, supervisors can become more effective leaders.

Culture is one dimension of the interpersonal process in supervision that is often overlooked. Most supervisors use a single interpersonal approach in most situations and do not take into consideration cultural differences among workers. The reality is that cultural diversity is a fact of life and supervisors can not ignore the issue of culture in their work environment. A major thesis of this chapter is that culturally sensitive supervisors can better establish the necessary conditions for effective supervisory relationships. They will not only help their workers to learn and grow in supervision but indirectly help the clients they serve. By being culturally sensitive they model the skills and knowledge base for working with different client groups.

This chapter will examine cross-cultural supervision. First it will provide an overview of intercultural communication and examine how culture affects the supervisory process. These effects will then be illustrated through the use of a case example. Finally the development of cultural competence and responsiveness among supervisors will be considered. By becoming both culturally competent and responsive, supervisors can individualize their approaches to staff members and better influence learning, development and performance. This, in turn, will help supervisors better accomplish the task-oriented functions associated with their job.

This chapter is not meant to provide a comprehensive treatment of all the ramifications of cross-cultural supervision, which is complex and a large field. Our aim is more limited: to focus on cultural issues in supervisory relationships and communications. Also we have not attempted to be comprehensive in our treatment of cultural groups, rather we have selected some specific examples for illustrative purposes.

## An Overview of Intercultural Communication

Before proceeding further, it is important to discuss the concept of culture and how it influences communications and interactions. Culture is a set of values, beliefs, behaviours, modes of communication and thought processes that is learned and exhibited by a specific group (O'Neil, 1984). Each element helps to form the way people think and feel about life experiences. It is best thought of as a filter through which a person views his or her environment. Porter and Samavor (1985) believe that culture and communication are inseparable since communication behaviours are developed within the culture in which people are raised. Different cultures, therefore, support different communication practices (Porter and Samavor, 1985).

In understanding the impacts of culture and communication it is important to realize that people retain their culture and traditional beliefs, values and customs in varying degrees when they emigrate. Once the initial shock has worn off, people begin the process of learning and adapting to the new culture. The behaviours associated with this new culture may be quite different from those learned in the original culture. The process of acculturation or adaptation will vary for each individual or family. Some will quickly adapt to mainstream society, accept the new culture's customs and become involved in the host culture and its institutions such as education, recreation and politics. Others will take a longer time to acculturate. Acculturation does not necessarily correlate with length of residence in Canada, nor does integration in one area mean assimilation in all areas (Okabe, Takahashi and Richardson, 1990). For example, a third generation immigrant may be integrated linguistically but may resort to traditional remedies during times of illness.

In their "Model of Intercultural Communication," Porter and Samavor (1985) present a useful model for understanding many of the underlying interpersonal dynamics in intercultural communication. They state that there are three core characteristics that combine to influence intercultural communication: perception, verbal behaviours and non-verbal behaviours. Figure 1 adapts Porter and Samavor's model and shows how culture influences communications and interpersonal processes.

### Perceptions

Perceptions underlie communications and interactions. This is the process by which people select, evaluate and organize information about

```
┌─────────────────────────────────────────────────────────────┐
│ Figure 1: A Model of Intercultural Communication             │
├─────────────────────────────────────────────────────────────┤
│                                                               │
│        Values          World View      Social Organization   │
│                                                               │
│                       Perceptions                            │
│                                                               │
│                                                               │
│                       Intercultural                          │
│                       Communication                          │
│                                                               │
│                                                               │
│           Verbal                      Non-verbal             │
│      Language   Thinking      Gestures Proximity Time  Facial │
│                                                    Expressions│
│                                                               │
│   After Porter and Samavor (1985)                            │
│                                                               │
└─────────────────────────────────────────────────────────────┘
```

the world around them. Perceptions act as a filter through which the world is viewed. Through the process of perception, people select information from a wealth of data and experiences; they pay attention to some and discard others, then organize and interpret this information into a frame of reference.

This frame of reference, which influences communications, consists of the following elements: values, world view and social organization (Porter and Samavor, 1985). Values are peoples' feelings and attitudes about life that influence and dominate the way people interact. Cultural values are derived from the environment within which people live. Values specify which behaviours are important and provide a code of conduct; they are expressed through verbal and non-verbal behaviours. For example, many people in Canada have been taught by their parents to say "please" when asking for something and "thank you" when receiving something. Manners are valued by people and provide a guide for individual and group behaviour.

Every culture also has a world view—a set of assumptions which explains the nature of mankind. It deals with people's orientation towards life. Examples of world view includes complex philosophical issues such as God, humanity or religion. World views influence values and affect how cultural groups think, make decisions, behave and define events (Sue, 1981). According to Porter and Samavor (1985), "our world view helps locate our place and rank in the universe...and represents the most fundamental basis of a culture" (p. 28).

An example of world view as an intercultural variable which affects many practices, attitudes, values and interpersonal communicative behaviours may be seen in many traditional First Nations cultures where there is a strong the concept of equality of land and a view of earth as Mother Nature. In traditional native view, the earth is the mother of all, therefore individual ownership of land is not culturally appropriate. Time is viewed as a circular in character, like the seasons, and therefore is not rigidly structured. Events begin when everyone is present. These views are quite different from many Western cultures where land is to be acquired and events are expected to start at a scheduled time.

Each culture also has its own unique social organization. Social organization refers to the manner in which a culture organizes itself and its institutions such as family, school and work. For example, in Japanese society conformity to rules of conduct and family wishes takes precedence over individual needs. The father is the person with the most authority, with the daughters ranked lowest within the family (Okabe et al., 1990). Also, as seen in many Asian cultures, children learn early in life the importance of family. In these cultures there is a great emphasis on not letting down one's parents; children and families gear their behaviours and decisions to parental expectations. In Canadian society kinship and friendship are regarded as basic human attachments while in countries such as Japan, relationship to the work group is of primary importance and people's social life is usually concentrated primarily within the place of work. With group consciousness so developed there is little room for individualization (Nakane, 1970).

These cultural differences are illustrated in a research study in which Michael Morris, a behavioural researcher at Stanford University, found that Westerners tend to interpret human behaviour individualistically, while Asians interpret actions in a social context. He showed a videotape of one fish leaving a group. Asian students interpreted the scene as the fish being ousted from the group while American students viewed the fish as choosing to leave the group. (*Globe and Mail*, June 21, 1995).

## Verbal processes and thought patterns

Verbal processes include not only spoken language but patterns of thought, which then gives meaning to the language people use (Porter and Samovar, 1985). Language is the primary way a culture communicates its values and beliefs and influences the way people think. Each culture has its own labels, word symbols and meanings. For example, in Japan the word "*hai*" or "yes" in its primary context simply means the other person has heard what was said and is thinking about a response. It is considered to be rude to not make an immediate reply. In Canadian society, by contrast, a "yes" response means agreement. Such differences can be quite confusing and lead to serious misunderstandings.

According to Porter and Samavor (1985), every culture also follows its own pattern of thought or way of thinking. For example, in Western cultures truth is viewed as an external reality, waiting to be discovered, while in Eastern cultures truth is not external but will often reveal itself as a situation develops. Thus people from Western cultures will tend to be active and assertive when dealing with controversial issues, while those from the East often value waiting, letting events unfold. Without understanding the cultural issues involved, each culture may negatively judge the other's approach to a problem.

## Non-verbal processes

While cultural groups do transmit a great deal of information through spoken words, they also communicate through the unspoken language of gazes, expressions, body movements and physical space (Knapp, 1978). Porter and Samavor (1985, p. 26) state: "as a component of culture, nonverbal expression has much in common with language...each is a coding system." Non-verbal communication is very strongly based in culture. For example, the use of gestures, space, facial expressions, tone of voice, rate of speech and gesturing with hands are culturally determined. Without understanding the cultural background of an individual, it is all too easy to misinterpret non-verbal communication. Many Canadians of European background feel comfortable socially talking with others at a distance of four feet. On the other hand, Arabs, Latin Americans, Africans and Indonesians prefer to stand closer to people when conversing. As a result, these ethnic groups may perceive European Canadians as cold and distant. In contrast European Canadians may view these ethnic groups' behaviour as intrusive and infringing on their personal space.

In the same way, cultural groups develop non-verbal means of communication for expressing thoughts and feelings. Knapp (1978) found that persons of European background rely heavily on eye contact, which in their culture demonstrates listening. Thus, in Canada, many people are taught from birth to maintain eye contact as a way of demonstrating respect and interest. Yet, some cultures, like many First Nation tribes, use more peripheral vision when discussing problems, eye contact is not practiced. Among some groups direct stares are considered hostile. As may be seen, non-verbal communication operates under very complex rules. Without understanding these, it is all too easy to misinterpret non-verbal behaviours.

## How Culture Impacts the Supervisory Process

One key issue often overlooked in supervision is cultural diversity. Despite the often unspoken assumption that all social workers are basically similar, there are important differences arising from cultural diversity. Until recently in the human services, cultural blindness has been the guiding response; the yardstick of middle-class values and customs was frequently used as a standard for understanding and working with people (Pinderhughes, 1989). Indeed, social work practitioners have traditionally been concerned with developing a "generalist" framework to be applied to all cultural groups (Lum, 1992).

Since Canada is an increasingly diverse society, social workers also come from a variety of cultural backgrounds. They bring to the workplace differences in culture, language, physical appearance and identity. Some have recently immigrated, while others come from families that have lived in Canada for many generations. Cultural differences may not always be visible, but all have been conditioned by their cultural history as attitudes, values and beliefs pass from generation to generation.

Culture pervades every aspect of work life: values, ethics, attitudes towards others and interpersonal relationships. As long as social workers and supervisors from different cultures encounter one another, there will be differences in the way they communicate information, ideas and feelings. When not understood, differences can result in confused and negative perceptions towards others; they can create barriers to communication and result in conflicts. Such conflicts can prompt supervisors and social workers to behave in dysfunctional ways, compromising both the interpersonal processes and concrete tasks of supervision.

It is obviously important to understand how culturally based perceptions and experiences affect the supervisory process. The more a supervisor knows about a worker's cultural background, the greater the opportunity to engage in a constructive supervisory process. As role models, supervisors need the ability to understand and communicate effectively across cultural barriers, to demonstrate an openness to and acceptance of differences and to help staff members to develop these same skills and attitudes.

## Views of self and role

The supervisory process is anchored in communications between supervisors and workers. The obvious and visible part of this relationship is communication about substantive matters: exchanging information, providing feedback and making requests. At the same time, as in all human communications, there is a less visible but equally important aspect to supervisory communications. Both supervisors and workers hold a sense of self and a view of their roles and responsibilities and these two are communicated, often in a non-verbal manner. Both supervisors' and workers' views of self are influenced by their culturally based experiences. This sense of self, in turn, influences their perceptions and expectations.

Most Canadians' sense of self is shaped by the Western cultural value of individualization and independence. However, individuals in many other cultures have a sense of self that is shaped by a cultural view which values interdependence rather than individualization. Most Canadian supervisors will likely value and encourage independent functioning on the part of their workers while supervisors from Eastern cultural backgrounds will tend to value team work and emphasize the importance of interdependence. Obviously, these differences in views of self, if not understood, can easily lead to misunderstanding and conflict.

The culturally shaped sense of self can influence workers' perceptions and expectations of their work role. For example, in South Asian, European and Arab cultures men are traditionally viewed as leaders, providers and decision-makers while women are considered to be homemakers and caregivers. As may be surmised, male social workers from such traditional societies are not likely, at the outset, to feel comfortable when supervised by a woman. They may be reluctant to engage in the supervisory relationship or even resist and challenge female supervisors. Correspondingly, women from these cultures may initially feel uneasy in leadership positions, especially if called upon to supervise men.

A culturally influenced sense of self and perception of role can result in misunderstandings and create difficulties in the supervisory process. Effective communication is the means through which supervisors and social workers can reach an understanding of each other, learn more about each other and gain trust in one another. Clear, accurate communications help to build the supervisory relationship and avoid misunderstandings.

## Communication pitfalls

Although most people in the helping professions possess effective communication skills, difficulties can arise when supervisors and workers do not take into consideration culturally influenced communication patterns. In such situations, the very means intended to bridge cultural misunderstandings—communication—can actually further divide.

The following examples illustrate the influence of cultural background on communication and show how misunderstandings between supervisors and workers can easily result from a lack of understanding of these culturally based communication patterns.

Most Canadians believe that eye contact is important to demonstrate attention and respect. In Arab countries, too, eye contract connotes interest. On the other hand, traditionally raised West Indian adults and children learn that direct eye contact with elders and persons in authority is not polite. Unless knowledgeable about West Indian culture, the Canadian supervisor may misinterpret the avoidance of eye contact. Indeed, Glasgow and Adaskin (1990) have found that people brought up in traditional West Indian culture may be viewed as bored, evasive or fearful for not maintaining eye contact.

Another key issue is the strong value social work places on expressing thoughts and feelings. Typically, supervisors encourage workers to share their feelings. Yet this style is not appropriate to all cultural groups. For example, expressing feelings and concerns may run contrary to the cultural background of Native social workers, and what may appear as resistance and a lack of openness is actually a case of cultural difference. Communication styles that emphasize minimal encouragers, summarization, restatement and reflection of feelings—very common communication skills in Western cultures—will be of limited use with Native social workers who may feel uncomfortable discussing personal issues. Instead, supervisors should display trustworthy behaviours such as being attentive, responsive and respectful to the worker, provide structure and direction to the interview and demonstrate respect for the native social worker's cultural identity (LaFromboise, Trimble, Mohatt, 1993).

Words too have different meanings in different cultures. For the Japanese, direct expression of disagreement or conflict is discouraged as interpersonal harmony and cooperation are highly valued. Confusion and misunderstanding can occur when a supervisor does not understand that a Japanese social worker may express disagreement subtly, by looking doubtful, but still respond positively to the supervisor's comments or suggestions to indicate that he or she has heard the statement.

Other examples could be provided of situations where culture influences the meaning of communications. Indeed, it is important not to generalize too broadly across specific cultural groups. For example, Canada is home to a variety of Aboriginal peoples including status Indians, non-status Indians, Metis and Inuit. In turn, the status Indians belong to one of 596 bands on 2283 reserves (Dickason, 1994). Although these groups may share basic core values and beliefs, there are important cultural differences from tribe to tribe, and the extent of acculturation varies. Thus, it can not be assumed that verbal and non-verbal communications have the same meaning across the entire Aboriginal population.

## CASE ILLUSTRATION

Jack became the supervisor in a program which was changing its mandate and operations due to cuts in funding. It was decided to reorientate programming direction towards family support interventions and to increase case level and program level evaluation activities in order to meet funders' accountability requirements. Senior administration asked Jack and his team of social workers to design a training program and train staff to meet the new mandate.

Jack is an energetic, enthusiastic person who thinks fast and gets staff motivated. He is highly organized and is meticulous in his work; he approaches all tasks systematically and logically. His supervisory style leans towards authoritarian as he likes his staff to listen to him and expects staff members to conform to policies and expectations. However, Jack is popular with staff members because of his charisma and energy, at the same time they would like him to provide more guidance and support, especially when contentious issues occur. In times of conflict, they have found it hard to figure him out as he rarely expresses his thoughts and feelings and tends to be quiet and pensive. Jack is well liked by administration because of his organizational skills, ability to visualize new trends and proven ability to get the job done.

Jack's family on his mother's side came from China in 1900; now fourth generation, the family is well acculturated into Canadian society. Jack's mother spoke little Chinese and was a very outgoing, vivacious individual. She liked to follow the fashions of the day and was active in the community. His father, on the other hand, came from China as a young man. He had to pay a head tax to live in Canada and was not allowed to bring any of his family from China. Jack's father lived in Toronto where he worked in the restaurant business. He married Jack's mother when he was forty and continued to work hard, often admonishing Jack that "to be successful you need to do well in school and work hard." Jack's father set an example of hard work; indeed, Jack seldom saw him except on his rare days off.

Jack remembers a number of cultural celebrations from his childhood. He remembers holidays such as Chinese New Year and the dragon and moon festivals. He looks back with particular fondness to the banquets and lion dances. He remembers little of his grandparents except that they spoke Chinese to him and always brought Chinese candy when they visited. Jack recalls that throughout his childhood many of his nine aunts and uncles lived with his family at one time or another. Now they all live within a few blocks of each other. His playmates and closest friends were his cousins, who were also the only other Chinese children in the school he attended.

The staff members in Jack's unit come from different ethnic backgrounds. One social worker, Fatima, comes from an Iranian background. In Iran, the family had belonged to an affluent urban class. Fatima never had to do household chores since there were servants in the home. Back home the family had confined themselves to their own social class and would not socialize with persons from lower classes. When Fatima was still an adolescent, the family had to leave Iran because of political persecution.

In Canada, Fatima's parents attempted to maintain their cultural traditions. Fatima, on the other hand, attempted to adopt North American ways to gain popularity with her peers, but her parents frowned on this lifestyle. They continued to stress the value of their cultural traditions and emphasized the importance of a university education for her brother and her. They were expected to achieve high grades and to do well in all areas of their lives. Ultimately, Fatima received her M.S.W. and her brother became a lawyer.

At work, Fatima is friendly and agreeable with some people and usually defers to people in authority. However, Jack has observed Fatima becoming impatient when people do not come to the point quickly or understand her explanations. She has been abrupt in dealing with some co-workers, saying: "What are you trying to say?" or "Get to the point." Several of her colleagues feel that Fatima talks down to them. Jack also has the feeling of being talked down to, although Fatima has always been overtly polite to him.

Fatima is not particularly concerned about timelines. She is rarely at work on time and is not punctual for meetings. Even when late for a meeting, she will stop to socialize with certain colleagues. The lack of concern about timelines extends to completing job responsibilities on schedule. The quality of Fatima's work is excellent, but she often misses deadlines.

Jack has found Fatima difficult to supervise. Although he considers her to be creative, skilled and knowledgeable, particularly in evaluation techniques, she does not seem to respond well to his feedback. He is particularly irritated by her failure to keep to timelines and has spoken to her several times about being on time for meetings and respecting deadlines. When they get into a discussion, Jack finds Fatima's style of communication irritating and difficult to accept.

Jack has sensed that, with each encounter, his relationship with Fatima has become more strained. They seem to have less respect and liking for each other. He is suspicious of Fatima's motives and senses that she, in turn, does not trust him. At the same time, Jack realizes that Fatima could be a valuable contributor to the project, particularly in establishing evaluation procedures. He realizes that with his own energy and strengths in organization and implementation and Fatima's knowledge and skills in evaluation, they can compliment one another and make an effective team. His challenge is to find a way to communicate more effectively with Fatima in order to promote a better working relationship.

Jack and Fatima are like two ships in the night; they may pass through the same waters, but they do not affect each other. This is not a constructive situation. A productive supervisory relationship is interactive and requires positive personal relationships as well as effective communications. The following section will address some of the issues involved in cross-cultural supervision and describe some of the skills required for culturally competent supervision. These skills could contribute to bettering the supervisory relationship between Jack and Fatima.

## THE CULTURALLY COMPETENT SUPERVISOR

Because social services employees are culturally diverse, the supervisory process has become increasingly complex. Attention to culture and its impact on the supervisory process increases the probability of more effective supervision. Cultural sensitivity can help supervisors understand people and communicate effectively, thereby reducing the possibility of misunderstanding, conflict and tension arising from cultural differences. Culturally competent supervision involves knowledge, attitudes, self-awareness, communication skills and helping staff members develop cultural competence.

### Knowledge

At a general level, culturally competent supervisors need an understanding of the role of culture in interpersonal communications and relationships, and in the supervisory process specifically. It is important that they understand how people's cultural backgrounds help shape their personalities and behaviours and how culture filters communications and perceptions. Supervisors also need to be aware of the potentially distorting effects on communications when those cultural differences are not understood or misunderstood. In short, supervisors need an understanding of the issues discussed in earlier parts of this paper as a general knowledge base for culturally competent supervision.

At the more specific level, individuals engaged in interactions with people from different cultures need as complete an understanding as is possible of the specific world views, perceptions, communication and behaviour patterns fostered by that culture. Because the supervisory process is one that is highly interactive, supervisors need to develop an understanding of the cultural backgrounds of the individuals they supervise. Understanding the meaning of the general world view as well as verbal and non-verbal behaviours supported by a culture helps to increase the possibility of more constructive interactions between supervisors and workers.

As the case example suggests, Jack did not really understand Fatima's cultural background and consequently misinterpreted her communications and behaviours. Predictably, relations between Fatima and him deteriorated. By understanding the cultural background that shaped Fatima's communication and behaviour patterns, Jack could have helped Fatima to better adjust to the culture of the agency, while at the same time creating a better understanding among staff members of Fatima's interpersonal style.

## Attitudes

People often regard cultural differences as posing barriers to effective communications and relationships. Indeed, where cultural differences are not understood they can raise fear and mistrust. Consequently, a natural reaction is to view differences in a negative manner. A more constructive attitude is to regard the differences inherent in diversity as an asset. As steel is strengthened by combining iron and carbon so, too, the staff complement of an organization can be strengthened by employing individuals from different cultural backgrounds. This perspective requires accepting diversity and valuing it; looking at cultural differences not as sources of problems but rather as sources of strength. Such acceptance leads to a framework where it is accepted that everyone comes from a cultural background, not just minority social workers.

Attitudes of acceptance and openness are indispensable to effective cross-cultural supervision. These attitudes lead to a desire to understand each worker as an individual rather than as a stereotype viewed through barely understood cultural filters. Acceptance and openness also lead to flexibility in the supervisory approach. The objective is to assist each worker to develop his or her unique potentials rather than attempt to make everyone fit into the mould of the dominant culture.

In the case illustration above, Jack interacts with Fatima from his own cultural frame of reference and has little understanding of hers. Conformity is valued in Asian cultures and the agency culture values timeliness. Thus Jack expects Fatima to conform to the official start of the workday, even when no meetings are scheduled. A more flexible approach would involve helping Fatima to meet expectations about timeliness when important events are scheduled as well as becoming more flexible about the starting time of the workday when there are no formally scheduled events. In short, the supervisor could help the worker adapt to the needs of the organization and at the same time adapt the organization to the needs of the worker. This approach leads to a more productive and helpful supervisory relationship by recognizing workers' cultural values rather than treating those differences as negative performance indicators.

## Self-awareness

People's values are shaped by their cultural experiences. When interacting it is impossible for supervisors to be value free as values influence their attitudes, perceptions and behaviours. It is important for supervisors to be aware of their own cultural background and to be willing to examine how these can potentially impact the supervisory relationship. Cultural values that can enter the supervisory relationship include those relating to work ethics, work roles and interpersonal relationships. Supervisors need to be aware of how their own cultural values will impact their perceptions and judgments of workers and work situations.

In the case example, although acculturated to Canadian society, Jack still maintains some Asian values of conformity and respect for authority. His approach tends to be authoritarian and "by the book." He is not fully aware of how these values influence his expectations of his workers. Jack tends to judge negatively workers who argue an issue too strenuously or who do not show proper respect for policies and procedures. By examining his own culturally based values, and how these may affect his judgments and perceptions, Jack might have discovered that some of his perceptions of Fatima were not based on performance but on his own culturally based expectations.

## COMMUNICATION SKILLS

Attitudes of openness, acceptance and of valuing diversity all have to be communicated as part of the interactional process between supervisors and workers. Effective communication skills are essential to the creation of the positive working climate. Effective supervisors, therefore, have a wide modality of verbal and non-verbal responses. They can send and receive messages accurately, even through cultural filters. As can be expected, skills in both non-verbal and verbal communications are important.

As was discussed in earlier sections, the meaning of non-verbal communications can only be accurately understood within a cultural context. When Fatima comes late for work, she does not intend to communicate disrespect or a lack of motivation about her work. Coming late is acceptable and not an important matter in her culture. Because Jack is not skilled in deciphering this non-verbal behaviour within Fatima's cultural context, he tends to interpret it within the context of his own and the agency's values where such behaviours indicate disrespect and a lack of motivation.

It is clearly important for supervisors to develop competence in understanding non-verbal communications. Supervisors can not understand the meaning and ramifications of all non-verbal behaviours within all cultures, but they should be aware that the meaning of non-verbal behaviours is wrapped in cultural meanings. Thus, they should refrain from judgment and make every effort to learn about staff workers' cultures.

Similar issues arise in the case of verbal communications. Styles of verbal communication, for example, vary from culture to culture. In Western society, directness is highly valued yet, in many Asian cultures, directness is considered to be rude and disrespectful. In the case illustration, Jack's staff members are generally pleased with his performance, but they find it difficult when, in times of heated discussion, Jack becomes thoughtful and addresses the issues in an indirect manner. They have thus interpreted this behaviour as indicative of a lack of confidence and openness on the part of Jack. The workers do not realize, and Jack himself is probably unaware, that Jack's style of communication is probably based in his cultural background. Since Jack is in a leadership position, he needs to gain greater awareness of how he reacts in conflict situations. He can then attempt to adjust his own style in these situations, engaging with his staff and addressing the issues more directly.

### Helping staff develop cultural competence

In the last example, we showed how Jack could adjust his communication style to more effectively relate to staff members in situations of conflict. This approach was suggested because Jack is in a supervisory position and it is our view that those in leadership positions should take the initiative in facilitating intercultural communications. However, effective intercultural communications are not unidirectional. To the extent that all staff members within a work unit or organization can acquire cross-cultural competence, bridges can be built from all sides, resulting in greater harmony and productivity.

When organizations employ workers from different cultural backgrounds, it is not enough to simply bring them together and hope for the best. Casual contact among different cultural groups may actually reinforce stereotypes or create new ones. It is an organizational responsibility to develop intercultural awareness and skills among staff members so that all can contribute to a workplace that supports and encourages cultural sensitivity and understanding.

As key staff members, supervisors carry a special responsibility for developing cultural competence among staff members. First, supervisors should model, through their own sensitivity and skills, appropriate, respectful and effective cross-cultural relationships. In their role as teachers, they should address the role of culture in interpersonal relationships and the skills required to effectively bridge cross-cultural barriers. Further, they should assist and support staff members in their efforts to increase their cultural competence.

Opportunities to contribute to the development of cultural competence on the part of staff members may arise at various times and in various ways. When workers are dealing with clients or when issues arise between staff members, supervisors can help workers identify any underlying cultural issues. Supervisors can also encourage reflection and discussion about cultural issues in staff meetings and other forums. Finally, supervisors can represent, at more senior levels in the organization, specific training needs in the cross-cultural area.

## DEVELOPING A CULTURALLY COMPETENT ORGANIZATION

The supervisory position is particularly important in fostering cultural competence in the workplace. As important as their role is, however, supervisors can not do it alone. There must be a commitment at the organizational level to help and support supervisors' and other staff members' efforts.

A number of strategies are available at the organizational level. These include making an explicit commitment to valuing differences in the workplace. It is also important that the diversity of the workplace and of the clientele that the organization serves be reflected at senior staff levels, including governing and advisory boards. Training and education are key to developing cultural competence within an organization; this is explored in further detail below.

Providing multicultural training and education to staff members involves a number of objectives. First, it is important to help staff members become comfortable with differences that exist among them. Second, training can assist supervisors and workers to gain an understanding of themselves and their own cultural values and biases while becoming sensitive to other cultures. Third, training can provide workers with an appreciation of issues in intercultural relationships. Finally, education and training can help to build staff members' knowledge and skills in cross-cultural communications.

Coverage of multiculturalism can be provided through formal courses or through in-service workshops. Instructional strategies may include: experiential and self-awareness exercises, role playing and simulations, modelling and observational learning, diaries, logs and supervised experiences.

The following are some of the core components for multicultural training (Corey, Corey and Callanan, 1993; Sue, 1981; Pedersen, 1986; Ridley, Mendoza, Kanitz, 1994):

1. Beliefs and attitudes of culturally competent workers:
   - Workers become aware of their own cultural attitudes, values and beliefs and how these affect working and helping relationships;
   - Workers learn to appreciate cultural diversity and develop a belief that diversity can contribute to both working relationships as well as to effective service provision.
2. Knowledge of cultural issues:
   - Workers learn to understand the cultural factors that may influence working and helping relationships;

- Workers learn to understand the value assumptions of different cultural groups;
- Workers acquire knowledge about specific cultural history, values, customs and communication styles; and
- Workers develop an awareness of effective cultural communication methods.
3. Cultural skills:
- Workers learn to adapt or modify the skills needed to communicate and relate effectively with individuals from different cultures.

## SUMMARY

A key component of supervision is the interpersonal process that occurs between the supervisor and the social worker. Most supervisors use a single approach in relating to and communicating with workers and do not take into consideration their cultural backgrounds. Consequently, communications between supervisors and workers may be inaccurate and misunderstandings can occur.

When supervisors have a basis for understanding their own and their worker's culturally based attitudes, beliefs and communication styles, the supervisory process is more likely to be effective. Culturally competent supervisors use this awareness to ensure accurate communications and to help build effective relationships with their workers. The result is an enhanced supervisory process that can help workers develop and grow as professionals, which results in a more harmonious workplace and ultimately benefits clients through improved service provision.

## REFERENCES

Corey, G., Corey, M.S. and Callanan, P. (1993). *Issues and ethics in the helping professions* (4th ed.). Pacific Groves, CA:Brooks/Coles.

Dickason, O.P. (1994). *Canada's first nations: A history of founding peoples from earliest times.* Toronto, ON: McClelland and Stewart Inc.

Evera, I.P. and Lazar, A. (1994). The administrative and educational functions in supervision: Indications of incompatibility. *The Clinical Supervisor,* 12(2), 39-55.

Glasgow, J.H. and Adaskin, E.J. (1990). The west indians. In N. Waxler-Morrison, J. Andersen, E. Richardson (eds.), *Cross-cultural caring.* Vancouver, B.C: University of British Columbia Press.

*Globe and Mail*, June 21, 1995, A7.

Ing, C. (1990). The application of learning style research in the supervisory process. In J.P. Anglin, C.J. Denholm, R.V. Ferguson, A.R. Pence (eds.), *Perspectives in professional child and youth care*. New York: The Haworth Press.

Kadushin, A. (1992). Social work supervision: An updated survey. *The Clinical Supervisor*, 10(2), 9-27.

Kelly, K. (1995). Visible minorities: A diverse group. *Canadian Social Trends* (35) 2-14.

Knapp, M.L. (1978). *Nonverbal communication in human interaction* (2nd ed.). New York: Holt Rinehart and Winston.

LaFromboise, T.D., Trimble, J.E., Mohatt, G.V. (1993). Counselling intervention and the American Indian tradition: An integrative approach. In D.R. Atkinson, G. Morten, D.W. Sue (eds.), *Counselling American minorities*. Dubuque, IA: Brown and Benchmark. (Reprint from *The Counselling Psychologist*, 18(4), (628-654). Sage Publications).

Lum, D. (1992). *Social work practice and people with color: A process stage approach* (2nd ed.). Belmont, CA: Wadsworth.

Munson , C. (1983). *An introduction to clinical social work supervision*. New York: The Haworth Press, Inc.

Munson, C. (1989). Trends of significance for clinical supervision. *The Clinical Supervisor*, 7(4), 1-8.

Nakane, C. (1970). *Japanese society*. Los Angeles, CA: University of California Press.

O'Neil, J. (1984). *The general method of social work practice*. Englewood Cliffs, NJ: Prentice-Hall Inc.

Okabe, T., Takahashi, K. and Richardson, E. (1990). The Japanese. In N. Waxler-Morrison, J. Anderson and E. Richardson (eds.), *Cross-cultural caring*. Vancouver, B.C.: University of British Columbia Press.

Pedersen, P. (1986). Developing interculturally skilled counsellors: A prototype for training. In H.P. Lefley and P. Pedersen (eds.), *Cross-cultural training for mental health professionals*. Springfield, IL: Charles C. Thomas.

Pinderhughes, E. (1989). *Understanding race, ethnicity and power: The key to efficacy in clinical practice*. New York, NY: The Free Press.

Porter, R.E. and Samovar, L.A. (1985). Approaching intercultural communication. In L.A. Samovar, and R.E. Porter, (eds.), *Intercultural communication: A reader* (4th ed.). Belmont, CA: Wadsworth.

Ridley, C.R., Mendoza, D.W., Kanitz, B.E. (1994). Multicultural training: reexamination, operationalization, and integration. *The Counselling Psychologist*, 22 (2), 227-289.

Sarick, L. and Koring, P. (1995). Rise in immigration level planned. (1995, November, 2). *The Globe and Mail*. p. A6.

Sue, D.W. (1981). *Counselling the culturally different: Theory and practice*. Toronto, ON: John Wiley and Sons.

Sue, D.W. and Sue, D. (1981). Barriers to effective cross-cultural counselling. In D.W. Sue *Counselling the culturally different: Theory and practice*. Toronto, ON: John Wiley and Sons. (Reprinted from *Journal of Counselling Psychology*, 24, (420-429).

# CHAPTER 10

# Bridging the Gap:
# A Cross-cultural Counselling Program

*Magdalena Amestica, Hilde Houlding,*
*Elsbieta Kiegler and Hadassah Ksienski*

## INTRODUCTION

This chapter focuses on a practical partnership model for social service organizations that are struggling to meet the challenge of developing programs to effectively serve an increasingly diverse clientele. The model addresses the need to provide all members of an ethnoculturally diverse community access to counselling services offered by mainstream organizations and, conversely, to avert the pressure to create parallel service systems for immigrants.

The model was developed in response to the social and economic realities of the early 1990s, a period highlighted by massive cutbacks in both provincial and federal funding of social service programs. The cutbacks were accompanied by escalating pressure on community-based organizations to be more creative in managing their diminishing resources and still continue services at existing levels to the community's most vulnerable and under-served members. Further, new initiatives to promote multicultural organizational change sponsored by the provincial government and the United Way of Calgary required that mainstream service providers be equipped to meet the needs of diverse cultural client groups, which until recently were served by public agencies.

To assist community-based social service agencies in preparing to deal with the complex demands of multicultural clients, the United Way of Calgary required all member agencies to conduct a comprehensive barrier analysis. The United Way also required agencies to develop a three-year plan to reduce identified systemic barriers for potential consumers to access the agencies' mandated services. The directive to agencies was to be more inclusive, effective and efficient in service delivery. Agencies were asked to review program goals and to develop measurable outcomes. They were also asked to identify service priorities and improve client access to programs and services.

The two organizations that entered into partnership to meet the challenge were the Calgary Immigrant Aid Society (CIAS), which provides comprehensive resettlement services to newcomers, and the Calgary Family Service Bureau (CFSB), which is an established counselling service provider in the community that independently identified the organizational goals that provided the basis for the partnership. CIAS was looking for new ways to meet the ever-changing needs of the 7500 new immigrants who arrive in the city every year. These newcomers require access to appropriate counselling services for issues related to the immigration process, post-traumatic stress disorders and difficulties arising from being victims of torture.

The need for mental health services to address resettlement issues escalated as the numbers of immigrants multiplied beyond the existing capabilities of service providers. The provision of mental health services were piecemeal and distributed across several different providers. In addition, these services were either physically inaccessible to or culturally inappropriate for the majority of immigrants and refugees. CIAS staff lacked confidence in the ability of mainstream counselling services to address the population's needs. This lack of confidence was related to outcomes associated with the *boomerang effect*, where clients referred to mainstream agencies returned to CIAS complaining that they did not receive appropriate counselling services. Already, CIAS settlement and integration workers were facing an uphill battle to appropriately identify clients' distress, develop awareness of the potential benefits of counselling, and link clients with appropriate resources.

CFSB was also looking for new ways to meet the counselling needs of new immigrants and refugees. The expectation that mainstream counsellors would provide service to members of other cultures raised ethical and competency concerns with the bureau. In addition, management and professional staff at the bureau had been strongly committed to the culture- and language-specific model introduced in the early 1980s as an effective alternative to cross-cultural counselling. For example, culture- and language-specific programs were available to the Chinese, Hispanic and Vietnamese communities; the disadvantage to this model was that it was resource intensive so that only a limited number of communities would be served.

However, this service structure provided no incentive for staff to seek training in cross-cultural counselling. The bureau needed to revamp its service delivery structure and to develop services that were culturally appropriate. It also needed to explore effective ways counsellors can relate to non-English-speaking immigrant clients through an interpreter. Significant cultural differences in family values and practices, and a lack of understanding of how to work with these differences, can create tension for counsellors and settlement and integration workers, as well as the immigrant clients.

The counsellors were looking for the appropriate forum within the bureau to address some critical needs: to express their need for training and becoming culturally responsive to clients; and to address the cultural biases inherent in Canadian counselling theories and practice. Already some counsellors were experiencing difficulties working with families whose cultural values conflicted with the feminist model of counselling.

## FACTORS PROMPTING THE PARTNERSHIP

Collaboration is defined as a process used to reach goals that could not be achieved as efficiently by any single organization (Bruner, 1991; Kagan et al., 1990). Gray's (1989) concept of collaboration as a vehicle for action learning guided the development of this project. The intent of this project was to shift the independently operating agencies providing specific services into a partnership with identified stake holders that would provide a wider selection of services. In the literature, collaborative partnerships are described as a continuum of organizational alliances ranging from informal operation to mergers.

For the partnership to be a successful one, prospective partner organizations were screened for certain criteria relative to the other organization:

- Clearly defined and distinct service mandates;
- Complementary service mandates;
- Clearly defined goals specific to its service mandates;
- Complementary goals;

- Compatibility in terms of organizational status and power;
- Collaborative partnership between the organizations would result in enhanced potential to achieve goals; and
- Strong potential for long-term benefits to both organizations, that is, increased levels of effective services to targeted client groups.

## Service mandates

CFSB has a mandate to provide counselling services to all persons in need of those services, and has expertise in the assessment of mental health issues, making appropriate resource referrals to community-based agencies, and ongoing consultation and debriefing on critical mental health issues. Similarly, CIAS has a service mandate to provide resettlement and cultural integration services to a diverse population of newcomers to Canada, such as the provision of interpreters and serving as cultural consultants to service providers.

## Complementary service mandates

The complementary nature of service roles and expertise of both organizations is self-evident. The overlapping service area for the organizations is working with immigrants. CFSB has a long history of providing generic counselling services to specific immigrant groups. On the other hand, CIAS employs settlement and integration workers representing twenty language groups and cultures. Settlement and integration workers not only serve as language and cultural interpreters to mainstream service providers, they are also the primary service provider to immigrants and refugees. They help newly arrived immigrants access needed resources from appropriate mainstream services. By pooling expert and skilled resources, both organizations hoped to transcend the barriers of language and culture to appropriately serve the immigrant community.

## Complementary organizational goals

Both agencies were committed to address systemic gaps in service, to remove barriers to services and to secure the necessary resources for underserved groups. CFSB wanted to improve access to and expand counselling services for monolingual multicultural individuals and families; to increase the number of culturally competent counsellors to develop a new approach to multicultural counselling. Likewise, CIAS wanted to enhance the skill levels of settlement and integration workers with respect to assessment, referrals and case management; and to do outreach through the design, development and implementation of *bridging* programs; to effectively promote its services among immigrant populations.

## Compatibility of status and power base

Significant differences in the power of partners to influence decision-making within the partnership and the wider community have been implicated in the literature as major factors adversely affecting emerging partnerships. There were no significant power and status differential issues between the two partner organizations in this project. Both organizations have well-established, multi-service mandates, diverse funding bases and long service records. However, in terms of responding to the directive to demonstrate increased access for clients from diverse cultural groups, CIAS had more experience working with immigrant populations and, as a consequence, better standing and credibility in the immigrant communities.

A status issue that needed to be addressed to minimize its potential to frustrate the partnership was the difference in the perceived status of professional counselling staff at CFSB, and the paraprofessional status of settlement and integration workers at CIAS. The response was to develop a team that would optimally combine the expertise of counsellors with the community knowledge, rapport and language skills of settlement and integration workers.

## Enhanced potential for both organizations to achieve their goals

For both Calgary Family Service Bureau and Calgary Immigrant Aid Society, it was clear that the partnership would only enhance their goal of providing counselling services to multicultural and monolingual clients unfamiliar with "talking therapy" as a beneficial intervention. Front-line staff of both organizations would participate in a structured "action learning" training program designed to promote team-building. They would also be oriented to a service model based on an understanding and appreciation of each organization's roles and expertise, the imperative for a multicultural perspective to shape new counselling approaches, and the importance of an enhanced cultural awareness sustained through an ongoing commitment to self-examination and agency-wide evaluation.

## Strong potential for long-term benefits

The period and the process of partnership development was also a period and process of learning for staff at the two organizations. They participated actively in identifying and reducing barriers to service created by differences in culture or language. Service protocols were developed, reviewed and adopted. Examples of projects that have emerged from the partnership contract between CIAS, CFSB and other social service providers are:

- Community-building projects with a strong mental health component to serve newly arrived immigrant and refugee groups (e.g., Serbian and Croatian immigrants from the former Yugoslavia);
- Expansion of existing services offered by the Calgary Language Bank and development of new specialized projects, e.g., Mosaic Family Resource Centre and Portable Solutions.

## PARTNERSHIP GOAL AND OBJECTIVES

The goal of the collaborative partnership was to reach underserved, visible minority individuals, families and communities using settlement and integration workers and counsellors working as teams. The goal-setting process began with a review of systemic gaps in service delivery in the area of counselling for immigrants and refugees. The need for such services was documented in *After The Door Has Been Opened*, the 1988 report of the Canadian Task Force on Mental Health Issues Affecting Immigrants and Refugees. The report also pointed to the indiscriminate nature of the stresses and strains of resettlement in a new country, which affect immigrants and refugees regardless of class, nationality or gender.

For many immigrants and refugees, the concept of counselling to relieve psychic stress is an alien one. In addition, many have been culturally conditioned not to "wash dirty linen in public;" hence, they are not used to seeking assistance from strangers. Further, even after they have been persuaded to "try" these services, many need information on available services and how to access them. Most existing ethno- or language-specific counselling programs, such as those serving the Chinese, Hispanic and Vietnamese communities and offered by CFSB, were developed in response to the size of total ethnic group to ensure the availability of a critical mass of clients who would support those services. Few programs were available to immigrant and refugee populations whose relatively small numbers could not support ethno- and language-specific services. Thus, by pooling resources of at least two organizations, it is hoped that social services would become available and accessible to all immigrant and refugee populations.

The partnership integration process presented a big challenge; some staff perceived the process as a threat to the established way that service was provided by both organizations. Several objectives were identified to facilitate goal accomplishment:

- Implement a cross-cultural, single-issue counselling model with a training component for the staff of the two agencies;
- Reduce agency-based cultural and language barriers to counselling;
- Expand awareness and openness towards alternative counselling approaches;
- Develop a referral process for both agencies; and
- Form a meaningful and sustainable working relationship between CIAS settlement and integration workers and CFSB counsellors.

## PARTNERSHIP STRUCTURE

Both partner organizations reviewed and approved statements articulating the common vision of the partnership. They also reviewed and approved the conceptual framework that would structure partnership policies and practices, including service delivery. CFSB assumed the responsibility of banker, that is, ensuring accountability of monies allocated by the United Way of Calgary to fund partnership projects and activities. Each partner agency was responsible for the allocation of adequate project resources, such as assigning staff, including the counsellors, settlement and integration workers, management and support services, to ensure that the agency would achieve stated service objectives. In addition, each agency appointed a project coordinator to administratively manage staff and service resources within the organization. The two coordinators worked as a team to oversee the implementation of the project, coordinate the community consultation and facilitate staff training.

Initially, three counsellors were assigned to the project for two hours a week. Within a year, four more counsellors were added to the project. The increase in number of staff designations to the project was a result of the client response that occurred.

The settlement and integration worker's role in the project was to identify needs, refer clients to the project, serve as interpreters and cultural consultants, provide follow-up services to clients and channel feedback from immigrant communities to counsellors. Counsellors were entrusted with assessing clients' presenting issues, providing culturally appropriate interventions, follow-up on clients and serve as consultants to settlement and integration workers. The clientele were previously under-served groups of immigrants and refugees and who needed ethnic- and language-specific counselling services.

The project was implemented in two stages. During the first stage the staff received multicultural competence training, and the second stage focused on team building and implementing the single issue cross-cultural counselling service. The single issue concept does not reduce the complexity of clients' service needs, but it does provide a single focus for intervention. The first stage took nine months, and the second stage has been a continuous process. Team building will need to continue to be a priority goal for partner organizations to sustain the partnership, to accommodate staff changes, to respond to continuous changes in service needs presented by a mobile client population, and to incorporate new knowledge and skills in the emergent field of multicultural competence.

## DEVELOPMENT AND IMPLEMENTATION OF THE TRAINING MODEL

Sessions designed to prepare staff for the changes associated with the establishment of the partnership were referred to as *training* sessions. Every effort was made to insure staff participation in all phases of the development of the new service model. Training goals included the following:

- Provide counsellors with information on various diverse cultures, with a particular emphasis on different cultural perspectives on the family—structure, function, roles and values;

- Develop the requisite skills for working effectively with an interpreter (that is, a settlement and integration worker) as a team (both counsellors and settlement and integration workers needed to learn new ways of using self and how to relate to each other in the counselling process.)
- Familiarize settlement and integration workers with community-based mental health resources so that appropriate client referrals would be made;
- Assist counsellors and settlement and integration workers in identifying and addressing systemic cultural biases inherent in counselling theories and practice;
- Assist counsellors to explore and practice intervention techniques that were easy to explain and understand (that is, techniques applied should be neither esoteric nor abstract in nature such as to make language translation difficult)
- Develop team building strategies.

During the initial phase of the project, partner agencies conducted a community-based focus group session to introduce the training model and to invite feedback and suggestions to enhance the training. This session included twenty-five social service providers, funders and educators. During the session, community members strongly supported the need for training to develop competency in multicultural counselling. In ensuing discussions, the ethics of providing services to members of other cultures without adequate training or knowledge of those cultures were discussed. The wider application of the training model to other collaborative ventures was also encouraged.

The training stage of the project started in February 1994 and ended in December 1994, when the team felt confident enough to begin implementing the service model. As a collegial training model based on "action learning," the process was structured to facilitate group process with all participants assuming responsibility for presentations relevant to their area of expertise. The peer learning approach reduced the tendency of partnerships to reinforce and perpetuate real or perceived power differentials between mainstream and immigrant-serving organizations. Further, the focus on process ensured that the staff of both organizations participated in all aspects of the training program.

## DEVELOPMENT AND IMPLEMENTATION OF THE SERVICE MODEL

The policy of the federal government to fund only essential services to immigrant populations, such as information-giving and interpretation services, continues to stymie any integrated planning and program development initiatives. Similarly, mainstream mental health services, which are under the jurisdiction of the provincial governments, have generally failed to address the mental health issues of newcomers. The arbitrary distinctions between resettlement and mental health mandates have resulted in the unique cultural and language needs of newcomers falling between the cracks, unmet. Thus, a partnership between a resettlement agency and a mainstream counselling agency was intended to address that gap.

The service model adopted requires both settlement and integration workers and counsellors to work effectively as a team. During the initial training phase, the focus was on the development of counsellor comfort and skills. The desirability of "specializing" in one culture was explored. This also meant that the counsellor would be paired with the same settlement and integration worker across clients. In a world of adequate resources, this would have been the preferred approach. However, given the range of diversity in the immigrant community and the limited number of counsellors available, the method ultimately selected was one where counsellors would have to see clients of diverse cultural backgrounds. Clients were assigned by the intake worker to the first available counsellor, who then teams up with the referring settlement and integration worker.

Settlement and integration workers had the task of informing ethnic communities of the availability of counselling services through the partnership arrangement. To achieve this task, information about available services was disseminated by word of mouth, that is, through face-to-face contacts with community members. Community leaders were also approached to refer clients. CIAS also used the mass media (radio, TV and newsletters) to promote the service. In addition, settlement and integration counsellors contacted former clients who were assessed as most likely to benefit from single-issue counselling services. Both organizations sought out other mainstream organizations and institutions (e.g., hospitals, social services agencies, schools, etc.) for help with disseminating information about the newly available services. These agencies were recruited on the basis of their experience with working with diverse populations, and their appropriate handling of previous referrals. Ample lead time was given to "prepare" the community, and these preparations began during the training stage of the project. This lead time factored into account that it would take some time for the immigrant community to become aware of the services offered, match services with personal needs and, finally, get comfortable with the idea of getting and receiving assistance from a community-based agency.

The first counselling session in most instances is held at CIAS offices. The settlement and integration workers are trained to recognize signs that a particular client could benefit from single-issue counselling sessions. They then make referrals. Frequently, they need to explain not only the service to clients but also the philosophical foundations of going outside of the family for help. They also take the time to explain how confidences will be preserved.

The decision to participate or to refuse service is ultimately the client's, and this norm is reinforced by the use of informed consent forms, written in a language in which a client is fluent. If they decide to avail themselves of the counselling services offered, they are actively involved in the development of a service plan. The settlement and integration worker is present and provides moral support to the client as they take the risk of reaching out to a counsellor.

Interestingly, many clients would not see a counsellor without the settlement and integration worker being present, even though they do not require language interpretation assistance. Clearly, these clients would not have accessed counselling services without support. However, after being introduced to the counsellor, it is not uncommon for them to ask the settlement and integration worker to leave. In other words, the settlement and integration worker is committed at, minimum, to attending the initial session. As for his or her attendance at later sessions, this is entirely contingent upon the client. Non-English-speaking clients require the presence of the referring settlement and integration worker and language interpretation assistance for the counsellor.

Timely access to services by clients was critical to the success of the project. Immigrants and refugees, as well as other families who are not acculturated, do not relate well to waiting lists or appreciate the fifty-minute client contact hour. CFSB, which has a long waiting list for counselling services, recognized at the inception of the project that it would be critical for the agency to provide priority access to clients referred to the project and, at the very latest, provide a counsellor within a week of the request. Most sessions are longer than the usual one hour session; this does not include the time required by counsellors and settlement and integration workers for team consultation and debriefing purposes.

Traditional collaborative arrangements tend to have traditional organizational structures to coordinate services across partner organizations, that is, administration and management efforts are top-down. However, in the case of this partnership project, management and coordinating efforts were staff-driven. Decision-making was based on the principle of maximizing service benefits to clients.

It took almost a year of operation before settlement and integration workers were able to effectively refer clients to counsellors and for counsellors to feel competent and comfortable working as a team with settlement and integration workers. During the initial phase of the project, the team met bi-monthly; currently, the team meets monthly to deal with case management issues and to keep track of ongoing efforts to evaluate the service model.

An effective partnership must be supported by effective problem-solving mechanisms at all levels of organization. Structured team meetings provided an adequate forum for staff to deal with problems as they emerge. Some problems may need additional time and/or management involvement in both organizations to facilitate problem resolution.

The reception, intake and information system staff, who are immediately and significantly impacted by new service projects, need to be kept well informed and actively involved in solving problems. Management in one partner organization has to be flexible and responsive to the service protocols and the need for up-to-date information of the other organization. Service procedures should be clearly formulated and understood by both parties to avoid problems, such as misunderstandings and misinterpretations, that lead to confusion and disruptions in service delivery.

## SERVICE OUTCOMES

Seventy-three clients were referred to the project during the first year of operation. Together with other collaborative accomplishments, there was definite evidence that the partnership project had been successful in achieving its goal: to reach underserved visible minority individuals, families and communities using settlement and integration workers and counsellors working as teams. The diversity of the clients referred to the program indicated that the project had the additional benefit of expanding traditional linkages that settlement and integration workers had with underserved groups. Besides clients from Poland (16), India (12), El Salvador (10) and Vietnam (5), immigrants from Bosnia, Croatia, Dominican Republic, Philippines, Costa Rica, Bangladesh, Lebanon and Kuwait were referred to the project and utilized counselling services.

Counsellors and settlement and integration workers endorsed the team approach to the provision of counselling services to newcomers. According to results from the "Evaluation of 'Diversity Through Partnership' Model" (a participant questionnaire administered in June, 1995), 78% of settlement and integration workers preferred the team approach. Thirty-three percent of clients rated their counselling and interpretation experience as "very satisfactory," 40% as "satisfactory." Fifty-five percent of settlement and integration workers confirmed that knowing the counsellor prior to having to work together helped the referral process.

Indicators most frequently reported by settlement and integration workers as helping to determine that the clients needed counselling were family conflicts, abuse issues, emotional health issues, suicidal ideation and couple concerns. Overall, client feedback on the effectiveness of the single-issue, cross-cultural counselling service was promising.

By the end of the second stage of the project, it became evident that the clients accessing the single-issue counselling service were distributed among three categories:

- Clients who understand English but are reluctant to converse in it because of a lack confidence in their ability to make themselves understood;
- Clients who require interpretation during the entire sessions; and
- Clients who require some interpretation and who are able to communicate without interpreters some of the time.

This confirmation of the effectiveness of the cross-cultural, single-issue counselling program in engaging all three categories of clients has promising implications for the continued application of this model and other cross-cultural counselling technologies as they emerge in the wider community.

The partnership between CIAS and CFSB provided stakeholders with an opportunity to pool their resources. With their combined assets the partnership was able to expand the range of services to immigrants and refugees, including access to mental health counselling services. The authors recognize that the planning and implementation of this collaborative partnership is only the first step in a long process. Continued commitment and determination will be required to sustain the gains already made in the adoption of an integrated approach to dealing with complex problems such as those associated with the provision of culture- and language-appropriate counselling services to first generation Canadians. The partner organizations learned some very important lessons about collaborative partnerships.

The training model provided the staff of the two organizations with a safe, structured process for exploring the potential and the constraints of cross-cultural counselling. It also served as a catalyst for expanding organizational and personal awareness of the changing face of our community. Both partners attribute their successful project efforts to the initial willingness to entertain change, in this case a major shift in their organizations' established ways of providing service to the project.

The project promoted the development of alternative counselling approaches using culture- and language- appropriate methods. Previously underserved groups now not only enjoy increased accessibility to services but also increased service participation rates. There was not enough time or opportunity for counsellors to actively explore alternate counselling approaches, but it did allow for the application and apparently successful use of experiential techniques.

Settlement and integration workers were concerned and apprehensive about working in an area that was to them relatively abstract. It was necessary to define their roles in the counselling session as concretely as possible, e.g., to provide culture and language translation services. It also helped these workers to participate in discussions on appropriate counselling techniques. Open and honest discussions around issues of diversity and the mental health and social service needs that such diversity generates provided those involved with a sense of empowerment and mutual support.

The cross-cultural, single-issue counselling service has the potential to provide an exemplary model for bridging the service gap between mainstream and culturally diverse organizations. This pilot project demonstrated that front-line service providers participating in an action learning approach to program development can produce innovative and creative alternatives to the established service delivery models. The target alternative model described in this chapter met a critical project goal: to increase accessibility by underserved groups to needed services. By presenting the partnership as an exploratory cross-cultural training opportunity, staff of both organizations did not feel threatened by the impending organizational changes that needed to take place. Instead, they were willing to entertain the vision and begin to seriously consider the steps necessary to reposition the organizations to accomplish the vision.

To facilitate an effective action learning process, both partners need to commit to and allocate accordingly the necessary time, energy, and resources needed by the project. Staff need affirmation and support while undergoing training. Training took longer than was initially anticipated due to the unexpected but welcomed greater staff interest. The necessary adjustments were made to accommodate additional staff. Another project modification was the adjustment needed to accommodate differences in time orientation between counsellors and settlement and integration workers. Settlement and integration workers developed a fluid sense of timing guided by the demands of the task rather than by deadlines and actual time, whereas counsellors tend to adhere to deadlines and actual time.

The number of staff from both agencies who were interested and participated in the training exceeded expectations. The mainstream counsellors and the settlement and integration workers were most cognizant of the difficulties involved in the proposed model and welcomed the opportunity to explore the possibilities of expanding their skills to meet the challenge. The training model served as a formal acknowledgment of the need for multicultural competence training to meet cross-cultural counselling needs. Further, the invitation to the staff of the partner agencies to design a service model was seen as managements' confidence in their abilities to work together to develop a cross-cultural service model for the community.

Another important lesson learned is that organizations need to be responsive to the learning needs of the staff and flexible in terms of expected outcomes. The learning needs of partners in the team-building process were different, and team-building sessions needed to be structured in such a way that they challenged participants to think and learn yet remained flexible enough to allow for questions and concerns to be aired and processed, or for sensitive issues to be discussed in an objective and non-threatening way. For example, settlement and integration workers are more likely to talk about cultural biases if asked to address this in their presentation about their own cultural heritage. Alternatively, if they are called upon to talk about their personal biases, they are probably going to be less forthcoming. In contrast, counsellors, unaccustomed to defining themselves in relation to cultural values and practices, tended to react defensively when asked to talk about cultural biases. Overall, the structure and focus of the training process was very effective in reducing resistance and facilitating problem solving. In retrospect, the process would have been more productive if the focus had been on identifying the cultural values and biases implicit in conventional counselling theories and practice.

In the "Evaluation of 'Diversity Through Partnership' Model" questionnaire, most settlement and integration workers responded to the inquiry relating to change in personal biases, whereas most counsellors did not answer the question. The few counsellors who did respond focused on their increased awareness of other cultures rather than on biases rooted in their own culture. In group discussion some counsellors identified cultural biases that would make it difficult for them to work with families from cultures with strong patriarchal family values. This admission indicated that the training process was successful in making some staff feel safe enough to share biases relevant to their work.

The training model did not live up to original expectations that it would provide opportunities for developing cross-cultural intervention strategies, but it was successful beyond expectations in team building. The training focused on defining and developing the core knowledge and skills required by the team, including skills that counsellors needed in order to work in tandem with an interpreter and the cultural awareness to provide culturally appropriate services. For settlement and integration workers, the goal was to understand the counselling process and to identify mental health issues that would warrant service referrals. Settlement and integration workers have benefited tremendously from being paired up with counsellors. They evidence the increased confidence that comes from having one's contributions valued and recognized.

To develop an effective partnership, both agencies need to be prepared to provide staff with the necessary authority to modify established service policies and procedures to respond to day-to-day needs. For example, new forms had to be designed and implemented; their utility and function needed to be understood and appreciated by those filling them out. Input and feedback from service providers in the design and implementation of the forms was time-consuming but vital.

A successful partnership depends on possessing effective mechanisms for problem solving at all levels of operation. The authority to develop and implement the project was delegated to group leaders appointed by the respective partners. Group leaders were able to resolve most problems at the group level. Senior managers were consulted about changes affecting other areas of operation, such as introducing the new referral and intake forms and the interpretation of policy relating to service eligibility guidelines. Consistent efforts were made by group leaders and senior managers to identify and address problems as they occurred.

The most exciting lesson learned by the partner organizations and the collaborative service team was that our vision of making mainstream counselling services accessible to all newcomers was attainable. Positive feedback from clients assured counsellors and settlement and integration workers that the service model is effective and appropriate for newcomers. Within one year, CFSB doubled its clientele from diverse cultures, and, for CIAS, gains made were in terms of greater competence in assessment, more meaningful and appropriate referrals and improved case management practices. These achievements were a direct result of the authority delegated to the group to establish its own time lines and to make the necessary decisions so that the project could be successfully implemented.

Collaborative partnerships are initially time- and process-intensive. However, preliminary outcomes of a project to introduce a major paradigmatic shift in service delivery in two medium-sized organizations support the contention that collaborative partnerships between agencies with complementary goals and service mandates enhance the effectiveness and efficiency of both organizations. The intensive time demands of collaboration, in terms of ongoing information sharing, consultation and problem solving, in and of themselves are quite a challenge to meet. Add to this the responsibility to ensure and sustain high standards of direct services and one begins to appreciate the pressure staff are experiencing. For this reason, empirical evaluations of the effectiveness and efficiency of collaborative approaches to service delivery are essential to assist service managers ensure that optimal time investments are being made to provide quality culturally appropriate services.

The development of effective multicultural counselling models is an imperative if we as a community are going to respond to the challenges presented by changing sociodemographic profiles. The collaborative training and service model developed here is one example of how to respond appropriately to the mental health and social service needs of diverse communities. By attending to these needs in innovative and creative ways, the hope is that, in the long run, the reduction of the risk of prolonged emotional distress or chronic mental illness through the timely provision of counselling services during the resettlement process will be achieved.

## REFERENCES

Bowhay, C. (1992). *Review of the literature on collaboration and consultation.* Alberta Mental Health and Calgary Board of Education, Collaboration Project Evaluation (Unpublished paper).

Bruner,C. (1991). *Thinking collaboratively: Ten questions and answers to help policy makers improve children's services* (3rd publication in the *Series on Collaboration*). Washington, D.C. Education and Human Resources Consortium.

Canadian Task Force on Mental Health Issues Affecting Immigrants and Refugees. (1988). *After the door has been opened.* Report of the Canadian Task Force on Mental Health Issues Affecting Immigrants and Refugees. Ottawa, Ontario: Health and Welfare Canada and Multiculturalism and Citizenship Canada.

Gray, B. (1989). *Collaborating: Finding common ground for multiparty problems.* San Francisco, CA: Jossey-Bass Publishers.

Kagan, S. L., Rivera, A. M., and Parker, F.L. (1990). *Collaboration in action: Reshaping services for young children and their families.* Bush Center in Child Development and Social Policy, Yale University (ERIC document 328363).

# CHAPTER 11

# Multicultural Organizational Change in a United Way Counselling Agency

*Robbie Babins-Wagner, Irene Hoffart*
*and Brian Hoffart*

## INTRODUCTION

Multicultural organizational change (MOC) is a process of dismantling visible and invisible barriers to the full social participation of non-dominant groups and establishing an organization responsive and responsible to the larger community (Thomas, 1987). This process is often challenging as it questions the basic values and assumptions of organizational functioning. As is the case with other previously researched change models (Dimock, 1981), the MOC process is successful when it is able to respond to organizational and societal needs. Each practical application of MOC brings with it new challenges and new learning and provides the foundation for further development and implementation. This chapter describes one such application in a not-for-profit counselling agency, its impetus, methodology, outcomes, learning and resulting recommendations.

## THE CONTEXT

Our society is changing. The rate of change is increasing geometrically, putting extreme pressure on individuals and organizations to respond to the newly emerging society. North America's aging population and globalization act as primary catalysts for MOC (Schwartz, 1993; London and Daft, 1992). The post-war baby boom and declining birthrates in the United States and Canada result in a rapidly aging population, and a larger workforce is necessary to the economic survival of each country. Expansion of the workforce can be accomplished by inviting other, previously excluded segments of the population to take part in the labour force (e.g., the disabled, women and ethnic or cultural minorities) and by encouraging immigration from other countries.

It has been suggested that we live in an information age. Technology simplifies long-distance communication and information exchange. Economic differences among countries become more apparent, lead to joint working opportunities and encourage immigration to the United States and Canada (Alberta Career Development and Employment, 1992). This is often referred to as a globalization: the distances among people who live in different parts of the world are made insignificant by technological advances (Schwartz, 1993).

Diversity can be defined as a multi-dimensional mixture where there is a variety of human qualities which include but are not limited to language, ethnicity and race, socio-economic class, religious and spiritual beliefs, sexual orientation, geographic origin, education and gender (Thomas, 1987). In short, diversity is "all the ways in which we differ" (Hayles, 1995). Aging population and globalization trends make valuing of diversity in all its forms a prerequisite to our societies' survival. As diversity has increasingly become part of our lives, its effects on the workplace have been under examination. The resulting findings demonstrate that it is the appreciation and celebration of differences rather than insistence on conformity that is imperative to the survival and success of any business or not-for-profit enterprise (Senge, 1990; Berry, 1991; Maznevski, 1994).

While the benefits of diversity are many, so are the challenges to enhancing its value in the workplace. This type of change is all encompassing and affects everyone's basic assumptions and stereotypes. It is important that the process of responding to diversity is motivated by strong political and economic leadership. In the not-for-profit sector, funding organizations can provide such an impetus.

## The United Way Response

In May 1990, the board of directors of the United Way of Calgary and Area established the Future Ways Task Force to assist them in the difficult job of setting funding priorities. This initiative responded to dramatic changes in Calgary (Canada's fourth largest city with a population of 750,000 and growing): growing demands on human service agencies, a continuing economy of restraint, and complex and rapid socio-economic as well as political changes. The report of the task force was approved in February 1991 and it was widely distributed in the community. Throughout work on the task force there has been active consultation with United Way member agencies, community agencies, consumers of services, United Way donors and community representatives.

Community consultation assisted in deriving six priorities, which were adopted in March 1991. These priorities established broad directions for funding and community building in and around Calgary. The priorities were intended to be complementary, interconnected and linked through the central principle of collaboration. The central direction was:

- To respond to the changing community through outreach, joint ventures, partnerships and/or initiatives that empower people.

The priorities included the following:

- To promote access for vulnerable groups to services, employment and education;
- To address systemic discrimination such as racism and sexism;
- To promote consumer focus in health and social services;
- To support self-help initiatives;
- To increase emphasis on prevention for vulnerable groups with particular focus on children, youth and people who care for them;
- To collaborate with consumers, agencies and funders to develop new planning and advocacy mechanisms for Calgary—where appropriate, United Way should advocate at a policy level on behalf of the poor and disenfranchised;
- To expand the resource base for community service.

The United Way of Calgary provided a great deal of support, education and consultation services to member agencies during this initial phase of the initiative. These services included a series of workshops with topics of agency accessibility, community consultation, developing outreach strategies for vulnerable groups, increasing consumer participation, supporting internal champions, developing action plans and dealing with resistance to organizational change. The workshops served to inform the agency workforce about the meaning of multicultural organizational change and to provide some tools to facilitate the process.

United Way member agencies were required to submit three-year action plans describing how they proposed to meet United Way's funding priorities, thus linking funding to the change process. The multicultural organizational change process was recognized as a strategy for meeting the funding priorities. The three-year action plan covered the period from January 1, 1994 to December 31, 1996.

## MULTICULTURAL ORGANIZATIONAL CHANGE OBJECTIVES

The United Way of Calgary and Area has been committed to multicultural organizational change (MOC) since June 25, 1990. The vision of MOC states that:

> The United Way of Calgary and Area be a model for multicultural change, reflective of the diversity of the community, culturally sensitive and free of cultural barriers. The goals for MOC are two-fold. Firstly, to foster and promote the full participation of ethnocultural groups in Untied Way by dismantling visible and invisible organizational barriers, and secondly, to develop a Catalyst-Connector Role for Multicultural Change among member agencies, non-member agencies, and the diverse communities. (Agger, 1993; Future Ways Taskforce, 1991)

The future ways and MOC initiatives began as separate initiatives in May and June 1990. In late 1994 the two were consolidated as part of the future ways process.

### Cluster model

The United Way of Calgary and Area adopted a cluster model in 1993 in order to implement its future ways, and later, MOC initiatives.

United Way funded agencies were invited to volunteer to participate in a collaborative process of MOC. The clusters are peer groupings of up to six organizations. Cluster 1 consisted of six large social service organizations, including the United Way; Cluster 2 is comprised of five medium and small agencies; Cluster 3 is comprised of five counselling agencies (Pastoral Institute was part of this cluster); Cluster 4 includes three women's shelters; and Cluster 5 consists of three agencies which serve clients in conflict with the law. The cluster model envisioned a process which would encourage effective, inclusive learning organizations. The representatives of each agency varied and included management, staff and board personnel. Their role was to facilitate the change process in their own organization on the basis of a planning framework developed in the cluster.

Key to this planning framework was a diagnostic process called a "barrier analysis." United Way of Calgary and Area and the Kahanoff Foundation put forward funds to assist each cluster in the process of MOC. The funds enabled each cluster to engage consultants to provide assistance in carrying out its barrier analysis. The aim of the barrier analysis was to identify organizational structures, cultures, systems and individual competencies that either facilitated or limited the change, and to begin developing action plans that build inclusive organizations. The barrier analysis components (see Figure 1 below) were recommended by the United Way.

Each cluster and individual agency planned and utilized their own tailor-made strategies. The cluster group met approximately once per month. The first meeting of Cluster 3 was held on January 21, 1993.

## The Pastoral Institute (PI)*

PI's involvement in the barrier analysis process began at the time of the community consultation and continued with its involvement with Cluster 3. The progression of change at the PI begins with a description of its historical roots.

PI of Calgary opened on July 1, 1962 under the direction of the Central United Church of Calgary. It embodied a dream for churches to participate more actively in a healing ministry which combined the principles of caring as espoused in the Judeo-Christian tradition and the knowledge and skills of the social sciences. Known at its inception as

---

\* The Pastoral Institute is now known as the Calgary Counselling Centre.

**Figure 1: Components of a Barrier Analysis**

1.    **Demographic Profile of Community**
   *Calgary*
   - age
   - language
   - visible minority status
   - religion
   - ethnicity
   - country of origin (if born outside of Canada)
   - length of residency in Canada
   - gender

   *Smaller Target Areas*
   - by geographic area
   - income/single parent, school, mental health, etc.

2.    **Demographic Profile of Agency**
   *Staff (contract, part-time, permanent, etc.)*
   - Manager
   - Professionals
   - Administration staff

   *Volunteers*
   - Board
   - Front-line

3.    **Demographic Profile of Consumers by Program**

4.    **Document Review**
   - Mission
   - Policy
   - Staff/volunteer descriptions
   - Training manual
   - Orientation manual
   - Advertising materials
   - Brochures
   - Forms

**5.  Internal Consultation**

**A. Priorities and Procedures for Staff and Volunteers**
- Written and unwritten norms of behaviour
- Competition process
- Interviewing techniques, short-listing
- Recruitment process
- Recognition process
- Employee relations
  (including performance, training, exit interviews)
- Training programs
- Orientation process

**B. Priorities and Procedures for Client Services**
- Intake procedures
- Front entrance and waiting rooms
- Intake forms `
- Referral process

**C. Other Organizational Norms**
*How are decisions made?*
*What are board and staff relations like?*
May include
- Management interviews
- Staff focus groups
- Volunteer surveys
- Board interviews
- Interviews with diverse staff

**6.  Community Consultations**
- Present and past consumers
- Non-consumers
- Waiting list
- Target groups (e.g., ethnospecific community, church groups, immigrant serving agencies)

the Institute of Family Services and Personal Counseling, the PI has an established history in the community of offering an array of services, ranging from direct intervention and prevention services to professional education. PI has sought to respond to the needs of persons from all walks of life who require personal counselling.

In 1967, PI began a training program in pastoral counselling education and, in May 1990, it was accredited as a teaching centre by the Canadian Association of Pastoral Practice and Education. In 1992, PI engaged a new clinical director who was given a mandate to enhance the overall quality of service delivery across all programs and services. While service delivery issues were being assessed and changes were being implemented, service demands were increasing and waiting lists grew. The increased demand for services was partially due to changes in the social service sector in Calgary. Government services were being cut back, and other services were tightening their service mandates. Many of these clients turned to PI for services. Some were new immigrants, and some were from religious groups not previously served at PI. More and more of the clientele were on welfare or from the ranks of the working poor.

The institute responded to the needs of clients by keeping the client as the central organizing force around which services were developed. With some increased staff (both contract staff and practicum students) and new ideas about how often to see clients (every second week rather than weekly, except for those clients who were in crisis) the two-month waiting list was eliminated. The education and training programs were expanded to include a broader range of practicums, internships and residencies in social work, psychology, marriage and family therapy, counselling, pastoral counselling and family nursing. PI continues to function with 9.5 full time staff (including a support staff of 4.5 individuals), twelve contract staff, twelve residents and thirty-five interns.

From 1962 to the early 1990s, staff, counsellors and trainees involved in the institute's programs and the agency's clientele were primarily from mainstream/majority cultural, religious, ethnic and racial backgrounds. However, as Calgary's demographics began to reflect an increasing multicultural component, PI began to consider how they might best meet the needs of an increasingly diverse clientele. Late in 1991, PI decided to become involved in the multicultural organizational change initiative spearheaded by the United Way of Calgary.

The United Way's MOC and future ways priorities were not new concepts for PI. From the agency's inception, an emphasis had been placed on prevention services for vulnerable groups, the empowerment of clients, accessibility of services, overcoming discrimination within the system, and collaboration with other organizations, agencies and services. Until 1991, energies in PI were directed primarily towards meeting the needs of mainstream consumers of services. The United Way initiatives pushed PI to reflect upon the continuing relevance of its mission given present-day service mandates, as well as future mandates, and to decide whether it would endorse the Untied Way initiatives at just a compliance level or whether it would truly endorse the principles undergirding the future ways and MOC initiatives. This deliberative process continued for months, passed and culminated in PI's Board adopting new mission, vision and values statements, as well as an updated service mandate in March 1994. PI became a member of United Way's cluster initiative (Cluster 3) in January 1993. Changes in the institute's mission statements over the years are shown in Figure 2 below.

## PASTORAL INSTITUTE'S GUIDING PRINCIPLES

The name "the Pastoral Institute" is oftentimes thought to be associated with Christian beliefs to the exclusion of other religious beliefs. The institute's guiding principles (see Figure 3 below) bring the organization in line with the future ways priorities and multicultural organizational change priorities. These principles also serve as the basis for understanding the meaning of "pastoral" counselling, education and prevention at PI (see Figure 3 below).

## THE PROCESS

There are five main assumptions behind the successful organizational change that guided the implementation of the process at the Pastoral Institute (Kanter, 1983; Thomas, 1991; Agger, 1993):

1. *The change process must be championed by individuals who make the final decisions.*
   Ongoing meetings with representatives of PI's management committee ensured informed commitment and participation at the top.
2. *The change process must involve all agency representatives and ensure that there is an opportunity to voice individual views.*

**Figure 2: Mission Statements of the Pastoral Institute pre- and post-March 1994**

**Prior to March 1994 the mission of the Pastoral Institute was:**

- The Pastoral Institute is dedicated to enriching and enhancing the quality of life through a triune thrust of training, education and counselling services. By promoting an atmosphere of acceptance and honouring the uniqueness of all persons, PI seeks to combine the insights of modern psychology with the riches of Judeo-Christian tradition in order to respond to emerging needs in the community.

- As Christ's mission of unconditional love began among the Jewish community and spread to incorporate the surrounding communities, so the Pastoral Institute began in 1962 as the resource for the local clergy and today seeks a broader pastoral outreach to all people, that is, the liberation of persons to life in all its fullness. The institute recognizes the value of the Christian tradition of providing care and endeavours to continue this tradition in a pluralistic society.

- Operating in an ecclesiastical context, PI enjoys the rare distinction of training persons for pastoral counselling service to the community. The Pastoral Institute adheres to high standards of counselling education and service delivery and aims to remain relevant and responsive to an evolving world.

**The new mission adopted by the board of directors in March 1994 is:**

The Pastoral Institute is dedicated to enriching life in our community by providing compassionate and affordable care through professional counselling, education and preventive services in an atmosphere that honours the uniqueness of every person and family.

At the outset letters introducing and describing MOC were distributed to all agency staff, volunteers, board members, interns and residents. Additionally, introductory meetings were

**Figure 3: Pastoral Institute's Guiding Principles**

*Principle 1* : All services of the Pastoral Institute are provided with a sensitivity and respect towards the religious faiths and practices of clients, volunteers, staff, students, interns, residents and board members. It is our intent to be responsive to human spiritual needs.

*Principle 2*: Spirituality is at the core of being human.

*Principle 3*: Religion is an individual's expression of spirituality through worship, practice and relationships within a faith group.

*Principle 4*: Individual needs for spiritual and religious care will be recognized and therapeutically supported.

*Principle 5*: The Pastoral Institute recognizes and supports the responsibility of faith communities for providing religious education.

*Principle 6*: All services of the Pastoral Institute are developed and offered in a context that provides caring, compassionate, moral and spiritual support.

*Principle 7*: Services of the Pastoral Institute will assist clients, volunteers, staff, students, interns, residents and board members to utilize their spiritual resources in accordance with these principles.

held with staff members and board members to provide further opportunity to respond to questions and concerns.

3. *The change process must highlight successes.*
   An inherent assumption of any organizational change process is that something is not working, and therefore must change. To counter this assumption, and to engender ownership and commitment to long-term implementation of change, successes

that occur throughout the process must be regularly identified. Organizational leaders and managers must then take responsibility to inform all in the organization of these accomplishments on a periodical basis. The implementation of the MOC described in this chapter was punctuated by periodic information on progress made and successes achieved.

4. *The change process must be informative and highlight advantages of change.*
   The diversity of agency participants led to a need to identify a variety of advantages. Some participants responded to societal and future-oriented advantages (as described in the context section of this chapter), others to more personal discussion (e.g., it is simply a good thing to do).

5. *The change process must be internally managed.*
   Multicultural organizational change must be implemented from the within, rather than forced by players or events outside of the organization. Although United Way provided initial impetus for change, it then became the agency's responsibility to take ownership and implement changes that are meaningful to both the workforce and agency clients. The consultant's role was to collect information and facilitate decision-making, rather than to take on an expert role by instructing and prescribing.

The project purpose called for a variety of methods to be utilized to facilitate the barrier analysis. Accordingly, when the analysis was conducted, it was partially based on the components for barrier analysis recommended by the United Way (see Figure 1). Information collected from a number of sources was to dovetail into several descriptive themes. Qualitative (individual interviews, focus groups and workshops) and quantitative (surveys) approaches were used to collect information about the agency board, management, staff and volunteers. The following describes the process and methodological approaches.

## Process and methodological approaches

The importance of ongoing involvement of PI stakeholders was described above. Although not formally used for data collection, meetings and interviews with stakeholders provided another opportunity to learn about the culture of the agency, building commitment, highlighting successes and exploring the advantages of change to PI. The bimonthly meetings at the agency were further supplemented by information collected during the monthly cluster meetings.

## Surveys

Surveys were used to collect data about agency representatives and agency clients. A questionnaire (workforce survey) developed specifically for the MOC process was administered to all agency staff, volunteers, and board members (PLAN:NET, 1994). Information was also collected from clients who received services at the agency in 1994. All surveys were accompanied by an introductory letter ensuring that issues of confidentiality and voluntary participation were addressed. See Table 1 for response rates.

| Table 1: Surveys — Response Rates | | | |
|---|---|---|---|
| **Population** | **Number Distributed** | **Number Distributed** | **Return Rate** |
| Staff, interns, residents | 40 | 18 | 45% |
| Volunteers (board included) | 46 | 19 | 41% |
| **Agency total** | 86 | 37 | 43% |
| **Active clients** | 525 | 228 | 43% |

## Workforce survey

The purpose of the workforce survey was threefold: it served as an evaluation instrument for United Way of Calgary (and was to be re-administered eighteen months after the initial distribution), it facilitated evaluation of MOC, and it served as a medium to collect information about the barriers to agency access. Two different versions of the questionnaire were designed, one to be administered to board members and volunteers and another to management and staff. Each questionnaire was divided into three parts.

The first part comprised questions about the respondents' perceptions regarding the agency and the community it served; it also attempted to capture respondents' sentiments regarding MOC. The second part of the questionnaire collected detailed demographic information about the respondents. The questionnaire also served as an initial intervention tool. Some of the questions raised issues that may not have been previously discussed (e.g., racism, sexism and conflict) and created further opportunities for discussion within the agency.

## Client surveys

An instrument was developed to collect information regarding client diversity and agency capabilities in sensitively responding to clients. This was accomplished by redesigning client intake forms and a post-treatment, follow-up questionnaire, which included questions on clients' perceptions of areas in which barriers to access or to receiving services at PI persist. The questionnaire consisted of two parts: one part seeking sociodemographic details, and the other part, focusing on service evaluation.

One of the aims of the MOC was to highlight variability of staff participation in organizational activities and representation of diverse groups among agency staff, volunteers and clients. The information collected provided client demographic data that could be compared to staff and community demographic distribution.

## Document review

MOC is a dynamic process, requiring that agency staff and volunteers develop skills to continually update and revise service records and documents as the organization becomes more responsive to changing community needs. The review was intended to provide an initial framework for future work to be carried out internally by the agency representatives. A document review training module conducted by United Way preceded the review process.

As part of the barrier analysis, PI by-laws and personnel manuals were reviewed. Document review checklists (Thomas, 1987; Simons, 1990) were used to determine potential obstacles to access by clients, barriers to full participation of staff and representation of various groups in the operations of PI. Focal areas included literacy level, use of language (e.g., outdated terminology), gender neutrality, recruitment, promotion policies, holiday and dietary requirements, marginalization of diversity and assumptions of what is normal and accepted practice. Document review outcomes further supported and contributed to identification of themes.

## Focus groups

Focus groups were used to collect in-depth information about the internal and external operations of the agency. This method of data collection is extremely useful when attempting to understand the inner workings of an organization (Morgan, 1993). Focus groups helped to analyze the agency's formal and informal systems and assisted in uncovering assumptions, biases and barriers to accessibility and diversity.

While the focus group schedule (see Figure 4 below) provided a framework for the process, participants' responses and previous experience with the organization itself guided examination of additional or more specific topics. As a result, probes and follow-up questions varied significantly among groups.

Four focus groups were conducted with a total of thirty-two participants. Where possible, an effort was made to constitute homogeneous groups and to include representaives from all levels of the organization. The groups included interns and residents, program staff, group facilitators and board members.

## Workshop

An agency-wide workshop provided an opportunity to report the findings to the staff, volunteers, residents and interns, to discuss these findings and to begin setting forth an action plan for continued change. Twenty-five staff, board members, volunteers, residents and interns participated in the six-hour workshop.

The findings included comparisons of demographic information among agency staff, volunteers, the larger community (United Way of Calgary and Area, 1993) and clients. The comparisons provided an opportunity to examine whether the socio-demographics of the larger community were adequately reflected among staff, volunteers and clients.

Critical issues or themes were extracted from the qualitative information collected during focus group sessions; these were supported

---
**Figure 4: Focus Group Schedule**

**All focus groups were based on nine primary questions:**

1. What groups of people does your agency serve?

2. Does the agency provide programs or services for specific diverse groups?

3. Can the group think of anything that makes it easy for diverse groups to access services at this agency?

4. Can the group think of anything that makes it easier for diverse client groups to fully benefit from this agency's services?

5. What, if anything, do clients need to do to be able to more easily access (or derive more benefit from) this agency's services?

6. What kind of training and development opportunities are available to employees? (volunteers)

7. Let's talk about what happens if someone complains about unfair treatment. How are such complaints handled?

8. To be successful in your work, are there any unwritten rules that you are expected to follow? What are some of these unwritten rules?

9. What do individuals from diverse groups need to do to be successful in your agency?
---

by the workforce survey findings, client information and document reviews. Themes were generated using inductive data analysis, defined by Lincoln and Guba (1985) as "a process for making sense of field data" (p. 202). Patton (1990), in describing the process, states that "inductive analysis means that patterns, themes, and categories of analysis come from the data. They emerge out of the data rather than being imposed on them prior to data collection and analysis" (p. 390).

During the workshop, the meaning of the issues to the agency and its representatives was processed in small, cross-level groups (three to seven participants). Each group was assigned a particular issue and asked to answer questions and present a summary of its discussion to the larger group. The questions explored areas successfully addressed by the agency as well as areas for future work. The final section of the workshop enabled participants to begin action planning on the basis of issues derived from the previous discussions. The small group format was used once again to begin planning specific activities.

## Process Findings and Outcomes

### Document review

Reviews of by-laws and the personnel manual showed that these important organizational records addressed diversity issues, but it also revealed areas for improvement. For example, the documents have consistently referred to regard for human rights as the central issue in agency functioning. Additionally, there are clearly identified provisions for the observation of any historical and religious events without loss of pay. Further, the agency by-laws make both male and female employees eligible for parental leave. These provisions indicate that a basic infrastructure was in place to facilitate the recruitment and employment of a diverse workforce.

On the other hand, several changes were indicated. For example, the new commitment to inclusive language meant the utilization of gender-neutral language. In many documents, references to chairman and he when both "he and she" are implied were quite common. Additionally, the term "family" appears frequently; however, no definition of the term is available. Change in terminology and language was expected to create a more comfortable work climate and a heightened sense of belonging among staff.

Further, the documents did not formalize or specify requirements for diversity training among staff, volunteers and interns. Similarly, staff qualification requirements did not specify language skills or experience working with or living in diverse communities. In addition, reflection of diversity in workforce composition was not mandated in organization documents. Inclusion of diversity as a requirement in hiring and training is an important component of the change process. Once legislated, changes to achieve these goals are easier to implement.

## Demographic comparisons

Socio-demographic analysis, comparing staff, volunteers, agency clients and community at large (United Way of Calgary and Area, 1993), was one method used to determine if agency staff, volunteer and client characteristics corresponded with the characteristics of the community it served. At a minimum, the agency's client profile should reflect the ethnocultural, gender, sexual orientation, income and disability characteristics of the wider community. In fact, agencies that endeavour to serve the most vulnerable groups generally carry a client load that includes more visible minorities, persons with disabilities, low income and poor people than is found in the general population. In addition, consumer access is encouraged when the agency's staff and volunteers include members of the same vulnerable groups.

As Table 2 below shows, with some exceptions, PI staff, volunteers and clients are largely white, Anglo-Saxon, Protestant and able-bodied individuals. Nevertheless, the agency's goal is to move towards more varied client ethnicity, as well as a relatively higher number of low income clients and single-parent families. In addition, PI needs to recruit more staff and volunteers born outside of Canada, especially those from third world countires.

## Critical issues

Compilation of findings from the focus groups and the document review resulted in identification of critical issues that were divided into five areas: view of diversity, client access, staffing and training needs, referrals and collaborations, and view of change. Participants' comments highlight each issue and are followed by plans for future activities.

## View of diversity

The organization's view of diversity assists in determining organizational readiness and need for change (Hall and Parker, 1993). The following comments support the need for diversifying the clientele. In fact, the organizational culture is already changing towards increased

| Variable | Staff | Volunteers* | Clients | Community |
|---|---|---|---|---|
| *Language* | | | | |
| English | 94.4 | 73.3 | | 83.7 |
| French | 61.2 | 36.8 | | 1.4 |
| German | 16.7 | 15.8 | | 2.0 |
| Spanish | 11.2 | 21.1 | | .8 |
| Chinese | 0 | 0 | | 3.3 |
| Other | 10.2 | 10.5 | | 11.82 |
| *Disability* | | | | |
| Hearing | 0 | 5.3 | | 3.3 |
| Other | 0 | 0 | | 20.7 |
| *Born Outside of Canada* | 22.2 | 26.3 | | 20 |
| *Visible Minority* | 5.6 | 5.3 | | 10.9 |
| *Ethnicity* | | | | |
| English | 44.4 | 21.1 | 10.2 | 26.2 |
| French | 0 | 5.3 | 3.9 | 9.4 |
| Other European | 16.7 | 15.8 | 19.5 | 64.7 |
| Latin/South American | 0 | 5.3 | .03 | .2 |
| Canadian | 11.1 | 15.8 | 3.9 | - |
| Jewish | 5.6 | 0 | .06 | 4.9 |
| American | 0 | 5.3 | - | .03 |
| Other | 0 | 0 | 12.4 | 9.59 |
| Unspecified | 16.7 | 21.1 | 40.1 | - |
| *Gender* | | | | |
| Female | 77.8 | 63.2 | 52.7 | |
| Male | 22.1 | 36.8 | 47.3 | |
| *Income* | | | | |
| Less than 5000 | 11.1 | 0 | 12.9 | |
| 5000 to 14,999 | 16.7 | 5.3 | 29.5 (to 15,000) | |
| 15,000 to 24,999 | 16.7 | 10.5 | 11.2 (to 20,000) | |
| 25,000 to 44,999 | 38.9 | 31.6 | 33.4 (to 50,000) | |
| 45,000 and over | 5.6 | 47.7 | 11.7 (over 50,000) | |
| *Religion/Spirituality* | | | | |
| Christian | 66.7 | 73.7 | 40.1 | |
| Agnostic/Atheist/None | 11.2 | 0 | - | |
| No Preference | 0 | 0 | 18.1 | |
| Jewish | 5.6 | 0 | .7 | |
| Other | 5.6 | 0 | 7.5 | |
| *Single parent families* | | | 25.7 | 3.5 |

* includes board members, direct and indirect service volunteers

acknowledgment of gaps in service and valuing diversity, suggesting the agency's readiness to begin the change process.

- We primarily serve the dominant culture, but our clients' diversity is increasing.
- Sometimes clients do not access our services because of their cultural background.
- For us it is sometimes difficult to know what do with diverse clients.
- We think that special attention to diverse clients in the reception area is important as an acknowledgment of their different needs in counselling.
- Our agency is a dynamic organization—it is always changing. The atmosphere of change is good for our agency, but it can also be unsettling.

## Client access

The issue of access for diverse clients depends on a variety of factors, ranging from the location of the building to something that is often taken for granted or overlooked because it seems innocuous, such as the agency's name. Information collected during the barrier analysis highlighted several elements restricting and enhancing access for diverse clients and, in turn, providing target areas for planning and change.

- Our reception area and offices may not be comfortable for our clients.
- Our location is central, neutral and wheelchair accessible. However, some may find parking, confidentiality and security a difficulty.
- Immediate service, flexibility in fees and in addressing the needs of parents make access to our services easier. Use of student counsellors, confidentiality risk with interpreters, cost of groups and our inability to speak a variety of languages may act as barriers.
- We know that the word "Pastoral" in the agency name may both hinder and facilitate access for some clients. If we change the

pastoral or traditional Christian orientation we may become more inclusive.

Action plans to improve client access to services are listed in Figure 5 below:

---

**Figure 5: Action Plans to Improve Client Access**

**Client access action plans**
- address the issue of space in the waiting room for those in wheelchairs
- change the faith symbols to include either none or more different denominations
- build an area for children  .
- hire parents/volunteers/ college practicum students specializing in early childhood to supervise children; set up time when baby-sitting is offered
- keep the name, but change the definition to encompass bringing services to anyone
- community outreach to specifically target various disabled and low income groups as well as single parents and religious groups
- obtain a more visible sign for the outside
- increase the size of the agency space
- set up a sign that says "see receptionist" in different languages

---

## Staffing and training needs

An organization is more accessible to diverse clients if its workforce is representative of the diversity of the target population, if there is opportunity for open discussion related to change and if everyone in the agency participates in ongoing, diversity-related training (Flamholtz, Randle and Sackmann, 1986). The institute's action plans for staff recruitment and training are briefly described in Figure 6 below.

Staff comments suggest a need to overhaul recruitment procedures to target professionals with diverse backgrounds and to increase training opportunities:

## Figure 6: Action Plans for Staff Recruitment and Training

**Staffing and training needs action plans**
- bring in more professionals from various cultures—examine transferability of various educational and experiential training, advertise to universities across Canada
- carry out exchange of information seminars with residents
- have available a resource person to call on for counselling with individuals of various backgrounds
- train interns/residents in related issues
- encourage ethnic volunteers and students to join the Pastoral Institute
- audit library resources to ensure availability of relevant books
- carry out open forums to discuss diversity-related issues once per month
- bring in guest speakers from different groups to act as liaisons and educational resources
- form a multicultural organizational change committee that would lead the change process and would work with the student liaison committee to make sure it meets students' needs
- include diversity issues into the orientation process

- Although we value and are working on recruiting diverse staff, volunteers, interns and residents, we presently have largely mainstream staff and volunteers.
- Although multicultural training opportunities have been increasing, we need more.
- We especially would like to learn about counselling with diverse groups and to increase our awareness of cultural issues.

### Referrals and collaborative efforts

Successful change processes must take place internally as well as externally. Internally, the organization changes its policies, procedures and services to better address client needs. Externally, organizations affect and are affected by others who wish to work with similar client groups. Connecting with organizations that service diverse client groups is imperative in improving access. Figure 7 lists action plans for improving referrals and collaboration with other community-based agencies.

**Figure 7: Action Plans for Improving Referrals and Collaboration**

**Referrals and collaborative efforts action plans**
- market to target ethnic clubs, or groups, (specifically Latin American, Asian, Sikh or Ismaili communities) immigrant agencies, community centres and churches
- obtain a master list of resource people for these communities
- carry out ongoing needs assessments by way of focus groups or other means
- carry out presentations to non-mainstream schools on various topics (e.g., violence)
- teach courses in the community (e.g., parent effectiveness training)
- carry out presentations to staff of non-mainstream agencies regarding the Pastoral Institute and its services (e.g., counselling in variety of languages, diversity of staff and language bank)
- establish an advertising campaign through mailings, personal contact, flyers, notices in community newsletters and church programs
- translate print materials into different languages
- establish an outreach committee with a mandate for an all-inclusive proactive marketing approach

The following comments from staff suggest a future focus on marketing to and building relationships with non-mainstream organizations.

- We collaborate with many Calgary agencies, but we primarily obtain referrals from mainstream organizations. We might be able to change this if our marketing targets diverse groups.

- We envision our agency as a training institute serving more diverse clients by establishing a continuum of services with non-mainstream agencies.

## Success indicators

The Pastoral Institute has been involved in Cluster Three activities including the agency and cluster barrier analysis since 1992. Agency involvement in the process resulted in a number of changes towards becoming a more inclusive and accessible organization. The following discussion historically summarizes the indicators of successful initiation of the multicultural organizational change process at PI.

## 1992 to the summer of 1993

By the summer of 1993, PI had achieved the following accomplishments as reported by an external evaluation team. The team had asked members of the cluster groups to assess the current status of their organization regarding the topics of policy development, board membership, organizational planning, managing change, personnel recruitment, volunteer management, staff and volunteer decision-making and communication, fund-raising, legal issues, marketing and community relations.

*Policy development*
- a written policy endorsing multiculturalism
- recruitment of staff of non-Christian religious affiliations
- recruitment of volunteers from visible minority groups
- establishment of partnerships

*Board membership*
- a board member participated in the workshops on diversity in order that all policy matters can be reviewed from a multicultural perspective

*Organizational planning*
- increased attention to matching client needs with provision of services, e.g., assessing the needs of clients regarding income security, accessibility, public transportation, etc.

- ongoing evaluation of organizational functioning vis-à-vis future ways and demographic trends

*Managing changes*
- monthly open forums held for all sectors of the agency to address change within the organization and to raise staff awareness of MOC issues
- in-service training for staff, interns, residents, practicum students and volunteers on cross-cultural counselling
- regular meetings of liaison committees; intern, residents and staff committees; and meetings with stakeholders
- participation in the cluster process
- networking with other agencies and community committees

*Personnel recruitment and management*
- admission of foreign-trained professionals into its training programs
- recruitment of visible minorities into its training programs
- employment of staff from a variety of cultures and religions

*Volunteer management*
- open policy of accepting all who wish to serve as volunteers (that is, attempting to form a diverse pool of volunteers from various ethnic, racial, religious and socio-economic backgrounds)

*Staff and volunteer decision-making and communication*
- open communication at various levels of the organization: board to staff, staff to board, volunteer to staff, staff to staff and administrative staff to management staff

*Fund-raising*
- diversifying membership of fund-raising committee

*Legal issues*
- participation by all management staff in MOC workshops

*Marketing and community relations*
- identify marketing and communications strategies that are multiculturally appropriate

*Strengths, weaknesses and priorities*
- address diversity and decrease barriers to service delivery.

## Fall of 1993 to June of 1994

The barrier analysis resulted in identification of further success indicators in terms of client access to services, staffing and training needs, and referrals and collaborative efforts.

*Client access*
- twenty-nine percent (29.5%) of clients currently served are in the lower income bracket ($5000-15,000).
- recruited a Spanish-speaking counsellor
- exploring establishment of interpreter/language bank for community to access
- targeting developmentally challenged persons as clients
- use of the term "partner" (rather than "husband" or "wife") in agency documentation in recognition of the fact that some clients are of same-sex sexual or bisexual orientation

## STAFFING AND TRAINING NEEDS

- availability of training in several different languages
- use of experts external to the organization facilitated the involvement of diverse group of experts
- continued diversity training workshops and multicultural presentations
- open forum to discuss multicultural issues

*Referrals and collaborative efforts*
- reformulation of mission statement to reflect full range of spiritual and religious beliefs
- availability of culturally competent counselling publicized among professional and prospective client groups

- Staff membership in various community-based committees (e.g., immigrant groups, planning group for multicultural youth, AIDS Calgary and the HAS Coalition- HIV/ AIDS Strategies Coalition)
- regular attendance of counselling agencies cluster meeting
- recruitment of volunteers representing non-mainstream agencies (e.g., Alexandra Centre in Calgary)

## Fall of 1994 to the present

In 1994, PI received a small project grant from United Way for "Training in Cross-Cultural Counselling: Competency in Counselling Services." The purpose of this grant was twofold:

1. To develop a training program for counsellors in mainstream agencies that focuses on developing cross-cultural counselling competency; and
2. To increase access to cross-cultural counselling services.

During the spring of 1994, an MOC assistant was hired on a provincial student temporary employment program grant (STEP). An extensive literature review was conducted which examined the current counselling context. The review included a comprehensive and critical examination of theoretical frameworks and models of multicultural practice and theories and models of training, to prepare counsellors for competent practice in a multicultural environment. When the STEP funding was exhausted, the individual continued to work in a counselling residency position throughout the balance of 1994 and all of 1995. The MOC assistant worked towards developing PI's multicultural counselling initiative. The goals, objectives and programs of the multicultural counselling initiative provide a broad framework for the next phase of PI's diversification process.

The ongoing commitment of PI to offer culturally competent services to all Calgarians has resulted in PI becoming increasingly known within Calgary's ethnocultural minority and mainstream populations. An increasing number of communities and groups are asking PI to help them develop programs to address the needs of culturally diverse groups and those most vulnerable to oppression and disenfranchisement.

## What is Next for Pastoral Institute?

The Pastoral Institute remains committed to focusing on the future ways priorities as outlined in this chapter. Data that is collected by PI on a continuous basis reflect that the agency is well on its way to meeting the future ways objectives. However, multicultural organizational change and future ways is an ongoing process. While PI has definitely embarked upon this process, there are still more activities to be accomplished.

The client population is changing; in particular it is more impoverished and vulnerable than in the past. Clients requesting service at PI are experiencing problems that are more difficult to solve as many of the traditional community supports are no longer available to Calgarians.

PI's services are increasingly being provided in the community, where access is easier for clients. The counselling staff participate in diversity training and cross-cultural competency training in order to enhance their clinical competency with an increasingly diverse client base. PI will continue to evaluate all service areas against the future ways criteria to ensure consistency with the future ways goals.

PI attempted to respond to each of the future ways priorities. This process resulted in a tremendous amount of change within PI and in relation to the communities it serves. The process of change has not always been easy; it has been laden with challenges and opportunities. The single most important discovery is that this type of change has been time-consuming for the agency. However, it has been worthwhile and far-reaching as it has had an impact on everyone within PI, from the board of directors, staff, contract staff, residents, interns, volunteers and consumers. The future ways process has also resulted in increased efficiency, increased community awareness of PI and increased energy to focus on the challenges ahead.

## Learning

The external environment played an important role in agency's ability to successfully engage in MOC. For example, PI's involvement was facilitated by Alberta's focus on decreased government spending, funders who value diversity and a changing client base. Absence of one of these elements, specifically funders' commitment, may have resulted in a very different outcome.

Agency leaders' ability to appreciate the need to respond to an increasingly diverse community with different needs, combined with the willingness to creatively obtain resources to finance change (e.g., in partnerships), are important components of a successful organizational change process. It was also critical to involve staff and volunteers in the planning and implementation of the change process to garner support and motivation for change. It was just as important to have managers' and board members' unequivocal endorsement of organizational change goals. As internal champions and agents of change, staff, board and volunteer representatives were responsible for continually noting and recording successes, managing and up-dating action plans as they are accomplished and communicating and disseminating all elements of MOC to staff and volunteers.

The benefits of diversity are many, but they are often not understood. Clarity around the benefits is important before the organizational change can be successfully implemented. This can be achieved by ongoing dissemination of printed information on the benefits of change as well as ongoing forums and meetings where information is verbally exchanged and processed. In addition to discussions of the numerous benefits to diversifying an organization (Senge, 1990; Berry, 1991; Maznevski, 1994), staff motivation can be increased by framing the change effort as adding value to the agency as well as to their own personal competencies, thereby enhancing their employability.

PI has a limited number of full-time counsellor positions, and it is a challenge to keep them filled by competent persons. Every year PI is challenged as it experiences significant turnover involving the majority of counsellors. This results in an ongoing education and training program to ensure the availability of not only skilled but culturally competent counsellors.

PI seeks to recruit a diverse student population. In the 1995/1996 academic year, PI piloted the first cross-cultural competency training program in Calgary. This program is compulsory for all staff and counsellors at PI and is open to community counsellors who wish to develop their skills and competencies.

The opportunities that the change process presented have been invaluable. PI has established a diverse advisory committee for the cross-cultural counselling initiative. The committee draws from a wide range of individuals of different ethnocultural backgrounds. In addition, PI's training and education programs have the privilege of providing training to a wide range of professionals including social workers, psychologists, marriage and family therapists and pastoral counsellors who will be working cross-culturally in the community.

## CONCLUSION

The process of change brought on by the future ways and MOC process has been challenging, exciting, exhausting and stimulating. The Pastoral Institute is not the same place it was three years ago when the process began. Interestingly, in a recent exploration of PI's archives, many of the current objectives, including the future ways and MOC objectives, fit into the original objectives of PI when it was established in 1962. One primary objective of the process had been to provide linguistically and culturally appropriate social services for ethnoculturally and racially diverse populations. PI is well on its way to meeting this objective.

## REFERENCES

Agger, N. (1993). *Managing diversity/MOC and organizational change: Our developing conception of the process.* Unpublished manuscript.

Alberta Career Development and Employment. (1992). *Immigration to Alberta, decade in review.* Alberta Career Development and Employment, Immigration and Settlement: Edmonton, Alberta.

Berry, J.W. (1991). *Sociopsychological costs and benefits of multiculturalism.* Working paper No. 24. Ottawa: Economic Council of Canada.

Dimock, D. G. (1981). *Intervention and collaborative change.* Office for Educational Practice, University of Guelph: Guelph, Ontario.

Flamholtz, E. G., Randle, Y. and Sackmann, S. (1986). Personnel management: The tone of tomorrow, *Personnel Management,* 66 (7), 42 - 48.

Future Ways Task Force. (1991). *Future ways: Direction and priorities for funding and community building,* Calgary, United Way.

Hall, D. T. and Parker, V. A. (1993). The role of workplace flexibility in managing diversity, *Organizational Dynamics, Summer.*

Hayles, V. R. (1995). Diversity journeys: Implementation and bottom line results. In Alberta Multiculturalism Commission, *Proceedings of Managing Diversity: Profiting from change.* Calgary, Canada.

Kanter, R.M. (1983). *The change masters: Innovation for productivity in the American corporation.* New York: Simon and Shuster, Inc.

Lincoln, Y. and Guba, E. (Eds.). (1985). *Naturalistic inquiry*. Beverly Hills, CA: Sage Publications, Inc.

London, A. and Daft, R. L. (1992). *Managing employee diversity supplement. 2nd Ed.* Orlando, Florida: The Dryden Press.

Maznevski, M. L (1994). Understanding our differences: Performance in decision-making groups with diverse members, *Human Relations*, 47 (5), 531 - 552.

Medeiros, J. (1991). *Family services for all. Study of family services for ethnocutural and racial communities in metropolitan Toronto.* Multicultural Coalition for Access to Family Services: Toronto, Ontario.

Morgan, D. L. Ed. (1993). *Successful focus groups: Advancing the state of the art.* Newbury Park, CA: Sage Publications.

Patton, M. Q. (1990). *Qualitative evaluation and research methods.* Newbury Park, CA: Sage Publications, Inc.

PLAN:NET. (1993). *Workforce Survey.* Unpublished survey.

Schwartz, R. M. (1993), (Ed.). Managing organizational transitions in a global economy. *Monograph and Research Series*, 57, Institute of Industrial Relations, University of California, Los Angeles, California.

Senge, P. M. (1990). The leader's new work: Building learning organizations. *Sloan Management Review*, 32(1).

Simons, G. F. (1990). *The questions of diversity: Assessment tools for organizations and individuals.* Amherst, MA: ODT Incorporated.

Thomas, B. (1987). *Multiculturalism at work: A guide to organizational change.* Toronto, Ontario: YWCA.

Thomas, R. (1991). *Beyond race and gender: Unleashing the power of your total workforce by managing diversity.* New York, NY: Amacom.

United Way of Calgary and Area, (1993). *Calgary in perspective: Demographic, social and economic overview.* Calgary, United Way of Calgary, Alberta.

# IMPLICATIONS OF MULTICULTURAL POLICY
## c) for evaluation
## and research

# CHAPTER 12

# Accountability in Multicultural Practice: Setting Competencies and Standards

## Gwat-Yong Lie

In the United States there is an accumulated body of empirical evidence attesting to the underutilization of traditional mental health facilities by ethnic and racial minorities. Of those who do make use of the facilities, many are likely to terminate prematurely at rates consistently higher than those evidenced by their white counterparts. According to Sue and Sue (1990), reasons for underutilization and premature termination include the biased nature of the services themselves. Services are antagonistic and lack relevance for the culturally different client (Sue and Sue, 1990).

One reason traditional mental health services have been inappropriate for the culturally different client is that service providers themselves have not been adequately trained to render culturally appropriate services. Sue and Sue (1990) note that many service providers graduate from programs that offer a monocultural perspective, i.e., the white, middle-class perspective. Such graduates are likely to analyze the experiences of their culturally different clients using the experiences and responses of the "typical" white and middle-class person as the norm. The end result is very often a tendency to pathologize experiences and behaviours that deviate or are different from the norm. This "disregarding of cultural variations" or "the substitution of model stereotypes for the real world" are examples of the tendency to "assume universal (*etic*) applications of their concepts and goals to the exclusion of culture-specific (*emic*) views" (Sue and Sue, 1990, p. 8-9).

The situation has its parallel in Canada. Even though Canada has committed to a social policy of multiculturalism, social service systems as well as educational institutions, for example, have yet to adopt a commitment to the preparation of multiculturally competent social service providers and educators. Among voluntary consumers of social services, visible minority and First Nations people are significantly under-represented (Christensen, 1986; Yelaja and O'Neill, 1990), and a frequently reported reason for their underutilization of mainstream social services is the lack of service providers who are culturally competent, and who are able to offer culturally appropriate interventions and other related services. As in the United States, responding to this gap is critical, for at least two principal reasons: (1) the fact of increasing racial and ethnic diversity of the population at large; and (2) empirical evidence that in addition to the common stresses experienced by everyone else, minority populations are more likely to encounter issues, such as immigrant status, poverty, cultural racism, prejudice and discrimination (Sue and Sue, 1990). Given the need to respond, the challenge thus becomes how best to respond to the call for multicultural services in the social services arena.

Ideally, the process should begin with a formal endorsement by representative organizations for social service professionals that a multicultural curriculum is indeed necessary. Following from this, a coordinated effort is made to design, develop and disseminate proposed curricula for review and refinement. Integral to the task of developing a multicultural curriculum is the decision around what particular competencies to emphasize. In addition, the professional collegia needs to determine the standards which training and educational programs must meet for accreditation purposes. Further, the issue of what mechanism to use to ascertain if the training culminates in the acquisition of the desired competencies needs to be discussed and decided. In short, accountability needs to be built into the system in order to answer queries about whether multicultural training does or does not produce a professional who is multiculturally competent to practice.

Accordingly, the purpose of this chapter is to: (1) explicate the utility of a multicultural perspective as opposed to a colour-blind perspective in social service delivery to culturally different individuals, families and communities; (2) describe a set of multicultural competencies and standards for selection and inclusion in professional training and educational curricula; (3) advocate the adoption of a language-sensitive approach to interviewing and intervention; and (4) argue the importance of a system of accountability for multicultural practice. With respect to objective (3) above, rather than reinvent the wheel, the work of the Association for Multicultural Counseling and Development (AMCD) is being referred to, with the hope that the standards and competencies identified by the association can serve as a starting point for the development of a set of competencies and standards appropriate to the Canadian context.

## THE COLOUR-BLIND CONTROVERSY

A popular approach for practitioners to apply in working with multicultural individuals, families, groups and communities has been the colour-blind strategy. As explained by Proctor and Davis (1994, p.316):

> Color-blind practice [is] assumed to control for client-worker racial differences, to foster the conveyance of "true regard" for minority clients, and to ensure that all clients [are] treated equally. The acknowledgment of racial difference [is] seen as akin to racism.

Associated with this view is the argument that the endorsement of multiculturalism simply feeds into and furthers the cause of the politics of segregation. Such causes, many still argue, simply serve to divide rather than unify (D'Souza, 1991; Woodward, 1991), and for these very reasons, multiculturalism as a social policy (as compared to a colour-blind policy) is still being received tentatively and warily.

The same logic prevails in professional training and education circles. There is still reluctance and/or resistance to the adoption of a multicultural perspective to training and instruction, on the grounds that differential treatment based on ethnicity or race, or any other visible trait, constitutes discrimination. For this reason too, it is not uncommon to encounter the situation where, "program professionals continue to see multicultural courses as less legitimate than other ... requirements" (Sue, Arredondo and McDavis, 1992, p. 477).

No matter that the practice is well intentioned, the colour-blind approach has its pitfalls. Proctor and Davis (1994) note that since race is reflected in skin colour and thus "visible," it cannot be ignored. The colour-blind method then, "is based on the pretense of the nonexistence of the obvious" (p. 316). In other words, colour-blind practice simply enables professionals "to avoid the cognitive and affective components of ... racial turmoil" (p. 316). From the client's perspective, because of its obvious nature, race invariably becomes "a major element in the client's self-definition and social reality" (p. 316). Thus, in not acknowledging the client's race in the therapeutic process, the practitioner is in essence denying the client sense of self. When this happens, the utility of the helping relationship is incontrovertibly compromised. In short, race and culture do matter.

The salience of race in the helping equation is even more compelling when one considers the changing socio-demographic profile of not only those who are most likely to avail themselves of professional social services but also those who are likely to provide those services. Canada is already a multiracial, multicultural and multilingual society. The likelihood of racially dissimilar professional and client coming together has increased exponentially over the last fifty years. What is disconcerting about the meeting is that both approach each other with "little understanding of each other's social realities and with unfounded assumptions and unrealistic expectations" (Proctor and Davis, 1994, p.321). The likely end results of such a mix were mentioned early in this chapter: underutilization of services and premature termination. To ignore these outcomes would simply be to deny culturally different clients the equal opportunity of benefiting from the services of service professionals.

The issue of race and ethnicity in the helping situation is further complicated by other confounding factors. For example, since "cultural diversity is manifest at the level of ethnic and immigrant composition" (Elliott and Fleras, 1992, p. 228), certain immigrant and refugee groups have experienced difficulties adjusting to Canadian society; "[f]or permanent residents, problems arise because of concerns over political power, economic well-being, and cultural survival" (p.245). Elliott and Fleras further note that, "[r]acial minorities....have long endured racial abuse and discrimination in the field of employment, education, housing, and government services" (p.248). This is not to imply that immigrants are a particularly vulnerable group, and that they, more than any other segment of Canadian society, are most apt to find themselves on social service rolls. But, as Milne (1990, p. 199) notes:

> While immigrants as a whole do not demonstrate a
> higher incidence of mental or emotional disorder than
> indigenes, certain contingencies surrounding migration

and re-settlement can result in the imposition of increased psychological stress on some individuals and groups in their efforts to adjust to a new environment.

In other words, the reality is inescapable. The professional faces a formidable challenge, "the development of a relationship qualitatively different than either party may have previously experienced with a racially dissimilar other" (Proctor and Davis, 1994, p. 315). Correspondingly, the imperative is undeniable. The training and education of service professionals must adopt a multicultural perspective.

## COMPETENCIES AND STANDARDS FOR MULTICULTURAL PRACTICE

An important part of the multicultural competence discourse is the challenge of convincing the professional collegium and ultimately society at large of the merits and benefits of multicultural training and education, and to incorporate the content into the core of professional training and educational curricula. Simply mandating such content without discussion and debate is certainly one way to effect compliance, but it is one made at considerable cost. It may only engender deep-seated resentment from service providers and the general populace. Worse, the target of such resentment is likely to be the very client needing the services.

On the other hand, if the issue of multiculturally competent services is framed in terms of a civil rights entitlement, the imperative to adopt a multicultural curriculum in professional training and education then rests upon an ethical obligation to render multicultural services to multicultural clients. As Sue, Arredondo and McDavis (1992, p. 480) contend, "professionals without training or competence in working with clients from diverse cultural backgrounds are unethical and potentially harmful." If the professional collegium is persuaded that, on ethical grounds, multicultural competence must be an integral component in professional training curricula, then the logical extension to this commitment must be the identification and implementation of a set of standards that becomes a part of the accreditation criteria.

Unlike many other training programs, multicultural training has no clear finish line, nor does it fit well with being conceptualized as a discreet element or stand alone module in a training curriculum. The nature of the training is such that,

.... becoming culturally skilled is an *active* process, that it is ongoing, and that it is a process that *never reaches an end point.* Implicit is recognition of the complexity and diversity of the client and client populations, and acknowledgment of our own personal limitations, and the need to always improve. (Sue and Sue, 1990, p. 164)

Ironically, this continuously evolving attribute of multicultural competence training and education is not unique or specific to the subject area. The other principal competencies that professional training and education demand also share the same characteristic. Because the state of knowledge is dynamic and never static, and the quest to know is never-ending, the need for continuing education and ongoing training thus becomes a perpetual reality.

In the quest for cross-cultural competencies and standards, Sue and Sue (1990) are widely recognized for having made an important contribution to the emergent conceptual framework. They identified three characteristics which distinguish the culturally skilled counsellor from one who is not so skilled. The first characteristic is counsellor awareness of her or his own assumptions about human behaviour, values and biases. Such a counsellor understands the impact of their own cultural conditioning on their perceptions of and behaviours with others. The second characteristic is the counsellor's ability to appreciate and understand the world view of his or her culturally different client. The third characteristic is counsellor commitment to the development and practice of "appropriate, relevant and sensitive intervention strategies and skills" (Sue and Sue, 1990, p. 170) for work with the culturally different client.

The other important axis of this multicultural conceptual framework is dimensions of competency. Sue, Arredondo and McDavis (1992, p. 481) note that three such dimensions are commonly identified: beliefs and attitudes, knowledge and skills. The first dimension addresses counsellor attitudes and beliefs about race and ethnicity, about the value of multiculturalism as a socio-political reality, and about the need to self-monitor for biases, prejudices and stereotypes. The second dimension addresses the knowledge base of the counsellor, which addresses the counsellor's comprehensive understanding of his or her own world view, those of the culturally different clients he or she works with, and the socio-political origins and current context of both. The third dimension, skills, refer to the counsellor's repertoire of intervention techniques and strategies for working with culturally different clients.

Using a 3 x 3 grid of counsellor characteristics (counsellor awareness of own assumptions, values, and biases; understanding the world view of the culturally different client; and developing appropriate intervention strategies and techniques) and dimensions of competency (beliefs and attitudes, knowledge and skills), Sue, Arredondo and McDavis (1992, Appendix A) offer a detailed conceptual framework of cross-cultural competencies and objectives. This is shown in outline form in the boxed text on the following pages.

These competencies could serve as minimum, "good enough" standards for multicultural competence. These, of course, would be subject to revisions and refinement with practice, experience and evaluation data to point to what needs to be revised and how it is to be revised.

Interestingly, Green's (1995) ethnic competence model identifies similar competencies compared to the Sue, Arredondo and McDavis's (1992) proposal above. His ethnic competence model addresses four core elements: (1) ethnographic knowledge base; (2) professional preparedness; (3) comparative analyses; and (4) appropriate intervention. The ethnographic knowledge base refers to understanding that allows the practitioner to identify what is salient in the client's culture and problem(s) or presenting issue(s). Professional preparedness addresses the personal meaning that race and culture has for the practitioner, along with its impact on the practitioner's professional relationships, particularly those with clients of a different cultural background. The issue of comparative analysis in Green's model refers to the ability of the ethnically competent practitioner to appreciate and understand that clients may subscribe to culturally different world views, and to respond with empathy and differentially (i.e., on an individual basis) in recognition and acknowledgment of, and respect for, the different perspectives. Finally, as with Sue, Arredondo and McDavis, Green recognizes the salience of differential intervention strategies, selectively applied, taking into account the cultural subtleties and nuances prescribed by each culture vis-à-vis presenting issues and help-seeking behaviours. In this regard, he predicts that "appropriate forms of intervention" will become the "front-line" work for future cross-cultural human services, whereby, "[m]ethods for learning about all these ...people and of meeting their needs appropriately may become a political demand as much as it is an ethical one" (Green, 1995, p. 48).

## Figure 1: Proposed Cross-Cultural Competencies and Objectives

**I. Counsellor awareness of own cultural values and biases**

*A. Attitudes and beliefs*

1. Culturally skilled counsellors have moved from being culturally unaware to being aware of and sensitive to their own cultural heritage and to valuing and respecting differences.
2. Culturally skilled counsellors are aware of how their own cultural background, experiences, attitudes, values and biases influence psychological processes.
3. Culturally skilled counsellors are able to recognize the limits of their competencies and expertise.
4. Culturally skilled counsellors are comfortable with differences that exist between themselves and clients in terms of race, ethnicity, culture and beliefs.

*B. Knowledge*

1. Culturally skilled counsellors have specific knowledge about their own racial and cultural heritage and how it personally and professionally affects their definitions and biases of normality-abnormality and the processes of counselling.
2. Culturally skilled counsellors possess knowledge and understanding about how oppression, racism, discrimination and stereotyping affect them and their work. They acknowledge their own racist attitudes, beliefs and feelings. Although this standard applies to all groups, for white counsellors it may mean that they understand how they may have directly or indirectly benefited from individual, institutional and cultural racism (white identity development models).
3. Culturally skilled counsellors possess knowledge about their social impact upon others. They are knowledgeable about communication style differences, how their style may clash or facilitate the counselling process with minority clients, and how to anticipate the impact that it may have on others.

*C. Skills*

1. Culturally skilled counsellors seek out educational, consultative and training experiences to enrich their understanding and effectiveness in

working with culturally different populations. Recognizing the limits of their competencies, they (a) seek consultation, (b) seek further training or education, (c) refer out to more qualified individuals or resources, or (d) engage in a combination of these.

2. Culturally skilled counsellors are constantly seeking to understand themselves as racial and cultural beings and are actively seeking a non-racist identity.

**II. Counsellor awareness of client's world view**

*A. Attitudes and beliefs*

1. Culturally skilled counsellors are aware of their negative emotional reactions towards other racial and ethnic groups that may prove detrimental to their clients in counselling. They are willing to contrast their own beliefs and attitudes with those of their culturally different clients in a non-judgmental fashion.

2. Culturally skilled counsellors are aware of their stereotypes and preconceived notions that they may hold towards other racial and ethnic minority groups.

*B. Knowledge*

1. Culturally skilled counsellors possess specific knowledge and information about the particular group that they are working with. They are aware of the life experiences, cultural heritage and historical background of their culturally different clients. This particular competency is strongly linked to the "minority identity development models" available in the literature.

2. Culturally skilled counsellors understand how race, culture, ethnicity and so forth may affect personality formation, vocational choices, manifestation of psychological disorders, help-seeking behaviour and the appropriateness or inappropriateness of counselling approaches.

3. Culturally skilled counsellors understand socio-political influences that impinge upon the life of racial and ethnic minorities. Immigration issues, poverty, racism, stereotyping and powerlessness all leave major scars that may influence the counselling process.

*C. Skills*

1. Culturally skilled counsellors should familiarize themselves with relevant research regarding mental health and mental disorders of various ethnic and racial groups. They should actively seek out educational experiences that enrich their knowledge, understanding and cross-cultural skills.

2. Culturally skilled counsellors should become actively involved with minority individuals outside the counselling setting (community events, social and political functions, celebrations, friendships, neighbourhood groups and so forth) so that their perspective of minorities is more than an academic or helping exercise.

## III. Culturally appropriate intervention strategies

*A. Attitudes and beliefs*

1. Culturally skilled counsellors respect clients' religious and/or spiritual beliefs and values about physical and mental functioning.

2. Culturally skilled counsellors respect indigenous helping practices and respect minority community's intrinsic, help-giving networks.

3. Culturally skilled counsellors value bilingualism and do not view another language as an impediment to counselling (monolingualism may be the culprit).

*B. Knowledge*

1. Culturally skilled counsellors have a clear and explicit knowledge and understanding of the generic characteristics of counselling and therapy (culture bound, class bound and monolingual) and how they may clash with the cultural values of various minority groups.

2. Culturally skilled counsellors are aware of institutional barriers that prevent minorities from using mental health services.

3. Culturally skilled counsellors have knowledge of the potential bias in assessment instruments and use procedures; they interpret findings keeping in mind the cultural and linguistic characteristics of the clients.

4. Culturally skilled counsellors have knowledge of minority family structures, hierarchies, values and beliefs. They are knowledgeable about community characteristics and the resources in the community and the family.

5. Culturally skilled counsellors should be aware of relevant discriminatory practices at the social and community level that may affect the psychological welfare of the population being served.

C. *Skills*

1. Culturally skilled counsellors engage in a variety of different verbal and non-verbal helping responses. They are able to send and receive verbal and non-verbal messages accurately and appropriately. They are not tied down to only one method or approach to helping but recognize that helping styles and approaches may be culture bound. When they sense that their helping style is limited and potentially inappropriate, they can anticipate and ameliorate its negative impact.

2. Culturally skilled counsellors exercise institutional intervention skills on behalf of their clients. They help clients determine whether a problem stems from racism or bias in others (the concept of healthy paranoia) so that clients do not inappropriately blame themselves.

3. Culturally skilled counsellors are not averse to seeking consultation with traditional healers, religious and spiritual leaders and practitioners in the treatment of culturally different clients when appropriate.

4. Culturally skilled counsellors take responsibility for interacting in the language requested by the client; this may mean appropriate referral to outside resources. A serious problem arises when the linguistic skills of the counsellor do not match the language of the client. This being the case, counsellors should (a) seek a translator with cultural knowledge and appropriate professional background or (b) refer to a knowledgeable and competent bilingual counsellor.

5. Culturally skilled counsellors have training and expertise in traditional assessment and testing instruments. They not only understand the technical aspects of the instruments but are also aware of the cultural limitations. This allows them to use test instruments for the welfare of diverse clients.

6. Culturally skilled counsellors should work to eliminate biases, prejudices and discriminatory practices. They should be cognizant of socio-political contexts in conducting evaluations and providing

interventions, and should develop sensitivity to issues of oppression, sexism and racism.

7. Culturally skilled counsellors take responsibility in educating their clients to the process of psychological intervention, such as goals, expectations, legal rights and the counsellor's orientation.

Source: Sue, Arredondo and McDavis, 1992

Practitioner-based characteristics that Green (1995) considers as essential for the promotion of ethnic competence include awareness of one's limitations; openness to cultural differences; adoption of a client-oriented, systematic learning style; appropriate utilization of cultural resources; and acknowledgment of cultural integrity. Thus, to become an ethnically competent professional, such a practitioner is aware of his or her own personal limitations and alert to environmental limitations. He or she is receptive and responsive to "new and perhaps challenging experiences" (Green, 1995, p. 91); in learning about others, the practitioner learns about self.

Additionally, the practitioner needs to be attentive to how "the counseling relationship fits into the client's normative expectations" (Green, 1995, p. 93), recognizing that cultural differences might account for different client responses. Another prerequisite trait is acknowledging that clients know a great deal about what is happening to them, and for the practitioner to adopt a role akin to that of a student. Further, when it comes to making resource referrals, instead of looking to mainstream resources, Green (1995, p. 95) suggests encouraging clients to draw on "the natural strengths inherent in their own traditions and communities...." Finally, an ethnically competent practitioner views all cultures as sources of "creative complexity" (p. 96).

## A LANGUAGE-SENSITIVE APPROACH

Typically, when the issue of language competency is raised, the discussion tends to be limited to the issue of whether, in order to be seen as competent, practitioners must acquire fluency in at least one additional language. In their model, Sue, Arredondo and McDavis (1992) see bilingualism as a plus, but they do not call for second language abilities as a competency requirement. They do recommend, however, that when the linguistic skills of the professional do not match those of the clients, the services of a translator be secured.

A different variation on the same theme is raised and discussed by Green. He addresses the issue of a language-sensitive approach as an integral aspect of cross-cultural work. Citing Spradley (1979, p. 17), Green contends that, "language is more than just a means for communicating about reality: it is a tool for constructing reality. Different languages create and express different realities" (Green, 1995, p. 118). Since different languages create different realities, Green concludes that "different uses of a single language create alternative realities as well" (1995, p. 118/9). On this account, the issue of "thinking self-consciously" (p. 118) about language—not just about how the client uses language to depict their concerns but also how the practitioner uses language in the therapeutic milieu—becomes critical to the helping process. This process of thinking self-consciously should form an integral part of the training and education of a multiculturally competent practitioner.

For example, Green cautions against the use of jargon and esoteric language by the practitioner, which would serve to alienate rather than enjoin the culturally different client. Jargon presumes professional expertise and is one way that power differentials are maintained, and it functions to "override and discount client speech preferences and the community and beliefs" (Green, 1995, p.118) . He also suggests that greater attention be given to the use of language by the client, citing as an example how a sociolinguistic analysis of a mental health interview by a researcher lent important insights to the client's sense of self. Briefly, he advocates taking an emic approach to listening, where clients define the problem and describe their experiences in terms and concepts that are meaningful to them. This would include understanding the client's use of metaphors and culturally specific expressions. In other words, the practitioner needs to have a good understanding of the meanings that clients attach to behaviour, events, other persons, words and settings in order to understand how they negotiate everyday living. One useful tool to help the practitioner transcend the limitations of culturally bound techniques in information gathering is the use of ethnographic interviewing from an emic perspective (Green, 1995).

In an ethnographic interview, the client becomes the expert and the cultural guide, defining the scope and depth of the presenting issues for the practitioner. The role of the practitioner is to "channel the flow of the interview by using linguistic features of the conversation as they are provided by the client" (Green, 1995, p. 133). There is no given format or procedure; the focus is on language, how the client uses it and what it suggests of the client's state of being and thinking. The challenge is to guide the interview using cues supplied by the client. Everything said is important and must be recorded accurately. Through content analysis, the descriptors, metaphors and behaviour sequences or scripts that people use to cope can be identified, and their relationship to each other examined and understood for their implications for service needs.

## EVALUATION OF MULTICULTURAL PRACTICE

In order for the multiculturally competent professional to be able to differentially apply culturally appropriate intervention strategies and techniques across clients from diverse cultural backgrounds, he or she needs to obtain feedback and collect information on any model or technique utilized in order to ascertain if these were indeed "culturally appropriate" and thus justified for continued use. It would be unethical to continue to use methods and techniques that were culturally inappropriate and thus ineffective. But what is practice effectiveness?

According to Blythe, Tripodi and Briar (1994, p. 160), practice effectiveness can be defined in relation to three conditions: (1) goal attainment, (2) the association between practice intervention and goal attainment, and (3) generality. Their definition of practice effectiveness in each of these three conditions is as follows:

(1) Practice effectiveness is the extent to which practice goals for a particular practice intervention are attained (effectiveness).
When more than one intervention is involved, practice effectiveness is the extent to which one particular intervention is relatively more successful than another intervention in achieving practice goals (relative efficacy).

(2) Practice effectiveness is the degree to which successful goal attainment is correlated with and/or causally related to the practice intervention(s).

(3) Practice effectiveness is enhanced when the relationship between practice intervention and goal attainment can be generalized over

time for a particular client, across clients for similar problems, and for clients with different problems in different environmental conditions.

Thus, central to the notion of practice effectiveness is the matter of whether goals for clients are met.

Goals specify what clients wish to accomplish and serve the following functions:

(1) Ensure that practitioners and clients are in agreement about objectives to be achieved;
(2) Provide direction and continuity to the helping process and prevent needless wandering;
(3) Facilitate the development and selection of appropriate strategies and interventions;
(4) Assist practitioners and clients in monitoring their progress; and
(5) Serve as outcome criteria in evaluating the effectiveness of specific interventions and of the helping process (Hepworth, Rooney and Larsen, 1997, p. 344).

Goal selection, invariably, is problem-based or issues-oriented. However, as Green (1982) notes, problem identification, linguistic idiosyncrasies in problem labelling, strategies for problem resolution and standards for knowing that a problem has been successfully resolved are culturally defined and, hence, culturally specific. For instance, each culture has its own explanations for the source of a problem, associated symptoms, the way to recognize and name these, and the course of the illness. In addition, Green notes that cultures also provide a sick role for those inflicted, prescriptions for treatment and definitions of successful treatment outcomes. For these reasons, it becomes incumbent on the practitioner to learn how people define problems, problem-solve within their own communities and what their expectations are in terms of successful outcomes.

Whose perspective of practice effectiveness should prevail—the client's, or the service provider's? Literature on strengths (see Saleeby, 1992) and empowerment (see Gutierrez, 1990, 1994) perspectives recommend that the client's perspective prevail. Multicultural practice, being client-centred in orientation, also advocates for adopting the client's perspective. This definition of effectiveness requires that goal-setting and goal-accomplishment activities actively involve the client. When the client's definition of effectiveness is taken, and when she or he has been instrumental in setting service goals, then interventions that are culturally appropriate are highly likely to result in desired outcomes. In other words, interventions are also very likely to be effective.

On the other hand, if the service provider's conception of success or efficacy is adopted, the likelihood of the intervention being both culturally inappropriate as well as therapeutically ineffective is extremely high. For example, a Chinese woman presents at a shelter for battered women having recently experienced a severe battering episode. Her immediate goal is to receive shelter and respite from the abusive situation. She intends to return home the next day giving her husband time to cool down. She is willing to receive counselling services and indicates that her goal is to learn how to better cope with the battering episodes. She explains that better coping would involve not having to turn to the shelter for help in the future. Leaving her batterer is not an option for her as that will only bring shame to the family.

A culturally competent service provider would reassure her that even though she may not use the shelter the next time an abusive episode erupted, the shelter would always be there if she needed. Together, client and service provider could explore means of protecting herself from serious injury during physical assaults and identify other resources that she could turn to for respite and shelter. These resources could include a trusted friend or relative.

On the other hand, if the service provider believes that the batterings are too frequent and regular to ethically endorse returning home to the abusive situation, then she may select work on enhancing self-esteem and leaving the abusive relationship as service goals. These goals may, in the eyes of the service provider, be culturally appropriate for the woman, although from the woman's perspective it may not be. The client is unlikely to appreciate the utility of the services and as a consequence is unlikely to follow through. Clinically, the intervention was ineffective.

A competency-based approach to the delivery of services would indicate that the competent multicultural practitioner must be someone who can "solve significant problems, devise new techniques, and evaluate both these new procedures as well as adaptations of older ones" (Barlow, Hayes and Nelson, 1984, p. 18), and be able to do so in a culturally meaningful and appropriate way. This approach begs the question:

should the training of the multiculturally competent professional be limited to activities to determine whether a desired client outcome was achieved—*clinical practice evaluation*—or should the training be rigorous enough such that, if the findings warrant it, significant contributions to the existing body of scientific knowledge are being made, i.e., *clinical research?* The distinction between the two concepts was made by Corcoran and Gingerich (1990) in recognition of the different level of uses to which resultant findings are put to.

According to Bloom, Fischer and Orme (1995, p. 15),

> The essence of successful practice is to help resolve
> client problems and to attain client objectives, without
> creating problems for others. Probably the most clear
> and socially accountable way of determining whether
> our practice is successful is through systematized,
> objective evaluation methods that can be replicated
> (repeated) by others.

These guidelines suggest that, at a minimum, the multiculturally competent professional should possess the requisite competencies to evaluate practice activities, which are necessary for reasons of professional accountability and for improved practice (Corcoran and Gingerich, 1990). Hence, because "[p]ractice evaluation provides empirically based feedback about change in a client's problem and the attainment of goals" (Corcoran and Gingerich, 1990, p. 32), practice evaluation appears to be the baseline qualification that multiculturally competent professionals should possess.

An important issue that needs clarification in the professional field is what constitutes a multiculturally competent intervention? Related to this are questions such as, does this entail the modification and adaptation of mainstream models and techniques for cultural relevance, or does this require developing a whole new way of intervening? Are both types of interventions equally appropriate and effective, or is one type superior? Again, the answers can only come if service providers are trained and willing to monitor and evaluate their practice with multicultural populations. There again, the onus for knowledge- and skills-building does not rest solely with the professionals working at grass-roots level. This responsibility ought to be shared with every person who has an investment in the success of the multicultural policy (e.g., educators, scholars and policy-makers), and its operationalization in the social service arena (including social service administrators and managers) into the provision of culturally appropriate service. Nonetheless, the fact remains that practitioners do play an important role in this critical process.

On the other hand, if data collected from rigorous evaluation studies prove that culturally configured methods and techniques to be unnecessary, then the profession, the field and society at large needs to know that. There again, unless well designed and carefully implemented evaluation studies are conducted, the query forever nags at society: are culturally appropriate techniques and methods in social service delivery justifiable and, if so, on what grounds?

## In Closing

A social service professional in an increasingly racially and culturally diverse milieu would be hard pressed to explain why he or she chose to ignore the call to become competent in delivering services to multicultural individuals, families, groups and communities. By the same token, professional organizations would be remiss if the training and educational curricula of member professionals do not reflect the multicultural perspective of the client or patient populations that they serve. Personal and organizational initiatives to acquire multicultural competencies, however, need to be supported and sanctioned by the profession and, in turn, society at large.

One form of professional endorsement of multicultural training and education is the selection and establishment of competencies and standards for training, education and practice. These competencies and standards serve as a means for quality assurance, accountability and professional credence. Prescriptions for competencies and standards evolve over time as they incorporate new knowledge about the dynamics of diversity and the concomitant skills needed to deliver appropriate services to diverse populations. Provisions for continuing education need to be made available. Being multiculturally competent, and the refining of those competencies, is a never-ending process. Already, another challenge for further growth and development as a multicultural practitioner has been issued.

Gould (1996) contends that becoming multiculturally competent is not simply about learning how to work with a particular ethnic or cultural group, learning about other cultural groups or even having the perspective of another culture. Drawing on Bennett's (1986) notion of total integration of ethnorelativism, Gould maintains that what is required is, "a framework that goes beyond encouraging intercultural learning and multicultural competency to building a multicultural identity for all groups" (p. 38). This compels all members of society to consider and hopefully break out of ethnic psychological captivity, a term she attributes to Hoopes (1979). To Gould, a paradigmatic shift "to a framework that informs thinking at a transcultural level rather than a model that merely provides specific strategies for ethnic-specific practice" (p. 30) is indicated. She argues that the shift is necessary to short-circuit the common approach to viewing multiculturalism, which is in terms of forced dichotomies, e.g., white people versus people of colour and established immigrants versus new immigrants.

Thus, multiculturalism needs to be reconceptualized as seeking to accomplish, "an understanding of social discourse in the cultural context—that is, a cultural dialogue" (Gould, 1996, p. 38). Taking a dynamic, non-linear perspective is critical because of the "multitude of equivalent cultural realities within society" (p. 37). Within this framework, "marginality" rids itself of its negative undertones (e.g., out-group and disaffected). Instead, marginality and conflict are looked upon as essential to the functioning of a healthy social system. Thus, the challenge to all, according to Gould, is to adopt a collectivist or all-inclusive perspective and to create an interrelated, complex, yet harmonious whole out of previously disparate parts. Against this backdrop, social service professionals function transculturally. She cites Bennett (1986, p. 27), to underscore the importance of adapting a transcultural perspective to multicultural practice:

> Today, the failure to exercise intercultural sensitivity
> is not simply bad business or bad morality, it is self-
> destructive. So we face a choice: overcome the legacy
> of our history, or lose history itself for all time. (Gould,
> 1996, p. 40)

In the final analysis, multicultural practice is all about working with individuals, families, group and communities of diverse backgrounds who have different ways of being, doing and viewing the world. Understanding those ways of being and doing facilitates knowing what to do, what to say, and how to be, such that one's behaviour promotes rather than impedes interpersonal relationship-building. For social service professionals this interpersonal skill is a prerequisite to becoming a culturally competent service provider who can work skilfully across cultures. In addition, if each service provider takes the responsibility of monitoring and evaluating what knowledge is essential, what type of skill is critical, what method or technique needs modification and what does not, he or she is engaging in and contributing to a steady process of knowledge- and skills-building. Over time and across professionals, these contributions become a vital source of information for the establishment of multicultural practice as a competent, credible and bona fide model of social service delivery. Alternatively, monitoring and evaluation may produce results that support the promulgation of a generic, nonculturally configured set of techniques and methods to serve all consumers of social services alike. Whatever the outcome, society in general has a right to know, and social service professionals have an obligation to find out.

## REFERENCES

Barlow, David H., Hayes, Steven C. and Nelson, Rosemary O. (1984). *The scientist practitioner: Research accountability in clinical and educational settings.* New York, NY: Pergamon Press.

Bennett, M.J. (1986). Towards ethnorelativism: A developmental model of cultural sensitivity. In R.M. Paige (ed.), *Cross-cultural orientation: New conceptualizations and applications.* Lanham, MD: University Press of America.

Bloom, Martin, Fischer, Joel and Orme, John G. (1995). *Evaluating practice: Guidelines for the accountable professional.* Boston: Allyn and Bacon.

Blythe, Betty, Tripodi, Tony and Briar, Scott (1994). *Direct practice research in human service agencies.* New York: Columbia University Press.

Christensen, Carole P. (1986). Cross-cultural social work: Fallacies, fears and failings. *Intervention,* 74, 6-15.

Corcoran, K. and Gingerich, W. (1990). Practice evaluation: Setting goals, measuring and assessing change. In Kevin J. Corcoran (ed.), *Structuring change: Effective practice for common client problems.* Chicago, IL: Lyceum Books.

D'Souza, D. (1991). *Illiberal education: The politics of race and sex on campus.* New York: Vintage Books.

Elliott, Jean Leonard and Fleras, Augie (1992). *Unequal relations: An introduction to race and ethnic dynamics in Canada.* Scarborough, Ontario: Prentice-Hall Canada, Inc.

Gould, Ketayun H. (1996). The misconstruing of multiculturalism: The Stanford debate and social work. In Patricia L. Ewalt, Edith M. Freeman, Stuart A. Kirk and Dennis L. Poole (eds.), *Multicultural issues in social work.* Washington, D.C.: NASW Press.

Green, James W. (1982). *Cultural awareness in the human services.* Englewood Cliffs, NJ: Prentice-Hall, Inc.

Green, James W. (1995).*Cultural awareness in the human services: A multi-ethnic approach.* Boston, MA: Allyn and Bacon.

Gutierrez, L.M. (1990). Working with women of color: An empowerment perspective. *Social Work,* 35(2), 149-153.

Gutierrez, L. M. (1994). Beyond coping: An empowerment perspective on stressful life events. *Journal of Sociology and Social Welfare,* 21(3), 201-219.

Hepworth, Dean H., Rooney, Ronald H. and Larsen, Jo Ann (1997). *Direct social work practice: Theory and skills.* Pacific Grove, CA: Brooks/Cole.

Hoopes, D.S. (1979). Intercultural communications: Concepts and the psychology of intercultural experience. In M.D. Pusch (ed.), *Multicultural education: A cross-cultural training approach.* New York: Intercultural Press. (As cited in Gould, 1996).

Milne, Winifred M. (1990). Factors affecting adaptation of immigrants and refugees to Canada: Implications for social work practice. *The Social Worker,* 58(4), 199-204.

Proctor, K. Enola and Davis, Larry E. (1994). The challenge of racial difference: Skills for clinical practice. *Social Work,* 39(3), 314-323.

Saleeby, D. (Ed.) (1992). *The strengths perspective in social work practice.* New York: Longmans.

Spradley, James P. (1979). *The ethnographic interview* . New York: Holt, Rinehart and Winston.

Sue, Derald W., Arredondo, Patricia and McDavis, Roderick, J. (1992). Multicultural counseling competencies and standards: A call to the profession. *Journal of Counseling and Development,* 70, 477 - 486.

Sue, Derald W. and Sue, David (1990). *Counseling the culturally different: Theory and practice.* New York: Wiley.

Woodward, C.V. (1991, July 18). Freedom and the universities. *New York Review of Books,* 41(13), 32-37.

Yelaja, S. and O'Neill, B. (1990). *Multiculturalism and social work education: Resources for change.* Waterloo, Ontario: Wilfred Laurier University Press.

# CHAPTER 13

# Developing Cultural Sensitivity in Social Service Research

*Judy Krysik*

We live in a society that leaves the responsibility for the ethical production and dissemination of research to the integrity of the researcher and the interpretation of published findings to the critical evaluation of the research consumer. Striving for cultural competence in social service research demonstrates a concern for the very relevance and validity of research. Culturally competent research is critical for displacing knowledge that has been oppressive to entire groups of people and for dispelling myths and negative stereotypes that are prevalent in our society. In addition, if we are to value the notion of diverse world views, then culturally competent research is critical for expanding our Euro-American, male-dominated knowledge base.

To be ignorant of our past leaves us vulnerable to repeat our mistakes. These words serve to remind us that the history of social science research is inundated with examples of its misuse. In 1968 for example, Arthur Jensen reported on the basis of IQ testing that whites were more intelligent than blacks and that intelligence was inherited. He concluded, therefore, that special training programs for blacks were a waste of resources (Dewdney, 1995). In 1989 J. Phillipe Rushton, a psychologist at the University of Western Ontario in London, reported that Asiatics, whites and blacks could be ranked in that order when it came to decreasing intelligence and less orderly behaviour (Dewdney,

1995). In 1994 Free Press released *The Bell Curve*, a controversial book authored by Richard Herrnstein and Charles Murray, which represents a continuation in the mission to empirically justify racial differences in intelligence. Despite the fact that such research has been heavily critiqued as pseudo-scientific, racist creed, its permanence and the damage it creates cannot be undone (Miele, 1995).

Research on race and intelligence is among the most blatant examples of cultural insensitivity and flawed research methodology. This type of research may be described as culturally destructive, that which refers to differences in race and ethnicity as a better than or worse than relationship. In the majority of research pursuits, however, cultural insensitivity is much more unconscious in intent and subtle to detect, for instance, research based on the assumption that culture makes no difference and that service provision is unbiased, or research that acknowledges culture but fails to address its relevance.

The purpose of this chapter is to present guidelines to aide in the production and critique of culturally competent research in the social services. Culturally competent research is not identified by whether the techniques of data collection are qualitative or quantitative, nor can it be distinguished by researchers who bring cultural perspectives to bear versus those who study a culturally diverse population. Developing cultural competence in research implies acknowledging and incorporating the relevance of culture at all phases of the research process, from selecting the research topic to reporting the findings.

## THE RESEARCH PROCESS

To produce culturally competent research one must focus on the knowledge and skills required at each phase of the research process (See Figure 1). Although the order of the research phases may vary depending on the research methodology, generally all six phases apply to some degree in every research endeavour. In a traditional quantitative research study, conceptual clarity about the research question precedes the collection and analysis of data. Qualitative research and research guided by feminist or participatory action principles do not, in contrast, generally use data collection and analysis to answer questions and test hypotheses. These approaches to research are more likely to be used to discover what the most important questions may be and to refine hypotheses. The more our collective research experience with culturally

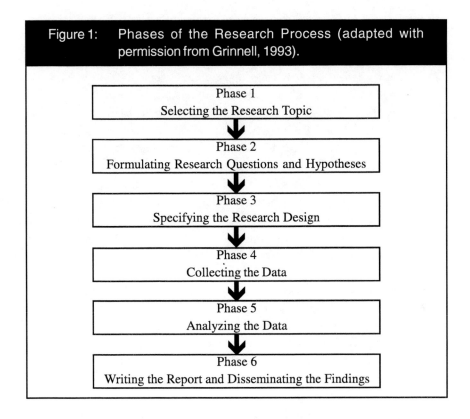

Figure 1: Phases of the Research Process (adapted with permission from Grinnell, 1993).

Phase 1
Selecting the Research Topic

Phase 2
Formulating Research Questions and Hypotheses

Phase 3
Specifying the Research Design

Phase 4
Collecting the Data

Phase 5
Analyzing the Data

Phase 6
Writing the Report and Disseminating the Findings

diverse groups grows, the more comprehensive our knowledge and skills in producing culturally competent research at each phase of the research process will become. The guidelines presented in this chapter, therefore, are meant to serve as a point of reference, not as a definitive list.

## SELECTING THE RESEARCH TOPIC

Selecting the research topic is the first step in any research study. A good research topic is one in which something in the situation is unknown and there is some reason for wanting to reduce the unknown (Rothery, 1993). Social work research topics are commonly selected by the researcher based on a combination of personal interest, a thorough review of related literature and expressed practice concern. Striving for cultural sensitivity in research topic selection, the researcher must be aware of the potential for biases in all three of these sources.

### Assessing self-awareness and personal bias

Unfortunately, it is impossible to be socialized in this society without being exposed to a myriad of opportunities to internalize negative beliefs and attitudes about those who are not members of one's cultural group (Grace, 1992). Throughout civilization, people have been separated socially, economically and educationally by ethnicity, race, gender and age. The results of this separation have been destructive myths, stereotypes and attitudes regarding diverse groups and their cultures. The memorabilia of racism is reflected in the hallmarks of popular culture, in musical lyrics, movies, advertisements, cartoons and literature.

Considering the embedded nature of racism in our society, we might question if those situated outside of a cultural group are capable of conducting culturally competent research. Although being a member of the cultural group studied is likely to confer certain advantages, such as language compatibility, a better understanding of cultural norms and increased acceptance and accessibility, it is no guarantee of cultural sensitivity or competence. Biases develop not only in relation to race and ethnicity but with regard to gender, age, socio-economic status and locality. The first step in working towards developing cultural sensitivity and competence in research topic selection, therefore, is to acknowledge one's own potential for cultural insensitivity. Engaging in a process of self-awareness is as important to the social service researcher as it is to the practitioner. Heightened self-awareness will help focus more careful attention on cultural sensitivity, both in the production and consumption of research.

### Assessing bias in the professional and academic literature

Biases in the literature can severely limit the generation of culturally competent research topics. Cultural biases in the literature characteristically assume three forms. First is the exclusion of diverse cultural groups. Because scholars have neglected to focus on minorities for so long, the number of available studies are few (Marlow, 1993). In addition to the overall lack of presence of minorities in the literature is the overgeneralization of existing studies. An example of overgeneralization would be a study that makes reference to Hispanics based on a sample of immigrants from Mexico.

The second form of cultural bias in the literature is a focus on negative attributes and the most disadvantaged (Beauvais and Trimble, 1992; Hill, 1978). Over time, this negative focus has led to the development and reinforcement of destructive stereotypes. Much of the literature on American Indians, for instance, pertains to alcohol and drug abuse, giving the impression that this problem is universal across the entire group. The tendency to define difference as pathology, and to rely on a unidirectional transfer of expertise, has functioned to delay knowledge development in the social service domains.

Third, a focus on negative attributes occurs at the expense of acknowledging the positive. Little is known, for instance, about the resilience of American Indians in the face of relocation and the loss of economic and cultural forms of acceptable behaviour (Padilla and Salgado de Snyder, 1992). And only recently has the idea of kinship care gained popularity as a preferred practice concept in child protection (Duer Berrick and Barth, 1994). The concept of kinship care has been central to the American Indian culture for generations, but unfortunately it has taken social service researchers decades to frame it as a concept worth pursuing.

## Assessing bias in social service agencies

Involving practitioners in the selection of the research topic acknowledges that they have important insights to contribute (Marlow, 1993). Bias may also exist, however, where research topics are derived from practice. American Indian children, for instance, are over-represented in Canada's foster care system based on their proportionate share of the total child population. Often, however, social service practitioners tend to emphasize individual parenting deficits and ignore the external and institutional factors such as poverty, poor education and loss of culture that impede healthy family functioning (Hill, 1978). This type of reductionism leads to a very narrow view of culturally diverse groups and the difficulties they face. Bias in social service agencies can also lead to the study of diverse populations only in typical contexts (Reinharz, 1992). For example, a typical context would involve the study of American Indians on reservations and the study of women in the context of motherhood. Studying populations only in typical contexts promotes stereotypes and masks within-group diversity.

### Acquiring rrerequisite knowledge

Given the potential for bias in the three most common sources of research topic selection, how does one achieve cultural sensitivity? One of the best ways to recognize and avoid bias, be it personal, written or institutional, is to invest time and effort in learning about the cultural group of interest. At a minimum, the researcher should acquire knowledge of: (a) cultural group history; (b) communication norms; (c) language preference for nonfamilial interactions; (d) the significance of religion or spirituality; and (e) the social meaning of gender. Conveying an attitude that is consistent with a willingness to learn, and respect and appreciation for cultural differences, is important in the process of acquiring necessary prerequisite knowledge (Grace, 1992).

### Differentiating between research *for* versus research *on*

In selecting a research topic it is useful to distinguish between research for versus research on a cultural group. Research for can be conceptualized as an altruistic activity, research pursued out of an unselfish concern for the welfare of others. Research for is consciously aimed at emancipating culturally diverse groups and enhancing their lives. Research for helps group members connect their personal experiences with the larger social context, captures how they struggle against and adapt to the dominant culture, and embraces within-group diversity. Bowman (1983) referred to this concept as functional relevance, promoting the expressed needs and perspectives of the group studied. Research on, in contrast, may be seen as an opportunistic activity, viewing the cultural group merely as a subject of study. The research process is considered as a means to an end rather than a process of creating empowering knowledge.

### Involving research participants

A second concept specified by Bowman (1983) that is important in developing cultural sensitivity in social science research is significant involvement. Significant involvement requires consulting members of the identified group in decision-making at each phase of the research process. The recruitment of a small but representative consultation and advisory group may be particularly helpful. To be effective, such an advisory group requires participation from a cross-section of cultural group members. A heterogenous group with representation from indigenous leaders, and variation in characteristics such as sex, age and economic status, will provide diverse viewpoints. The group should meet regularly to be updated on the progress of the research and to give feedback that will be used to guide future research activities. It is important that researchers do what they can to ensure that group members feel free to express their opinions in advisory committee meetings. Research topics selected with a concern for significant involvement may have a very different focus than research topics selected independent of such consultation.

Securing significant involvement requires special skills in communicating. Cultural group members may question the intentions of the researcher, especially of those from other cultures. It is incumbent upon the researcher to make the goals, methods, procedures and implications of the proposed research clear. A researcher who views the cultural group as having necessary expertise, and who demonstrates knowledge of the culture, respect for cultural differences and a willingness to learn and be helpful, is likely to communicate more effectively (Grace, 1992). This person stands a better chance of gaining access to information and developing cooperative alliances that will lead to the selection of a culturally competent research topic.

## Guidelines for Selecting the Research Topic

- Acknowledge personal biases.
- Assess for bias in the literature and express practice concerns.
- Avoid focusing on negative attributes and the most disadvantaged.
- Avoid studying a population only in typical contexts.
- Avoid ethnocentrism, defining difference as deviance or pathology.
- Learn about the culture, its history, norms, gender roles, language, religion, etc.
- Consult with cultural group members and include them in the process of topic selection.
- Recruit an intentionally heterogenous three- to five-member consultation and advisory committee that will meet regularly to be updated on the research and provide feedback.
- Examine the relevance of the research topic to the population.

# Formulating Research Questions and Hypotheses

The process of formulating research questions, and in some instances hypotheses, is a matter of moving from the general identification of a research topic to a greater degree of specificity. This phase is necessary for research to proceed with clarity and purpose. Whereas clear stipulations of the research questions or hypotheses are a prerequisite for quantitative study, it is often the product of qualitative research. The placement of this phase in the research process will vary, therefore, depending on the research approach.

## Evaluating conceptual relevance

Research questions and hypotheses are constructed from concepts that are used to focus and communicate the scope of the study. Differences in the conceptual meaning of values and behaviours, however, may not be captured in the language of the dominant culture. It is common for researchers to move into a cultural context where they have not had even cursory experience and to expect that all their concepts will have equivalent meanings, a practice that is sure to create confusion and misrepresentation (Beauvais and Trimble, 1992). The concept of wealth, for instance, has a variety of meanings across culturally diverse populations. To one culture it may mean money, to another the presence of children and to another spirituality. It is important, therefore, that researchers explore culturally specific meanings of concepts when formulating research questions and hypotheses.

Evaluating the relevance of research concepts to the population studied is also important. The concept of independence, for instance, is generally considered a healthy developmental task for adolescents in North American families. To a traditional Hindi family, however, adolescent independence is not only irrelevant but undesirable. What researchers with a dominant North American perspective might describe as an enmeshed and undifferentiated parent/child relationship may be considered healthy in the context of another culture. Likewise, Western researchers may view care for elderly dependents as a burden on adult children, however, filial piety, the responsibility to care for one's elders, is considered a virtue in traditional Chinese families. It is important that the researcher consult with members of the cultural group to attain clarity on the meaning and relevance of major concepts.

## Anticipating consequences

In quantitative research the questions asked, or not asked, may be as important as the answers generated. Research questions are practically relevant if there are gaps or contradictions in current knowledge that can be alleviated by answering them, and when pursuing them will contribute to more effective policy or practice decisions (Rothery, 1993). Some research questions, however, are more likely than others to lead to knowledge that will be used for unacceptable or harmful purposes. For instance, research questions that seek to rank order racial intelligence. Such questions may represent a significant risk to research participants. It is important that the researcher consider the potential for misuse of the data that will be generated and any harm, physical or psychological, such misuse might inflict on research participants or on members of their cultural group.

## Respecting privacy

All research is intrusive to some degree. Whether or not research is considered overly intrusive should be evaluated from the perspective of the research participant(s) not the researcher. In addition, some topics may be considered by cultural group members as too sacred or private for the public domain. Breaching the confidence or privacy of diverse cultural groups is likely to restrict future access by researchers to the population.

## SPECIFYING THE RESEARCH DESIGN

A research design is a blueprint for how a research project is to proceed. There is considerable debate among social service professionals as to whether qualitative or quantitative methods of research are more sensitive to culture. Research methods, however, are neither inherently sensitive or insensitive to culture; it is in their application that the "isms" of race, sex and age are perpetrated. While healthy scepticism is good, going so far as to drop all notions of either quantitative or qualitative study is not (Yllo, 1988). Both quantitative and qualitative research methods have a distinct role to play in the generation of knowledge. Qualitative methods, for instance, are not suited to providing information on the over-representation of American Indian children in the foster care system: the longer average number of years these children remain in foster

> ## Guidelines for Formulating Research Questions and Hypotheses
>
> - Explore meanings of concepts with the cultural group of interest.
> - Determine what values and measures of success are important to the population.
> - Assess to whom and how answering the question or testing the hypothesis will be useful.
> - Anticipate potential consequences of conducting the research, both positive and negative.
> - Explore whether members of the cultural group would consider the research overly intrusive or exploitive.
> - Consider issues of privacy from the perspective of the participant.
> - Reformulate the research questions or hypotheses to reflect feedback obtained from members of the cultural group and repeat the review process. Repeat this process until consensus is reached among cultural group members that the research questions and hypotheses are acceptable.

care and the higher average number of foster care placements they experience. Quantitative methods, in contrast, are not able to portray the experience of being an American Indian child in foster care. Reflecting the voices of research participants through qualitative research methods gives one an appreciation and understanding of life experiences that cannot be captured through quantitative methods. The choice of research method should be guided by the type of information required. Conflict over which research method is more sensitive to culture diverts attention away from important questions of researcher integrity and ethics.

## Measurement

There are only two ways to measure concepts, and that is to ask or to observe. Whether the subject of interest is behaviour, knowledge, attitudes or feelings, the objective is always to obtain valid and reliable data. The measurement options within these two approaches of asking or observing are only limited by the researcher's creativity.

*Standardized instruments.* Standardized instruments are popular measurement tools used in quantitative research, especially for research that is designed to evaluate social policies, social service programs and change in a single system. Before using a standardized instrument in a culturally diverse context, however, the researcher should search for psychometric information on whether the instrument is valid and reliable for use with the population of interest. Often this information will not be available, or claims of cultural sensitivity may exist without any testimony on how they were determined. In the absence of satisfactory psychometric information, the instrument should be reviewed with those who are knowledgeable about the culture and a preliminary trial, i.e., a pilot test, should be conducted to discover potential difficulties before the measurement task begins. Pilot testing should include debriefing procedures in which potential subjects can discuss their experiences with the standardized instrument and their interpretations of the items (Beauvais and Trimble, 1992).

Some standardized instruments have been developed specifically for use with culturally diverse populations. The Hispanic Stress Inventory, for instance, is a standardized instrument designed to assess psychosocial stress in the lives of immigrants from Latin America (Cervantes, Padilla and Salgado de Snyder, 1990). Reference librarians are often able to help researchers locate specialized and non-specialized standardized instruments.

*Questionnaires.* When standardized instruments are not available, or are limited in scope, the development of a questionnaire may be required. Questionnaire items may be either closed- or open-ended. Closed-ended questionnaire items offer participants a limited number of predetermined responses rather than allowing them to choose their own words as do open-ended questions. In choosing between open- and closed-ended questions, the researcher should consider which type, or combination of the two, is likely to be most relevant for members of the cultural group. An American Indian elder, for instance, may not want to communicate on a linear, quantitative level, which makes open-ended questions more relevant (Hill, 1978). The researcher must also acknowledge that brevity and parsimony are not equally valued in every culture.

When developing closed-ended questionnaire items it is important that careful attention be given to the wording of items. For instance, the question, "Do you believe that doctors who practice traditional Chinese medicine are as good as doctors who practice Western medicine?" may elicit a "no" response or even a nonresponse. While both responses are intended to convey disagreement with the foregoing statement, neither can accurately communicate the respondent's actual perception—that Chinese doctors are better than Western doctors. Again it is important to consult with cultural group members to develop the wording of questionnaire items and the range of appropriate responses.

*Observation.* Observational research is generally classified by the role of the researcher in the data gathering process, as such it includes both participant and non-participant forms. Non-participant observation is commonly used in studies of non-verbal populations, examining the influence of the environment on behaviours. This form of detached observation involves observing activities and events in a community, but the interpretation of what this means is left to the observer, who is apt to use her or his own frame of reference and value system to make the interpretation. In contrast, the participant observer who is immersed in the culture and actively participates and interacts with cultural group members, as opposed to just observing, is invariably going to appreciate what is going on from the perspective of the indigenous members. The participant observer's interpretation of events, ceremonies, etc. is more likely to be compatible with, if not similar to, those of the cultural group's members. Participant forms of observation attempt to interpret phenomena as shaped by their social context as opposed to being context free.

## Developing the sampling plan

Because obtaining data from an entire population is usually not feasible, sampling procedures are used to select a subset of individuals or other units that are considered representative. Two major types of sampling procedures are probability and non-probability. The objective of both is to reflect as close as possible the population of interest. Although probability sampling is generally considered preferable for this purpose, it requires the existence of a comprehensive list of all possible participants. The researcher interested in the study of diverse cultural groups will seldom have access to such a list and may have to rely on the various forms of non-probability sampling.

Two concepts to consider in attempting to draw a representative sample are heterogeneity and acculturation. Although there may be many well-documented commonalities, it is important to keep in mind the potential for within-group diversity. The African-American, Asian, Hispanic, American Indian and Pacific Islander communities are all marked by considerable within-group heterogeneity. There are, for instance, over 149 American Indian languages spoken in North America, excluding Alaskan natives (Red Horse, 1988). The term Hispanic takes into account people of Mexican, Puerto Rican, Central and South American origin, not to mention those from Spain and Latin America. Generally people in these subgroups have little knowledge of each other and are surprised and offended at the notion of being considered as members of a group (Klor de Alva, 1988).

Acculturation refers to the degree to which people from a particular cultural group display behaviour that is similar to that of the dominant society. Determining the state of acculturation involves an evaluation of such factors as cultural identification, residential status, immigrant status, language preferences, health practices and marriage patterns. Red Horse (1988) provides an excellent illustration of how American Indian families can be situated along a continuum of acculturation.

Being specific about who the cultural group of interest is and considering the degree of heterogeneity and acculturation are important when selecting a sample and relating the information back to the population. In sampling, researchers should attempt to capture the range of within-group diversity and avoid the tendency to overgeneralize and treat each group as monolithic.

## Choosing the data collection method

Choosing an appropriate data collection method is not just a matter of trying to fit a particular type of data collection to a particular research question or hypothesis. Cultural sensitivity involves selecting the data collection method or methods that will be most comfortable and relevant for the cultural group of interest. In deciding on a data collection method the researcher should consider language, literary ability and motivation to participate. Consideration of such factors may result in changes to the language used, the method of data collection and whether or not and how participants will be compensated. Making the participant primary in considerations involving data collection will positively influence the quality of the data and the degree of participation. Where possible it is best to use multiple data collection methods for increased confidence in the results (LeCroy, 1985). The use of multiple methods of data collection, however, requires a skilled researcher or a researcher who is able to coordinate a team of individuals with a variety of skills (Marlow, 1993). It also requires time and resources; therefore, it is important to be realistic about the objectives of the study from the start.

*Survey.* The survey method can be used to collect both quantitative and qualitative data. The survey can include closed- and open-ended questions as well as standardized instruments. It may be mailed, conducted over the telephone or administered face-to-face in individual or group formats. Survey research usually excludes or cannot make use of opportunities for clarification and discussion, it is therefore not recommended for the development of knowledge in areas where there is no or limited information.

*Interview.* Interviews are more free-flowing than a survey and vary in the degree of structure that they include. The semi-structured or unstructured interview is a principal method for encouraging the active involvement of research participants in the construction of data. It is marked by free interaction between researcher and interviewee. In recent years innovative approaches that allow the participant to define their own reality in their own language have been developed. Two innovative techniques include telling or dictating one's life story and drawing.

The focus group interview has become a popular method of qualitative data collection in recent years. This technique brings people together in small groups to talk about their perceptions, lives and experiences in free-flowing, open-ended discussion, which usually focuses on a single topic. A distinguishing feature of the focus group interview is the explicit use of group interaction to produce data and insights that would otherwise be difficult to obtain. The members of the group influence each other by responding to ideas and comments. If group membership is intentionally diverse, the focus group can provide a broad perspective.

*Secondary analysis.* The use of secondary data for the study of diverse cultural groups presents an alternative to the collection of original data (Hill, 1978). Secondary analysis is any further analysis of an existing data set which presents interpretations, conclusions or knowledge additional to, or different from, those already presented (Hakim, 1982). The use of secondary data decreases the reporting burden on the public.

For cultural groups with only a small number of members, the utilization of secondary data may avoid the problem of overstudy. Secondary analysis is commonly used with survey data such as the population census. In census-type surveys, the members of culturally diverse groups are often purposefully represented in larger numbers because probability proportionate to size or oversampling techniques were employed. Larger sample numbers facilitate the use of statistical techniques that are inappropriate with smaller numbers. Where cultural group members are under-represented, a statistical weighting procedure can be used. Weighting can be used to represent cultural groups in relation to the proportion of the population that they represent.

## PLANNING FOR DATA COLLECTION

The data collection method may be sensitive to the characteristics of a diverse population, but the way in which is administered may not. All of the researcher's efforts in selecting a research topic, formulating research questions and hypotheses and planning the research design will be of little value if the researcher is not able to collect valid and reliable data representative of the population of interest.

### Guidelines for Specifying the Research Design

- Select the research method that is most appropriate for the objectives of the study.
- Assess whether standardized instruments are valid and reliable for use with the population of interest.
- Ensure that closed-ended questions are phrased in a way that will allow for the entire range of responses.
- Where possible use multiple measures, considering those most comfortable and relevant for the population.
- Sample for the range of within-group diversity, do not assume homogeneity within ethnic, age or gender groups.
- Consider the degree of acculturation as a variable.
- Use secondary analysis where possible to lessen the reporting burden on the population.
- Consider weighting survey data to make the cultural group proportionate to the actual population or to over-represent.

### Characteristics of data collection personnel

Where data collection personnel are required, this involves consideration not only of culture but of language, gender roles and intergenerational role expectations (Marlow, 1993). In many cultures, the age, race and gender of the data collector may have a significant impact on the participants' responses. It is important, therefore, that the data collector be knowledgeable about cultural etiquette. Important cultural values may include, for instance, respect for authority and age (Grace, 1992). Being perceived as too casual or too young may close rather than open doors. It is important to consult with cultural group members in advance of the data collection phase to determine what style of personal interaction is likely to obtain the best results. Where language is a consideration, the most desirable interviewer would be one that is bilingual, preferably of the same ethnic or racial origin so that they might understand the nuances of the culture, i.e. dialect, patterning in responses and body language.

### Translating survey questions

Depending on language proficiency and preference, standardized instruments and questionnaires may require translation. One method of ensuring language equivalency is to use the back translation technique (Hill, 1978). Back translation requires translation of the original document into the language of the research participant's preference and subsequent translation by an independent translator back to the language of origin. The second translation is then compared with the original document for equivalency and adjustments are made accordingly.

### Compensating participants

One method of gaining cooperation and showing respect is to compensate research participants for any expenses they may incur with regard to their participation in the research study. Costs to the research participant can include transportation, child care, parking, etc. If possible, research participants should also be compensated for their time. In some cultures, gift giving may be more appropriate than monetary compensation, and the researcher should consult with members of the cultural group about the appropriate means of compensation in advance of the study.

Related to issues of compensation is sensitivity to time. The researcher should be honest and up-front about how much time participation in the research endeavour is likely to require. The researcher should also be sensitive to culture by collecting data at the most convenient and appropriate times for the research participants. This entails being aware of religious holidays, days of worship, planting and harvesting seasons, etc.

## ANALYZING THE DATA

Researchers have a responsibility to ensure that the techniques of data analysis are as appropriate as possible. This entails devising a plan for analysis and seeking consultation on analytical techniques and the interpretation of results where needed.

---

### Guidelines for Collecting the Data

- Consult with cultural group members on the administration of the data collection plan.
- Consider the data collector's race, gender, age and how these characteristics may influence research participants' motivation to participate and responses. Recruit accordingly.
- Be aware of communication norms specific to the culture.
- Use the back translation technique for questionnaires and instruments that require translation.
- Compensate participants for any expenses incurred and for their time if possible.
- Collect data at the most appropriate and convenient time for the population studied.

---

### Using control variables

Where variables such as age, gender, education and socio-economic status are controlled, there may be fewer differences found between cultural groups than expected (Madison, 1992). Sometimes it is the interaction between two or more variables such as age and ethnicity that can best explain a phenomenon. Using control variables and checking for interactions are important when attempting to explain variation.

Consultation with members of the cultural group in advance to determine what control variables are relevant is advised.

## Statistical versus practical significance

There is a tendency in social service research to equate statistical significance with practical or substantive significance (Hill, 1978). Statistical significance is the probability that a certain result will occur by chance. The likelihood of finding statistically significant results depends to a large extent on the size of the sample, i.e., the larger the sample the smaller the difference required to produce statistical significance. Thus, results may be proclaimed as statistically significant when the overall difference found is not substantive. Statistical significance also depends on the number of statistical tests conducted. The more statistical tests, the greater the likelihood that significance will occur as a result of chance alone. Controlling for multiple statistical tests can be achieved through the use of a correction factor such as the Bonferroni (LeCroy, 1985).

Researchers should be equally careful when concluding that results which are not statistically significance are not important. At times, the order in which variables are entered into multivariate equations can render important variables nonsignificant. And, just as large samples increase the likelihood of finding statistical significance, small samples decrease the likelihood, even when a true relationship may exist.

## Participant verification

Making sense out of the data is sometimes difficult in settings where different cultural groups are represented. No matter how careful the data collection process, its validity will be sacrificed if the researcher attempts to make interpretations that reflect personal, literary or social service agency biases. Consulting with cultural group members for feedback can help ensure the validity of findings, especially where they deviate from those expected. In qualitative analysis, cultural group members can participate in the research process by extracting themes and key concepts for coding the data.

Research reports put knowledge into a written and permanent form. It is important, therefore, to ensure that bias against certain groups is not perpetuated through research reports. To aide in this task the researcher should seek feedback from colleagues and members of the cultural group studied. Sometimes the most valuable feedback comes from those who are not immersed in the topic.

## Formatting the report

Whether written for publication or presentation, research reports should customarily include certain information. First, the researcher should state the values and assumptions that influenced the research. Second, the population of interest and the sampling method should be described, and where probability sampling is used, the response rate and implications for generalization should be reported. Third, the data collection method should be described, including how access and consent were established. Fourth, where percentages are reported, absolute numbers should also be provided. Reporting percentages perpetuates misconceptions about diverse cultural groups, especially where they are

### Guidelines for Analyzing the Data

- Consult with the population of interest to inform the choice of variables for analysis.
- Look for within-group differences, i.e., use gender, age, education, socio-economic status and residence as control variables.
- Obtain consultation on statistical techniques and interpretation of statistical results where necessary.
- Explore the order of variables entered into multivariate equations.
- Control for multiple statistical tests by using a correction factor such as the Bonferroni.
- Assess for substantive as well as statistical significance.
- Seek collaboration from members of the population to check the validity of the findings.
- In the analysis of qualitative data include cultural group members in the formulation of themes and categories for coding.

based on unrepresentative proportions. Finally, the researcher should make suggestions for how the findings might be used, including recommendations for further questions, hypotheses and methodologies. Whatever the avenue of dissemination, the researcher should always respect the participant's right to confidentiality: avoid disclosing names and locations unless given documented permission to do so.

## Raising sensitive issues

Raising sensitive issues provokes a level of discomfort the researcher may prefer to avoid. If the research results do not support the status quo, the report is likely to create a dynamic that will rebound upon the person who raised the issue (Marlow, 1993). This discomfort can be alleviated if the researcher has paid careful attention to cultural sensitivity throughout the research process, ensuring that the data are accurately presented and nonjudgmentally discussed. Careful consideration must be given to if and how sensitive issues should be disseminated. Checking with appropriate channels in the cultural community about the dissemination of sensitive issues should be the first step in the process (Beauvais and Trimble, 1992).

## Acknowledging limitations

There is no such thing as a perfect research study. Acknowledging the limitations of research is an important part of writing the report. If limitations are not outlined explicitly by the researcher, the reader may draw assumptions about the findings that are not warranted. The danger of this occurring can only be avoided by enhancing the reader's knowledge (Marlow, 1993). In particular, it is important that the researcher clearly differentiate between results and discussion, correlation and causation.

## Using sensitive and inclusive language

There is a fundamental uneasiness about language usage when it comes to diverse cultural groups (Dickstein and Hoopes, 1991). A contributing factor to this uneasiness is that the acceptability of terms changes over time. In recent decades, for instance, there has been a shift from Negro to black to African American. Similarly, confusion exists over the preferred usage of Latino, Hispanic or Chicano. Using the term

Spanish American to make reference to immigrants from Mexico will exclude and possibly offend Spanish-speaking American Indians. Although researchers may find this sensitivity to language frustrating and confusing, it should be seen as a sign of moving towards a more heightened sense of sensitivity to culture. The best insurance against offending cultural group members is to: (a) avoid grouping large numbers of people under one label; and (b) consult with members of the cultural group to determine their preferences. The principle of self-determination advocates that individuals have the right to choose their own labels.

## Ensuring accessibility

Information on practice with culturally diverse populations needs to be accessible. The medium of dissemination depends to a large extent on the intended audience: reports may be circulated informally; restricted to sponsoring agencies; presented at conferences; distributed through mailing lists; published in journals, books and monographs; and discussed casually. Being clear about the intended audience is important when choosing the avenue of dissemination. Knowing one's audience also provides information on how the research report should be written or presented. Consumers vary considerably in their ability to comprehend research concepts and in their desire for technical detail (Marlow, 1993).

In recent years a number of periodicals specific to the study of certain racial and ethnic groups have appeared. For example, *The Journal of Black Studies*, *Hispania*, and the *American Indian Quarterly*. If one of the objectives in conducting research, however, is to sensitize the general public to a certain issue, publishing the results in a mainstream rather than a specialized periodical may be more appropriate.

Sharing the final report with the research participants conveys an attitude of appreciation and respect. Where applicable, the report should be produced in the language of the participant's preference. A cultural group armed with research may feel particularly empowered and may choose to disseminate such information in creative ways, such as through the use of music, art, drama and dance. Partnering with cultural group members in the dissemination process can prove particularly effective.

## SUMMARY

Cultural competence is a goal towards which all social service researchers should strive. Opportunities for being sensitive towards

- Be clear about the values and assumptions influencing the research process.
- Specify the population studied, the sampling method used and its implications for generalization.
- Describe the data collection method including how access and consent were established.
- Report the response rate and its implications for the findings.
- Always respect confidentiality in publications and presentations.
- Report unexpected findings and sensitive issues only after consultation with members of the cultural group.
- Discuss limitations of the data and the findings.
- Provide suggestions for further research including alternative questions, hypotheses and recommended methodologies.
- Use inclusive and sensitive language.
- Write in a style comprehensible to the target audience, bilingual if appropriate.
- Evaluate submission to specialty versus mainstream publications.
- Distribute to participants and engage participants in the dissemination process.

issues of culture present themselves at every stage of the research process. Apart from making culture central to the research endeavour, how data are interpreted, where the results are presented and published, and how they may be interpreted, used and misused are important considerations. For the social science researcher interested in producing culturally competent research, investing time in learning about a diverse population, their history and cultural norms is essential. This includes finding out what questions need to be asked and what methods are most appropriate for asking them. Forging a positive alliance and enlisting the assistance of members of the cultural group are critical to the validity of the research process. Less resistance to research efforts is likely to be encountered in the long run if those who have a stake in the research are meaningfully included at each phase of the process and if they have some sense of ownership and control. Developing culturally competent research requires a shift in thinking about cultural group members as respondents and informants to considering them as consultants, participants and partners in the direction, design and conduct of social service research.

## References

Beauvais, F. and Trimble, J. E. (1992). The role of the researcher in evaluating American Indian alcohol and other drug abuse prevention programs. In M. Orlandi (ed.), *Cultural competence for evaluators: A guide for alcohol and other drug abuse prevention practitioners working with ethnic/racial communities*. Rockville, MD: U.S. Department of Health and Human Services.

Duer Berrick, J. and Barth, R. P. (1994). Research on kinship foster care: What do we know? Where do we go from here? *Children and Youth Services Review*, 16, 1-5.

Bowman, P. J. (1983). Significant involvement and functional relevance: Challenges to survey research. *Social Work Research and Abstracts*, 19, 21-26.

Cervantes, R. C., Padilla, A. M. and Salgado de Snyder, V. N. (1990). Reliability and validity of the Hispanic Stress Inventory. *Hispanic Journal of Behavioral Sciences*, 12, 76-82.

Davis, J. E.(1992). Reconsidering the use of race as an explanatory variable in program evaluation. In A. Madison (ed.), *Minority issues in program evaluation*. San Francisco, CA: Jossey-Bass.

Dewdney, A. K. (January 10, 1995). IQ tests: They're a stupid way to judge intelligence. *Calgary Herald*, A5.

Dickstein, R. and Hoopes, M. S. (1991). *Minority American women: A research guide*. Tucson, AZ: Southwest Institute for Research on Women.

Grace, (1992). Practical considerations for program professionals and evaluators working with African-American Communities. In M. Orlandi (ed.), *Cultural competence for evaluators: A guide for alcohol and other drug abuse prevention practitioners working with ethnic/racial communities*. Rockville, MD: U.S. Department of Health and Human Services.

Grinnell, R. M., Jr. (ed.). (1993). *Social work research and evaluation* (4th ed.). Itasca, IL: F. E. Peacock.

Hakim, C. (1982). *Secondary analysis in social research: A guide to data sources and methods with examples*. London: George Allen and Unwin.

Hill, R. B. (1978). Social work research on minorities: Impediments and opportunities. In D. Fanshel (ed.), *Future of social work research*. Washington, D.C.: National Association of Social Workers.

Klor de Alva, J. J. (1988). Telling Hispanics apart: Latin sociocultural diversity. In E. Acosta-Belen and B. R. Sjostrom (eds.), *The Hispanic experience in the United States*. New York: Praeger.

LeCroy, C. W. (1985). Methodological issues in the evaluation of social work practice. *Social Service Review,* 59, 345-357.

Madison, A. (1992). *Minority issues in program evaluation*. San Francisco, CA: Jossey-Bass.

Marlow, C. (1993). *Research methods for generalist social work*. Pacific Grove, CA: Brooks/Cole.

Miele, F. (1995). Skeptic magazine interview with Robert Sternberg on *The Bell Curve. Skeptic Magazine*, 3, 72-80.

Padilla, A. M. and Salgado de Snyder, N. (1992). Hispanics: What the culturally informed evaluator needs to know. In M. Orlandi (ed.), *Cultural competence for evaluators: A guide for alcohol and other drug abuse prevention practitioners working with ethnic/racial communities*. Rockville, MD: U.S. Department of Health and Human Services.

Red Horse, J. (1988). Cultural evolution of American Indian families. In C. Jacobs and D. Bowles (eds.), *Ethnicity and race: Critical concepts in social work*. Washington, D.C.: National Association of Social Workers.

Reinharz, S. (1992). *Feminist methods in social research*. New York: Oxford.

Rothery, M. (1993). Problems, questions, and hypotheses. In R. M. Grinnell, Jr. (ed.), *Social work research and evaluation* (4th ed.). Itasca, IL: F. E. Peacock.

Yllo, K. (1988). Political and methodological debates in wife abuse research. In K. Yllo and M. Bograd (eds.), *Feminist perspectives on wife abuse*. Newbury Park, CA: Sage.

# IMPLICATIONS OF MULTICULTURAL POLICY

d) for professional
   education, training and
   continuing education

# Multiculturalism, Racism and Social Work: An Exploration of Issues in the Canadian Context

*Carole Pigler Christenson*

## INTRODUCTION

Social work is commonly defined as a profession dedicated to enhancing, restoring or modifying the psycho-social functioning of people, individually, in families, in groups or in communities to enable them to reach their full potential in harmony with their environment and the wider society. Social services are the networks, formalized systems and organizations through which the profession attempts to operationalize these objectives. Social welfare refers to the policies, structures legislation, professions, programs, formal agencies and informal self-help groups that seek to ensure that people have access to the goods and services necessary to reach their full potential, while respecting the rights of others. Social work is the profession most closely associated with social services and social welfare.

This paper examines the response of the social work educators and professionals in Canada to the realities of a multicultural society, past and present. It begins with an overview of the Canadian context of multiculturalism, which has resulted in a uniquely Canadian response to pluralism. The ideologies that have shaped these responses and their effects on social work education and social work practice are then summarized. The final section of the paper considers current debates that are shaping the themes under discussion in universities, in professional associations, and in the literature. Elsewhere, I have given detailed examples of the types of theoretical material and practice experience that should be incorporated into core courses in the Canadian social work curriculum (Christensen, 1991). The issues presented here offer examples of the emerging issues that students are seldom challenged to explore in meaningful depth.

The major premises of this paper are that: 1) social work has yet to incorporate multicultural realities as integral factors in the provision of social services when envisioning the social welfare of Canadian society, past and present; 2) failure to deal with racism and its ramifications remains a major stumbling block preventing the changes necessary for social work and social services to bring the promise of social welfare to all Canadians.

## THE EARLY HISTORY OF MULTICULTURAL CANADA

Students of social work, like all others in Canadian society, have incorporated many myths about Canadian history. This lack of knowledge is directly related to the manner in which many of the clients that these students will serve may be perceived, assessed and treated. Two of the most prevalent and damaging myths are: 1) Canada had only two "founding" people, the British and the French; 2) only recently have people of colour, originating from the Third World, been part of the Canadian mosaic. Consequently, many people whose ancestors came to Canada from one to three centuries ago are asked daily, "Where are you from?" simply on the basis of skin colour. Social work educators have contributed to the myth of a "white" Canada by omitting mention of the social welfare experience of people other than the British and the French.

In fact, Canada has always been multicultural. It is increasingly being acknowledged that the earliest European settlers encountered Aboriginal peoples with extremely varied forms of government, language, cultural and religious traditions, and lifestyles based on available resources (e.g., nomads, fishers, farmers, hunters). Furthermore, it is also being acknowledged that the early European settlers borrowed many ideas about communal responsibility for social welfare from Aboriginal peoples such as the Iroquois, whose sophisticated confederacy suggested that all people are equal in the eyes of the creator and should therefore be respected for their common human qualities. Collective responsibility for all people in a given community contrasted sharply with the European experience of feudalism and indentured servitude. Based on European belief systems about race, serious efforts were made to enslave Aboriginal peoples, and more of them experienced this condition than Africans for a time.

Although recent political events have resulted in Euro-Canadians beginning to acknowledge Aboriginal peoples' contributions there is, as yet, little recognition of the contributions of early settlers who were not of European descent (Christensen, 1995). For example, although it is a well-documented fact that Matthew deCosta, a black man, translated the Micmac language for Samuel deChamplain, only deChamplain is credited for the "discovery" of the east coast of Canada. Canadian historical accounts generally fail to acknowledge slavery under French and British rule, which lasted from 1628 to 1833.

Similarly, black settlements of parts of Nova Scotia, New Brunswick and Ontario by freed black loyalists from the United States between the late 1700s and the 1800s are ignored, as are black pioneers in parts of Western Canada in the early 1900s. Black settlers were farmers, labourers, artisans, cowboys and, in the case of Vancouver's James Douglas, the first governor of the newly formed provincial legislature. It is often stated that Asians are newcomers to Canada, but they have been an integral part of this country, particularly on the west coast, since the mid-1850s when people of Chinese, Japanese and South Asian (Indian) descent worked in the mines and built the railroad. Restrictive and racist immigration clauses limited the entrance of European Jews, even during the Nazi persecution era. Southern and eastern Europeans were less welcome than northern Europeans before the 1950s. Although the preferred immigrants were from Great Britain and France (in Quebec), immigrants and refugees who had white skins were indistinguishable from the British and the French and tended to "blend in" by the second generation when their children were no longer audible minorities.

To the extent that they were accepted by the dominant cultural groups, minority and Aboriginal Canadians made important contributions. However, the plight of people from continents other than Europe has never been easy in Canada. Historical records are replete with atrocities against Aboriginal peoples, riots directed against blacks and Asians, and overt and "subtle" institutional forms of racism (Bolaria and Li, 1991; Hughes and Kallen, 1974).

Historically, the social welfare of minorities in Canada has been ignored and neglected. Historical accounts of Canadian social welfare, social services and social work almost invariably fail to mention the presence and plight of Aboriginal peoples, immigrants and minorities altogether. This indicates the extent to which these groups were marginalized and excluded. Social work, despite its lofty ideals, was no less prone to incorporating racist ideology than any other profession (Christensen, 1996).

## Ideological Issues Shaping Social Work and Social Welfare

An ideology may be defined as a set of assumptions, beliefs, values, and perceptions that help members of a group to make sense of their world, and to organize, maintain, and transform power relations in a given society. Social work, social services, and social welfare cannot be viewed separately from social, economic and political ideologies which shape and continuously transform it.

A review of Canadian texts indicates that formal social work,, social services, and social welfare have been shaped mainly by ideologies associated with the English Poor Laws and the Church (Roman Catholicism in Quebec), modified by the North American social welfare movement (Mullaly, 1993; Turner and Turner, 1995). The Protestant work ethic was also imported, suggesting that work is a divine vocation in and of itself and that material success is a sign of God's favour. The ideology of rugged individualism is still prevalent in social work's insistence that well-functioning people are independent and self-sufficient, an ideology incorporated in definitions of well-being and in our goals for our clients. Canadian society and the social work profession have yet to resolve the dilemma left by the legacy of the simplistic belief that the undeserving poor are responsible for their plight and are, therefore, not as deserving as those who are willing to work hard (Delaney, 1995). Clearly, oppressed groups were never considered part of the opportunity structure, and social welfare provisions were not intended for them. Presently in Canada, it is far from certain that social work education includes information on hierarchical structures of modern societies and their influence on the complex systems (e.g., the media, governments) that, in turn, influence equally complex human interactions and responses. Apparently, the result is that social work graduates often find it difficult to be "nonjudgmental" towards those labelled culturally and racially "different." Moreover, many social work theorists continue to suggest individual or familial solutions to systemically based problems that affect population groups in predictable (and preventable) ways (e.g., discrimination in hiring which leads to low income).

In the social sphere, Canada is generally viewed, of necessity, as incorporating a pluralistic ideology. There are many belief systems, attitudes, values and world views held by people from many ethnic, cultural and racial backgrounds. As a country covering a wide geographic area, Canada is also diverse in lifestyles (e.g., rural, urban), degrees of economic disparity by region, and climatic conditions that influence lifestyles (Fleras and Elliot, 1992). This ideology is reflected in the social work profession and by advocates of social welfare, since a wide range of attitudes and belief systems is tolerated among professionals. Furthermore, schools of social work expose students to diverse viewpoints and emphases explaining human behaviour from the structural to the psychodynamic; curricula include community and organizational development as well as family growth and development over the lifespan. In addition, there is content on communication styles and characteristics of normal and abnormal behaviour. Professors of social welfare may hold any number of viewpoints along a continuum from liberal to conservative, and they are generally free to express their opinions.

Economically, Canada is expected to prosper as a country blessed with natural resources. Nonetheless, it is plagued by many of the same ills that are now affecting all of North America and the Western world (e.g., recession, free trade adjustments and the influence of a global economy and multinational corporations). Statistics frequently quoted by government sources indicate that nationwide some 10% of workers are unemployed, but these figures are generally not reported for various racial categories. However, studies indicate that, on average, unemployment rates for Aboriginal peoples on reserves is three times or more that of Euro-Canadians (York, 1992). A recent study using census data to examine the conditions of the black family in Canada indicates that one-third of black children live in households earning below $20,000 compared to 22.2% of non-blacks (Christensen and Weinfeld, 1993). The importance of determining indices for particular categories is apparently very important.

Unlike the United States, Canada as we know it did not result from pioneers who created a revolution. Rather, French and British settlers determined that both cultural groups had certain rights and responsibilities for the collective good. Thus the ideology of compromise and negotiation was born early in the Canadian psyche. The primacy of the ideology of compromise is considered by many to be uniquely Canadian, stemming from having two founding nations vying for power and control. This continues to be the root of conflict in the political arena. Canada seems periodically to teeter on the brink of dissolution over the very bicultural and bilingual issues which have been its strength (differentiating Canada from the United States) and its weakness. It has been noted that much of what has passed as factual about Canadian social work and social welfare refers, in fact, to the experience of those living in English-speaking Canada. Canada differs from the United States in other important ways. French-Canadians and other Quebecers have had a unique experience influenced by the Roman Catholic church, the philosophy of existentialism, social freedoms, emphasis on the family unit and a collective spirit. Yet another difference between Canada and her closest neighbour is that, due to the existence of two recognized founding peoples representing linguistic groups with different religious convictions, Catholic and Protestant, the separation of church and state was impractical. Church-related programs remain an important part of the social service sector. Although Canada denied her multicultural and multiracial past internally for a very long time, from an external perspective membership in the British Commonwealth has given Canada an ideology of tolerance and an association with fifty other independent nations representing many ethnic, cultural and racial groups.

From the perspective of oppressed groups, colonialism and the ideology that accompanies it has had the most influential impact on Canadian social welfare. It has had an ongoing impact in all spheres—social, economic and political. Colonialism led the British and French settlers to feel entitled to Aboriginal people's land and resources. It also justified slavery in Canada until 1833 (Winks, 1972).

## EFFECTS OF RACIST IDEOLOGY ON SOCIAL WORK

The minority groups in Canada that have been marginalized and overtly excluded from social, economic and/or political structures at specific points in time (e.g., the Japanese) and those who have remained marginalized over several generations (e.g., blacks) have benefited from the provisions afforded to all by the development of the welfare state. Since the Great Depression, efforts have been made to cushion citizens against personal hardship caused by forces beyond their control. Since 1948, when the Canadian government instituted family allowances (baby bonuses) as a universal program, social welfare programs have served to allow a more equitable distribution of the wealth collected from tax dollars than was possible in a strictly dog-eat-dog world. Until recently, the following benefits have been taken more or less for granted by most Canadians: basic income programs of old age security, unemployment insurance and family allowances, all designated as federal responsibilities under the British North America Act (Canada's constitution). All other programs (e.g., public assistance, or welfare) were administered by provincial governments. This included the provision of subsidized medical care, prior to the Canada Health Act of 1983. At that time, the federal government instituted transfer payments to force provinces to comply with federal standards for health care (i.e., patients could not be charged extra fees for medical services) or face the loss of dollar amounts in federal government subsidies. Education also falls under provincial jurisdiction and is heavily subsidized, even at the post-secondary level, supposedly to ensure the widest possible access to programs, including university-level programs, of which social work programs are one of many.

Like the United States, however, Canada has incorporated the ideology of racism into the very fabric of society and, therefore, into all aspects of social work and social services, severely impacting the lives of people who are not of European descent. It is noteworthy that Canada has never had a civil rights movement acknowledging the past or present inequities experienced by racial minorities (although the Japanese were compensated for having been interned and having their properties confiscated during World War II). The rights of French Canadians have dominated political discourse ever since confederation.

Despite the current debate about the value (or lack thereof) of multiculturalism as a defining ideology for present-day Canada, social work students and professionals should be ever cognizant of the recency of the official recognition of this fundamental fact of Canadian life. Pluralism as part of the public discourse did not occur until 1970, and even then it came as part of the ever-present discussion about the two founding nations. As a result of the protest of those who are of neither British nor French origin, Book IV of the Royal Commission on Bilingualism and Biculturalism pointed to the contributions of the other ethnic groups, and a year later, in 1971, Prime Minister Trudeau proclaimed that Canada was a multicultural society within a bilingual framework (Christensen, 1995). The Multiculturalism Act was passed in 1988, and in 1991 the Department of Multiculturalism and Citizenship was created as a full-fledged entity separate from the Department of the Secretary of State. The most recent change came in 1993, when the department was merged with a new department called Heritage Canada. Although federal government policy defines multiculturalism as "a characteristic of Canadian society in general, and of its whole population, rather than pertaining only to non-charter groups," this view is not shared by the separatist government of Quebec, which promotes an assimilationist model. Neither is this view embraced uniformly by Euro-Canadians outside of Quebec (Tepper, 1994). At present, terms such as "ethnic," "mosaic," "multicultural" and, in Quebec, "cultural communities," are most commonly associated with visible minorities.

Although developing an identity within the context of a country professing democratic ideology valuing fair play and opportunity, the social work profession did not seek to alleviate the unique distress of Aboriginal peoples, blacks and Asians during its formative years. In fact, social services were segregated on the basis of race and religion (Christensen, 1990). Some minorities were allowed to amass a degree of wealth through access to the employment sector and financial markets and establish separate, parallel, social services (e.g., Jewish social services, Chinese benevolent associations). Those who had difficulty negotiating loans could not enter the business sector. Meanwhile, negative myths and stereotypes about racial and ethnic groups were incorporated into social science literature and social work theories. Today, the theoretical base of the profession remains essentially monocultural (i.e., Anglo-conformist), middle-class and assimilationist. Evidently, social policy decision-makers and educators are no less prone to racism and discriminatory practices than other segments of society.

Canada is often referred to as having embraced the ideology of a social democracy. However, Henry, Tator, Mattis and Rees (1995) have suggested that, in reality, the prevailing ideologies discussed above have resulted in democratic racism. As ideology, democratic racism presents two conflicting sets of values that are congruent. The same people who profess commitment to the principles of freedom, equality, fairness, justice, collective responsibility, autonomy and compassion often exhibit conflicting attitudes and behaviours, including negative feelings about minorities and differential treatment and discrimination against them.

## Effects of democratic racism on social work and social welfare

Democratic racism is an ideology that has affected social work educators and the social work profession. The profession claims to be committed to helping all people to reach their full potential in harmony with the environment and the wider society. The principles on which the profession is said to stand include: enhancing the well-being and quality of life for all clients, individuation, non-judgmental attitude and starting where the client is. The values that students of social work are expected to adhere to as they are socialized into the profession include: acceptance, self-determination and respect for all people. However, conflicting belief systems, values and discriminatory behaviours exist simultaneously.

During the past decade there has been a proliferation of studies documenting that racism and cultural insensitivity are prevalent throughout the social service sector, creating access barriers that have just begun to be acknowledged (Christensen, 1985a; Doyle and Visano, 1987; Canadian Task Force, 1988). These findings are not surprising, given that these same barriers have been identified in social work education (Canadian Association of Schools of Social Work, 1991).

Racism is also manifested in the lack of ethnic, cultural and racial diversity among social work professionals employed in social services and in universities, and in the levels at which those who are employed are placed (Christensen, 1993; Henry, Tator, Mattis and Rees, 1995). Few people who are not of European ancestry are in decision-making positions that might allow them to help their institutions to offer culturally appropriate services and a welcoming environment. Barriers exist not only for recent immigrants and refugees who may have difficulties with language and cultural adaptation, but also for Aboriginal peoples and for Canadian minorities of longstanding. These groups have identified various forms of institutional racism and discrimination when they seek services (Head, 1986; Sirros, 1987), and students of social work claim to experience the same in schools of social work (Canadian Association of Schools of Social Work, 1991; Christensen, 1994). There is ample evidence that, due to the conditions of democratic racism, equitable and accessible social services and social work education remain an ideal that has not yet materialized for racial minorities in Canada, universal entitlement notwithstanding.

With respect to the wider society, the right-wing agenda of recent governments has changed the context for social work practice. While mainstream agencies have failed to structure services so that all people would be well-served, the benefits from universal programs are also threatened in the present climate of restraint. Not unlike Ronald Reagan and Margaret Thatcher, Brian Mulroney, then the "Progressive Conservative" prime minister of Canada, targeted the most vulnerable groups in society in his cost containment and cost reduction measures. As a result, the policies and programs associated with the welfare state have been under attack during the past decade; social programs benefiting the poor have been cut while tax benefits have gone to the wealthy and to corporations (Mullaly, 1992). Unemployment insurance and social assistance caseloads have increased, and public sector hiring freezes, retrenchment in the corporate sector, hospital closings and privatization of public services in certain provinces have contributed to a general state of malaise among the poor and the middle classes. The poor have been further victimized by the ongoing debate between the federal and provincial governments about who will be responsible for the shortfall when cost-sharing programs are not adequately funded. The current Liberal government led by Jean Cretien has reduced payments to the provinces for health, education, unemployment insurance, social assistance programs and churches and voluntary organizations, e.g., food banks, soup kitchens, which have been expected to take up the slack.

There is now a direct connection between attitudes towards immigrants and government policies of restraint. The response to the economic pinch being felt by those often referred to as "ordinary Canadians," (synonymous in the minds of the majority as Euro-Canadians) has been to blame immigrants for many woes experienced by society. According to popular perception, one can tell an immigrant by the colour of his or her skin. It therefore becomes easy to see who is to blame for high levels of unemployment. One hears the familiar arguments: they are taking all of our jobs; keeping our young people out of universities; building monster houses in our neighbourhoods, costing us in taxes for English as a Second Language (ESL) classes, etc.

When all else fails, the construction of deviance is always present and affects new and old visible minority immigrant groups alike. In its simplest terms, deviance may be defined as any behaviour that violates societal expectations. In Canada, the dominant Anglo-conformist model is acknowledged as the norm against which all others are measured. Visible differences in skin colour are still used as the basis on which to impute that certain individuals and groups hold deviant values that determine deviant behaviours. Such expectations held by social workers often create a myth of deviance for those whose values and lifestyles are neither known nor understood. Instead, social workers need to be mindful that many visible minorities viewed as immigrants have a history of several generations or several centuries in Canada. They have, of course, fully incorporated Canadian values, even if holding on to perceived positive aspects of the cultures of their ancestors.

With regard to recent immigrants, the point system determines whether independent immigrants will be accepted—considerable points are given for education and skills, the ability to speak French or English, and having a job waiting in Canada. In recent years, an entrepreneur category was created for wealthy, would-be immigrants. As a result, many immigrants coming to Canada from the Third World are better educated, or economically better off, than the average Canadian. This, too, is cause for tension. These immigrants apparently pose a particular psychological and social threat. It is said that they are too ostentatious and arrogant. As one Chinese student said, "We cannot win in this game. When all Chinese immigrants were poor we were resented. Now that many recent Chinese immigrants from Hong Kong and Taiwan are well off, we are still resented."

Since the relaxation of overtly racist immigration policies in the 1960s, increasing numbers of immigrants have come from the Third World (Staffford, 1993). Today, people from Asia, Africa, Latin America and the Caribbean comprise the largest group of immigrants (81%) entering Canada (Immigration Consultations, 1994). That such groups continue to be perceived as "other" is manifest in several ways and, in both official and unofficial parlance, is cause for concern. Canadian government sources coined the term visible minorities in the 1970s to refer to all people of non-European descent whose skin colour makes them immediately identifiable. Quebec government officials initiated use of the term *allophone* for those who are neither of British nor French origin; and more recently, anti-ethnic prejudice and racism, closely connected to the separatist movement, have led those of French Canadian origin to refer to themselves as *pur laine* (pure wool). Immigrants of European origin, on the other hand, are popularly referred to as originating from traditional source countries.

## The Response of Social Work Educators and Practitioners

The fact that a number of studies have documented the deleterious effects of the lack of attention to issues relating to ethnicity, culture and race among educators and practitioners has resulted in the publication of Canadian-based works suggesting solutions to the current state of affairs.

### Current trends in social work education

In 1989, the then Secretary of State for Multiculturalism, Walter McLean, gave impetus to an invitational conference to consider social work's response to immigrants and refugees. This led to the publication of a book of papers that, for the first time, named and discussed issues affecting immigrant and refugee settlement nationally (Yelaja, 1990). Also in 1989, the Task Force on Multicultural and Multiracial Issues in Social Work Education was formed by the Canadian Association of Schools of Social Work (CASSW) in recognition of the need for schools to respond to demographic realities and to Canada's multiculturalism policy.

Two years later, publication of the task force report, entitled *Social Work Education at the Crossroads: The Challenge qf Diversity* (Canadian Association of Schools of Social Work, 1991), provided a wake-up call to this nationwide body which accredits schools of social work in Canada. Using a survey questionnaire and face-to-face, on-site interviews, the task force examined social work education across Canada in terms of students' preparation for work with diverse ethnic, cultural and racial groups. The survey of students, administrators, professors, field instructors and community representatives indicated that social work education failed to provide students with the necessary opportunities to acquire the knowledge, attitudes and skills for current demographic realities, whether in the classroom setting or in the field work practicum. This document was tabled at the delegates assembly of the CASSW, to which all schools send representatives. The highlights of these recommendations are briefly summarized since the recommendations of the task force now constitute one of the many bases for accrediting and re-accrediting schools of social work. The recommendations resulting from this nationwide survey covered issues in the areas of organizational structures, policies, content, students, faculty, field education and community; they will be summarized in this order.

## 1) Organizational structures

Although administrators were generally positive about introducing needed organizational changes to make schools more accessible to minority and Aboriginal students, the necessary policies to support verbal commitments were uneven across the country. To conform to federal contract compliance regulations, most universities have since adopted equity policies for hiring faculty. Such policies affect women (and have apparently benefited them most), Aboriginal peoples, visible minorities and the disabled. Affirmative action policies for students from certain backgrounds (e.g., Aboriginal, minority) have been put in place at some schools. Lack of administrative leadership, organizational inertia (often based on questioning the seriousness of inequity and racism in a particular school) and the lack of realistic timetables for change were viewed as the greatest threats to accomplishing the stated desire to respond to critical ethnic, cultural and racial issues.

## 2) Curriculum content

The task force recommended that schools should review their curricula to ensure that they are infused with appropriate cross-cultural and anti-racist content. It was also recommended that the development of appropriate teaching materials and training programs for instructors of social work (to enable them to become aware of their own biases and to impart the necessary knowledge, values and skills) should be a priority.

## 3) Students

Student admission policies and procedures should be sensitive to differences in educational opportunity due to systemic inequities and should credit students' abilities beyond grade point averages. Policies should be developed to deal with problems of institutional racism, discrimination and paternalism encountered by minority and Aboriginal students. All students should be exposed to multicultural course content and anti-racist social work practice.

## 4) Faculty

The task force recommended that schools should avoid having only one minority professor. Having only one visible minority places undue stress on that person and is unlikely to reflect the realities of multiculturalism in a given area. Faculty should be encouraged to undertake non-exploitive research about issues of race, ethnicity and culture in social work education. Schools should design programs to train existing faculty and field instructors for effective and culturally relevant practice.

## 5) Field work

Engagement in outreach efforts in ethno-specific agencies was recommended in order to develop opportunities for field practice with minority populations. Students also need to recognize and deal with issues of culture, ethnicity and race as they arise in mainstream agencies. Taking local conditions into account, insofar as possible, all students should have opportunities to work cross-culturally and should be evaluated on their ability to work with people from backgrounds other than their own.

## 6) Community

Community representatives were quite willing to enter into formal partnerships with schools (e.g., for curriculum development, field instruction) as long as arrangements are reciprocal and mutually beneficial. Such arrangements should recognize the social service contributions and expertise of people actually performing social work tasks, including advocacy, in diverse community agencies (often in the non-governmental sector). It was suggested that schools should be directly involved in advocacy work.

In the aftermath of the tabling of the above report, it is important to note that the CASSW delegates' assembly has, in two successive years, overwhelmingly passed resolutions suggesting that the task force recommendations be implemented. To date, there has been limited concrete change during the five years since the report was tabled (Durst, 1992; Christensen, 1994). Notable efforts have been made at several universities (for example, the University of Manitoba, 1994; Université du Québec à Montreal, 1994). A significant outcome of the task force report is that its recommendations are now formally taken into account during the accreditation process. It remains to be seen whether the impetus to carry out needed changes will be more in evidence in the coming years.

## Contributions to the literature

Social work education in Canada has always been greatly influenced by literature emanating from the United States. This has been problematic for several reasons: 1) faculty who are not familiar with the true history of Canada's immigrants are prone to incorporate the literature from the United States to, for example, learn more about Hispanic or black cultures that do not "fit" in Canada (e.g., the majority of the Canadian black population is comprised of recent Caribbean and African arrivals, is predominantly urban and meets, or exceeds, levels of education of the average Euro-Canadian); 2) such incorporation has meant that the biases and stereotypes in American literature and research, as well as theoretical formulations of the issues, may also be incorporated by Canadian educators; and 3) for decades, American social science literature has accepted racist concepts regarding black/white differences as real, and has based volumes of studies on belief systems using white Americans as the norm. People in that country appear to view the world in terms of black and white races, and use the terms in "scientific" work as if white people all share one culture, and as if for black people culture and race are one and the same. In the Canadian literature, similar misconceptions abound in studies of Aboriginal peoples.

Recently, there has been a proliferation of literature emanating from Canadian social workers researching current issues (Bergin, 1988; Burrell and Christensen, 1987; Christensen, 1985a; James and Muhammad, 1992; Medeiros, 1991), describing the Canadian context (Berry and Laponce, 1994; Yelaja, 1991), offering original practice models (Christensen, 1985b) and/or incorporating old and new theoretical formulations for a Canadian readership (Herberg, 1993; Mullaly, 1993). In addition, resources for change have begun to be developed and have been brought forth at recent CASSW annual conferences (Yelaja and O'Neill, 1990). In addition, the Canadian journal for professional social workers, *The Social Worker,* has published a number of articles dealing with issues affecting Aboriginal peoples and minorities. A special issue of the CASSW national journal, *Social Work Review,* was entitled "Social Work and Multiculturalism (1991)."

## CONCLUSION

A common thread that may be discerned in much of the specifically Canadian literature dealing with issues of culture, race and ethnicity is urgency. Canadian educators and practitioners fear the kinds of unrest that can be observed in race riots, militia and other extremist movements that are reported in the news from the United States. Even as they struggle to differentiate themselves from their neighbours to the south, they cannot help noticing that both countries were born of a colonial past, and many feel threatened by the challenges of cultural, ethnic and racial diversity. Canada too has skinheads, overt racists and an undetermined number of people distressed by seeing the "face" of Canada changing at an ever-accelerating pace.

In the midst of scepticism about whether we can "get it right," there is also excitement because of the opportunity waiting to be seized. In many ways, the nature of our work places social workers in an enviable position. We touch people where they live, and work with them when and where it really matters. Should we choose to rekindle the spark that allowed us to articulate noble principles and values that cut across cultures, social work educators and practitioners can be instrumental in helping to build a future in which all people may indeed be able to reach their full potential in harmony with their environment.

## REFERENCES

Bergin, B. (1988) *Equality is the issue: A study of minority ethnic group access to health and social services in Ottawa-Carleton.* Ottawa: Social Planning Council of Ottawa-Carleton.

Berry, J.W. and Laponce, J.A. (eds.) (1994). *Ethnicity and culture in Canada: The research landscape.* Toronto: University of Toronto Press.

Bolaria, B.S. and Li, P. (1991). *Racial oppression in Canada.* Toronto: Garamond Press.

Burrell L.F. and Christensen, C.P. (1987). Minority students' perceptions of high school: Implications for Canadian school personnel. *Journal of Multicultural Counseling and Development,* 15, 3-15.

Canadian Task Force on Mental Health Issues Affecting Immigrants and Refugees. (1988). *After the door has been opened.* Report of the Canadian Task Force on Mental Health Issues Affecting Immigrants and Refugees. Ottawa: Health and Welfare and Multiculturalism and Citizenship Canada.

Canadian Association of Schools of Social Work. (1991). *Social work education at the crossroads: The challenge qf diversity.* The Report of the Task Force on Multicultural and Multiracial Issues in Social work Education. Ottawa.

Christensen, C.P. (1996). The impact of racism on the education of social service workers. In C. James (ed.), *Perspectives on racism and the human services sector: A case for change.* Toronto: University of Toronto Press.

Christensen, C. P. (1995). Chapter 11, Immigrant minorities in Canada. In J. C. Turner and F. J. Turner. (eds.), *Canadian social welfare,* 3rd Edition. Scarborough, Ontario: Allyn and Bacon.

Christensen, C.P. (1994). Rethinking social policy for a multicultural and multiracial society. In *Rethinking social welfare: People, policy and practice.*Proceedings from the Social Policy Conference, St. John's, Newfoundland: Memorial University.

Christensen, C. P. (1993). Undue duress: Minority women in academia. *The Journal of Ethno-Development,* 3, 3, 77-85.

Christensen, C.P. (1994). *Linking schools of social work to Aboriginal students and communities: Exploring the issues.* Vancouver, British Columbia: UBC School of Social Work.

Christensen, C.P. (1990). Towards a framework for social work educators in a multicultural and multiracial Canada. In S. Yelaja (ed.). *Toward a framework for the settlement and integration of new immigrants to Canada.* Waterloo, Ontario: Faculty of Social Work, Wilfred Laurier University, and Centre for Social Welfare Services.

Christensen, C.P. (1985a). The perceived problems and help-seeking preferences of Chinese immigrants in Montreal. *Canadian Journal of Counselling,* 21, 4, 189-199.

Christensen, C.P. (1985b). A perceptual approach to cross-cultural counselling. *Canadian Counsellor,* 19, 2, 63-81.

Christensen, C.P. and Weinfeld, M. (1993). The black family in Canada: A preliminary exploration of family patterns and inequality. *Canadian Ethnic Studies,* XXV, 26-44.

Delaney, R. (1995). The philosophical base. In J.C. Turner and F.J. Turner (eds.), *Canadian social welfare,* 3rd Edition. Scarborough, Ontario: Allyn and Bacon.

Doyle, R. and Visano, L. (1987). *Access to health and social services by members of diverse cultural and racial groups.* Reports I and 2. Toronto: Social Planning Council of Metropolitan Toronto.

Durst, D. (1992). The road to poverty is paved with good intentions: Social interventions and indigenous peoples. *International Social Work,* 35(1), 191-202.

Fleras, A. and Elliot, J.L. (1992). *Multiculturalism in Canada: The challenge of diversity.* Scarbourough, Ontario: Nelson Canada.

Head., W. (1986). *Black women's work: Racism in the health system.* Toronto: Ontario Human Rights Commission.

Henry, F., Tator, C., Mattis, W. and Rees, T. (1995). *The colour of democracy: Racism in Canadian society.* Toronto: Harcourt Brace and Company, Canada.

Herberg, D.C. (1993). *Frameworks for cultural and racial diversity.* Toronto: Canadian Scholars' Press.

Hughes, D. and Kallen, E. (1974). *Anatomy of racism: Canadian dimensions.* Montreal: Harvest House.

James, C. and Muhammad, H. (1992). *Children in childcare programs: Perception on race and race related issues.* Toronto: Multicultural and Race Relations Division, Children's Services, Municipality of Metropolitan Toronto.

*Immigration Consultations 1994, Discussion Document.* (1994). Ottawa: Citizenship and Immigration Canada.

Medeiros, J. (1991). *Family services for all.* Toronto: Multicultural Coalition for Access to Family Services.

Mullaly, R. (1993). *Structural social work: Ideology, theory, and practice.* Toronto: McClelland and Stewart Inc.

Sirros, C. (1987). *Rapport du comité sur l'accessibilité des services de santé et des services sociaux du réseau aux communautés culturelles.*

Stafford, J. (1993). The impact of the new immigration policy on racism in Canada. In V. Satzewich (ed.), *Deconstructing a nation: Immigration, multiculturalism and racism in '90s Canada.* Halifax, Nova Scotia: Fernwood Publishing.

Tepper, E. L. (1994). Immigration policy and multiculturalism. In J. W. Beffy and J. A. Laponce (eds.), *Ethnicity and culture in Canada: The research landscape.* Toronto: University of Toronto Press.

Turner, J.C. and Turner, F.J. (eds.). (1995). *Canadian social welfare,* 3rd Edition. Scarborough, Ontario: Allyn and Bacon.

Winks, R. (1972). *The blacks in Canada: A history.* Montreal: McGill Queen's University Press.

Yelaja, S. and O'Neill, B. (1990). Introduction. In S. Yelaja (ed.), *Toward a framework for the settlement and integration of new immigrants to Canada.* Waterloo, Ontario: Faculty of Social Work, Wilfred Laurier University and Centre for Social Welfare Studies.

York, G. (1992). *The dispossessed: Life and death in native Canada.* Toronto: Lester and Orpen Denys.

# CHAPTER 15

# Anti-Oppressive Social Work:
# A Model for Field Education

*Narda Razack*

## INTRODUCTION

Social work education is transforming to respond to the needs of a diverse society (Dominelli, 1996; Longres, 1991; Kolb Morris, 1993; Gold and Bogo, 1992). Transformation requires redressing the powerful, historical legacy of oppression evident in pedagogical and practice approaches (Chau, 1991; Thompson, 1993; Maroccio, 1995). The practicum and field placement course is a critical nexus for this transformation—paradoxically perhaps the most critical site because of the partnerships between the university, social work practitioners and community agencies. This location provides an important opportunity to acknowledge and incorporate different knowledge and expertise needed for anti-oppressive social work practice in a constantly changing society. Collaborating with a range of communities where practice involves innovative approaches with diverse groups further informs and enriches social work education in an increasingly global context.

Field education has been historically located on the periphery of social work education (Schneck, Grossman and Glassman, 1991). Although students report that the practicum is the most significant course in their social work program, the field has not generally been accorded full academic status (Schneck, 1995). In difficult economic times, the field, which demands more resources than in-class courses, can suffer setbacks.

And yet, the practicum course provides students with the bridge for theory and practice.

Field education has the potential for new learning, and it lays the groundwork for an anti-oppressive framework for practice. Such an approach requires philosophical, organizational and methodological changes. Field education departments in all schools of social work differ in organization and structure although they share an overarching objective in the integration of knowledge, skills and experiences. The field is ideally located to incorporate an anti-oppressive framework because of the involvement of student, faculty, field instructor, community and agency. This chapter describes the efforts of one school of social work to develop anti-oppressive principles in its practicum curriculum. The first part of the paper provides a brief overview of the literature on anti-discriminatory practice as it relates to field education and a critical perspective around oppression. The second section details the model that has been developed and concludes with some implications for social work education and practice.

REVIEW OF THE LITERATURE

There has been a groundswell of needs assessments, studies and research that identify the need to infuse the curriculum with content relating to the oppression of marginalized groups (Carillo, Holzhalb and Thyer, 1993; Task Force CASSW, 1991; Yelaja, 1988). Curriculum transformation poses particular challenges for faculty given the historical, traditional, Eurocentric theories and practice approaches (Rossiter, 1995; Singleton, 1994). There are articles which document the need for an anti-racist curriculum (Macey and Moxon, 1996; Dominelli, 1988) and pedagogical principles to assist in developing an anti-oppressive focus (Christensen, 1992; Chau, 1991; Gordon, 1995).

Tully and Greene (1993) studied the coverage of articles relating to cultural diversity in social work education and reported that practice skills received the greatest attention (60.4%), while the area most neglected related to the field practicum (1.3%). They pointed out the obvious anomaly that students are usually exposed to diversity in placement yet there was little or no preparation with respect to cultural awareness and preparation for practice. Since 1991, the year Tully and Greene's study was completed, there has been more attention to cultural diversity and anti-racist practice in the literature (Dominelli, 1996; Thompson, 1993;

Hugman, 1996; Kolb Morris, 1993; Van Soest, 1994a, 1994b). However, most of the current literature focuses on the need to understand cultural frameworks of the clients (Christensen, 1992; Insoo and Miller, 1992) and the importance of ethnic sensitive social work practice (Razack, Teram and Rivera, 1995; Longres, 1991; Haynes and Singh, 1992). Nonetheless, searches of library resources failed to identify any literature concerning the management of field education in general (Kilpatrick and Holland, 1993). Literature which includes significant analysis of field education with respect to diversity and anti-racism is limited to analysis of specific components of field education. The discussion encompassed in this article, therefore, should be of interest because it describes the process involved for the field education department to provide a comprehensive approach to anti-oppressive social work practice.

## ANTI-OPPRESSION AND FIELD EDUCATION

Salcido, Garcia, Cota and Thomson (1995) describe their efforts to include a cross-cultural training model at integrative seminars in field education. Gonzalez del Valle, Merdinger, Wrenn and Miller (1991) discuss an integrated model designed for practice with the Spanish-speaking community. Razack, Teram and Rivera (1995) relate the process and benefits in providing placements for a few students each term in multicultural agencies. These articles focus on particular components of field education and fail to incorporate systemic and systematic change. The focus of this discussion will be on ways in which an anti-oppressive framework can be inscribed in all areas of the field education process.

Rogers (1992) describes principles relating to field education and "ethnically-sensitive anti-discriminatory practice." Guidelines are thus established for students to understand issues around ethnic-sensitive practice. These principles, while relevant to the overall process of anti-oppression practice, neglect the pivotal role of the field department in facilitating a comprehensive approach to anti-discriminatory practice with all the constituents. In order for the practicum to reflect the diversity in society, there has to be an understanding of the importance of culture, community, race (racism), oppression and the need to ensure that there is a process for realizing change and challenge.

Black, Maki and Nunn (1994) report on the difficulties in providing accurate descriptions of the relationship between field instructor and student who have different racial and ethnic backgrounds. Social workers typically identify with an image of justice and empathy, and they may find it particularly difficult to acknowledge and recognize their own racism and lack of understanding of anti-racist social work practice. Van Dijk (1987, p. 358) interprets his interviews with white Caucasians on the issue of racism:

> ....the better educated are just as prejudiced in their interactions, but tend to be so in a more indirect and subtle way, especially in the domains in which their own interests are perceived to be threatened...the better educated, the elite, follow strategies of positive impression formation. Their self-image features a component of (ethnic or other forms of) "tolerance," which must be upheld especially in public, and in contacts with strangers (such as interviewers).

Further data indicate that field instructors, whether minority or non-minority, discuss the racial and ethnic backgrounds of clients more frequently with minority students than did field instructors with majority students (Black et al., 1991, p.15). Students with minority field instructors also stated that they were better prepared to work with clients from other ethnic groups. Their research suggests that non-minority supervisors felt that they had more than adequately prepared their students to work with groups other than their own. However, the students' rating of their performance around supervision and preparation of student to work with minority groups was lower.

Given the fact that the field department has such a critical role, it is imperative that change occurs at all levels in order to ensure the delivery of a curriculum that incorporates justice, ethics and inclusion. This chapter describes the process of attempting to ground the practicum within an anti-oppressive framework. In this process, the major constituents involve students, field supervisors and faculty. The field is at the cutting edge of education and practice and the practicum must not be viewed only as a place for students to bridge theory and practice, but also as an important area to ensure that anti-discriminatory practice is actively taught. Field education can provide an important place where issues of diversity and oppression can be included in all aspects of planning, organizing, instructing and implementation of the placement.

As a result, all participants—student, field instructor, agency, faculty and agency personnel—will be encouraged to address issues of difference, not simply from a cognitive approach but through discussion and practical application. The field can thus be viewed as the place where "practice can inform and reform knowledge."

## A reflection on oppression

There are many people in our society who experience different forms of oppression as a result of the behaviour of those who exert their power through subordinating and excluding others. Oppression signifies a lack of economic and institutional power. Pharr (1988) identifies common elements of oppression and the dominant societal norms that dictate rightness and righteousness that all are to be judged by. Those who do not fit are relegated to the margins. It is through this process that the "other" is created and made to feel invisible, isolated, tokenized and violated. Rodwell and Blankebaker (1992) use wounding as a metaphor to understand oppression in order to develop cross-cultural sensitivity. They provide an analogy of child abuse for students to understand cultural wounding.

The principles of anti-oppressive field practice are based upon an acknowledgment and understanding of the prejudice and oppression inherent in traditional values and beliefs. This admission is necessary because social workers have been taught an essentially Euro-American model of social work and practice in an environment which is systematically and institutionally oppressive to a vast number of people. Some agencies have provided opportunities for reflection through workshops and conferences. However there has not been consistent training for field instructors to facilitate a reflective process with students for discussions of prejudice and discrimination. If these discussions do not occur at all levels of the placement process, this reflection towards an understanding of a person's well-being will continue to be damaging and oppressive for students, practitioners and more importantly the client(s).

The focus for the next millennium should be on the needs of those who continue to be oppressed and marginalized in society. These groups tend to be disproportionately represented on caseloads within social service agencies and the object of policies and community development projects. Field instruction should also encompass the particular needs of the minority student and the clients. Although immigrants and visible minorities have a long historical presence in this country, there is still marked discrimination in practices (Seebaran and McNiven, 1979).

## A MODEL OF CHANGE

Given the entrenched nature of oppression and the oppressive practices that result, it is imperative that the field adopt educative principles towards an anti-discriminatory framework for practice. Five major questions will be introduced for discussion to guide the conception, philosophy and implementation of such a framework. The change process in one department will be discussed with an awareness of different contexts and approaches in other social work field departments. However, efforts will be made to highlight ways to adopt various principles together with critiques and accommodation for additional perspectives.

### 1. How can placements expand to include diverse settings and what are the issues towards achieving this goal?

Recent studies indicate the need for practicum placements to expand to include ethno-specific agencies (Task Force, 1991). In order to respond to this directive and to our diverse student body, I, as the practicum coordinator, invited executive directors and/or representatives from ethno-specific agencies to an inaugural meeting at the university. We outlined our goals towards inclusion in the field and listened to their needs for an anti-racist and anti-oppressive curriculum necessary for students to participate in their programs. The Multicultural Advisory Committee was formed following this meeting, which comprises members from various ethno-specific community agencies, faculty and the practicum coordinator. The primary objective is for the practicum department to reflect an anti-oppressive framework that would result in the integration rather than the token representation of ethno-specific placements into our field curriculum. This approach ensures that minority and non-minority students are not simply placed at ethno-specific agencies, but that there is an infrastructure of support and education. The advisory committee members have field students and provide feedback for change and participate in all other school activities.

Students can request a split placement at ethno-specific agencies to observe and learn about cross-cultural issues. I was very fortunate to be the first student to begin a split placement at a multicultural agency, which contrasted sharply and distinctly from my other placements at traditional agencies (See Razack et al., 1995). My learning opportunities were maximized because of these varied experiences, yet the school regarded the mainstream supervisor as the only person qualified to evaluate my performance. We agreed to shift our thinking around formal supervision by recognizing, respecting and valuing the qualifications, knowledge and expertise of experienced workers at these non-traditional agencies. Supervision of split placements and others is augmented when necessary through consultation and collaboration with the faculty field advisor, practicum coordinator and the agency.

The practicum committee also serves an important function in promoting the objectives of anti-discriminatory practice and is representative of a diverse community. This committee assists with the production of our newsletter, *Field View*, published at the beginning of each term. The newsletter is another medium to ensure the message of diversity as faculty, visiting professors, field instructors and students are encouraged to provide articles. Innovative and international placements are also highlighted as are field events. Some of the above changes can easily be incorporated into any existing structure despite the differences in student body regarding numbers, diversity or approach.

Multicultural and innovative placements pose a challenge and require ongoing work to maintain because of the general lack of importance placed on work within these agencies and the absence of "professional" titles. However, if students have the opportunity to experience practice in these agencies and continue to hear the message about global practice, the desire for such placements will increase. There must be commitment from the entire department to facilitate ongoing change.

## 2. How can field instructors be more aware of oppression and what are the issues?

The field agency and field instructor are also critical to the facilitation of an anti-oppressive framework. Field instructors are invited to attend seminars at the school during the course of their role with students. The presenters are asked to include an analysis of racism and oppression in their presentation, and the coordinator provides information pertaining to the philosophy and expectation of the department. Presenters include field instructors, faculty, community workers and students, and the topics relate to current practice issues.[1] These seminars have resulted in lively discussions that create further opportunities for inclusive practice. Our university is located in a large metropolis, and agencies are shared among three area universities as well as colleges. As a result, there is a huge turnover with field instructors and agencies, which makes long-term planning and education difficult. The seminars have been a successful educational alternative.

Students report great anxiety around the practicum course (Rompf, Royse and Dhooper, 1993), and this anxiety can be further exacerbated for minority students in placement if there is a denial of differences or subtle and blatant forms of discrimination. The field instructor has a powerful influence on the student as a professional (Schneck, Grossman and Glassman, 1991; Bogo and Vayda, 1987; Shulman, 1983). The supervisor should ensure, therefore, that the students have appropriate orientation to the placement setting in order to minimize anxiety and possible feelings of exclusion. The role of the field instructor within the program is critical to facilitate change and growth, especially in areas demanding personal and professional commitment. Field instructors should begin the process of inclusivity from the pre-screening interview by ensuring that there is a discussion about work with diverse populations, the agency's mandate around anti-harassment and sexual exploitation. Moreover students should feel empowered to enquire about practice and supervision knowledge in the area of diversity.

Over the past year I have facilitated workshops, presented at seminars and participated in discussions that were focused on the theme of anti-oppression principles in field education. These situations have been uncomfortable because the participants, whether minority or non-minority, were divided on the subject of beginning a discourse around anti-oppressive practice at the pre-screening interview. According to Williams (1991), "the cold game of equality staring" becomes stark and burdensome when facilitating such discourse. Field instructors felt that a discussion of anti-racism/oppression would make the minority student feel marginalized. Some minority field instructors and students concurred. It is obvious that the context and construction of new ideas and approaches need further deliberation. To simply acknowledge the colour of a student in an initial interview without awareness and education around inclusivity will indeed be marginalizing and very disconcerting. During and, more intensely, after these workshops I felt uneasy and disheartened with the learning paradigm around oppression.

This internal struggle persisted because I remember my experiences as a minority student where there was a whole denial of my cultural identity, and my otherness was felt very sharply on a daily basis—in the classroom, at the field interview and at my mainstream placement. My initial disappointment at the first few workshops stemmed from the fact that the majority field instructors did not recognize the denial that exists within themselves around issues of oppression or how deeply entrenched oppression is within marginalized groups. Also, as minority workers and students, we have had to learn from theorists whose pedagogical principles and cognitive awareness did not include the lives of marginalized groups in society. As a result, we have either become so immersed in an oppressive system that it becomes too tiresome to continue to challenge for change or we may have internalized our oppression so deeply that current approaches to practice become effective measures for competency as a social worker. Oppressive practices are manifested in subtle and even blatant ways in placement. For example, students may be given only clients who belong to their own ethnic groups. Although these students may prefer working with their own groups, it is important for field instructors to discuss preferences with the students before making such an assumption. These are examples of the kind of issues inherent in our discussions at all seminars.

It is critical that field instructors pay attention to the language and behaviours that may be part of the culture of the agency helping those who require service. Many times students report their disillusionment when the incidental chatter of workers includes casual derogatory remarks about particular clients and families. Students report that they feel powerless to challenge their field instructor/supervisor or other agency personnel for fear of backlash because of the power differential and the evaluative nature of placements. Students who are members of the group that is the target of oppression will feel judged and devalued by the negative comments. Field instructors must be helped to feel comfortable discussing organizational issues, including the political realities that relate to funding constraints, increasing caseloads and the resulting effects as workers face burnout and display feelings of abuse and oppression within a system over which they also feel powerless. Our field instruction seminars provide opportunities to discuss several of these issues and could be easily integrated at educational fora in field education departments.

3. How can students be made more aware of oppression and what are the issues?

The curriculum of our school was recently revised with an objective of integrating issues of systemic inequalities.[2] As a result, students have some exposure to challenging oppression and racism in their work. These objectives are met in several ways in the field curriculum. All students attend a practicum orientation seminar, which covers a wide range of topics including innovative learning at non-traditional agencies and the importance of thinking and working cross-culturally. Seventeen years ago, Weeks (1981, p. 7) elaborated on the merits of placements at innovative settings:

> Field placements in innovative community settings involve maintaining broad boundaries for social work practice. They offer students alternatives to therapeutic work with individuals and families....They allow group work, community development and organizing to be central rather than peripheral social work methods....Advocacy...and systems brokerage are considered as valuable and important as counselling and therapy.

Students need to understand bureaucratic structures and be able to work effectively in these settings while learning to critically reflect on practice to acquire an analysis that goes beyond application of a learnt theory for a particular situation (Goldstein, 1993). There is a radical shift in practice approaches as traditional clinical settings are being challenged to embrace community perspectives and link families with resources.[3] Practicum graduates are also invited to these seminars to share their placement experiences with reference to their learning of anti-oppression principles for practice. These seminars occur in most schools and are an ideal place to remind students of inclusive practice.

A discussion of anti-oppressive principles is also important during the individual interview the student has with the field coordinator to determine strengths and areas of interest and discuss potential placement choices. Forms for students were revised to recognize split placement opportunities and remind students about practice with diverse groups. Practicum students must attend two integrative seminars each term with their faculty field advisor. The seminars provide a further mechanism for those students who do not have opportunities at their placement to effectively begin to question the exclusionary nature of practice. Students are encouraged to critically analyze the organizational structure of their placement agency and provide ways to incorporate discussion around the challenges in working with a diverse population. It is hoped that all students who have been involved in courses relating to anti-oppression, attended orientation seminars, interviews and other meetings in preparation for the field, will feel more able to discuss practice issues with a diverse population at a pre-screening meeting and in their placement agency. This model facilitates this dialogue through different steps of this process.

### 4. How can faculty be more aware of oppression and what are the issues?

At field coordinators' meetings, faculty commitment or lack of it is always a point of discussion.[4] Kilpatrick and Holland (1993) conducted a research study to identify strengths and problems in the area of field education. The most important criteria for improving field education related to the involvement of faculty. Although each school has different requirements regarding faculty advising, information and participation in field education can be facilitated through faculty meetings, seminars, newsletters and internal dialogue.

Faculty members are included at field instruction seminars as facilitators and participants. Visits to the field have been reduced from three to one, and each faculty must now hold two integrative seminars per term for all practicum students. These seminars are mandatory and provide opportunities to discuss issues relating to organizational change and practice with marginalized groups. All faculty members met initially to formulate the guidelines and approach to these seminars and again for evaluation. We need to continue these meetings to ensure that anti-oppressive principles continue to be actively discussed. Salcido et al. (1993) expanded the format of integrative seminars to include an experiential component with videotapes and found that this had a more positive effect in the area of skills acquisitions than the traditional seminar approach. We are conducting a study of the effectiveness of these seminars to improve and make change.

All the faculty members in our department have a group of practicum students each term and, therefore, have ongoing discussions with the coordinator as well as more general discussions at faculty and council meetings. This collaboration again gives prominence to the field and creates further opportunities for inclusion of anti-oppressive principles. Faculty members also share annual membership on the practicum and multicultural committees. They are also asked to present at seminars and at workshops in the community around field education. These efforts help to promote the field departments as vital components of the curriculum and social work education.

5. What can the practicum coordinator do to ensure that department is committed to the importance of the role of the field in promoting anti-oppression in practice?

Field education is in a constant state of flux and change mainly because of the historical lack of recognition of its importance to the curriculum (Kilpatrick and Holland, 1993). After the tenured field coordinator retired several years ago, the department agreed to hire a practicum coordinator on a limited term contract. During the first year, discussions concerning the position were ongoing and the contractually limited appointment was changed to a tenure track appointment with open competition. The change in position is an important one and signals more status and credence to the role of field education within the university and in the wider community.

As the new coordinator, it was important to understand the position of field education not only to this school but to social work in general. This appointment came at the heels of program reviews that emphasized the need for the expansion and integration of ethno-specific agencies for student placements. Some efforts have been noted in other schools in extending cultural diversity to field education. Razack et al. (1995) describe the process involved in providing one-day multicultural placements for a few graduate students. Courses around cultural diversity provide students with a framework for sensitive practice (Salcido et al., 1995; Rogers, 1992). It was apparent that fundamental changes to the field department and to the school were needed in order to deliver a program based on anti-oppression principles. The field coordinator must represent the need to change the structure and approach to the department and be firmly committed through actions and practice. It is also important to liaise with a range of agencies and make concentrated efforts to visit non-traditional settings and provide opportunities for exchange of ideas.

Forms for agencies and students reflect our commitment to diversity. The practicum manual has been significantly changed to include an anti-oppressive focus. Evaluation and progress reports have been re-written to fit traditional and non-traditional practice approaches and have moved away from a distinct clinical focus. These changes further emphasize our commitment and acceptance of traditional and non-traditional ways of practice in a diverse society. It is imperative that the department regard field education as a vital component of the curriculum. Recognizing the pivotal role of the field is essential in creating an infrastructure to facilitate an anti-oppressive framework for practice. The practicum is now a regular item on the agenda of every faculty meeting, which helps to ensure that everyone is aware of changes, initiatives and developments. In this school, faculty have significant roles and membership on all committees.

Through a small grant the Multicultural Advisory Committee produced an instructional videotape, *Beginning Inclusivity: The First Interview*.[5] This videotape consists of short scenarios of a pre-placement interview with a field instructor and student to ensure that there is a beginning discussion of diversity from personal and/or professional perspectives. This videotape is beneficial for students, educators and practitioners as the scenarios point to the difficulty of change and provide ways to discuss sensitive issues. This videotape has been presented at seminars and conferences and is a marketing tool for the school, and the idea could be easily adapted to suit particular needs and demands. It is also suitable for practice courses and for field instruction seminars. Community agencies have also found the material useful for staff professional activities. The field coordinator needs to be informed about curriculum developments and practice issues. Further plans include forums, workshops and research opportunities between the department and the community.

## IMPLICATIONS FOR SOCIAL WORK PRACTICE

This field education model is described from the perspective of one school but with a recognition and belief in its adaptability. This approach reflects an ethical and moral response to the need to integrate an anti-oppressive approach to the practicum. It seems illogical to wait for the academy to fully reflect anti-racist and anti-oppressive pedagogical principles in the classroom in order to influence changes in the field. The challenge towards incorporating an anti-racist/anti-oppressive curriculum is arduous and still not a priority for many educators and practitioners, for reasons that may relate to fear of change, anxiety, tradition and resistance. The classroom effectively remains a private domain that comes up for public scrutiny only through occasional evaluations.

In social work there are challenges to the traditional power differential between the knower and the known; between the power paradigm inherent in the lecturer and the student; and, more importantly, the power imbalances between the social worker and the client. There are many workshops around the power dynamics in field instruction that speak to the imbalance of power between the student and field instructor (Rogers, 1992). All of these areas should be under continuing personal and professional scrutiny to ensure that there are mechanisms to understand and avoid opportunities for oppression and subordination of others.

Moffat (1996, p. 48) discusses a reflective process whereby the social work student can reach "an understanding of a person's well-being in practice." This process assumes that the student/worker will be able to recognize oppressive behaviours and be reflective in order to understand how oppression affects others. However, if within the student/field instructor realms of education and experiences there was little or no focus on anti-oppressive principles, how then can the "person's well-being" be understood? What is the mechanism provided for student/instructor discourse around oppressive practice? It becomes critical, therefore, to provide the structure and space not only for reflection but for honest and necessary discussion and analyses of oppression. Reflection should lead to dialogical enquiry where issues will be discussed and a new level of understanding and practice can ensue. The field education process, in contrast to the traditional classroom, provides different and significant opportunities for the introduction of material related to oppression in critical discussion with all its constituents: student, faculty, field instructor, administration, agency and community.

Freire (1970) refers to the common approach to pedagogy as the "banking" concept, where education is carried out by teacher "for" learner or by teacher "about" learner. He contrasts this to the teacher working "with" the learner "mediated by the world—a world which impresses and challenges both parties, giving rise to views or opinions about it" (p.82). Working with the learner is vital in field instruction in order to facilitate discussions of sensitive issues. Social work is viewed as a caring and helping profession. In today's society, social work educators are struggling to educate and prepare students for the realities of practice. I have often challenged the "given" in social work that empathy should be enough when working with clients. I know that empathy does not generally facilitate a discussion around oppression and, even if this discussion happens, it is only in the context of being empathic relative to the given situation and not through an examination of the political implications of imperialism, colonialism or racism. If the field instructor has been trained to listen, acknowledge pain and give corrective feedback without an analysis that includes attention to systemic inequalities, then this may result in a further disservice to the student and the client.

The field department simply cannot afford to maintain a peripheral position in the curriculum because of the availability of opportunities through the links with all areas of the profession. The structure for change is permissible, affordable, attainable and sustainable. Field coordinators need to advocate the importance of the position and the role of the field in order to first have the commitment to change. Innovation and enthusiasm are also important elements to sustain efforts and create commitment. Inviting the community to collaborate, participate in meetings, sit on school councils, search committees and other important functions gives the department prominence and encourages a wide degree of participation. There are numerous opportunities for critical reflection and enquiry around themes relating to oppression, racism, colonialism and the resulting marginalization of groups. The framework presented in this article has generated many opportunities for research projects that are critical to field education. One area of research that needs critical attention relates to the position of minority students in mainstream agencies with non-minority instructors. The field can make concrete and practical adjustments, and the process of change can then be documented for research and scholarship purposes. The field then "administers" and simply "does" and becomes a critical area where "practice can reform knowledge."

## CONCLUSION

Anti-oppression principles deserve ongoing debate, challenge and collaboration. The integration of these principles requires particular attention in the development of the practicum. This development needs to be documented and evaluated for teaching and practice purposes since there is no model to fully eradicate oppressive practices. Anti-oppressive practice needs to include introspection and private inner confrontation and must also be compelling enough to brave interactive discourse and admission to vulnerabilities and cultural wounding.

Goldstein (1993, p. 181) points out that "any serious changes in field education would significantly disturb and even alter all other aspects of the curriculum." This model has significantly transformed the practicum department and influenced social work education and practice. Each division of field education needs to play a critical role in anti-oppression/racist analysis in order to reflect inclusivity and appreciation of differences. This anti-oppressive framework incorporates the roles of students, field instructors, faculty, community and administrators through institutional and systematic change processes.

## ENDNOTES

[1] Some topics include: anti-oppressive principles for field education—panel discussion with perspectives on race, sexuality, disability and Aboriginal settings; the integration of theory and practice; politics and social work; the effective cross cultural field instructor; racial power dynamics in field supervision.

[2] Some of the core courses include: anti-discriminatory practice; identity and diversity; power, organization and bureaucracy.

[3] Recent conversation with educational coordinator in a health care setting.

[4] Field coordinators from the area universities meet monthly and the national group meets annually at Learned Society Meetings.

[5] This videotape was made possible through a minor research grant and is available through the department.

## REFERENCES

Black, J., Maki, M. and Nunn, J. (1994). Does race affect the social work student-field instructor relationship. Paper presented at the Conference of Field Education, Calgary, Alberta. June.

Bogo, M. and Vayda, E. (1987). *The practice of field instruction in social work.* Toronto: University of Toronto.

Canadian Association of Schools of Social Work. Social work education at the crossroads: The challenge of diversity. Report of the Task Force on Multicultural and Multiracial Issues in Social Work Education, (Ottawa, 1991).

Carrillo, D., Holzhalb, C. and B. Thyer. (1993). Assessing social work students' attitudes related to cultural diversity: A review of selected measures. *Journal of Social Work Education*, 29(3), Fall.

Chau,K. (1991). Social work with ethnic minorities: Practice issues and potentials. *Journal of Multicultural Social Work.*1(1), 23-39.

Christensen, C.(1992). Training for cross-cultural social work with immigrants, refugees, and minorities: A course model. *Journal of Multicultural Social Work,* 2(1), 79-97.

Dominelli, L. (1988). *Anti-racist social work: A challenge for white practitioners and educators.* London: MacMillan Press.

Dominelli, L. (1996). Deprofessionalizing social work: Anti-oppressive practice, competencies and postmodernism. *British Journal of Social Work,* 26(2), 153-175.

Freire, P. (1970). *Pedagogy of the oppressed.* New York: Continuum.

Gold, N. and Bogo, M. (1992). Social work research in a multicultural society: Challenges and approaches. *Journal of Multicultural Social Work,* 2(4), 7-21.

Goldstein, H. (1993). Field education for reflective practice: A re-constructive proposal. *Journal of Teaching in Social Work,* 8(1/2), 165-182.

Gonzalez del Valle, A., Merdinger, J., Wrenn, R. and D. Miller. (1991). The field practicum and transcultural practice: An integrated model. *Journal of Multicultural Social Work*, 1(3), 45-55.

Gordon, E.B. (1995). Educating for empowerment:Teaching policy and practice with individuals with disabilities. *Arete*, 20(1) Spring, 65-69.

Haynes, A. and Singh, R. (1992). Ethnic-sensitive social work practice: An integrated, ecological, and psychodynamic approach. *Journal of Multicultural Social Work,* 2(2), 43-52.

Hugman, R. (1996). Professionalization in social work: The challenge of diversity. *International Social Work*, 39(2), 131-147.

Insoo, K. and Miller, S. (1992). Working with Asian American clients: One person at a time. *Families in Society:The Journal of Contemporary Human Services.* pp. 356-363

Kilpatrick, A. and T. Holland. (1993). Management of the field instruction program in social work education. *Journal of Teaching in Social Work*, 7(1), 123-136.

Kolb Morris, J. (1993). Interacting oppressions: Teaching social work content on women of colour. *Journal of Social Work Education*, 29(1), Winter, 99-110.

Longres, J. (1991). Toward a status model of ethnic sensitive practice. *Journal of Multicultural Social Work,* 1(1), 41-56.

Macey, M. and E. Moxon. (1996). An examination of anti-racist and anti-oppressive theory and practice in social work education. *British Journal of Social Work*, 26(3), 297-314.

Maroccio, K. (1995). Identifying oppression in language: The power of words. *Canadian Social Work Review*, 12(2), Summer, 146-158.

Moffatt, K. (1996).Teaching social work practice as a reflective process. In N. Gould and I. Taylor (eds.), *Reflective learning for social work*. Brookfield, VT: Ashgate Publishing Co.

Pharr, S. (1988). *Homophobia: A weapon of sexism*. Inverness, CA: Chardon Press.

Razack, N., Teram, E. and Rivera, M. (1995). Cultural diversity in field education: A practice model for enhancing cross cultural knowledge. In G. Rogers (ed.), *Social work field education: Views and visions*. Dubuque, IA: Kendall/Hunt.

Rodwell, M. and Blankebaker, A. (1992). Strategies for developing cross-cultural sensitivity: Wounding as metaphor. *Journal of Social Work Education*, 28(2) Spring/Summer, 153-165.

Rogers, G. (ed.). (1995). *Social work field education:Views and visions*. Dubuque,IA: Kendall/Hunt.

Rogers, G. (Jun 1992). Teaching and learning ethnically-sensitive anti-discriminatory practice: Field placement principles for Canadian social work programmes. Paper presented at the CASSW 1992 Annual Conference, P.E.I.

Rompf, E., Royse, D. and Dhooper, S. (1993). Anxiety preceding field work: What students worry about. *Journal of Teaching in Social Work,* 7(2), 81-95.

Salcido, R.M., Garcia, J., Cota, V. and C.Thomson. (1995). A cross cultural training model for field education. *Arete*, 20(1), Spring, 26-36.

Rossiter, A. (1995). Entering the intersection of identity, form, and knowledge: Reflections on curriculum transformation. *Canadian Journal of Community Mental Health,* 14(1), Spring, 5-14.

Schneck, D., Grossman, B. and Glassman, U. (eds). (1991). *Field education in social work: Contemporary issues and trends*. Iowa: Kendal/Hunt.

Schneck, D. (1991). Ideal and reality in field education. In Schneck, D., Grossman, B. and Glassman, U. (eds), *Field education in social work: Contemporary issues and trends*. Iowa: Kendal/Hunt.

Schneck, D. (1995). The promise of field education in social work. Keynote address in Rogers, G. (ed.), *Social work field education:Views and visions*. Dubuque, IA: Kendall/Hunt.

Seebaran, R. and McNiven, C. (1979). Ethnicity, multiculturalism and social work education. *Canadian Journal of Social Work Education,* 5(2,3), 125-131.

Shulman, L. (1983). *Teaching the helping skills: A field instructor's guide*. Illinois: Peacock.

Singleton, S. (1994). Faculty personal comfort and the teaching of content on racial oppression. *Journal of Multicultural Social Work,* 3(1), 5-16.

Thompson, N. (1993). *Anti-discriminatory practice.* London:The MacMillan Press.

Tully, C. and R.Greene. (1993). Cultural diversity comes of age: A study of coverage, 1970-1991. *Arete,* 18, Summer, 37-45.

van Dijk, T. (1987). *Communicating racism: Ethnic prejudice in thought and talk.* CA: Sage.

Van Soest, D. (1994a). Impact of social work education on student attitudes and behaviour concerning oppression. *Journal of Social Work Education,* 32(2), Spring/Summer, 191-202.

Van Soest, D. (1994b). Social work education for multicultural practice and social justice advocacy: A field study of how students experience the learning process. *Journal of Multicultural Social Work,* 3(1), 17-28.

Weeks, W. (1981). *Innovative community settings: A guide to social work field instruction.* School of Social Work, McMaster University.

Williams, P. (1991). *The alchemy of race and rights.* Cambridge: Harvard.

Yelaja, S. (ed.) (1988) *Proceedings of The Settlement and Integration of New Immigrants to Canada Conference.* Centre for Social Welfare Studies:Waterloo, Ontario.

# CHAPTER 16

# Structuring a Learning Environment: Guidelines for Becoming Competent in Cross-Cultural Practice

*Gayla Rogers and Helena Summers*

## INTRODUCTION

The need for multicultural competence in social service delivery has never been more urgent. An environment for learning multicultural, cross-cultural social work practice can be structured in a number of ways and take place in a number of settings. Becoming competent in this arena is not restricted to a college classroom and is in fact less likely to occur using traditional teaching methods that are hierarchical, such as lectures and didactic approaches with little or no discussion. It requires more than good intentions on the part of the learner and needs to be directed and facilitated in such a way that over time the learner becomes engaged in a self-reflective process that is shared with others.

Transforming one's belief systems and incorporating other perspectives leading to new ways of seeing, thinking, feeling and acting that may prove more inclusive, differentiating and integrative are both interactive and inter-subjective processes (Mezirow, 1991). Developing competence in cross-cultural social work practice to reflect the above involves a planned approach to learning that includes a curriculum and teaching/learning methods appropriate to this unique subject matter and to the learners. Although the learning needs to be purposely structured, it can take place in the workplace or classroom, as a formal class, practicum or informal workshop, as a course for degree requirements, or as continuing education. It can evolve from a few committed individuals wanting to develop themselves personally and professionally to an organizational mandate and policy for staff development and training, or it can be part of a degree or diploma program with required and elective course offerings.

What is not negotiable is that this learning takes place at a personal as well as a professional level. The learning must include strategies for personal change and strategies for professional change. These two types of changes are interrelated since addressing personal biases is a prerequisite for transforming practices, services and organizations; these broader transformations will, in turn, support further individual change (Hayes, 1994). This chapter provides a framework for examining the processes and strategies of both the personal and professional development of cultural competence. It includes salient content and concepts as well as issues and processes involved in structuring a learning environment conducive to preparing practitioners for cross-cultural social work practice.

## AN AGENDA FOR CHANGE

A personal change agenda is composed of ingredients that facilitate change in perceptions and beliefs that impact interactions and relationships on a daily, personal basis. Colin and Preciphs (1991), for example, discuss six connected elements that promote personal change in racist behaviours and attitudes: awareness and acknowledgment of racism, commitment to change, understanding and valuing diversity, self-awareness and reflection, affective learning, and developing and evaluating new behaviours.

A professional change agenda focuses on how we can work with others to create broader changes through our practices and service delivery systems. Some useful strategies have been developed by anti-racist and feminist educators (Das Gupta, 1993). For example, Thomas (1984) identifies similarities and differences between anti-racist education and multicultural education and describes the key principles of anti-racist education. Multicultural education, he suggests, has emphasized the sharing of information about different cultures and the fostering of appreciation for them as ways of increasing social equity. Anti-racist education, in contrast, focuses on the nature and origins of unequal power relationships among different groups of people and on the ways in which racist beliefs and actions justify these inequities.

Thomas' five principles can provide a foundation for specific anti-racist, feminist teaching and learning strategies as well as a framework for efforts to challenge racism and sexism in institutions and professional organizations (Hayes, 1994). The first principle articulated by Thomas (1984) is to expose racist and sexist beliefs and stereotypes and to examine ways the media, the family and other social institutions spread them. The second principle is to treat culture as complex and dynamic involving multiple factors such as gender, class, age, sexual orientation, etc., in peoples lives, and to reject simplified and romanticized generalizations about customs or lifestyles. The third principle is to recognize the role of the economy and the systems delivering education, health care and social services in fostering inequities. The fourth principle is to acknowledge that both the oppressed and the oppressors must be engaged in overcoming inequities and possess skills to both challenge racism and deal with resistance to change. The fifth principle is to recognize that collective action is necessary to address institutional racism.

Structuring learning directed at personal and professional change involves dealing directly with issues of prejudice, power and privilege in addition to general information regarding cultural diversity. The challenge for educators and learners is to integrate the complex ways in which multiple forms of oppression overlap and intersect without universalizing about similarities or romanticizing about differences. Sensitivity to diversity is about valuing the differences while seeking common elements in peoples' struggles against oppression, discrimination, marginalization, subordination and exclusion; it is about giving voice and making connections. It is about becoming culturally competent.

## WHAT IS CULTURAL COMPETENCE?

Cultural competence refers to skills and knowledge that incorporate an understanding and appreciation of cultural differences and similarities within, among and between groups in all interactions and phases of work. A major feature of being culturally competent involves an awareness of how social work practices, both at the individual and system levels, must change to accommodate the history, culture, lifestyles and experiences of diverse, disadvantaged, oppressed groups (Hanson and Lynch, 1990). What is essential in demonstrating cultural competence is an attitude of openness to cultural variability and to the relativity of one's own values

(McGoldrick, Pearce and Giordano, 1982). Cultural competence can be viewed as a goal towards which educators, practitioners and their respective systems can strive.

Becoming culturally competent can be viewed as a developmental process with five elements: 1) valuing diversity; 2) making a cultural self-assessment; 3) understanding the dynamics when cultures interact; 4) incorporating cultural knowledge; and 5) adapting practices to the diversity in the setting (Cross, Bazron, Dennis and Isaacs, 1989, p. 19). Thus, becoming culturally competent is a developmental process involving assessment, support building, developing resources, setting goals and outlining action steps to structure effective learning experiences for the realities of a diverse and pluralist society. There is a growing literature based on empirical findings and conceptual developments to help educators and learners find content on ethnic and racial minorities, women, lesbians and gay men, persons with disabilities and other oppressed populations at risk of discrimination (Bial and Lynn, 1995; Chau, 1990; Gladstein and Mailick, 1986; Ifill, 1989; Ho, 1991; Marshak, Oritz Hendricks, and Gladstein, 1994; McRoy, Freeman, Logan and Blackmon, 1986; Reesor, 1992). This literature provides an invaluable contribution of techniques, strategies, methods, issues, trends and concerns regarding the preparation of culturally competent practitioners.

## WHY SOCIAL WORKERS NEED TO BE CULTURALLY COMPETENT

Practitioners with little cultural awareness may find it difficult to understand the impact of oppression and discrimination on the lives of various groups. "The 'use of self' nature of social work practice...requires that [practitioners] in our profession know themselves as thoroughly as possible as a prerequisite to effective interpersonal helping" (Manoleas, 1994, p. 44). Teaching models which focus on interpersonal components of culturally sensitive practice and cross-cultural empathy encourage both learners and educators to self-assess and self-define prior to cross-cultural interactions (Garland and Escobar, 1988; Nakanishi and Rittner, 1992; Pinderhughes, 1989; Proctor and Davis, 1994; Sue, 1981).

During the last two decades, due to a liberalization of immigration policies, Canada has opened its doors to Third World and non-white refugees and immigrants who were previously discriminated against (Christiensen, 1995). These policy changes have created a dramatic impact on the cultural profile of the population. For example, in British Columbia in 1986, seven out of every 100 people were members of a visible minority. By the year 2001, thirty-nine out of every 100 people are projected to be members of a visible minority (Province of B.C., 1991). In support of multiculturalism, Canada, in 1971, became one of the first countries in the world to have a multiculturalism policy. In 1988, multiculturalism was formally declared by the enactment of An Act for the Preservation and Enhancement of Multiculturalism in Canada. Educating students for multicultural practice has become a mandated goal for accredited schools of social work since the adoption of the multicultural and multiracial educational policy standards by the Canadian Association of Schools of Social Work in 1992 (see Christensen, 1991).

Social work programs are challenged to implement the policy statements, and agencies are scrambling to provide multicultural training for social workers, relevant services to clients and to eliminate barriers to equitable access. It is also argued that service needs are complicated by clients who are immigrants or refugees with language barriers, and when prejudice and stereotyping override other more valid mechanisms used to form opinions and make decisions. All of these factors pose a challenge to practitioners' effectiveness and competence, making it all the more essential to learn cross-cultural social work practice. Before we address these issues, it is necessary to understand concepts related to cultural competence.

## RELATED CONCEPTS

Since the 1960s, Canada has described itself as a cultural mosaic. This description is very different from the melting pot metaphor used in the United States. The concept of cultural pluralism is implied in the ideal of a cultural mosaic. Cultural pluralism, as defined by Herskovits (1972) and Rappaport (1977), embraces a mutual respect for the existence of cultural differences among racial and ethnic groups and recognizes the strengths inherent in those differences. This definition must be expanded to include the notion of mutual respect and appreciation of strengths when the cultural differences relate to those individuals and groups who are gay, lesbian or bisexual, old or physically or mentally challenged. Cultural pluralism, expanding Kellen (1956), supports the rights of groups different from the powerful dominant group to maintain their uniqueness while contributing to the richness of the whole.

Cultural ethnocentrism, on the other hand, views the mainstream (white, North American, able-bodied, male, heterosexual, Christian, young to middle age and middle to upper class) culture as superior to all others. This perspective advocates the perpetuation of the dominant culture and values it as the single standard against which merits of other groups are to be gauged. These two concepts are at either end of a value continuum for viewing the cultural differences of clients (Chau, 1990).

Biculturation refers to the ability to live simultaneously in two cultures (Velasquez and Velasquez, 1980). It involves the ability to effectively bridge the gap between one's culture of origin and the dominant society. The idea of people holding a dual perspective (Norton, 1978) reinforces the notion that minorities not only live in and are subjected to the influences of the dominant cultural environment but are also embedded in their own culture. This gives different meanings to their problems, struggles and ability to ask for and receive help. The variations of world views, values and cultural beliefs causes an incongruence between the norms and expectations of the two cultural environments. Although Norton was referring to ethnic minorities, the notion of dual perspective is equally applicable to all non-dominant culture individuals and groups. The degree of incongruence often varies according to the extent of biculturation an individual is able to manage (de Anda, 1984). Consider the increasing complexity and further potential for incongruence if we attempt to include the multiple cultures many of us try to juggle and hold simultaneously.

The concept of cultural dissonance refers to the stress and strain of cultural incongruence (when two or more cultures clash or oppose each other) and to the internal conflict caused by the social and cultural ramifications of being different (Chau, 1990). It occurs when minorities seek to cope with their life situations while under the pressure to conform to the often conflicting and incongruent requirements of their own and the dominant culture.

These concepts help us to understand the complexity of thinking about and practising with diverse populations. We also require an historical perspective to place these concepts and our practices in context. Examining how our "thinking about" and "knowing how" has evolved assists us in the complicated process of personal and professional learning, growth, development and change.

Canadians are known worldwide for their prosperity, peaceful cohabitation and fostering equality and human rights. During the 1960s, many Canadians viewed the racism in the United States that resulted in the civil rights movement as foreign, and prided themselves on being colour blind and non-racist. In actuality, racism always existed, but it would not be exposed until twenty-five years later, when cultural communities became more visible, vocal and diverse. This exposure of racism becomes an opportunity for further uncovering and dismantling of the entrenched institutional racism and accompanying individual and often violent racist behaviours.

## Institutional racism

In learning multicultural practice, it is important to become aware that racism and ethnocentrism are destructive and oppressive at an individual and institutional level. What most compels our work is that we view these "isms," along with sexism, ageism, anti-Semitism, classism, heterosexism and ableism, as forms of abuse that result in psychological, physical and emotional consequences for victims. On a societal level, the academy, along with the media, economic and legal systems, are institutions that influence the fabric of society, and as such play a role in perpetuating racism. Unfortunately, institutionalized racism is habitual and implicit—it is taken for granted. The media, for example, in pre-Nazi Germany routinely created images of Jews as opportunistic parasites. This profoundly contributed to the institutionalization of German anti-Semitism, which greatly supported Hitler's rise to power.

In North America, during the period of colonization, the conquest of lands and the subjugation of First Nations people was implicitly rationalized by portraying them as heathens and savages. Colonial agents, greatly influenced by a missionary mentality, were further convinced that they were justified in forcing Aboriginals to adopt Western ways. During the forties, fifties and sixties, social workers were indoctrinated by a positivistic, Eurocentric curriculum in the guise of enlightened thought about, for example, certain child-rearing practices. They operated as agents of social control in the "sixties scoop" of First Nations children. These apprehensions and placements in white homes contributed to the further destruction of First Nations cultures, languages and spirituality (Summers and Yellowbird, 1995). In learning multicultural practice, learners, particularly if they are from the dominant culture, need to be aware of how our institutions portray and perpetuate the "truth" of the dominant culture.

## Whose truth?

There are, of course, radically and subtly differing perspectives named "truth" depending upon who is writing or telling the story. The tellers' perspectives on how life is, or was, or ought to be, have evolved out of their various cultural traditions and life experiences. It is imperative for multicultural social work practitioners to learn the "truth" about truth, since they will be dealing with such multiple realities. In interactions with clients, workers will need to be conscious of how their own cultural traditions and the reality of the dominant culture inform their own truths.

We in the Western world have been socialized to value universality in knowledge building. Universality is promoted when ways of understanding people, ideas and events are seen as applicable to all, even when the knowledge is derived from only a select group, namely white, male, Anglo Europeans (Flannery, 1994). According to Lyotard (1991), universality is the search for a master narrative, an objective depiction of universal truth, often referred to as the scientific approach. True knowledge is built when a scientific approach is used to collect facts about some particular phenomena. This desire to seek and find universal truth involves faulty generalizations whereby data collected from persons of a particular kind or group are generalized as the standard for all (Collard and Stalker, 1991; Minnich, 1990).

Another problematic aspect of the pursuit of universal truth is related to the power exercised by those who gather, determine and disseminate these truths. This power is hidden by the assumption that the knowledge builders and those whose lives are being studied are interacting. It is concealed by the assumption that anyone can participate in knowledge building. This is not the case. There is not, and has not been, mutual influence. Rather, the knowledge builders use their own lenses to determine truth. Their ways of viewing life are influenced by their own culture, values and expectations. (Flannery, 1994, p. 19)

Thus, the presumption of universality results in errors of reasoning in which "only one group is being generalized from" and in power relationships where "one group speaks for, of, and to all of us" (Minnich,

1990, p. 53). These universal truths are inculcated personally and institutionally, profoundly influencing and colouring our responses to others and to the world around us.

### "Already always" responses

Our government policy of multiculturalism contains certain inherent dilemmas we need to address before learning appropriate, effective multicultural practice. The first dilemma is that a fear of difference, ranging from mild to extreme, is pervasive. A variety of economic, political and social forces may contribute to this universal fear of "others." Thus, while undesirable, it is not surprising that in the face of our benchmark Multicultural Act there has been tension and backlash from the dominant populace.

Multicultural practice learners, particularly when members of the dominant culture, also need to be aware of any backlash within themselves and become skilled in the paradoxical experience of standing outside of their particular culture. This "opening of an open mind" will help the practitioner take responsibility for any internal reactions to clients' unfamiliar ways of being. By an open mind we mean the ability to be in a continually questioning and reflective mode. To achieve this awareness and develop such skills, learners identify and repeatedly bring to the level of consciousness their "normal," albeit unwelcomed responses, that may occur, even with the best of intentions. For example, a practitioner reveals that she was taught as a child that males with long beards are dirty and untrustworthy. As a learner, this practitioner identifies that she feels disgust and fear when confronted by men with long beards. This unwelcome response, if left unidentified and unchanged, will undoubtedly create problems in working with Hassidic Jews or Sikhs. These "already always" responses to difference occur as a "voice in one's head," that is, beneath the level of consciousness (Derrida, 1978). Maintaining an open mind and taking responsibility for our "already always" responses is a difficult state of consciousness to achieve.

During the developmental process of learning multicultural practice, learners begin to identify their habitual "already always" and "fear of other" responses to a whole range of differences represented by human diversity so that they can by changed. These responses exist because we are all unwitting adaptations of experiences of race, class, culture, family, ethnicity, gender, sexual orientation, etc. that continue to unconsciously affect us until we identify and challenge them. This work is important because it enables a more open perspective rather than a moralistic and blaming posture when communicating with people we have disagreements with. Learning multicultural practice, as with any complex skill acquisition, involves a developmental process that occurs over time. To be able to understand another culture, to stand outside of our own and to have understanding even for those with whom we profoundly disagree, we first need to thoroughly explore and understand how our own culture has affected us (Latting, 1990; Manoleas, 1994). In doing so we validate and value—give voice to—a new narrative.

## Giving voice

To give voice requires us to acknowledge different realities and understand that there are different ways of interpreting reality (Sheared, 1994). This assumes that there is more than one way of knowing and constructing meaning from experience. It also assumes that connectedness, through dialogue with others, is essential to the process of validating what is known. Collins (1990, p. 312) suggests the narrative method is one way of finding meaning, but in so doing she insists the story is "not torn apart in analysis, and trusted as core belief, not admired as science."

Belenky, Clinchy, Goldberg and Tarule (1986) describe several ways in which women construct their realities about truth, knowledge and power. They delineate stages through which women proceed, from silence to an ability to construct knowledge. These stages demonstrate that women can move from a position of subordination to a place in which they share equal voice in the decisions and choices that are made. It is, however, through discourse that learners have the opportunity to challenge the knowledge constructed by others and to deconstruct their own stories. Through the dialogue, learners explore alternative ways of viewing the world and begin to voice their understanding of the ways in which they have learned to operate and function in relation to others.

## Deconstructing personal stories

Multicultural practice learners must develop awareness and then actively challenge their own cultural learning and belief systems. In order to do this, learners engage in a process of unlearning the prejudices and stereotypes inculcated from childhood. Unlearning and relearning must consciously take place and be an ongoing process as practitioners realize and accept that becoming culturally competent is an ongoing, developmental process.

> While you are learning, you are also unlearning. Prejudices, misconceptions and falsifications have to be carefully stripped away. Some will be obvious from the beginning, some will succumb to intelligent research and reading, while others crumble under the influence of experience with the people. However, there are deep-seated and popular prejudices which are difficult to undo. They have been knit into the dominant ideology and help to keep racism alive and well. (Collier, 1993, p. 50)

One teaching method uses triads where learners alternate between the roles of questioner, learner and coach to facilitate questioning, self-disclosure and respectful honest dialogue among participants. During this peculiar process of appropriate detachment and engaged curiosity, learners explore all aspects of their own stories, deconstructing them so that they can transparently observe them and, when necessary, assist each other to construct new beliefs (White, 1993). In this process, the learners may discover and unlearn the reactionary forces within themselves. Such awareness and practice may later empower them to bridge universes so that they can honour the diversity of people from different cultures and, ironically, better understand the dominant culture. This developmental work will also facilitate the learners' ability to challenge clients, when required, in an effective and compassionate manner. This is particularly important since clients may be perpetrators as well as victims of discriminatory, oppressive, racist or sexist thoughts and actions.

## Making use of concepts and context

Using these concepts (i.e., discrimination, oppression, racism and sexism) and appreciating the context of personal and professional interactions has significance in preparing social workers for learning culturally competent practice across a range of differences. First, it raises awareness of the ideals of cultural pluralism as a basis for designing services and delivering practices. Second, it shows how cultural ethnocentrism creates attitudes, thoughts and behaviours that reinforce prejudicial interventions based on a single set of dominant culture standards carefully camouflaged as universal truths.

Third, it helps practitioners to understand that there may be a range of viable responses and solutions to client problems, since relevant solutions and responses are often influenced by culture and context-specific world views. For example, if possible alternative solutions and responses are drawn from a particular cultural milieu, then it is more likely that these natural supports and indigenous community resources will provide access to the strengths found in particular cultures and communities.

Fourth, it encourages practitioners to view the clients' needs or problems in terms of their experience of cultural dissonance or degree of "multiculturation." In other words, social workers can consider how clients cope with the stress, demands and influences of the different cultural environments to which they are connected or affiliated while trying to exist in harmony with the dominant culture.

And fifth, practitioners need to also ensure they understand their clients as individuals and not assume, expect or ascribe certain attitudes, meanings and behaviours based on belonging to or coming from certain groups. Given this understanding, you are now in a position to examine and address the dilemmas and challenges inherent in multicultural cross-cultural social work practice.

## DILEMMAS AND CHALLENGES

Honouring diversity, even what we disagree with, is crucial and difficult to achieve especially when there are vast differences in cultural discourses between "us" and "them." Once learners genuinely and transparently accept diversity, a new challenge develops in creating appropriate bridges and boundaries. How can social workers be accepting of diversity, while at the same time not accepting certain elements of heterogeneity that may be unacceptable to their spirit and to the law? A significant challenge in developing a multicultural consciousness lies in the dilemma of honouring differences while maintaining certain positions which conflict with those differences. In the heart of multiculturalism, all cultural realities of individuals and groups are understandable. How then does a practitioner deal with unappealing, even abhorrent pieces of the mosaic that may include Eurocentric patriarchy, spousal abuse, bride burning and female genital circumcision?

In the larger picture of human adaptation, anthropologically we may understand, for example, the Somali practice of female circumcision. However, on a local level, this act becomes female genital mutilation and is unacceptable under Canadian law. Yet, any time we are critical of a non-dominant cultural practice, the possibility exists that the criticism may be discriminatory. Within a context of diversity can one ever take action and not let one's self be open to accusations of discrimination? How can one differentiate between culture, tradition and abuse? How does a practitioner remain absolutely committed to diversity, yet act as a change agent, promote equality and social justice, express value disagreements and not be viewed as racist?

A challenge for social work lies in creating methods to assess what works and what does not work in the dominant and non-dominant cultures without resorting to the use of an absolutist and positivistic framework. How can social workers take a strong stand without having a transcendental position to come from? This is an unusual place to operate from in the world. Practitioners, skilled at multicultural practice, need to become skilled at understanding and assessing policies, laws, cultural practices and advocating for change on several fronts. We certainly must be social justice advocates and work to change dominant culture prescriptions, laws and social work practices when they are racist, discriminatory or otherwise inappropriate to the goal of establishing harmonious multiculturalism, as well as draw the line on certain abusive non-dominant culture practices. Paradoxically, we must do this work unreservedly, honouring all diversity, if we are to maximize the possibility of mutuality and minimize harm in the pursuit of preferred multicultural goals.

How do educators and learners resolve many of the dilemmas described above? It may appear impossible to be accepting of all realities while at the same time making demands for change. If we have many realities and no grand narratives to rely upon, how can a social worker justify action? What becomes of right and wrong, ethics and morality? A useful way of addressing these dilemmas lies in creating an extraordinary type of balancing. This may be provided by a middle-way framework we have adapted from nonlinear postmodern theory and Buddhist thought to provide guidance in multicultural practice social work education. This framework is presented after an examination of the relevance of postmodern thought to multicultural practice.

## CONTRIBUTIONS FROM POSTMODERN THOUGHT

Postmodern thought asserts that human history cannot be captured by grand narratives or dominant cultural stories. Grand narratives invariably reflect the dominant cultural values, discourses, knowledge base and institutions. Following from this, there is no objective or privileged literal reality or truth. There are only realities and truths constructed from the point of view of the teller based upon his or her own culture, race, class, gender, etc. (Fraser and Nicholson, 1990; Leonard, 1994). It is a myth that we can ever be impartial, value free and detached from the historical social relations in which we all participate. The best we can hope for is to be aware of and responsible for a partial view of reality from our own perspective, which we all view through the filters of our own race, class, gender, culture and ethnicity.

> Where there is a conscious mind, there is a point of view. This is one of the most fundamental ideas we have about minds—or consciousness. A conscious mind is an observer, who takes in a limited subset of all the information there is. (Dennett, 1991, pp. 101-102)

While a postmodern perspective may initially appear unsettling for many Westerners taught to know the "truth," it can be emancipating and educative in learning and teaching about multiculturalism, where different positions are equally understandable. Thus, postmodern ideas translate well into a framework for diversity education where the learner must grasp that there is not any one single way of viewing or understanding the world, despite what their previous educational and ethnocultural learning may have taught them, despite what the "already always" response in their heads and bodies may assert.

The basic dilemma, of course, is that although we may see and accept life as multiverse, in a practical day-to-day world we need to take stands. While different people have different truths, unfortunately one person's truth acted out in a particular behaviour may harm someone on the other side of that truth. Passivity based on universal acceptance is not usually useful, particularly in social work contexts. Yet, how do we say "yes" and "no" at the same time when normally human consciousness precludes this? Since Western knowledge is based on dualistic thinking, the us/them dichotomy has made it difficult for people to reach out and embrace difference. We have learned to fear, or judge as wrong, people who are not like ourselves or what we know. Generally, we live in a dualistic world where we objectify distinctions, make them into absolutes and overlook the profound interrelationship between all things and all beings. So we have two basic and logically exclusive domains: profound relationship and fragmentation or separateness. Leaning too far over on either side becomes a problem in relation to achieving potent social action.

## A middle-way framework

The middle-way framework we have adapted from postmodern and Buddhist thought is useful in multicultural education for resolving the dilemmas described above. The middle-way is a term borrowed from Mahayanan Buddhism (Sprung, 1979) and is congruent with our understanding of postmodern thought. The middle-way, or *madhyamika*, asserts paradoxically that there is no essential or substantial nature to reality. Yet reality, as we routinely experience it, certainly exists. The development and use of a middle-way for our purposes involves a delicate balancing. In practice it facilitates seeking the common ground; being validating and respectful of others; not making people wrong, though not necessarily agreeing with them; and taking practical and perhaps difficult stands.

Acting in a middle-way is like riding a bicycle. Here the rider never achieves stationary balance, but rather, upon mastery, achieves ongoing balance, oscillating back and forth, tipping and leaning forward between bisected spaces, creating completion in the process. In relation to multicultural practice, the basic manner in which we bisect space is between accepting all realities as perfectly normal and understandable— given human adaptation and tradition—yet in practice not accepting some realities, making distinctions and taking action. The balancing, integration and completion of the two is an overarching middle-way.

In using a middle-way framework, there may be two sides to consider. On the one side, a profoundly holistic and relational perspective is created. This perspective validates all points of view in the profound and thorough inter-relatedness of existence. Thus, what is disliked, even abhorred, also remains understandable in a holistic context of life. This view, however, does not preclude the social worker from taking action when necessary. The other side includes making distinctions in our localized experience of day-to-day living. Thus, practitioners still do what, in their assessment, needs to be done. In a middle-way, one side informed by the other in an oscillating synchronicity decreases the possibility of harm and opens up a wider range of options. In a middle-way, differences that naturally arise in our domain of distinctions are balanced by the bigger holistic compassionate picture. In practice, this is challenging to achieve. It is like moving back and forth, using two very different parts of the brain. In multicultural practice, this is demonstrated by taking a stand against a behaviour or action while genuinely and transparently not invalidating the person. This perspective increases the chance of remaining in relationship despite conflict. Dialogue to find common ground has more opportunity to flourish.

The middle-way framework balances the many voices of diversity with the dominant culture voice while maintaining the integrity of each. The challenge in inter-cultural and intra-cultural communication is in opening up dialogue where there is respect for the other person's humanity, even if there is not agreement with the person's ideas or action. Multicultural practitioners need to be able to hear the client's story in a way that they have never listened before. They are open to changing their perspective and at the same time willing to make a demand for work. Just as multicultural practice learners discover their own biases and prejudices through dialogue, multicultural practitioners engage in a culturally appropriate modified version of a similar questioning and dialogue with clients. Such a process honours differences, empowers clients and assists both participants to grow, learn and arrive at liberating goals.

Experienced multicultural practitioners continue the developmental process of learning multicultural practice through rigorous ongoing consultation, questioning and dialogue with peers and supervisors regarding personal reactions to interactions with client systems. The ability to be genuinely curious, engage in rigorous questioning and tolerate not having objectivistic answers are important skills in developing multicultural practice competence.

## DEVELOPING A MULTICULTURAL PERSPECTIVE

Complacency is an obstacle in developing a multicultural perspective. If practitioners are to adequately meet the demands of an increasingly diverse client population, their supervision and education must reflect societal realities. Reality indicates that the theoretical myth of sameness leads to the erroneous belief in the homogeneity of particular cultural groups, gender socialization, sexual orientation, physical challenge and other sources of discrimination (Hardy, 1991). The dominant values do not work for everyone, minority and mainstream students alike. To overcome this, learners should identify the obstacles to exploring how their practices and their use of knowledge and skills might vary as a result of racial, ethnic, cultural and other differences.

### Barriers to learning

Institutionalized racist norms act as a barrier to learning and buffer us from even acknowledging the existence of discriminatory and oppressive practices. Dominelli (1988, pp. 71-72) identifies seven strategies that perpetuate individual, institutional and cultural racism and block learning. These have been extended to include other forms of discrimination in addition to racism.

1) *Denial*: the refusal to accept that racism [or other "isms"] exists.
2) *Omission*: the refusal to see the relevance of race [gender, ethnicity, class, age, ability, sexual orientation] in most situations.
3) *Decontextualization*: an acceptance that racism [or other "ism"] exists in general but the refusal to believe it permeates everyday activities.
4) *Colour blindness*: treating people of colour [or those with other obvious difference] as if they were not, thereby negating their experience of racism [sexism, ableism, ageism].
5) *Dumping*: blaming the victim by holding people of colour responsible for racism [and people with other differences responsible for the corresponding "ism"].

6) *Patronizing*: although mainstream ways are considered superior, other ways are tolerated.

7) *Avoidance*: there is an awareness that race [or gender, ethnicity, class, age, ability, sexual orientation] is a factor but opportunities for addressing it are avoided.

In response to these strategies, learning has been geared specifically to raising the consciousness of the dominant group. The intention is to remove/reduce the barriers to learning and help practitioners undertake anti-discriminatory and anti-oppressive action. However, members of the non-dominant culture also need to address internalized racism and the other "isms" that have affected them.

Difficulties do exist in working across all types of difference, not just racial difference. Those who share the experience of oppression, whatever form it takes (e.g., sexism, ageism, racism, etc.), have certain experiences in common. Those who are outside the experience of oppression have a difficult time understanding what it means to be disadvantaged. Factors like race, class and gender have historically been a significant part of deep divisive social structures that have engendered conflict, tension, hostility and mistrust between whites and blacks, the haves and have nots, males and females (Narayan, 1989). Add to this the divisions between heterosexuals, homosexuals and bisexuals, the able-bodied and the disabled, youth and elderly, the complications not only multiply, they increase exponentially. Overcoming these difficulties in communicating and establishing relationships requires more than good intentions on the part of mainstream, advantaged practitioners.

Narayan (1989) suggests there are three ways in which those outside the experience of oppression fail to appreciate the pervasiveness and cost of its impact. The first way is by minimizing the emotional costs of oppression. An empathetic and caring outsider (i.e., a dominant culture practitioner) may feel anger at a perpetrator and sympathy with the victim after witnessing or hearing about an incident that is racist or sexist, but they can not possibly grasp the full scope of its effects. The victim, on the other hand, may have a range of feelings: anger at the perpetrator; a deep sense of humiliation; a sense of being soiled; hatred for the whole group of which the perpetrator is a part; rage at society for producing a history that sustains and condones such attitudes and behaviours; anger and shame at the powerlessness and inability to retaliate; a strong sense of solidarity with those who face the same problems; and, maybe, even pity and sadness for the stupidity of the perpetrator. This complex array of emotions extracts a cost that even an empathetic outsider can not begin to compute.

The second way involves missing the subtle manifestations of oppression. Someone who has not experienced oppression first-hand is likely to understand only the general and common ways oppression is manifested. For example, openly racist or sexist remarks are easy to detect. But when attitudes are expressed more covertly, such as under-valuing the work done or a contribution made, dismissing concerns or not being taken seriously, an outsider may fail to notice what is happening. Therefore someone who has experienced oppression is far more likely to know the extent to which oppression permeates society and the subtle ways it operates.

The third and final way in which outsiders fail to grasp the meaning and cost of oppression is by not making connections or failing to see oppression in other contexts. For example, male practitioners who have been sensitized to the silencing of their female counterparts in team meetings may fail to see this phenomenon in informal gatherings. Those who have experienced oppression are likely to be more vigilant in making these connections and seeing it across contexts.

These failures have in common the inability of those outside the experience of oppression to fully understand and respect the emotional responses of oppressed individuals and groups. This results in some individuals and groups being particularly vulnerable to the insensitivity and ignorance emanating from culturally incompetent practitioners with whom they are expected to work and trust. Awareness of these problems will help well-intentioned practitioners focus more careful attention on the implications of what is said, since goodwill alone is not sufficient to guarantee that perceptions and comments are not offensive. Those who experience oppression should not be required to educate others about their offensive behaviour.

## Gaining personal insight

Shulman (1993) suggests that if learners are to strengthen their ability to practice with diverse populations, they need to come to terms with their own sexist, racist, ageist, homophobic attitudes and stereotypes. An effective learning environment permits these views to be expressed, even though they may not be politically correct or represent the "wrong" social work values. Comments that reflect personal bias should be seen as a learning opportunity, a chance to help learners explore and transform the stereotypes and biases they have integrated from their families and communities. This assumes, however, that the educator is able to identify and engage in discourse about the subtle and not-so-subtle manifestations of stereotypical perceptions and personal bias. Additionally, educators should be able to articulate and model their own professional development processes in identifying the "isms" that they have had to struggle with (Latting, 1990).

Effective cross-cultural education must go beyond simple descriptions of cultural differences to create greater self-awareness, insight and sensitivity. It is argued that the process of self-assessment and self-awareness increases sensitivity to others, especially cultural, ethnic and racial sensitivity (Burgest, 1989). Through this process of gaining personal insight and awareness, practitioners develop a potential for confronting negative stereotypes, myths and assumptions which handicap the ability to work across differences and establish effective relationships.

Clear, precise communication helps develop effective trusting work relationships amongst educators and learners who differ in terms of characteristics like gender, ethnicity, race, class, age, ability and sexual orientation. Practitioners, especially those who are mainstream, who see themselves as non-judgmental, sensitive and caring individuals may have difficulty admitting to such practice blunders as making assumptions based on skin colour and using culturally insensitive assessment and treatment approaches. If educators have opened the lines of communication in this area, practitioners will be enabled to admit these mistakes and submit them to a reflective dialogue with their colleagues.

Practitioners must recognize that they may never be totally free of prejudices and biases if their existence is denied (Proctor and Davis, 1994). Knowledge, acceptance and sensitivity to cultural and human diversity are prerequisites for effective cross-cultural learning. In the educator-learner relationship, when they are of different cultures, problems of prejudice, bias, racism and ethnocentrism may emerge along with language difficulties, lack of insight, insensitivity and lack of knowledge of the other's culture (Ronnau, 1994). This may lead the educator and learner to approach each other with little understanding of their respective social realities and with unfounded assumptions and unrealistic expectations (Proctor and Davis, 1994). This poses a formidable challenge to the learning relationship. The anxiety that is mobilized in interaction with culturally different others can be neutralized by recognizing that changes are needed for effective cross-cultural interaction, learning how cultural identity and issues of power and powerlessness impact on human functioning, and identifying how their behaviour affects service delivery (Pinderhughes, 1989).

Educators must be sensitive to the fact that those who have or are experiencing various forms of discrimination have more complex and in-depth understanding of the ways in which oppression operates and the costs it extracts from those who experience it. Therefore, educators may need to spend extra time engaging learners in order to overcome basic mistrust. For example, supervision in neutral office space gives practitioners a greater sense of control, and taking the time to build a relationship before assessing and judging practitioners' learning objectives and plans might avoid premature dilemmas in supervision.

Environments with little heterogeneity in their staffing profile may look upon minority practitioners or students as the resident experts. These individuals then bear the burden of educating other staff and supervisors about their history of oppression and injustice, as well as the richness and strengths of their culture. This may well result in the person feeling exploited in yet another instance. Social work practitioners must incorporate knowledge of cultural norms and cultural variability with practices that respect and account for individual differences such as age, gender, ability, personal style and sexual orientation. Inherent in this combination is the need to understand the effects of oppression, discrimination, racism, colonization, Anglocentric explanations of human behaviour and unequal or restricted access to economic and political power, services and resources.

## Learning from clients

If we accept that there is no room for positivistic grand narratives, then students and practitioners can further contribute to the development of multicultural practice by being open to the hearing and telling of all stories that arise from practice. By confronting existing narratives that constrain opportunities for liberation, new ones that expand opportunities can be created. The client's wisdom, vision, stories and lived experiences provide valuable opportunities for all to learn and grow in a multiverse of open discourses. Practitioners can make great contributions to multicultural practice by having the courage to bring to the discourse the voices, wisdom and insights of their powerless and oppressed clients, as well as the best of their own cultures within a context of respect and dignity for all.

### The diversity within

Just as there is diversity between cultures, there exists difference and diversity within cultures. For example, a social worker, when working with a father who felt it was his Koranic obligation to administer corporal punishment to his daughters to instil the value of remaining sexually pure, found a religious leader from the local mosque who could offer the family a different interpretation of the Koran. In this definition of fatherhood, the use of physical discipline was not condoned and gentler guidance was called for (Markowitz, 1994). Social workers sometimes make the mistake of downplaying or being unaware of the degree to which subgroups within ethnic categories differ. They believe that once they have worked with a family from one ethnic group, they are now skilled at working with that group since they mistakenly believe that all people from that group are similar. Consequently, differences, cleavages, disputes and animosities between various subgroups get overlooked (Christensen, 1986).

To the above analysis we would add that besides there being diversity within each cultural, ethnic or racial group, diversity exists within each individual. There are many different inner voices with their "already always" responses which reflect racism, bias and prejudice. These voices come from our families, cultures, genders, classes, ethnic groups, religions and professional disciplines. At any moment we can decide which voices we are going to give power to. In becoming a competent multicultural practitioner, it is necessary to continually acknowledge that these voices exist and engage in ongoing reflective dialogue about them.

## THE LEARNING PROCESS CURRICULUM

Herberg (1993) identified a set of culturally and racially sensitive skills required for professional competence of human service practitioners. We have combined our work with these skills, the Cross et al. (1989) cultural competence elements and Manoleas' (1994) outcome objectives for cultural competence into a curriculum covering the knowledge, values and skills to be included in educational programs or staff development training for practitioners in the context of preparing them to be culturally competent.

## 1. Provide a safe environment to explore diversity dilemmas

An educator must recognize that both she or he and the learner have cultures. There is a skill in knowing when and how to raise the possibility that miscommunication and lack of competence may be due to cultural differences. It is necessary to have the ability to raise subject matter and openly discuss taboo topics. In a situation where people feel threatened by a taboo on the topic, issues of power should be assumed to interfere. The educator, in raising and sustaining discourse on such topics, models to the learner how it can be done in addition to directly addressing the dilemma and the power differential. Through discourse, learners are encouraged to challenge the knowledge constructed by others. In dialogue, learners explore alternate ways of viewing the world and are encouraged to voice their understanding of the ways in which they have learned to function in relation to others.

## 2. Increase awareness and gain insight regarding the sources or causes of dilemmas

Socialization through childhood and adolescence is a powerful source of influence. A culturally competent practitioner appreciates that values are often hidden from full conscious control. Learning that takes place in childhood often remains unchallenged in the adult person's behavioural repertoire. Gaining insights into the sources or causes of differences around race, culture, ethnicity, gender, sexual orientation or disability can be simultaneously satisfying and painful.

Introspection allows practitioners to become skilled in critical self-reflection. This will facilitate raising awareness of their own discomfort with certain differences and challenging their self-image as an unbiased person. Because the mind tends to simplify events by using generalizations about instantly visible categories such as age, gender and race, the taboo nature of these makes it less likely they will be critically examined. The ability to identify our "already always" responses and tune into our stereotypical thinking are crucial skills. Practitioners need to unwrap their own feelings of guilt, jealousy, ignorance, anger and/or fear towards certain groups. At the same time, they need to learn to avoid being defensive and needing to be right. They learn that there is no need to be culturally competitive. Deconstructing personal stories with racist beliefs and constructing new middle-way beliefs facilitate this process and empower the learner to bridge universes.

### 3. Identify challenging issues and situations

Practitioners must learn to be comfortable with a wide range of situations and people and to acknowledge that values and behaviours can be understood in relation to the culture with which people identify. They learn that there are differing perspectives named "truth," created from peoples' various cultural traditions and life experiences which, of course, have been influenced by pervasive institutionalized racism. The practitioner learns to accept that there are no standards by which one can measure any culture's worth in absolute terms. They realize that many of the common assessment and diagnostic tools are limited when applied to non-dominant cultures or ignore the impact of cultural factors on organizational or client functioning altogether. In doing so they may challenge the accepted practice methods and the delivery system regarding the systemic barriers to diverse populations. They may also demonstrate proactive, anti-discriminatory practice leading to a more culturally competent organization and system of care.

### 4. Exploring alternatives

Being able to enter another person's cultural frame of reference implies the ability to apply a generalizable model to any given situation and then to search for the unique and particular elements. It means being able to understand the middle-way, both cognitively and affectively, so as to be able to take potent stands without invalidating anyone. It implies searching for, not assuming that you understand the meaning of events, circumstances and relationships. For example, practitioners must be aware of any cultural explanations of the response to someone in authority and a position of power that differs from the dominant belief system. Practitioners may fail to recognize that communication patterns and interactional behaviours with a client or a supervisor may reflect culture-bound attitudes and beliefs about the way a client or a supervisor is to be treated.

## 5. Acquire new ways of thinking and acting in response to dilemmas

As advocates, social work practitioners may have to argue for culturally diverse learning opportunities that can be made available for students from within or from other systems. This includes raising awareness of discriminatory and oppressive practices and institutionalized forms of racism, sexism, ageism, ableism and heterosexism that create barriers to access. Learners who themselves are disadvantaged and non-dominant may require extra help from educators and supervisors in negotiating the bureaucratic maze of the organization and in getting connected to other systems or programs.

## CONCLUSION

The literature concerning multicultural practice learning has evolved over the last several years. There are varying opinions about how one learns this work. One view is that to be effective you need to study each culture individually, and for some time, before you are qualified to work within it (Lum, 1986; Pedersen, 1983). Others suggest that you cannot learn multicultural practice because you need to be from the particular culture, ethnic or racial group to be effective, or need to engage cultural consultants in your work (Waldegrave and Tamasese, 1993). Many have argued that students and practitioners need to learn about themselves and how their own culture has shaped their lives, even when they thought that it had little influence, before engaging in multicultural practice (Devore and Schlesinger, 1991; Garland and Escobar, 1988; Razack, Teram and Sahas, 1995; Van Soest, 1994). The thinking is that once you have identified the basic elements about your own culture and how you learned or were influenced by them, you will have developed some information and basic skills that are transferable. Much of what we have discussed supports this later view. To be consistent, however, with keeping away from "grand narratives," we recommend a variety of approaches. In a particular situation, one of the above approaches may work better than another, while in another situation a combination of approaches may be more effective.

Engaging in multicultural practice is like embarking on a roller coaster ride. It will raise some fundamental philosophical questions about who you are and how you see yourself. Sometimes it will be scary and sometimes it will be exciting. Ultimately it may be fulfilling, rewarding and will result in empowerment for your clients and society. This work challenges the core of our belief systems. To engage in this work is also to become part of the multicultural movement. A movement that we predict will join with and contribute to the feminist movement in the transformation of social work education and practice.

For the social work knowledge base concerning multicultural practice to expand productively, it needs ideas, discoveries and a focus on inclusiveness (Chau, 1991). Each way of knowing will contribute, deepen and add increased dimensions to it. Multicultural practitioners will pose newer and better questions in an ever-expanding process of knowledge creation. By privileging any grand narrative, we run the risk of tyranny (Lyotard, 1991). Certainly the current situation is unacceptable where the development of knowledge, based on grand theory, contributed to the rank ordering of difference and perpetuated Eurocentric "truths" and discrimination in society. What is true becomes each person's "truth," and the academics' or practitioners' "truth" may be no more valid or useful, depending on the context, than the clients'. Instead of creating more universals, we suggest that the profession will be empowered by the acceptance of multiverses, keeping in mind that in a middle-way, stands will need to be taken in relation to liberating goals.

As we explore alternative ways of being, inventing and creating new knowledge bases, learners will need perseverance. History teaches us that within the scientific community many scientists have had work ignored or repressed, sometimes for decades, because what they taught destabilized the accepted positions in the university and scientific hierarchy. "The stronger the 'move' the more likely it is to be denied the minimum consensus, precisely because it changes the rules of the game upon which consensus had been based" (Lyotard, 1991, p. 63). Multicultural social work practice not only challenges accepted positions but also involves giving voice and validity to those voices that have been previously excluded.

# REFERENCES

Belenky, M., Clinchy, B., Goldberg, N. and Tarule, J. (1986). *Women's ways of knowing: The development of self, voice, and mind.* New York: Basic Books.

Bial, M. and Lynn, M. (1995). Field education with students with disabilities: Front door/back door: Negotiation/accommodation/mediation. In G. Rogers (ed.), *Social work field education: Views and visions.* Dubuque, IA: Kendall/Hunt.

Burgest, D. (1989). *Social work practice with minorities* (2nd ed.). Metuchen, NJ: The Scarecrow Press.

Chau, K. (1990). A model of teaching cross-cultural practice in social work. *Journal of Social Work Education,* 26(2), 124-133.

Chau, K. (1991). Social work with ethnic minorities: Practice issues and potentials. *Journal of Multicultural Social Work,* 1(1), 23-41.

Christensen, C. (1986). Cross-cultural social work: Fallacies, fears, and failings. *Intervention,* 74, 6-15.

Christensen, C. (1991). *Social work education at the crossroads: The challenge of diversity.* Report of the Task Force on Multicultural and Multiracial Issues in Social Work Education. Ottawa: Canadian Association of Schools of Social Work.

Christensen, C. (1995). Immigrant minorities in Canada. In J. Turner and F. Turner (eds.), *Canadian social welfare policy,* 3rd ed. Scarborough, ON: Allyn and Bacon.

Colin, S. and Preciphs, T. (1991). Perceptual patterns and the learning environment: Confronting white racism. In R. Hiemstra (ed.), *Creating environments for effective adult learning.* New Directions for Adult and Continuing Education, no. 50. San Francisco: Jossey-Bass.

Collard, S. and Stalker, J. (1991). In R. Hiemstra (ed.), *Creating environments for effective adult learning.* New Directions for Adult and Continuing Education, no. 50. San Francisco: Jossey-Bass.

Collier, K. (1993). *Social work with rural peoples* (2nd ed.). Vancouver: New Star Books.

Collins, P. (1990). The social construction of black feminist thought. In M. Mason, E. Mudimbe-Boyi, J. O'Barr and M. Wyer (eds.), *Black women in America: Social science perspectives.* Chicago: University of Chicago Press.

Cross, T., Bazron, B., Dennis, K. and Isaacs, M. (1989). *Towards a culturally competent system of care: A monograph on effective services for minority children who are severely emotionally disturbed.* Washington, D.C.: Georgetown University Child Development Center.

Das Gupta, T. (1993). Towards an antiracist, feminist teaching model. *New Horizons in Adult Education,* 7(1), 33-51.

de Anda, D. (1984). Bicultural socialization: Factors affecting the minority experience. *Social Work,* 29(2), 101-107.

Dennett, D. (1991). *Consciousness explained.* Toronto: Little, Brown and Company.

Derrida, J. (1978). *Writing and difference.* Chicago: University of Chicago Press.

Devore, W. and Schlesinger, E. (1991). *Ethnic-sensitive social work practice,* 3rd ed. New York: Merrill.

Dominelli, L. (1988). *Anti-racist social work: A challenge for white practitioners and educators.* London: Macmillan.

Flannery, D. (1994). Changing dominant understandings of adults as learners. In E. Hayes (ed.), *Confronting racism and sexism.* New Directions for Teaching and Learning, no.61 (pp. 17-26). San Francisco: Jossey-Bass.

Fraser, N. and Nicholson, L. (1990). Social criticism without philosophy: An encounter between feminism and postmodernism. In L. Nicholson (ed.), *Feminism/postmodernism.* New York: Routledge.

Garland, E. and Escobar, D. (1988). Education for cross-cultural practice. *Journal of Social Work Education,* 24(3), 229-241.

Gladstein, M. and Mailick, M. (1986). An affirmative approach to ethnic diversity in field work. *Journal of Social Work Education,* 22(1), 41-49.

Hanson, M. and Lynch, E. (1990). Honoring the cultural diversity of families when gathering data. *Topics in Early Childhood Special Education,* 10(1), 112-131.

Hardy, K. (1991). The theoretical myth of sameness: A critical issue in family therapy training and treatment. In G. Saba, B. Karrer and K. Hardy (eds.), *Minorities and family therapy.* New York: Haworth.

Hayes, E. (1994). Developing a personal and professional agenda for change. In E. Hayes (ed.), *Confronting racism and sexism.* New Directions for Teaching and Learning, no.61 (pp. 77-89). San Francisco: Jossey-Bass.

Herberg, D. (1993). *Frameworks for cultural and racial diversity: Teaching and learning for practitioners.* Toronto: Canadian Scholars' Press.

Herskovits, M. (1972). *Cultural relativism: Perspective in cultural pluralism.* New York: Random House.

Ho, M. Keung (1991). Use of Ethnic-Sensitive Inventory (ESI) to enhance practitioner skill with minorities. *Journal of Multicultural Social Work,* 1(1), 57-67.

Ifill, D. (1989). Teaching minority practice for professional application. *Journal of Social Work Education,* 25(1), 29-35.

Kellen, H. (1956). *Cultural pluralism and the American ideal.* Philadelphia, PA: University of Philadelphia Press.

Latting, J. (1990). Identifying the "isms": Enabling social work students to confront their biases. *Journal of Social Work Education*, 26(1), 36-44.

Leonard, P. (1994). Knowledge/power and postmodernism: Implications for the practice of a critical social work education. *Canadian Social Work Review*, 11(1), 11-25.

Lum, D. (1986). *Social work practice and people of color.* Monterey, CA: Brooks-Cole.

Lyotard, J. (1991). *The postmodern condition: A report on knowledge.* Minneapolis, MN: University of Minnesota Press.

Manoleas, P. (1994). An outcome approach to assessing the cultural competence of MSW students. *Journal of Multicultural Social Work,* 3(1), 43-57.

Markowitz, L. (1994). The cross-currents of multiculturalism. *The Family Therapy Networker,* 18(4), 18-27.

Marshak, E., Oritz Hendricks, C. and Gladstein, M. (1994). The commonality of difference: Teaching about diversity in field instruction. *Journal of Multicultural Social Work*, 3(1), 77-89.

McGoldrick, M., Peace, J. and Giordano, J. (1982). *Ethnicity and family therapy.* New York: Guilford.

McRoy, R., Freeman, E., Logan, S. and Blackmon, B. (1986). Cross-cultural field supervision: Implications for social work education. *Journal of Social Work Education*, 22(1), 50-56.

Mezirow, J. (1991). Conclusion: Toward transformative learning and emancipatory education. In J. Mezirow and Associates (eds.), *Fostering critical reflection in adulthood.* San Francisco: Jossey-Bass.

Minnich, E. (1990). *Transforming knowledge.* Philadelphia: Temple University Press.

Nakanishi, M. and Ritter, B. (1992). The inclusionary cultural model. *Journal of Social Work Education,* 28(1),27-35.

Narayan, U. (1989). Working together across differences. In B. Compton, and B, Galaway (eds.), *Social work processes,* 4th ed. Belmont, CA: Wadsworth.

Norton, D. (1978). *The dual perspective: The inclusion of ethnic minority content in the social work curriculum.* New York, NY: Council on Social Work Education.

Pedersen, P. (1983). Intercultural training of mental health providers. In D. Landis and F. Brislin (eds.), *Handbook of intercultural training: Issues in training methodology,* Vol. 2. New York: Pergamon.

Pinderhughes, E. (1989). *Understanding race, ethnicity, and power: The key to efficacy in clinical practice.* New York: Free Press.

Proctor, E. and Davis, L. (1994). The challenge of racial difference: Skills for clinical practice. *Social Work,* 39(3), 314-323.

Province of British Columbia, Immigration Policy Branch. (1991). *Immigration to B.C.: Facts and figures.* Victoria, BC: author.

Rappaport, J. (1977). *Community psychology: Values, research and action.* San Francisco, CA: Holt Rinehart and Winston.

Razack, N., Teram, E. and Sahas, M. (1995). Cultural diversity in field work educations: A practice model for enhancing cross cultural knowledge. In G. Rogers (ed.), *Social work field education: Views and visions.* Dubuque, IA: Kendall/Hunt.

Reesor, L. (1992). Students with disabilities in practicum: What is reasonable accommodation? *Journal of Social Work Education,* 28(1), 98-109.

Ronnau, J. (1994). Teaching cultural competence: Practical ideas for social work educators. *Journal of Multicultural Social Work,* 3(1), 29-42.

Sheared, V. (1994). Giving voice: An inclusive model of instruction. In E. Hayes (ed.), *Confronting racism and sexism.* New Directions for Teaching and Learning, no.61. San Francisco: Jossey-Bass.

Shulman, L. (1993). *Teaching the helping skills: A field instructors guide,* 2nd ed. Alexandria, VA: Council on Social Work Education.

Sprung, M. (1979). *Lucid exposition of the middle way.* London: Routledge and Kegan Paul.

Sue, D. (1981). *Counseling the culturally different.* New York: McGraw Hill.

Summers, H. and Yellowbird, M. (1995). Building relationships with first nations communities and agencies: implications for field education and practice. In G. Rogers (ed.), *Social work field education: Views and visions.* Dubuque, IA: Kendall/Hunt.

Thomas, B. (1984). Principles of antiracist education. *Currents: Readings in race relations,* 2(3), 20-24.

Van Soest, D. (1994). Social work education for multicultural practice and social justice advocacy: A field study of how students experience the learning process. *Journal of Multicultural Social Work,* 3(1), 17-28.

Velasquez, J. and Velasquez, C. (1980). Application of a bicultural assessment framework to social work practice with Hispanics. *Family Relations,* 29(4), 598-603.

Waldegrave, C. and Tamasese, K. (1993). Some central ideas in the "just therapy" approach. *Australia New Zealand Journal of Family Therapy,* 14(1), 1-8.

White, M. (1993). Deconstruction and therapy. In S. Gilligan and R. Price (eds.), *Therapeutic conservations.* New York: Norton.